ANCIENT ITALY AND SICILY

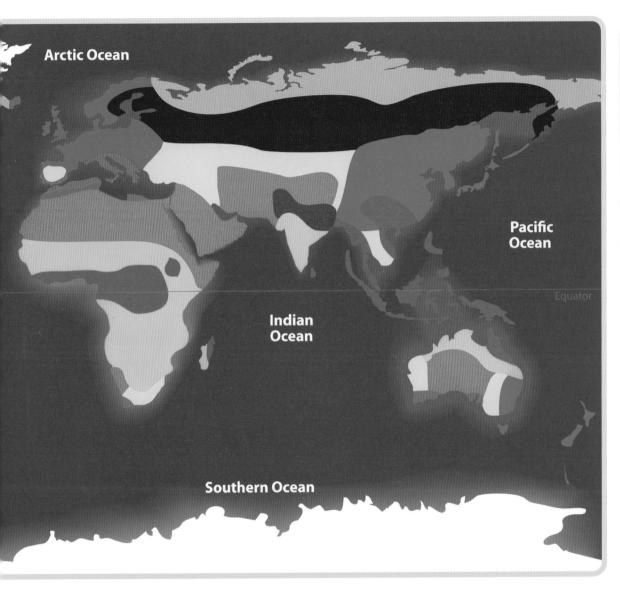

Arctic Ocean

Pacific Ocean

Indian Ocean

Equator

Southern Ocean

☐	Ice sheet
	Tundra
	Taiga
	Alpine
	Temperate forest
	Rain forest
	Savanna
	Desert
	Grassland
	Mediterranean
	Marine

This map shows the major land biomes around the world. They are surrounded by the marine biome, the largest habitat on Earth. In addition to the marine biome—the open ocean—there are also separate water biomes at coastal areas, at coral reefs, and in swamps, lakes, and rivers. Animals have adapted to live in all these places, even in the most challenging and hostile conditions.

ROAR ANIMAL PLANET

Although an alarming number of animal species are in danger of becoming extinct, there are also some success stories. Golden lion tamarins are small, cool-looking monkeys that live in Brazil. They were critically endangered by the 1970s. Then 200 were discovered in the small patches of forest along the Atlantic coast. Their habitat was being destroyed for logging, farming, and industry. A huge conservation effort began to breed tamarins in captivity. Today, tamarins have been reintroduced to the few remaining patches of Brazilian forest, and there are now 1,200 or more in the wild. Tamarins' long-term future cannot be guaranteed, but they are much safer now than they were before.

◀ Potter wasps use tiny pellets of mud to build exquisite pot-shaped nests for their eggs. They stock the nests with insects for their young to feed on.

HABITATS IN DANGER

All over the world, animal habitats are in danger. Some of the major threats are:

CLIMATE CHANGE Earth is getting warmer. The temperature of the oceans is rising, melting the sea ice. The habitat of polar bears and other animals that depend on ice is shrinking fast.

DEFORESTATION Humans are clearing trees to make space for homes, farms, mines, and roads. Cutting down trees for timber has already destroyed huge areas of precious rain forest.

POLLUTION Poisonous chemicals from cars and factories are polluting the air and water; millions of tons of plastics and other garbage are collecting in massive patches on ocean surfaces, destroying habitats and killing wildlife.

ANIMAL FEATURES

ANIMALS ALL HAVE SPECIAL FEATURES to help them survive in their particular habitats. In nature, elaborate feathers, fur coats, sharp claws, hooked beaks, and long legs are not simply for show. They are adaptations for attracting mates, keeping warm, self-defense, running, and catching prey—all vital for staying alive.

Only animals that adapt to their conditions are likely to survive. Very small birds called finches live on the Galápagos Islands of South America. Over time, each species of finch has developed a different-shaped beak to help it ingest a different type of food. Some have thin, sharp beaks for eating insects and grubs. Others have large, claw-shaped beaks for eating fruits and buds. These adaptations help finches avoid competition for food and allow them a better chance of survival. This type of change over time is called evolution.

Cactus finch

KEY FEATURES

VERTEBRATES

MAMMALS ▶

- Have hair on bodies
- Give birth to live young
- Feed young on milk

◀ BIRDS
- Have feathers on bodies
- Have beaks instead of jaws
- Most can fly

REPTILES ▶

- Have dry, scaly skin
- Most lay eggs
- Most live on land

◀ AMPHIBIANS
- Most are born in water
- Most adults live on land
- Have smooth, moist skin

FISH ▶

- Have bodies shaped for swimming
- Most are covered in scales
- Live in fresh and salt water

INVERTEBRATES

◀ ARTHROPODS
Insects
- Have bodies with three parts
- Have six legs
- Some have wings

Arachnids
- Have bodies with two parts
- Have eight legs
- Do not have wings or antennae

Crustaceans
- Have hard exoskeletons
- Most breathe using gills
- Have two antennae

OTHER INVERTEBRATES ▶
- Have soft bodies
- Some lack distinct shape
- Live in water environments

A LOOK INSIDE

FROG

◀ *A frog moves by jumping, using its extremely long back legs. To cope with the stresses and strains of leaping, it has a short, stiff spine rather than a long, flexible one.*

FISH

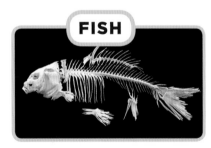

▲ *A fish's body is adapted to life in water. Muscles attached to its spine produce a side-to-side movement as it swims. Its fins and tail help it push and steer through the water.*

BIRD

◀ *A bird's body is built for flying, with light, hollow bones; front limbs evolved into wings. The muscles needed for flight are fixed to a large breastbone.*

SNAKE

▶ *A snake has a small skull and a long spine. This makes it flexible, and able to move by slithering, climbing, and burrowing.*

A CLOSER LOOK

Take a close look at this magnificent polar bear. It lives in the Arctic, and its body is perfectly designed for life in the cold. A thick fur coat covers even most of its feet, and it has a 4-inch (10.2 cm) layer of blubber underneath its skin. Small ears and a short tail keep its body from losing too much precious heat. All these features help the polar bear stay warm even when temperatures drop to below −34°F (−37°C). In fact, they're so effective that polar bears are more likely to overheat than get too cold.

A polar bear's white coat helps camouflage it against the white ice when it is hunting seals to eat. But, strictly speaking, its fur is not white—it's colorless. The hairs are hollow (to trap warm air) and they scatter light, reflecting it back to the eye so the fur appears white.

EARS Small ears cut down on heat loss.

COLOR Fur color provides camouflage.

HEAD A small head cuts down on heat loss.

SNOUT A long snout heats freezing air before it hits the lungs.

BLUBBER Thick blubber keeps it warm in water.

FUR Thick fur keeps it warm on land.

FEET Fur on the soles of the feet help with warmth and grip.

PAWS Large paws spread out the bear's weight on ice.

CLAWS AND TEETH Sharp claws and teeth are used for catching prey.

WEBBING Webbed front paws are used for swimming.

13

EVERYTHING AN ANIMAL DOES can be called behavior, from simple things like the way it finds and eats its food to more complex activities such as building a home or attracting a mate. Most of this behavior is instinctive—animals naturally know what to do without being taught—but a few animals are able to learn from experience and work out solutions to problems.

Many animals show social behavior and live in groups of some sort, such as flamingos in huge flocks and bigeye trevallies in massive schools. Living together has many advantages—namely, there is safety in numbers. Animals can produce and raise their young together, work together to find food, and defend themselves better against enemies. Some groups are highly organized, with a definite ranking of individuals with different statuses. Others are looser collections of animals belonging to the same species.

Communicating with one another is very important, whether animals live in groups or alone. Calls and sounds, body language, scents and smells, and striking colors and patterns are all signals that animals use to send information to one another. These signals enable them to find food, attract mates, mark out territories, defend themselves and their homes, and ward off enemies.

Animals use their senses to receive information about the world around them. Depending on how they communicate, some of their senses may be sharper than others. For example, animals that have good eyesight often have lots of color variation and use visual signals. Animals that communicate mainly with sound need good hearing. Many animals use scent trails to mark out their territories or leave other messages; they have a sharp sense of smell.

SUPER SENSES

Like we do, animals use the five senses of sight, smell, touch, taste, and hearing. In addition, some animals have enhanced or altogether extra senses that humans do not share.

Keen night vision
Bush babies have extralarge eyes. that help them hunt at night.

Supersensitive hearing
Barn owls hunt using their hearing to locate prey.

Unique tasting ability
Catfish have whiskers called barbels that sense prey.

Unusual touch technique
Stick insects navigate their environments by touching with their antennae.

Electroreception
Platypuses use sensors in their beaks to detect electric signals made by prey.

Chemoreception
Cats use special organs in the roofs of their mouths called Jacobson's organs to detect chemicals and heighten their sense of smell.

Thermoreception
Boas have heat pits in their jaws that pick up infrared heat given off by prey.

Echolocation
Bats use echolocation—bouncing sounds off objects to detect them—to find prey and navigate in the dark.

Many animals, including birds, make long journeys between their feeding and breeding sites. This is called migration. They are able to find their way there and back each year without getting lost. Some birds navigate using the position of the sun and stars, plus landmarks such as mountains or coastlines. Some even use Earth's magnetic field.

Surprisingly Human

When an elephant dies, the other members of its herd stay beside its body for several days, refusing to leave their relative. They seem to mourn its passing, and even to cry tears. They may rip up trees and grass and drop them on the body, similar to how people bury the dead at a funeral. Even many years after a death, elephants may stop by the place a loved one died and touch the bones with their trunks.

Lions live in family groups called prides that are made up mostly of related females and their young, with one or two adult males. A pride cooperates to hunt prey that would be too large for a single lion to tackle. The females also help raise one another's cubs, including nursing one another's babies.

WHAT DO ANIMALS EAT?

ALL ANIMALS NEED ENERGY to go about their daily lives. They get their energy from food, and they have ingenious ways of finding it. Some animals are active hunters, stealthily stalking their prey. Others sit and wait for food to pass by. A huge variety of foods are eaten. Some animals are carnivores—they eat meat. Within this category, there are smaller groups, such as insectivores, which eat insects. Other animals are herbivores—they eat plants. Omnivores are animals that eat both plants and other animals. Humans and black bears are examples of omnivores.

What an animal eats and how it finds its food shape the way it looks, moves, and behaves. Animals have adapted to make use of the food available in their particular habitats. They have special features for hunting, such as claws and fangs, or long beaks for reaching inside flowers to drink nectar. Some are carefully camouflaged, so that they can hide from possible predators or sneak up on their prey by surprise. The ways in which animals find their food also determine how they live. For example, wolves live and hunt in packs, enabling them to catch bigger prey than they could do singly.

WHAT'S ON THE MENU?

KRILL

◄ *An excellent swimmer, the Atlantic puffin dives up to 200 feet (60 m) beneath the ocean's surface and speeds through the water in search of food. When it spots small fish it likes, it grabs several in its strong beak.*

BAMBOO

▶ *Giant pandas eat bamboo and very little else. They use their hands and feet to grip stems, then nibble away at the leaves. Sadly, the bamboo forests in China where pandas live are being destroyed.*

BLOOD

◄ *Several animals feed on blood, including leeches, fleas, and vampire bats. A leech has suckers at both ends, with jaws at its head. When it bites, it injects a chemical that numbs the wound and prevents the blood from clotting.*

▶ *Nectar is a sweet liquid found deep inside flowers; it is the favorite food of some birds, insects, and bats. A hummingbird hovers in front of a flower, then sticks its long, pointed bill inside to get a drink, like sipping on a straw.*

NECTAR

Orcas are skilled hunters and ferocious meat eaters. Off the coast of Argentina, they hunt for sea lion pups. An orca lurks in the water, observing the pups learning to swim. Then, suddenly, it launches itself out of the water. Sometimes it catches a pup in its jaws. Most often, the pup gets away.

TABLE MANNERS

No knife and fork? No problem. Animals have interesting and unusual ways of eating food.

An aye-aye has long, thin middle fingers like twigs. It taps on tree bark, then listens for insects moving below. It rips off the bark with its teeth and hooks prey with its finger.

A chameleon has a long, sticky tongue that it keeps curled up in its mouth . . . until it spots an insect. Then it shoots out its tongue at lightning speed.

Flamingos feed with their heads almost upside down, sweeping their bills from side to side in the water.

A crown-of-thorns starfish has no table manners. It feeds by forcing its stomach out through its mouth over the coral it eats. It then makes special juices that digest the coral.

A UNIQUE FEEDING STYLE

Animals use many different techniques for finding and delivering food. Honeypot ants have a unique method. They collect and store nectar in their abdomens to feed others in the nest.

Wood mouse

Humpback whale

Humans

Burchell's zebra

Rhesus monkey

TOP TRAITS

Mammals have hair or fur. ▶ Mammary glands in mammal ears called the anvil, the hammer, and the stirrup. ▶ Mammals the environment is. ▶ Like all vertebrates, mammals have backbones. ▶ There are

MAMMALS

mothers produce milk used to feed young. ▶ Mammals have three bones in their middle are warm-blooded: They maintain their body temperature no matter how cold or hot about 5,420 species of mammal on Earth, making it a relatively small animal class.

MAMMALS ARE INCREDIBLY DIVERSE, ranging from the tiny bumblebee bat, which weighs about 0.1 ounce (3 g), to the 100-ton (90.7 metric tons) blue whale, the largest animal on Earth. Mammals get around by walking on two or four feet; some primates even walk on their knuckles. Mammals also hop, jump, climb, fly, glide, and swim. Mammals live on every continent, having adapted to every habitat from blazing desert to frozen tundra. They live on the ground, underground, in trees, in water, and in the air.

EVOLUTION

Mammals first evolved more than 200 million years ago, but during the Age of Dinosaurs, they were overshadowed by the the huge reptiles. When the dinosaurs became extinct around 66 million years ago, mammals survived.

Without dinosaurs as competition, mammals grew larger and evolved special features that allowed them to tolerate a variety of habitats—warm fur for cold areas, big ears to radiate heat in the desert. Huge animals such as Indricotherium (32–23 million years ago); Smilodon, the saber-toothed tiger (2.5 million–10,000 years ago); and the woolly mammoth (200,000–10,000 years ago) arose. They all eventually vanished—but their descendants are today's mammals.

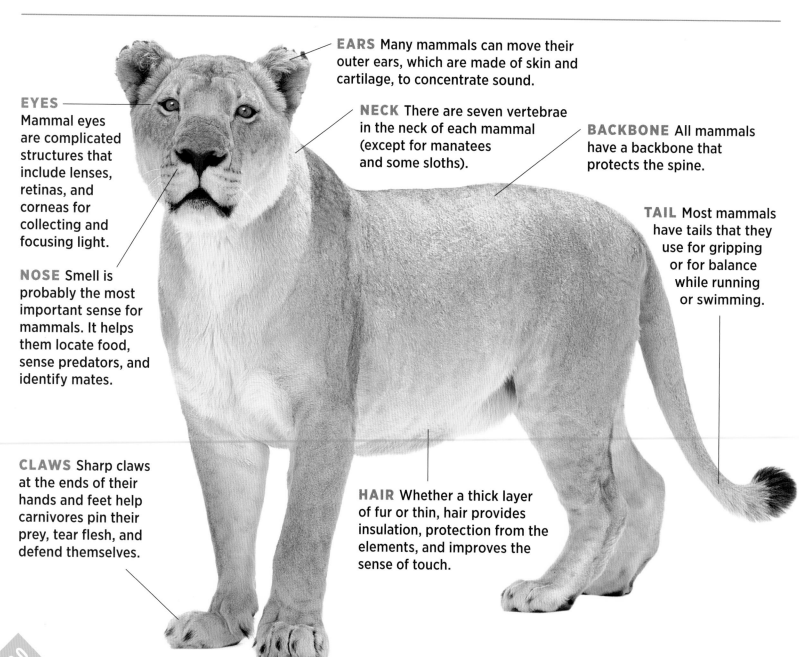

EARS Many mammals can move their outer ears, which are made of skin and cartilage, to concentrate sound.

EYES Mammal eyes are complicated structures that include lenses, retinas, and corneas for collecting and focusing light.

NOSE Smell is probably the most important sense for mammals. It helps them locate food, sense predators, and identify mates.

NECK There are seven vertebrae in the neck of each mammal (except for manatees and some sloths).

BACKBONE All mammals have a backbone that protects the spine.

TAIL Most mammals have tails that they use for gripping or for balance while running or swimming.

CLAWS Sharp claws at the ends of their hands and feet help carnivores pin their prey, tear flesh, and defend themselves.

HAIR Whether a thick layer of fur or thin, hair provides insulation, protection from the elements, and improves the sense of touch.

SENSES

Like all creatures, mammals understand the world around them through their senses: vision, hearing, smell, taste, and touch. Like other animals, mammals' senses evolved to suit their lifestyles. Hunters such as cats and seals have extra sharp hearing, sense of smell, and night vision to find prey at night.

Moles, which live in dark, underground environments, do not have great vision, but they have developed a strong sense of touch to help them feel around in these low-light conditions.

Bats and whales have an extra sense, called echolocation, that lets them interpret low-frequency sounds so they can locate prey. They do this by sending out signals that bounce off moving objects.

ENDOTHERMIA

Mammals are endothermic, or warm-blooded, which means they can generate their own warmth in colder environments and cool themselves off in hotter environments. Their bodies do this automatically, slowing down or speeding up metabolism so that they stay as warm in cold climates and as cool in warm climates as they need to. Some mammals have developed special body parts to help deal with heat and cold, such as the weighty layers of blubber that keep whales and seals insulated in freezing water, and the big ears that emit heat for fennec foxes and jackrabbits in hot desert regions.

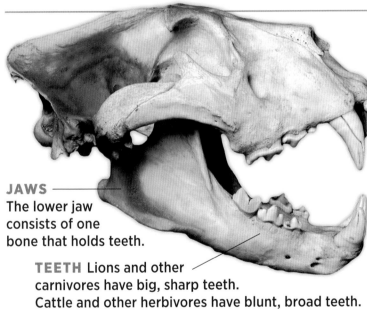

JAWS
The lower jaw consists of one bone that holds teeth.

TEETH Lions and other carnivores have big, sharp teeth. Cattle and other herbivores have blunt, broad teeth.

BLOWHOLE Whales and their relatives live underwater but have lungs and need to breathe. They must surface to take in air and expel carbon dioxide from blowholes on the tops of their heads.

FLIPPERS AND FINS
Mammals that live in water use flippers and fins to help them swim and stay balanced.

ON THE INSIDE

SKELETON Five types of vertebrae make up the skeleton: cervical (neck), thoracic, lumbar, sacral, and caudal (tail).

SKULL A mammal has two small knobs at the base of its skull that fit into the top vertebrae of its backbone.

BRAIN Only a mammal has a neocortex in its brain. This aids in language, perception, and thought.

LUNGS Mammals breathe in oxygen and breathe out carbon dioxide. Air is taken in through noses and mouths; diaphragms and rib cages expand and contract to push air to and from the lungs.

WE ARE MAMMALS: Human beings fall into the mammal class and share characteristics with the other species in the class. We have hair on our bodies; human moms produce milk in their breasts to feed their babies; and we have three bones in our middle ears—only mammals have these traits. We are also warm-blooded vertebrates, like all mammals.

Like many mammals, we are born with a strong instinct to join with other members of our species and to bond with our children; these behaviors have helped mammals survive and succeed, because each species protects and comforts its members.

GIVING BIRTH

Mammals give birth in one of three ways. The monotremes—including platypuses and echidnas—lay eggs. Marsupials—kangaroos, opossums, wombats, koalas, and many others—bear tiny infants, sometimes smaller than a grain of rice; a marsupial infant immediately crawls into a furry pouch on its mother's body, where it eats and grows until it can survive independently. All other mammals carry fetuses in their wombs, then give birth to live babies. Some of these babies are able to eat, walk, and run within minutes of emerging from the womb; others need extra care from their mothers for days, weeks, or months.

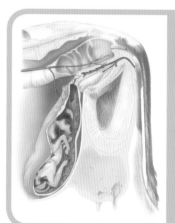

WOMB

MOST mammals give birth to live babies, rather than laying eggs. A baby develops in the female's womb and is nourished by the mother's blood supply through the placenta.

LACTATION

Every mammal species produces milk for its young; this process is called lactation (the Latin word lac means "milk"). Milk is produced in mammary glands; it contains the right mix of nutrients for each species. The first liquid that comes out after a baby is born is called colostrum. This contains enzymes that make the baby immune to some diseases. Mammal babies are born with the instinct to suckle; a healthy baby that is placed near its mother will move to the mother's nipples and begin to nurse. The dayak fruit bat is the only male mammal that produces milk.

LIVE ACTION: BROWN BEAR

A mother brown bear stirs in a dark den. Before entering the den last winter, she had eaten three times her needs every day. Now, three months later, the store of extra fat is gone. A tiny cub, born during the big sleep, rests by her side.

The bears' keen senses catch the scent of leaf buds and hear the splash of fish in a faraway stream. Hungry, the pair leaves the den to find food. Suddenly, a mountain lion appears and separates mother and cub. Frightened and enraged, the mother slashes the cat with one huge paw, sharp with claws, to protect her cub. The mountain lion dashes away, wounded.

BABY BONDING

Because of the way that mammals are born and fed in infancy, their mothers have to be near them for a period of time. This nearness leads to strong bonding between mammal mothers and babies. Fathers in some species also care for the young, but not as often or as devotedly as mothers. Koala mothers chew food for their babies; mother rabbits and deer protect their offspring by hiding them; bears will attack any animal that comes near their cubs. Chimpanzees remain connected to their offspring for life, and in some species, such as elephants, the connection lasts through generations: Females form herds with their children and grandchildren.

SOCIAL MAMMALS

Some mammals, including many members of the cat family, prefer to live alone. But most mammals, including humans, are social and spend most of their time with other members of their species.

Mammal groups have many names, such as herd, mob, pride, and tribe. In bonobo groups and elephant herds, females dominate. Among chimpanzees and many hooved animals, males are the leaders. Sometimes the groups are made up mostly of females and children, and the males join only during mating season.

Mammals often form strong bonds with their herd mates; they hunt or forage together and share food. Some, such as zebras, will defend members of their group that are attacked by predators.

BIG OR SMALL, BROWN OR GRAY—all marsupials have one remarkable feature in common: their babies called joeys, are tiny when they are born—some are smaller than jellybeans. They breathe through their skin because their lungs are undeveloped. After birth, they crawl through their mothers' fur towards her teats. There, they latch on and eat and grow until they're ready for the outside world. In many (but not all) species this growth takes place in a furry pouch called a marsupium (MAR-sou-PEE-um).

Of about 330 species of marsupials, 70 percent live in Australia and surrounding islands; some in South and Central America; and just one (Virginia opossum) in North America. Most prefer wet areas and woodlands. Most are herbivores; a few, like the Tasmanian devil, eat meat.

Experts believe that the first true marsupials evolved in North America about 90 million years ago and migrated to Australia.

KOALA
Phascolarctos cinereus

SIZE: male: 15–26 pounds (7–12 kg); female: 11–18 pounds (5–8 kg)
HABITAT: Eucalyptus woodland; eastern Australia
FOOD: Eucalyptus leaves and shoots

Koalas look cute and cuddly but are shy and avoid humans and each other. They make unpleasant sounds and move higher into trees when approached. They have large paws for gripping branches and gray or brown fur. The eucalyptus leaves and shoots they eat—about 1 pound daily—are not very nutritious. They have energy to stay awake for only five or six hours each night.

GOODFELLOW'S TREE KANGAROO
Dendrolagus goodfellowi

SIZE: 15–18 pounds (7–8 kg)
HABITAT: Rain forest; New Guinea, Indonesia
FOOD: Silkwood leaves, fruits, flowers, grasses

Tree kangaroos have developed features that help them live in trees: wide feet and long tails for balancing on tree branches, plus sharp, curved claws for climbing. Goodfellow's tree kangaroo has a digestive system that allows it to break down many kinds of plants efficiently. It was named after Walter Goodfellow, a British zoologist.

SNACK ATTACK

Koala babies—called joeys—need a special kind of help from their moms. Koala joeys don't have the bacteria that adult koalas use to break down the poison in eucalyptus leaves. The young eat their mother's poop to introduce helpful bacteria to their digestive systems.

TAMMAR WALLABY
Macropus eugenii

SIZE: 9–20 pounds (4–9 kg)
HABITAT: Grassland, coastal shrub; New Zealand, Australia
FOOD: Leaves, grasses, seeds

Wallabies are similar to kangaroos, but smaller. Like other kangaroos and wallabies, tammar wallabies have strong legs that they use for hopping and defense. Their long, muscled tails help them balance. Wallabies are noisy; they vocalize and stamp their feet to scare off predators and to communicate with each other.

COMMON WOMBAT
Vombatus ursinus

SIZE: 44-77 pounds (20-35 kg)
HABITAT: Forest, coastal scrub; southeastern Australia, Tasmania
FOOD: Grasses, mosses, shrubs

Wombats like to be alone. Each one burrows a tunnel from 6 to 60 feet (1.8-18.3 m) long; they leave the burrows at night to find food. When they sense danger, they run back at up to 25 miles per hour (40.2 kph). Among the world's largest burrowing animals, wombats survive in burrows without food for several days.

RINGTAIL POSSUM
Pseudocheirus peregrinus

SIZE: 1-2 pounds (0.5-1 kg)
HABITAT: Brush forest, coastal scrub, rural garden; Australia
FOOD: Leaves, flowers, fruits

Living together in nests called dreys built between tree branches, ringtail possums will communicate with each other in high-pitched squeals. They rarely descend from the trees and use their long tails to swing from branch to branch. Their diet of leaves is hard to digest, so they often eat their feces to wring more nutrition from it.

Surprisingly Human

Many mammals produce a hormone of love and bonding called oxytocin. During pregnancy, the amount of this hormone will increase. Studies show that female mammals with greater levels of oxytocin gaze at their offspring more frequently, watch them more carefully, and retrieve them from danger faster.

QUOKKA
Setonix brachyurus

SIZE: 6-9 pounds (2.5-4 kg)
HABITAT: Thicket, scrub; Rottnest Island, off western Australia
FOOD: Grasses, leaves, seeds, roots

Friendly little quokkas live in family groups. They use strong back legs to climb trees. Living on an island with no fresh water, they have developed the odd ability to drink saltwater.

EASTERN GRAY KANGAROO
Macropus giganteus

SIZE: male: 110-146 pounds (50-66 kg); female: 37-88 pounds (17-40 kg)
HABITAT: Open woodland, grassland, forested mountain; eastern and southern Australia
FOOD: Grass, leaves, seeds, grains

The eastern gray kangaroo has the super strong back legs that make kangaroos the only large animal that gets around by hopping. Kangaroos live in large groups called mobs. The males often fight with each other by using their front limbs to box and push; they sometimes kick with their legs. Kangaroos can jump up to 6 feet (1.8 m) high. They have excellent hearing and can move their ears in different directions.

ALL CATS EVOLVED 33–66 MILLION YEARS AGO from a group of small, meat-eating tree-dwellers called miacoids. Cats belong to the Felidae family; smaller cats are members of subfamily Felinae. The 13 Felinae genera live wild in many habitats on all continents except Australia and Antarctica.

Cats are carnivores with great hunting skills—climbing, jumping, and swimming. They have sharp claws, sharp senses of hearing, smell, and night vision. Most are nocturnal. Many have spectacular fur with bold markings.

A few species live in groups; most are loners. They communicate with unique sounds—purring, meowing, roaring—and body language. Most cats mark their territory with their scent by urinating. Females give birth to one or multiple kittens (small cats) or cubs (big cats) that can't walk or open their eyes. Mothers care for them until they become independent.

SAND CAT
Felis margarita

SIZE: 3–8 pounds (1.5–3.5 kg)
HABITAT: Desert; northern Africa, Middle East, central Asia
FOOD: Rodents, rabbits, birds, reptiles

The sand cat is the only cat that lives in true deserts. It is superbly adapted to that habitat: Its light brown fur is good camouflage, and it has hair on its foot pads for walking on hot stone and sand. It can live without drinking water, extracting moisture from its prey.

DOMESTIC CAT
Felis catus

SIZE: 9–13 pounds (4–6 kg)
HABITAT: Indoors; worldwide
FOOD: Meat, fish, dairy

Humans have kept cats as pets for at least 4,000 years; there were cat goddesses in ancient Egypt. Today, hundreds of millions of housecats (over 100 different breeds) control pests, provide companionship, and entertain us.

Even pampered housecats can survive in the wild, using their superb hearing and climbing ability to hunt. Though still wild, cats develop affection for their owners. Studies show that owning a cat improves both physical and psychological health.

Surprisingly Human

Some people think that civilized humans started personal grooming—but lots of animals, especially cats, do it. All felines clean themselves for several hours daily, licking their fur to remove dirt with their sandpaperlike tongues.

JAGUARUNDI
Puma yagouaroundi

SIZE: 10–20 pounds (4.5–9 kg)
HABITAT: Rain forest, woodland, grassland; southern United States, Central America, northern South America
FOOD: Small mammals, birds, reptiles

Jaguarundis look like weasels, with long, narrow bodies, short legs, and small heads. They come in a variety of colors, from near black to red to tawny yellow. They travel and hunt during daylight, covering large areas. They are good jumpers, leaping high off the ground to catch birds. Females gives birth in dens.

CARACAL
Caracal caracal

SIZE: **18–42 pounds (6–19 kg)**
HABITAT: **Grassland, thicket, woodland; Africa, central and southwestern Asia**
FOOD: **Birds, small mammals, reptiles, fish**

The caracal's speed is legendary; these medium-size cats jump in the air and catch birds in flight with their large paws. Persian and Indian royals often captured caracals and made bets on their success in killing birds. Caracals also swim fast to catch fish. Their name comes from a Turkish word meaning "black ear."

LEOPARD CAT
Prionailurus bengalensis

SIZE: **3.5–15 pounds (1.6–7 kg)**
HABITAT: **Forest, shrubland, grassland; Asia**
FOOD: **Rodents, birds, amphibians**

The most common wild cat in Asia, all twelve subspecies of leopard cats have beautiful spotted fur and are often killed for their pelts. Leopard cats don't play with their food; they pounce and kill quickly.

CANADA LYNX
Lynx canadensis

SIZE: **10–37 pounds (4.5–17 kg)**
HABITAT: **Coniferous and mixed forest, tundra; Canada, western and northeastern United States**
FOOD: **Snowshoe hares, birds, fish**

The Canada lynx has wide feet that it uses like snowshoes in its icy habitat. This large, strong cat is a patient hunter, often lying in wait for hours. Its life is tied to its perferred prey, the snowshoe hare. When not hunting, the Canadian lynx rests under trees or rock ledges.

OCELOT
Leopardus pardalis

SIZE: 18–35 pounds (8–16 kg)
HABITAT: Tropical forest, marsh, grassland; southern United States, Central and South America
FOOD: Small mammals, birds, reptiles, fish

The largest and one of the most beautiful of the small spotted cats, the ocelot is a skilled hunter, climber, and swimmer. Males stake out and patrol territories where a few females live. Ocelots, though always rare, maintained a population of several hundred in the southwestern United States until their habitats were destroyed by development. Today, fewer than 100 of them live north of the Mexican border.

Animal Antics
Most cats, from tigers to tabbies, play. They stretch, climb, jump, unroll toilet paper, tangle yarn, bat balls, and hide in cabinets and boxes. Some animal behaviorists say cats are practicing hunting when they play.

THE MOST FEARED ANIMALS of the jungle, big cats are extraordinarily skilled hunters with sharp senses and strong, fast bodies. They are beautiful creatures, with brightly colored fur, bold markings, and penetrating eyes. Some experts call only members of genus *Panthera*—lions, tigers, leopards, jaguars—big cats; others include cheetahs and cougars, which are not quite as big. Recent evidence shows that the first big cats appeared in Asia about 6 million years ago.

Big cats live in jungles, forests, grasslands and mountains in Asia, Africa, and South America; a few extend to eastern Europe and the southern United States. All are meat-eaters; some also eat fish and eggs. They eat plants only if nothing else can be found. They scent-mark their territory with their urine.

Babies are called cubs. Mothers care for cubs for a few years until they become independent. Most big cats are nocturnal, and most active at dusk and dawn.

SIBERIAN TIGER
Panthera tigris altaica
SIZE: male: 397–675 pounds (180–306 kg); female: 220–368 pounds (100–167 kg)
HABITAT: Forest; eastern Russia, China
FOOD: Bears, deer, wild pigs, salmon

The world's largest cats and the only cats with stripes, tigers are extraordinary hunters. They mark their territory with urine and hide in wait for prey, then pounce. Their speedy, slender bodies are designed for attack, with powerful forearms, sharp claws, and massive jaws that deliver crushing bites. Tigers rarely eat food they haven't killed themselves and teach cubs to stalk. They are also excellent swimmers.

COUGAR
Puma concolor
SIZE: male: 79–265 pounds (36–120 kg); female: 64–141 pounds (29–64 kg)
HABITAT: Forest, desert, swamp, mountain; North and South America
FOOD: Deer, elk, cattle, raccoons, other vertebrates

Cougars are fast, agile stalkers and kill prey both larger and smaller than themselves. They are ambush attackers, hiding and then pouncing. Cougars are called by many names, including puma, mountain lion, and panther. Their cubs have spots, which disappear as they mature. Cougars can't roar, but they can purr.

SNOW LEOPARD
Uncia uncia
SIZE: 55–165 pounds (25–75 kg)
HABITAT: Mountain steppe, forest scrub; Russia, central and southern Asia
FOOD: Sheep, deer, goats, dogs, other vertebrates

Thick fur keeps these cats warm, and big noses help them breathe the thin air in their cold mountain habitats. They can jump a distance of 50 feet (15 km), using their super long tails for balance.

 FUN FACT

Big cats are the only animals that can roar. Lions, tigers, leopards, and jaguars have cartilage—the flexible material that makes up the human ear and nose—in their larynx that enables the roar. Lions have the most cartilage and are thus the loudest.

 **ANIMAL PLANET ROAR** Because fewer than 450 Siberian tigers are left in the wild, the International Fund for Animal Welfare has been collecting orphaned tiger cubs in eastern Russia and taking them to protected areas. After making sure that they are healthy and have skills to survive, they release them into the wild.

BENGAL TIGER
Panthera tigris tigris
SIZE: male: 397–569 pounds (180–258 kg); female: 220–353 pounds (100–160 kg)
HABITAT: Tropical and subtropical forest; Indian subcontinent
FOOD: Wild boar, water buffalo, other vertebrates

Bengal tigers are slightly smaller than Siberians. Most have deep gold or orange fur with black stripes. Bengal tigers are the national animal of India and Bangladesh. Though only about 2,500 still exist in the wild, they are the most common wild tiger.

SUMATRAN TIGER
Panthera tigris sumatrae

SIZE: male: 220–309 pounds (100–140 kg); female: 165–243 pounds (75–110 kg)
HABITAT: Forest; Indonesian island of Sumatra
FOOD: Deer, pheasant, porcupine, other vertebrates

Only about 400 members of this subspecies exist in the wild; three other subspecies are already extinct. The smallest of the tiger subspecies, Sumatran tigers have darker fur and thicker stripes. As with all tigers, each cat's stripes are unique, like fingerprints. They avoid areas marked by human activity.

CLOUDED LEOPARD
Neofelis nebulosa

SIZE: 24–51 pounds (11–23 kg)
HABITAT: Tropical forest, woodland; India, Nepal, southeastern Asia, southern China
FOOD: Large and small mammals, birds

Amazing climbers that sometimes hang upside-down from trees, clouded leopards can stalk prey from the ground or from above. They have unusually long canine teeth, similar to those of saber-toothed tigers. Clouded leopards are not related more closely to leopards than they are to other big cats.

ASIATIC LION
Panthera leo persica

SIZE: male: 353–419 pounds (160–190 kg); female: 243–265 pounds (110–120 kg)
HABITAT: Dry deciduous forest; Gir National Park and Wildlife Sanctuary, western Gujarat, India
FOOD: All kinds of meat, from tiny to huge animals

Apex predators, lions have strength and keen senses that allow it to rule. And male lions are the only cats with crownlike manes. Lions are the most social big cats. Females live in tight packs called prides. Males live in groups and court the females, sometimes fighting to the death over a mate. Females are the main hunters and care for the cubs. The African lion subspecies lives in sub-Saharan Africa.

JAGUAR
Panthera onca

SIZE: 150–300 pounds (68–136 kg)
HABITAT: Rain forest, grassland, woodland; southwestern United States, Central and South America
FOOD: Large and small mammals, fish, snakes

The jaguar's name is said to come from a native South American word meaning "beast that kills with one leap." The largest cats in the Americas, jaguars have the strongest bite of any big cat and are the only cats that kill by piercing their prey's skulls and brains. Most have spotted fur, but some are solid black.

CHEETAH

The cheetah stands out—literally, as its fur is unique in providing no camouflage in its habitat. But what it is best known for is its speed. It has enlarged nostrils and is able to take in more oxygen than other cats, allowing it to run faster and catch more elusive prey.

ABOUT ME!

I'm a cheetah cub. My mom looks after me. My dad likes to hang out with the other dads in a group called a coalition. They make sure we have enough room to eat and hunt. I love to wrestle and play with other cubs. This will help me learn to hunt for food when I get older.

7 FACTS ABOUT THE CHEETAH

- ▶ Is a daylight hunter, unlike other big cats
- ▶ Accelerates from 0-60 miles per hour (0-96 kph) in 3 seconds
- ▶ Has excellent eyesight
- ▶ Spots are called rosettes
- ▶ Lives in African grasslands
- ▶ Has up to eight cubs in a litter
- ▶ Long tail is used for steering and balance

THE MEMBERS OF THE CANIDAE FAMILY, called canids or canines have compact, speedy bodies and walk on the toes of their four feet. Most have long snouts, shiny noses, and bushy tails that they use to communicate. They are almost all carnivores and use their pointy teeth to crack bones and slice flesh. They also eat berries and fish. Two species specialize in eating insects.

Canines have sharp senses of hearing and smell, allowing them to track prey for miles. Some species such as wolves are social animals, forming packs to hunt, and others are more solitary. Parents prepare dens where pups are born and most fathers stay to care for the young.

The gray wolf, one of the first of the modern canines, appeared about 500,000 years ago. Canidae includes 13 genera and about 35 species. Members live on every continent except on Antarctica.

COYOTE
Canis latrans

SIZE: **15–46 pounds (7–21 kg)**
HABITAT: **Forest, grassland, desert, swamp; North and Central America**
FOOD: **Small mammals , plants, garbage**

Coyotes are recognized by their distinctive *yip-yip-yip* sound. Clocked at 40 miles per hour (64 kph), they're one of the fastest land animals in North America. Coyotes sometimes partner with American badgers to hunt; the coyotes chase down ground squirrels that run, the badgers dig out those that hide in burrows. They're more successful together than each would be alone.

FENNEC FOX
Vulpes zerda

SIZE: **2–3 pounds (1–1.5 kg)**
HABITAT: **Sandy desert; northern Africa**
FOOD: **Insects, rodents, birds**

The smallest of all canids, fennecs are all ears. Their huge, thin-skinned ears emit heat on hot desert days, and their thick fur warms them during cold nights. Fennecs mate and stay with their family units for life.

DOMESTIC DOG
Canis lupus familiaris

SIZE: **1–198 pounds (0.5–90 kg)**
HABITAT: **Indoors; worldwide**
FOOD: **Meat, fish, bones**

The first animals that lived with people, dogs started bonding with early humans over 10,000 years ago. There are close to a billion dogs in over 400 breeds in the world today. Dogs benefit people by protecting them, herding other animals, cleaning up garbage, and warning of attackers. Dogs can be trained to respond to human commands and perform tasks such as sniffing bombs. They have super sharp hearing and smell, plus emotional senses that make them loyal and comforting.

ARCTIC FOX
Vulpes lagopus

SIZE: male: 7–20 pounds (3–9 kg); female: 3–7 pounds (1.5–3 kg)
HABITAT: Arctic tundra; northern Europe, northern Asia, North America
FOOD: Lemmings, marine mammal carcasses, sea birds, fish, berries

Plush white fur warms the Arctic fox, even the bottoms of its feet and tip of its tail (which it wraps around its face, like a scarf). The fur changes color with the seasons; white in winter, gray-brown in spring. This fox uses especially sharp hearing to find prey in vast landscapes it inhabits.

DINGO
Canis lupus dingo

SIZE: 22–44 pounds (10–20 kg)
HABITAT: Forest, plain, mountain, desert; southeastern Asia, Australia
FOOD: Rabbits, rodents, wallabies

Dingos descended from an Asian version of the gray wolf; they were introduced to Australia over 4,000 years ago. They eat whatever is available and often prey on farm animals. They howl to communicate with pack members.

GOLDEN JACKAL
Canis aureus

SIZE: 11–33 pounds (5–15 kg)
HABITAT: Desert, grassland, forest; Africa, Europe, Middle East, Asia
FOOD: Birds, mammals, fish, reptiles

Jackals are scavengers; they eat garbage and dead animals. But they are also excellent hunters with strong, slender bodies and long legs that they use to travel long distances. Jackals mate for life. They will bring food to mates by swallowing it so it won't be stolen and then spitting it up.

GRAY WOLF
Canis lupus

SIZE: male: 66–120 pounds (30–54.5 kg); female: 51–121 pounds (23–55 kg)
HABITAT: Forest, tundra, prairie; northern North America, Europe, Asia, Africa
FOOD: Large hooved animals, small mammals, livestock, berries

The largest canid, gray wolves have excellent senses and fascinating social and communication skills. Most live in packs (there are some lone wolves). Within each pack, a dominant male and female breed and lead. All members care for the young. All pack members understand body language such as baring teeth in warning, raising tails to show danger or attention, or tail-wagging when relaxed.

The gray wolf's comeback is a conservation success story. Habitat destruction as well as overhunting had reduced populations to near zero in the United States and Europe. But since the 1970s, protection laws have allowed them to thrive in the wild again.

BEARS

APEX PREDATORS—ANIMALS THAT are prey for no animals—bears themselves are omnivores. Though they eat meat and fish, their diet is mostly berries, nuts, and other plants. They live in wooded areas, and different species have adapted to all climates, from polar to tropical. Most have superlative vision, hearing, and smell. Bears generally have big, bulky bodies, flat faces with conical snouts, and flat feet so they can walk upright.

Cold climate bears hibernate during winter, when food is scarce. Their respiration and heart rate slows down and they sleep in dens without eating or drinking until spring. Most species give birth during hibernation and keep the cubs with them, still sleeping. Mothers are fiercely protective.

The eight bear species are members of the Ursidae family. They evolved from small, raccoonlike mammals that appeared in North America about 35 million years ago.

BROWN BEAR
Ursus arctos

SIZE: 176–1,323 pounds (80–600 kg)
HABITAT: Forest, mountain, alpine meadow; northern regions of Eurasia, North America, and Russia
FOOD: Plants, salmon, small and large mammals

There are at least 16 subspecies of brown bears. All eat berries, nuts, and roots, but they also eat a great deal of meat and salmon. Hundreds of bears gather to catch salmon with their huge paws as they swim upriver. Brown bears hibernate in winter when food is scarce. They sleep in dens or caves for six months without eating, drinking, or urinating.

SLOTH BEAR
Melursus ursinus

SIZE: male: 176–320 pounds (80–145 kg); female: 121–209 pounds (55–95 kg)
HABITAT: Tropical forest and grassland; Indian subcontinent
FOOD: Insects, especially termites, honey, eggs, fruit

Shaggy-coated sloth bears have light-colored patches on their chests. They pierce termite and ant nests with curved claws, blow away dust, and suck out insects. Mothers carry cubs on their backs when they first leave the den.

SPECTACLED BEAR
Tremarctos ornatus

SIZE: male: 220–340 pounds (100–155 kg); female: 132–180 pounds (60–82 kg)
HABITAT: High-altitude forest and grassland; Andes mountains of South America
FOOD: Plants, rodents, insects, birds

Named for spectacle-like white patches around its eyes, this large black bear eats cacti and other thorny plants. It also strips bark off trees and eats the pulpy wood underneath. Spectacled bears spend most of their time in trees, using branches to build platforms for resting. They're also called Andean bears.

ASIATIC BLACK BEAR
Ursus thibetanus

SIZE: male: 220–440 pounds (100–200 kg); female: 110–275 pounds (50–125 kg)
HABITAT: Temperate and tropical forest; Asia, eastern Russia
FOOD: Mostly plants, including nuts, fruits, berries and insects

These bears are very similar to American black bears, and scientists believe they had the same ancestor and split about 4 million years ago. Asiatic black bears have crescent-shaped white patches on their black fur and are called moon bears. Those who live farthest north hibernate in winter.

AMERICAN BLACK BEAR
Ursus americanus

SIZE: male: 104–551 pounds (47–250 kg); female: 86–375 pounds (39–170 kg)
HABITAT: Forest, woodland; North America
FOOD: Berries and other plants, insects, carrion, calves of hooved animals

There are twice as many black bears as any other species. Some are cinnamon, reddish-brown, or blue-gray. They find food cleverly, digging and climbing with their short claws. Their large paws can open screw-top jars. Mothers give birth while they hibernate in dens; the cubs stay snuggled next to them, nursing, until spring.

GRIZZLY BEAR
Ursus arctos horribilis

SIZE: 220–700 pounds (100–317 kg)
HABITAT: Forest, meadow; northern North America
FOOD: Vegetation, nuts, seeds, fish, hooved animals, small mammals, carrion

One of the biggest brown bear subspecies, grizzlies are identified by a large hump between their shoulders and very long claws. They have a particularly keen sense of smell that can detect food for miles.

During Bear Awareness Week—the third week of May—naturalists and park rangers remind us how important bears are to our ecology, celebrate the strength of these creatures, and help protect their wild habitats.

SUN BEAR
Helarctos malayanus

SIZE: 60–143 pounds (27–65 kg)
HABITAT: Tropical forest; southeastern Asia
FOOD: Insects, honey, fruit

Also known as honey bears, these bears have jet-black fur with distinct light patches on their chests; the patches sometimes look like suns. They stick their extremely long tongues into beehives or insect nests to extract food. Sun bears are the smallest bear species.

POLAR BEAR
Ursus maritimus

SIZE: male: 661–1764 pounds (300–800 kg); female: 330–661 pounds (150–300 kg)
HABITAT: Icy region; Arctic Circle
FOOD: Ringed seals, birds, whales

Polar bears are the largest carnivorous land animals on Earth. Their efficient digestive systems let them devour huge amounts of food and store it for times of scarcity. Their weight is distributed over four large legs so they don't crack thin ice. The soles of their feet are bare to provide suction. Their pointy claws are like tiny icepicks. Polar bears spend their time in or near water; they can stay submerged for two minutes.

FUN FACT

Polar bears have super fur. Its pure white appearance makes them invisible against snowy landscapes. Polar bear fur covers every body part except their nose and the bottoms of their feet. The individual hairs are hollow and trap air for extra insulation.

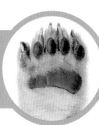

GIANT PANDA

Giant pandas are considered national treasures in China, but they are an endangered species with only about 1,000 left in the wild. Solitary animals that avoid each other, giant pandas only meet during mating season. They eat more than 40 different types of bamboo, but their chosen food has very little nutrition, so they have to spend two-thirds of their day eating. They consume anywhere from about 30-80 pounds (13.5-36 kg) of bamboo daily to get the energy they need.

7 FACTS ABOUT THE GIANT PANDA

- ▶ Weighs up to 300 pounds (136 kg)
- ▶ Inhabits bamboo forests in Central China mountains
- ▶ Sleeps in hollow logs or tree stumps
- ▶ Eats a diet which is 99% bamboo, plus some meat
- ▶ Has an extra finger (a modified wrist bone) for stripping leaves
- ▶ Has largest molar teeth of any carnivore
- ▶ Infants are born white, develop color later

ABOUT ME!

I'm a newborn giant panda. I am tiny; I weighed about 4 ounces (100g) at birth. I am helpless, so my mother is very protective; she will even eat my poop so predators won't be attracted by its scent. I stay with my mother for around 18 months. Usually when I leave it's because my mom is pregnant again.

SMALL CARNIVORES

CARNIVORA, THE MEAT-EATING ORDER of mammals, includes almost 300 species. About 100 of those are large, well-known animals in the canine, feline, and ursine families; another 33 are seals. There are about 170 species of smaller carnivorous mammals that fall into groups like weasels, otters, genets, civets, raccoons, and mongooses. Many of these are not strictly meat-eaters, but they have teeth and digestive systems that can handle meat.

Small carnivorous mammals are a diverse group. They live all over the world, and there are species that have adapted to every habitat. Much of the wildlife in North America—raccoons, weasels, and skunks—falls into this category. They range in size from the least weasel that weighs under an ounce (25 g) to otters that weigh over 100 pounds (45 kg). Like larger carnivorous mammals, most have sharp claws, good senses, and good hunting skills.

HONEY BADGER
Mellivora capensis

SIZE: **13–26 pounds (6–12 kg)**
HABITAT: **Scrubland, rain forest; Africa, Asia, Indian subcontinent**
FOOD: **Small mammals, insects, honey, amphibians, fruit.**

Honey badgers have an ingenious way of obtaining honey. They send a stench from their anal glands into beehives. They eat the escaping bees, then break open the hive for the honey. Unlike other badger species, honey badgers are loners, except that cubs stay with mothers for over a year.

STRIPED HYENA
Hyaena hyaena

SIZE: **55–120 pounds (25–55 kg)**
HABITAT: **Arid mountainous region, scrub woodland; northern Africa, Middle East through India**
FOOD: **Carrion, seeds, fruit, insects, birds, fish, mammals**

Like other hyenas, striped hyenas resemble dogs but are closely related to cats. They kill large prey by working in pairs and hanging on with their powerful jaws. They can puff up their hair to make themselves look larger.

NORTHERN RACCOON
Procyon lotor

SIZE: **4–22 pounds (2–10 kg)**
HABITAT: **Forest, suburb, city; North America**
FOOD: **Plants, small animals, garbage**

Raccoons can be instantly identified by their facial mask. Some scientists theorize that the patches under their eyes reduce glare and improve night vision for these nocturnal animals. Raccoons are known for their flexibility. They live all over—coasts, mountains, woods, cities—and eat anything. The word raccoon comes from a Powhatan word meaning "one who rubs, scrubs, and scratches with hands." Highly intelligent, they can remember how to solve a problem three years later.

Surprisingly Human

Raccoons don't have opposable thumbs, but they have extremely dexterous front paws with long finger that can turn doorknobs, unscrew jars, and untie knots. They can open trashcans even if the lids are latched.

MEERKAT
Suricata suricatta

SIZE: 1–2 pounds (0.5–1 kg)
HABITAT: Grassland, scrubland; southern Africa
FOOD: Mainly insects; also small animals, plants

A type of mongoose, meerkats—sociable, big-eyed, standing upright—live in groups called mobs in complex burrows with many entrances. At dawn, the meerkats emerge together and bask in the sun. One meerkat stands guard as they play, dig, and forage. They vocalize to each other all day. Everyone in the group cares for the pups.

RED PANDA
Ailurus fulgens

SIZE: 7–15 pounds (3–7 kg)
HABITAT: Mountainous forest; Nepal, India, Bhutan, Myanmar, southern China
FOOD: Mostly bamboo; possibly small amounts of fruits, lizards

Red pandas are not in the bear family, but—like giant pandas—they mostly eat bamboo. Also like giant pandas, one of bones in their wrists sticks out and acts like an extra finger. They are solitary, crepuscular (most active at dusk and dawn), and good climbers. Red pandas resemble raccoons, and their reddish fur camouflages them against the rust-colored moss in their habitat. They make only a few sounds, but one of them combines a quack with a snort.

STRIPED SKUNK
Mephitis mephitis

SIZE: 2.5–15 pounds (1–6 kg)
HABITAT: Grassland, woodland, populated area; North America
FOOD: Insects, small mammals, plants

Skunks are small, but they have a fantastic defense system: they can shoot a horrible-smelling oily liquid from under their tails, hitting targets ten feet away with accuracy. Larger animals—except dogs—avoid them because the spray is caustic, difficult to remove, and can cause blindness. Strictly nocturnal, skunks hide during daylight hours.

FUN FACT

Skunks spray as a last resort, after first hissing and running. They have a tiny amount of foul liquid in their bodies; once they use it all, it takes ten days for them to produce more.

ERMINE
Mustela erminea

SIZE: male: 2–12 ounces (56–360 g); female: 1–6 ounces (25–180 g)
HABITAT: Open area, forest, marsh; northern Eurasia, North America
FOOD: Small mammals

These skillful hunters, also called stoats and short-tail weasels, hide and then pounce and bite their prey's neck. Males and females stay in separate territories when not mating. Their fur turns from reddish to white in winter.

COMMON GENET
Genetta genetta

SIZE: 2–7 pounds (1–3 kg)
HABITAT: Rocky terrain, forest, scrubland; Africa, Middle East, Europe
FOOD: Wood mice, lizards, small mammals, birds

Genets are usually loners, but they are good communicators. They growl to show aggression and click to warn of danger; mothers and offspring hiccup, purr, and mew. Genets hunt on the ground, but they chase prey by climbing trees with their catlike claws or squeezing their bendable bodies into very tight spaces.

SEA OTTER

Sea otters have the perfect coat for their cold, wet environment; with up to one million hairs per square inch it is the densest fur on Earth. They groom constantly to keep the coat clean because dirt and oil ruin its insulating effect. Sea otters dive deep in the ocean to find shellfish, their favorite food. They use rocks to open the shells, and are among the very few mammals (such as humans, apes, and monkeys) that use tools. Sometimes sea otters float on their backs and use their chest as a table to prepare food.

8 FACTS ABOUT THE SEA OTTER

- ▶ Spends almost all its time in water
- ▶ At under 100 pounds (45 kg), it is the smallest marine mammal
- ▶ Swims in groups called rafts
- ▶ Lacks blubber, but its dense fur insulates it
- ▶ Inhabits rocky ledges and kelp forests
- ▶ Lives on the coasts of North America
- ▶ Can dive more than 150 feet (46 m) to find food
- ▶ Uses its tail as a rudder and its back feet as flippers to move in the water

ABOUT ME!

I'm a baby sea otter. My mom will feed and care for me until I'm three months old. At first, she'll wrap me in kelp and leave me on the water surface. Then when I'm about two months old, she'll teach me how to dive for food. If a predator comes along, she'll grab me by the neck and dive down to protect me.

PINNIPEDS

SEALS BELONG TO A GROUP of mammals called pinnipeds (pin-uh-PEDZ); the word *pinniped* means "having feet," and these semi-aquatic mammals have bodies and senses that allow them to live both in water and on land. There are three types of pinnipeds—walruses; true seals, also called earless seals; and eared or fur seals, which include sea lions—33 species in all. They descended from an ancestor that was also common to bears and weasels. They split about 30 million years ago.

Pinnipeds have heavy agile bodies covered in insulating blubber. Some species spend more time on ice floes; others spend almost all their time in the water, even giving birth underwater. Most are social, gathering on ice floes to feed and care for their young. They eat fish, crustaceans, and cephalopods, and can dive deep to find them.

HARBOR SEAL
Phoca vitulina

SIZE: male: 154–331 pounds (70–150 kg); female: 132–243 pounds (60–110 kg)
HABITAT: Coastal water, rocky beach, estuary; northern Atlantic and Pacific Oceans, Baltic and North Seas
FOOD: Fish, shellfish

Young harbor seals play together, and females sometimes give birth in groups. Pups are born with dark fur; they shed the pale, soft fur of most newborn pups while they're still in their mothers' wombs. An earless species, they are also called common seals.

SOUTHERN ELEPHANT SEAL
Mirounga leonina

SIZE: male: 3,306–8,818 pounds (1,500–4,000 kg); female: 661–1,984 pounds (300–900 kg)
HABITAT: Rocky beach, open ocean; islands off southern South America, Antarctica
FOOD: Squid, fish, crabs

Southern elephant seals are the largest of all pinniped species. Males are up to eight times the size of females, the biggest difference in all mammals. Males have long noses that look like elephant trunks. They spend more time on land than other species. But they are great divers, descending 1,000-7,000 feet (300-2,200 m), and sleep underwater. Hundreds gather on rocky ledges to sunbathe.

HARP SEALS
Pagophilus groenlandicus

SIZE: 265–298 pounds (120–135 kg)
HABITAT: Coastal water, pack ice; Arctic Ocean, northern Atlantic Ocean, Greenland
FOOD: Fish, marine invertebrates

Adult harp seals have black marks on their upper bodies. Pups have thick white fur that they later shed; they are often slaughtered for it. Thousands of females gather on ice floes to give birth, but each mother recognizes her own pups by their scent. Mothers will leave their pups for days to find food.

SNACK ATTACK

Seals need a thick layer of blubber to keep warm in their cold habitat. Seal pups need to add it quickly to survive, and they gain up to five pounds a day. That's because their mother's milk is up to 50 percent fat, the highest fat content of any milk. Human milk is about 4 percent fat.

CALIFORNIA SEA LION
Zalophus californianus
SIZE: male: 606–860 pounds (275–390 kg); female: 201–243 pounds (91–110 kg)
HABITAT: Sandy beach, rocky area; remote islands off west coast of North America
FOOD: Fish, including anchovies and mackerel; cephalopods

California sea lions are intelligent; seals in aquarium shows are usually from this species. They are also trained by the U.S. Navy to detect bombs. They are the fastest seals, capable of bursts of 25 miles per hour (40 kmh). They can hunt in water for 30 hours straight and can also move swiftly on land.

LEOPARD SEAL
Hydrurga leptonyx
SIZE: 661–1,102 pounds (300–500 kg)
HABITAT: Pack ice, ice floes; Antarctic coasts and sub-Antarctic areas off Africa, South America, Australia
FOOD: Krill, penguins, other seals

Leopard seals are exceptional hunters, with strong jaws and long teeth. They draw their snakelike heads back to strike prey. They are the third-largest seal, and the only seal that eats other seal species. Leopard seals are fast on land and in water. They are usually solitary, but females join groups when they give birth.

WEDDELL SEAL
Leptonychotes weddellii
SIZE: 882–1,323 pounds (400–600 kg)
HABITAT: Icy water; Antarctica and surrounding islands
FOOD: Fish, squid

Weddell seals spend most of their time beneath the ice. To breathe, they find thin areas and chew through it, which damages their teeth. They have good vision in the dark, make sounds underwater, and can hold their breath for an hour.

FUN FACT
Walruses and seals use their sensitive whiskers to locate prey. Movement in the water causes a vortex. Whiskers can detect this vortex from a distance, and pinnipeds follow it to find the moving animal.

WALRUS
Odobenus rosmarus
SIZE: male: 1,764–3,307 pounds (800–1,500 kg); female: 1,323–1,874 pounds (600–850 kg)
HABITAT: Beach, rocky ledge, ice floe; Arctic Circle
FOOD: Shellfish, octopus, slow-moving fish

Walruses are enormous, covered in a thick layer of insulating blubber to keep them warm. They gather in huge groups called herds; males and females stay apart except when mating. Walrus tusks are up to 3 feet (1 m) long, and their skin is super tough to prevent other walruses' tusks from injuring them. Walruses use tusks to defend themselves, to break holes in ice, and to push themselves from water to ice, which is called "tusk-walking."

PRIMATES—THE GROUP TO WHICH humans, apes, monkeys, and prosimians belong—began as tree-dwelling animals, and many of them still are. Most live in tropical areas. Primates have larger brains than most mammals, and their vision is better than their sense of smell. Primates are omnivores; many of them prefer fruit. Primates form complex social structures and bond with their young.

Big apes are the biggest primates. They are the most intelligent land animals on Earth; most are able to create and use tools, remember tasks, and solve complex problems. Relationships among them differ; some stay within two-parent families. Chimpanzees live in male-dominated groups, while bonobo groups are dominated by females.

Early primates probably evolved about 80 million years ago. Hominids—early versions of apes and humans—were first seen about 20 million years ago.

MOUNTAIN GORILLA
Gorilla beringei beringei
SIZE: male: 309–452 pounds (140–205 kg); female: 154–251 pounds (70–114 kg)
HABITAT: Tropical forest; Virunga volcanoes and Bwindi Impenetrable National Park in eastern Africa
FOOD: Foliage, fruit

The second largest of the apes, the mountain gorilla has a shaggy, dark coat. They're called silverbacks because the hair on the males' backs turns a silvery color as they age. Like many primates, they walk on their knuckles and the soles of their feet, which is called knuckle-walking. Each has a unique nose shape. These gorillas live in stable family groups. They fold foliage on the ground for sleeping. Gorillas are emotional, showing joy and laughter, grief, and sadness.

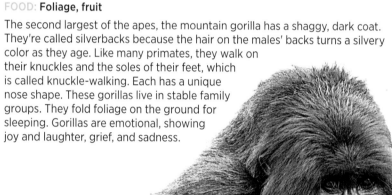

BONOBO
Pan paniscus
SIZE: male: 82–134 pounds (37–61 kg); female: 60–84 pounds (27–38 kg)
HABITAT: Rain forest; Democratic Republic of Congo
FOOD: Fruit, leaves, small vertebrates

Bonobos and chimpanzees are humankind's closest relatives. Smaller and less aggressive than chimpanzees, bonobos live in trees in groups of up to 100. Females are leaders in bonobo society and develop strong relationships with each other. When ready to breed, females move to other groups, which creates a more diverse genetic pool for the species.

SIAMANG
Symphalangus syndactylus
SIZE: 22–26 pounds (10–12 kg)
HABITAT: Tropical lowland forest; Sumatra, Malaysia, Thailand
FOOD: Fruit, leaves, insects, small vertebrates

This is the largest gibbon species, twice the size of some others. Siamangs have sacs in their throats that enable them to sing with loud, deep voices. Males and females sing duets that are heard from almost a mile away.

CHIMPANZEE
Pan troglodytes
SIZE: male: 75–154 pounds (34–70 kg); female: 57–110 pounds (26–50 kg)
HABITAT: Dry to humid woodland; western and central Africa
FOOD: Fruit, leaves, insects

Sharing 98 percent of genes with humans, chimpanzees are intelligent and social. They stay in the area they were born; mothers and offspring are together for life. Chimpanzees use tools (sticks and rocks) to dig and crack nuts. They communicate with calls and body language and have learned sign language in captivity.

Animal Antics Chimpanzees, especially young ones, love to play. They chase each other up trees, wrestle on the ground, and tickle each other. The running and climbing is good practice for when they need to find food and escape predators.

HUMANS ARE PRIMATES, TOO
Modern humans evolved about 200,000 years ago. Chimpanzees and the closely related bonobos are the animals that are most like humans. More than 98% of their DNA is the same as ours. We are in the same family—Hominidae. Modern humans have much larger brains than other species and less hair than other primates. Human skeletons are adapted to walking on two feet, and jaws and teeth are smaller than other primates. Humans are the only species that makes fire, grows food, and changes its environment significantly.

SUMATRAN ORANGUTAN
Pongo abelii
SIZE: male: 110–198 pounds (50–90 kg); female: 66–110 pounds (30–50 kg)
HABITAT: Tropical rain forest, swamp; Sumatra
FOOD: Fruit, especially figs; insects

Asia's largest primates (except for humans), Sumatran orangutans live in trees and rarely descend to the ground. They follow fruit trees, especially figs, moving to wherever the fruit is ripening. They support the ecology of the forest by spreading seeds. Orangutans are intelligent, using tools and communicating with calls. Its name means "man of the forest."

SILVERY GIBBON
Hylobates moloch
SIZE: 9–20 pounds (4–9 kg)
HABITAT: Rain forest; Java
FOOD: Fruit, leaves, flowers

Gibbons live in trees, swinging from branches with long arms and curved fingers. They jump gaps of 50 feet (15 m); their shoulders are adapted for catching hold. When they walk on two feet they raise their arms for balance. They live in tight family groups. Males scream at approaching strangers.

BORNEAN ORANGUTAN

Swinging through the jungle with long arms, calling out loudly to avoid collisions with others, finding and using tools to secure food and shelter—orangutans have skills and personality. Though they are not social, orangutans have a culture and maintain family bonds—mothers and children stay close for up to eight years.

These beautiful, spirited animals need and deserve our protection; they are endangered. The native lowland forests of Asia are being cut down and replaced with oil palms, destroying their habitat.

ABOUT ME!

I'm a Bornean orangutan. I use sophisticated construction know-how to build a nest for myself every night. I am careful to choose the right branches, bending and weaving them, then covering them with lighter, leafy branches to make a strong, comfortable resting place. The process takes me only about five minutes.

7 FACTS ABOUT THE BORNEAN ORANGUTAN

▶ Is the largest tree-dwelling animal
▶ Has 32 teeth like a human
▶ Is the only great ape found outside Africa
▶ Is active during daylight hours
▶ Uses branches to swat mosquitoes
▶ Builds a new nest every night
▶ Its name means "man of the forest"

THERE IS INCREDIBLE DIVERSITY within the roughly 130 species of Asian and African monkeys. Most live in trees, but some, including baboons, are mainly land dwellers. They inhabit a wide range of habitats, from tropical rain forests to deserts to cool mountains. Though they eat many plants, some are omnivores. Their bodies have striking features, like the mandrills' bold colors and the long, shaggy hair on colobus monkeys. They all have tails.

Most monkeys live in groups led by females, with just a male or two. Daughters stay with their mothers for life; males come and go to other groups. Babies are born well developed and immediately cling to their mothers.

Prosimians, a primate group that include lemurs, tarsiers, and lorises, are mostly nocturnal and more primitive than monkeys. Their brains are smaller, and they are less social, living singly or in small groups.

GOLDEN SNUB-NOSE MONKEY
Rhinopithecus roxellana

SIZE: male: 33–86 pounds (15–39 kg); female: 13–22 pounds (6–10 kg)
HABITAT: High mountain forest; western and central China
FOOD: Lichens, bamboo shoots, bark, fruit

These beautiful monkeys chatter constantly. They're extremely social, belonging to families that join other families in troops. Mothers care for infants, but other family members help. Golden snub-nose monkeys spend most of their time in trees, and can climb higher very quickly when threatened. Unlike many primates, they can tolerate snow in the high altitudes where they live.

Surprisingly Human

A 2014 study at University of Oxford showed that human and macaque brains are similar in many ways, especially in how language is handled and the way decisions are made.

PHILIPPINE TARSIER
Tarsius syrichta

SIZE: **3–6 ounces (85–170 g)**
HABITAT: **Dense vegetation in rain forest; Philippines**
FOOD: **Insects, spiders, lizards**

Small, shy, and brownish-gray, with bat-shaped ears, tarsiers' dominant feature is their big eyes. They have great vision and hearing, which make them excellent hunters. Their young learn to hunt by the time they are 45 days old.

FUN FACT The tarsier's eyes are bigger than its brain. It has the biggest eyes, relative to its body size, of any mammal.

JAPANESE MACAQUE
Macaca fuscata

SIZE: **15–26 pounds (7–12 kg)**
HABITAT: **Subtropical, subalpine, and temperate forest; Japanese islands**
FOOD: **Leaves, fruit, berries, flowers, seeds, insects**

Macaques are covered in dense fur except on their faces and backsides. They live in large troops that can number as many as 150. They are very vocal, chattering in shrill voices. Japanese macaques (snow monkeys) live further north than any other primate species.

VERREAUX'S SIFAKA
Propithecus verreauxi

SIZE: 7–15 pounds (3–7 kg)
HABITAT: Dry forest, rain forest;
Madagascar
FOOD: Leaves, fruit, flowers

Sifakas are one of many lemur species in Madagascar. They have beautiful long-haired coats and hop with arms above their heads, in trees and on the ground. Sifakas live and forage in groups. When they are alarmed, their call sounds like *shif-auk*, which is where they got their name.

MANDRILL
Mandrillus sphinx

SIZE: male: 68–73 pounds (31–33 kg); female: 26–29 pounds (12–13 kg)
HABITAT: Rain forest, subtropical forest; central-western Africa
FOOD: Fruits, seeds, insects, small animals

Mandrills are among the largest monkeys in the world . They have red, blue, and yellow stripes and patches. Males have bolder colors; each group's dominant male is usually the most striking. Groups of about 40 forage together, grunting and chirping noisily until the dominant male barks an order for them to stop. When ready to mate, females' backsides swell.

CHACMA BABOON
Papio ursinus

SIZE: male: 46–97 pounds (21–44 kg); female: 26–37 pounds (12–17 kg)
HABITAT: Woodland, savanna, semi-desert; southern Africa
FOOD: Plants, seeds, fruits, fungi, lichens, small vertebrates

Like all baboons, chacmas have doglike muzzles. They eat many kinds of food—mostly plants, but also meat and occasionally small livestock. They live in groups that interact with other groups of baboons; there are set vocalizations for communicating within and between groups. Males court females by grooming them or helping to care for the young.

PROBOSCIS MONKEY
Nasalis larvatus

SIZE: male: 35–49 pounds (16–22 kg); female: 15–26 pounds (7–12 kg)
HABITAT: Mangrove and rain forests; Borneo
FOOD: Leaves, fruits, seeds

The big, sausagelike nose in the middle of the male proboscis monkey's face makes its voice louder, which impresses females and intimidates males. These monkeys spend most of their time in trees, but they are also excellent swimmers; they leap from trees into water with loud bellyflops. They live in groups, with one male and several females. Females compete over the dominant males. Babies have black fur and bright blue faces when they are born.

NEW WORLD MONKEYS

ABOUT 40 MILLION YEARS AGO, monkeys migrated from Africa to South America, possibly on a land bridge that existed at that time. Once there, they spread out; now, five families, divided into 19 genera and over 100 species, live in rain forests and tropical forests from southern Mexico through Central and South America.

New world monkeys have flatter noses than old world monkeys and prehensile tails, which means that they can grasp things with them, a very useful ability. They range in size from the tiny pygmy marmoset (about 5 ounces, 150 g) to the southern muriqui (30 pounds, 13 kg). Like the monkeys of Asia, they are mostly herbivores and specialize in fruit, including gums and resins. They live in fairly large groups and are able to learn new behavior and teach it to their offspring.

CENTRAL AMERICAN SQUIRREL MONKEY
Saimiri oerstedii

SIZE: **1–2 pounds (0.5–1 kg)**
HABITAT: **Tropical forest, floodplain, mangrove swamp; Costa Rica, Panama**
FOOD: **Fruits, leaves, buds, gums, insects, small vertebrates**

Small creatures with black and white faces and reddish coats, these monkeys jump from branch to branch very much like squirrels, using their tails for balance. Central American squirrel monkeys live in groups, but unlike other monkey groups, neither males nor females dominate. They often forage with capuchin monkeys.

HUMBOLDT'S WOOLLY MONKEY
Lagothrix lagotricha

SIZE: **7–22 pounds (3–10 kg)**
HABITAT: **Humid forest; northern South America**
FOOD: **Fruits, seeds, leaves, flowers, insects**

Named for their short and thick hair, woolly monkeys have bare faces and a bare spot on their tails that helps them grip branches. They can even pick up food with their tails. Woolly monkeys dwell in male-dominated groups. Monkeys living in each group form strong bonds and often socialize, vocalize, and play.

Surprisingly Human

Capuchin monkeys are being trained to help the disabled, especially people with spinal cord injuries. They can follow commands to do things like turn pages, scratch itches, and insert straws into cups.

CRESTED CAPUCHIN MONKEY
Cebus robustus

SIZE: **2–11 pounds (1–5 kg)**
HABITAT: **Tropical lowland forest; Brazil**
FOOD: **Fruits, plants, insects, frogs**

There are two groups of capuchin monkeys: the gracile group have round skulls, and the robust group have crests and stronger jaws. All capuchins are intelligent and good at manipulating objects with their hands. They use tools, such as stones for cracking nuts, and copy problem-solving behavior after seeing it. Laboratories use them to study animal intelligence. Capuchins are tree-dwellers. They live in groups with several females and their offspring, plus a few males.

BLACK SPIDER MONKEY
Ateles paniscus

SIZE: male: 12–22 pounds (5.5–10 kg); female: 14–24 pounds (6.5–11 kg)
HABITAT: Tropical rainforest; eastern South America
FOOD: Fruits, leaves, flowers

Spider monkeys have prehensile tails, which means that they can be used for grasping. They hang from branches with their tails so that their long hands and feet are free for finding and eating food. They excel at climbing, swinging, and running on two feet. Their calls sound like dogs barking or horses whinnying.

GOLDEN MARMOSET
Leontopithecus rosalia

SIZE: 1–2 pounds (0.5–1 kg)
HABITAT: Tropical rain forest; southeastern Brazil
FOOD: Fruits, flowers, nectar, insects

Golden marmosets, also called golden lion tamarins, have silky manes surrounding dark faces; their color comes from sunlight and pigments in their diet. They have long, flexible fingers with sharp nails that they use to filter small animals from foliage and cling to tree trunks like squirrels. Marmosets live in close-knit groups that share food they forage by day. They move every night.

Marmoset fathers share in child care. The father is usually the one who carries the offspring until they can walk. The father may groom and feed the offspring.

RED TITI MONKEY
Callicebus discolor

SIZE: 1–2.5 pounds (0.5–1.1 g)
HABITAT: Rain forest; Peru, Ecuador, Columbia
FOOD: Fruits, leaves, insects

Red titi monkeys live in trees and are active during the day. They have long, soft hair and jump from branch to branch—they are called "jumping monkeys" in German. They mate for life and pairs vocalize in unison.

BALD-HEADED UAKARI MONKEY
Cacajao calvus

SIZE: 4–7 pounds (2–3.5 kg)
HABITAT: Tropical rain forest; western Brazil, eastern Peru, southern Columbia
FOOD: Fruit, nuts, leaves, insects, nectar

A bright red face on a bald uakari monkey shows that it doesn't have malaria (which would make it pale) and is therefore a good mate. These small monkeys have very short tails and strong jaws that open nuts that other species can't access. They live in groups of up to 100.

HORSES, ZEBRAS, RHINOCEROSES, and tapirs all have odd numbers of toes on their hooves and simple digestive systems. In prehistoric times, before grass was available for eating, odd-toed hooved animals were among the most successful species. Later, when grass spread, animals with sophisticated digestive systems (such as cows and sheep) that could process grass flourished, while the odd-toed group became less prominent.

But several odd-toed species still exist. Graceful, well-muscled horses have long, slender legs and are built for speed. They are herbivores; they have broad, flat teeth with grinding surfaces that can chop grass finely. In the wild, they form female-dominated herds. Zebras and horses are in the same genus, *Equus*.

Tapirs and rhinoceroses are closely related but very different from the hooves up. They are stout and slow, with heavy legs. They are also herbivores.

GREATER ONE-HORNED RHINOCEROS
Rhinoceros unicornis
SIZE: 4,000-6,000 pounds (1,800–2,700 kg)
HABITAT: Swamp, grassland and forest near water; India, Nepal, Bengal
FOOD: Grasses, fruit, leaves

This huge animal has large and leathery skin folds that serve as armor and regulate temperature. Its horn is made out of keratin, the compound that is in human fingernails and hair. Rhinoceroses are usually loners, but they bathe together to keep cool. They are good swimmers and run up to 34 miles per hour (55 kph). Their vision is poor, but their senses of hearing and smell are excellent.

DOMESTIC HORSE
Equus ferus caballus
SIZE: 838–1,213 pounds (380–550 kg)
HABITAT: All habitats, worldwide
FOOD: Grasses, oats, hay

Horses evolved from a smaller animal about three million years ago, and were domesticated about 5,500 years ago. They retain features they learned when they were wild; they can run very fast, hear very well, and sleep both standing up and lying down. Over 300 breeds of horses are used for agriculture, recreation, law enforcement, and transportation.

Demand for rhinoceros horns, which are used in herbal medicine, has led poachers to kill thousands of rhinoceroses. Rangers are fighting back, declaring war on the poachers. They set up surveillance and carry weapons to stop the slaughter.

KIANG
Equus kiang
SIZE: 551–970 pounds (250–440 kg)
HABITAT: Grassland; Tibetan Plateau of southwestern China
FOOD: Grasses, sedges

The largest type of wild ass, kiangs are herbivores like all members of the horse family. They have short hair in summer, but their coats turn long and shaggy in winter. They form large, loose herds of females and babies. Stallions leave the herd and are loners. When attacked, kiangs form a circle and kick viciously.

BRAZILIAN TAPIR
Tapirus terrestris

SIZE: 331–551 pounds (150–250 kg)
HABITAT: Rain forest; South America
FOOD: Leaves, shrubs, reeds, fruits

Tapirs use their super long snouts—which are extensions of their lips and noses—to pick fruit and strip leaves from bark. They are strong swimmers and runners; they run like galloping horses. Tapirs run to water when prey chases them. They are solitary animals that graze at night.

GREVY'S ZEBRA
Equus grevyi

SIZE: 769–994 pounds (349–451 kg)
HABITAT: Semidesert, grassland; Kenya, Ethiopia
FOOD: Tough grasses, leaves

Grevy's zebras have bigger, rounder heads and ears than plains zebras. They also have different social habits: Plains zebras form large, solid herds, but Grevy's zebras are usually solitary. Grevy's zebras are the largest animal in the *Equus* family. Newborns can run 45 minutes after birth.

AFRICAN WILD ASS
Equus africanus

SIZE: 441–606 pounds (200–275 kg)
HABITAT: Desert, semidesert; northeastern Africa
FOOD: Grasses, bark, leaves

Ancestor of the domestic donkey, African wild asses have short, compact bodies and big ears, through which they emit body heat. They can live without water for several days and rehydrate in just a few minutes. They are fast, have excellent hearing, and make a lot of noise, especially when they gather in herds.

PRZEWALSKI'S HORSE
Equus ferus przewalskii

SIZE: 441–750 pounds (200–340 kg)
HABITAT: Steppe and shrubland; Mongolia, China, Kazakhstan
FOOD: Grasses, other plants

Officially declared extinct in the wild in 2008, specimens from zoos and breeding stations have been reintroduced successfully in Asia. These short, muscular horses have never been tamed and ridden; they are the last truly wild horses.

PLAINS ZEBRA
Equus quagga

SIZE: 386–849 pounds (175–385 kg)
HABITAT: Grassland, savanna, woodland; Africa
FOOD: Grasses, herbs, shrubs

Zebra stripes—vertical on the body, horizontal on hindquarters—help them blend into crowds of zebras, so predators can't attack single zebras. Stripes may help these very social animals recognize each other. Zebras sleep standing up, and tend to sleep in groups to be safer from predators. When attacked, they face the predator and bite and kick, then circle and protect wounded herd mates. Zebras have a very efficient digestive system, so they can survive on very little nutrition.

Zebras communicate with sound and body language. They'll snort and bark to warn of predators. And they move their ears to communicate: ears up is a greeting, pulled back is a threat.

ELEPHANTS

THE ELEPHANTIDAE IS THE LAST remaining family of the Proboscidea order. There are scores of extinct species in the order. Elephants live in South Asia and sub-Saharan Africa, usually near water. These herbivores maintain their impressive size by eating all day.

Intelligent and social, elephants live in groups made up of females and children. Mothers stay with their calves for several years. Males don't stay around, except during mating season.

ROCK HYRAX
Procavia capensis

SIZE: 4–11 pounds (2–5 kg)
HABITAT: Rocky area of desert, savanna, and scrub forest; sub-Saharan and northeastern Africa
FOOD: Grasses, shrubs, fruits

Little hyraxes are related to massive elephants. They share several features, such as front teeth that keep growing like tusks and long pregnancies. They like to rest and hide in rock crevices, usually with another hyrax standing watch.

The Partnership to Save Africa's Elephants is fighting the ivory trade that has reduced world elephant populations drastically. The partnership aims to stop the killing and trafficking of elephant tusks, the most important source of ivory, by promoting the enforcement of current laws and by educating the public. Their message: If no one buys ivory products, no one will kill elephants to make them.

AFRICAN FOREST ELEPHANT
Loxodonta cyclotis

SIZE: 5,952–13,228 pounds (2,700–6,000 kg)
HABITAT: Tropical rain forest, swamp; west and central equatorial Africa
FOOD: Leaves, fruit, bark

Forest elephants are smaller than African bush elephants. Like all elephants, their lips and noses extend to form a trunk. They use their trunks to breathe, to take in water and spray themselves, to lift heavy objects, and to make trumpeting calls. There are fingerlike attachments on the trunk that can be used to pick up small items.

AFRICAN BUSH ELEPHANT
Loxodonta africana

SIZE: 6,614–13,228 pounds (3,000–6,000 kg)
HABITAT: Savanna, grassy plains, forest, desert; Africa south of the Sahara Desert
FOOD: Grasses, woody plants

The largest land mammals on Earth, elephants (and their tusks) keep growing throughout their lives. Their heads make up about one quarter of their total weight. In an average day, they eat 440 pounds (200 kg) of food, drink 170 quarts (160 l) of water, and defecate 18 times. Herd animals, elephants vocalize with loud trumpeting and low-frequency sounds. They have the most smell-related genes of any animal and are often called the best smellers in the animal world.

Surprisingly Human

Elephants show kindness to other animals and to people. They go out of their way to avoid hurting people, sometimes backing up in tight spaces. They will guard and protect injured animals and people

FUN FACT
African bush elephants are very large animals, but they are afraid of little bees.

54

GIRAFFES

SO TALL, BLOTCHES AND PATCHES, EVEN-TOED HOOVES

WHEN IT COMES TO HEIGHT, giraffes take the prize. Their legs are taller than most humans, allowing them to run swiftly. They rarely sit and even give birth while standing up (their babies survive the drop.)

Giraffes have four toes on their hooves, which makes them related to other even-toed hooved animals such as camels and cows. They descended from antelopelike mammals that lived in Eurasia at least 10 million years ago.

OKAPI
Okapia johnstoni

SIZE: 441–772 pounds (200–350 kg)
HABITAT: Rain forest; Democratic Republic of Congo
FOOD: Leaves of more than 100 species of tree, charcoal

Okapis are close relatives of giraffes, with long necks and markings across their fur. Okapis sometimes eat toxic leaves; they also eat burned wood, which is an antidote to the toxins in the plants. Like elephants, okapi mothers communicate with babies through infrasonic (low-frequency) sounds that humans can't hear.

ROTHSCHILD'S GIRAFFE
Giraffa camelopardalis rothschildi

SIZE: 2,500–2,800 pounds (1,134–1,270 kg)
HABITAT: Protected areas; Kenya, Uganda
FOOD: Foliage, seed pods, apricots

One of the most endangered giraffes, fewer than one thousand Rothschild's giraffes exist, mostly in wildlife preserves. Dark brown-orange patches are connected by creamy outlines on their fur; their lower legs are pure white. They have five hornlike growths called ossicones on their heads.

MASAI GIRAFFE
Giraffa camelopardalis tippelskirchi

SIZE: male: 2,000–3,000 pounds (907–1,361 kg); female: 1,300–2,000 pounds (590–907 kg)
HABITAT: Savanna; Kenya, Tanzania
FOOD: Leaves, branches

Each giraffe subspecies has different markings. Masai giraffes have oak leaf-shaped dark blotches on their creamy skin. They are the tallest giraffes and therefore tallest of all land mammals. Because they are so tall they have high blood pressure and a heart that beats up to 170 times a minute.

ANGOLAN GIRAFFE
Giraffa camelopardalis angolensis

SIZE: male: 1,764–4,200 pounds (800–1,930 kg); female: 1,213–2,601 pounds (550–1,180 kg)
HABITAT: Savanna, scrub, woodland; sub-Saharan Africa
FOOD: Woody plant leaves (especially acacia), seeds, pods

Giraffes' super long necks contain seven vertebrae, just like humans and most other mammals. But giraffe necks have special joints that make them flexible enough to reach treetops. Giraffes join in loose herds but are not territorial. Males roar at and fight with each other, but are usually gentle. Zebras and wildebeests often join them to benefit from their good hearing and strong vision, both of which can alert to predators.

SNACK ATTACK
Giraffes use their long tongues to browse for food in trees and woody bushes. They eat thorny leaves and tough berries. These don't hurt their tongues because they secrete thick, slimy saliva that provides protection.

ASIAN ELEPHANT

Asian elephants live in groups of about 20 females and children called herds; the oldest female is the leader. Males leave the group, but return occasionally.

Elephants form close bonds with one another; they greet by bumping trunks or rubbing their bodies together. Children play by chasing each other and trunk-wrestling. Baby Asian elephants follow the herd by holding onto the tail of their mother or sister. When a baby is in danger, the adults will form a circle around it to provide protection.

8 FACTS ABOUT THE ASIAN ELEPHANT

- ▶ Is the largest land animal in Asia
- ▶ Has smaller ears and rounder backs than African elephants
- ▶ Eats mostly grass, also leaves, bark, shrubs, and crops such as bananas
- ▶ Only males have tusks; females have incisor teeth called tushes that barely protrude from the mouth
- ▶ Lives 60-70 years
- ▶ Has 60,000 or more muscles in its trunk
- ▶ Has an excellent memory
- ▶ Is endangered due to habitat destruction and hunting

ABOUT ME!

I'm an Asian elephant. I'm smaller than my African relatives, but my brain is bigger. I'm one of the smartest animals in the world. I can use tools and perform many tasks: I scratch my back with branches, throw large objects with my trunk, and clear forests by moving trees with my tusks.

LIKE MANY EVEN-TOED hooved animals, camels are large plant-eating mammals that have multi-chambered stomachs that allow them to chew their food several times before it's fully digested. This process is called rumination, and the animals are called ruminants.

The camel family includes two true camels that live in deserts and four South American species that live in mountainous areas. All are well adapted to their climates.

GUANACO
Lama guanicoe

SIZE: 254–309 pounds (115–140 kg)
HABITAT: Desert grassland, shrubland, forest; South America
FOOD: Grasses, shrubs, cacti

Swift and graceful, guanacos are ancestors of llamas and the largest members of the camel family in South America. They have warm woolly coats and blood that's suited for mountain regions. Guanacos live in herds dominated by females, with one male for protection. Their young, called chulengos, can run with the herd right after birth.

WILD BACTRIAN CAMEL
Camelus ferus

SIZE: 1,323–2,205 pounds (600–1,000 kg)
HABITAT: Desert and arid plain; Gobi Desert
FOOD: Shrubs

The only camels left in the wild, two-humped Bactrians survive for long periods without food or water and can drink 50 quarts (47 liters) of water when they find it. They are among the only mammals that can tolerate drinking saltwater.

FUN FACT
Baby camels stay with their mothers for two years or more. They call to their mothers with a sound that sounds like a lamb's *baaa*.

LLAMA
Lama glama

SIZE: 287–342 pounds (130–155 kg)
HABITAT: Originally mountainous regions of South America; now domesticated throughout the world
FOOD: Grasses, leaves, shrubs, seeds

Incas in South America used long-necked llamas for food and to carry loads. Their blood has a high red cell count that makes them able to live in high altitudes. Farmers all over the world employ llamas to protect their livestock, as they will circle a herd and stomp on invaders. There are distinct social ranks within llama herds.

DROMEDARY CAMEL
Camelus dromedarius

SIZE: male: 882–1,323 pounds (400–600 kg); female: 661–1,191 pounds (300–540 kg)
HABITAT: Desert; northern Africa, Middle East
FOOD: Foliage, desert vegetation

One-humped dromedary camels are incredibly adapted. Their eyelashes and self-closing nostrils protect them from sandstorms; their tough, flat hooves handle hot sand; and their kidneys can sustain water loss that would kill other animals. Their hump stores up to 80 pounds (36 kg) of fat, which they can convert to water. Humans have domesticated camels for almost 4,000 years, due to their ability to carry huge loads over long distances as well as their docile personalities.

COWS, GOATS, AND ANTELOPES are among the over 140 members of the Bovidae family. They are also called bovines or bovids. All have a similar body type, and are herbivores and ruminants. They have stomachs with several chambers, and they chew and rechew their food, passing it from one stomach to another. This system has allowed bovines to become one of the most common animals on Earth.

WILD YAK
Bos mutus
SIZE: 672–2,205 pounds (305–1,000 kg)
HABITAT: Alpine tundra, grassland, cold desert; Tibet, southwestern China
FOOD: Grasses, sedges

These massive animals survive the thin, cold air of high altitudes with their thick, matted coats and large lungs that can take in more oxygen. Their bulky frames and sharp horns make them look dangerous, but they are friendly except when defending their young. They are domesticated worldwide, and their dung is used as fuel.

ASIAN WATER BUFFALO
Bubalus bubalis
SIZE: 551–2,646 pounds (250–1,200 kg)
HABITAT: Woodland near river, wet grassland, swamp; Bhutan, Nepal, India, Thailand, Myanmar, Cambodia
FOOD: Grasses, herbs, fruits, bark, aquatic plants

These huge beasts have been domesticated in much of Asia and even brought to North Africa, Australia, and South America; they're used as plow animals and for meat and milk. There are still wild water buffalo (*Bubalus arnee*). Social animals, they live in female-dominated groups and spend much of their time wallowing in the mud. They have impressive horns, sometimes measuring 6 feet (2 m) wide.

DOMESTIC COW
Bos taurus
SIZE: male: 2,000–3,307 pounds (907–1,500 kg); female: 600–2,500 pounds (272–1,134 kg)
HABITAT: Meadow; worldwide
FOOD: Grasses, other plants

About 10,000 years ago, humans began domesticating wild animals in the cow family. Researchers have found that modern cows may descend from as few as 80 cows. Today there are more than 1 billion cows on the planet. These animals are raised for meat, milk, and leather. There are dozens of breeds, from small Jerseys to large Angus. Male cows are called bulls. The species from which they were domesticated has been extinct for more than 300 years.

Surprisingly Human
Cows are pregnant for about nine months, just like humans. Cows' milk has more protein and less fat and sugar than human milk. It is just right for calves, as the nutrients in human milk are just right for human infants.

AMERICAN BISON
Bison bison
SIZE: 701–1,984 pounds (318–900 kg)
HABITAT: Grassland; national parks and wildlife areas of North America
FOOD: Grasses, sedges, flowering plants

Huge herds of wild bison once migrated thousands of miles from Mexico to Canada every year to find fresh grass as the seasons changed; today, they live only in wildlife preserves in female-dominated groups. They have massive heads on bulky bodies and sharp horns. Surprisingly fast, they can run up to 40 miles per hour (64 kph). They graze a few hours each day, then rest.

GOATS

HORNS AND BEARDS, BROWSERS, SURE FEET

GOATS, DOMESTIC AND WILD, are known for curiosity and agility. They climb on the steepest terrain and will eat anything. Herbivores and ruminants, goats brows shrubs rather than eat grass. Males have sharp horns; males and females have beards. Both wild and domesticated goats become aggressive during mating season.

Domesticated in Iran at least 10,000 years ago, goats have four-toed hooves. They are members of the Bovidae (cow) family.

SAANEN GOAT
Capra aegagrus hircus (Saanen breed)
SIZE: **134–161 pounds (61–73 kg)**
HABITAT: **Domesticated; Europe and North America**
FOOD: **Grasses and other plants**

Saanen is one of many breeds of goat raised for milk and cheese. They were first bred in Switzerland's Saanen Valley and were exported across Europe in the 1890s. They were selected for sturdiness, easy milking, and milk quality.

MOUNTAIN GOAT
Oreamnos americanus
SIZE: male: 133–181 pounds (61–82 kg); female: 126–157 pounds (57–71 kg)
HABITAT: Rocky alpine or subalpine area; Alaska, western Canada, northwestern United States
FOOD: Grass, woody plants, lichen, moss

Both male and female mountain goats have curvy black horns—bigger on males—that grow new rings each year. Females give birth on steep cliffs to keep predators away. Parents care and protect the kids for a year, then chase them away. Male goats dig shallow beds for resting. They rub themselves in the dirt to remove parasites, which is why they often appear dirty.

NUBIAN IBEX
Capra nubiana
SIZE: **55–154 pounds (25–70 kg)**
HABITAT: **Dry rocky area; northeastern Africa, Middle East**
FOOD: **Herbs, shrubs, leaves, fruits**

Nimble and steady, Nubian ibexes navigate rocky cliffs in the morning and evening, but rest during the hottest part of the day. Their light coats reflect the sun, keeping them cool. When threatened by predators like vultures and leopards, they rear up on their legs and point their long, sharp horns at the attacker. Females also have horns, but they're smaller.

MARKHOR
Capra falconeri
SIZE: 71–243 pounds (32–110 kg)
HABITAT: Mountain forest; Afghanistan, Pakistan, India, Uzbekistan, Tajikistan
FOOD: Grasses, leaves

Markhors are distinctive because of their long hair, black beards, and dramatically twisted horns on males and females. They're aggressive, especially when fighting for mates by crashing their horns against each other.

SHEEP ARE MEMBERS of the Bovidae (cow) family. Wild and domestic sheep all fall into one family, but there are several hundred breeds. Sheep are good flockers, moving together in groups of more than 1,000. They have excellent memories and wide-range vision.

As ruminants with four-chambered stomachs, sheep chew and rechew their food, passing it from one chamber to another.

ARGALI SHEEP
Ovis ammon

SIZE: 140–400 pounds (64–181 kg)
HABITAT: Dry mountain area, steppe valley, rocky outcrop; central Asia
FOOD: Grasses, herbs, sedges

Argalis are the largest wild sheep; there are nine subspecies that live in different regions within the range in Asia. The males have elaborate corkscrew-shaped horns that are up to 13 percent of their total weight; female horns are smaller. Males fight noisily over females during mating season; they all get along peacefully at other times.

THINHORN SHEEP
Ovis dalli

SIZE: male: 161–249 pounds (73–113 kg); female: 101–110 pounds (46–50 kg)
HABITAT: Dry mountain region; western Canada and Alaska
FOOD: Grasses, shrubs, sedges

Males and females of this species each have different horns; the males' are big and curly, the females' are short and thin. Males and females live in separate herds except when mating. Each group has several home territories where they go in different seasons. When birthing, females go to high ground that is inaccessible to predators.

Animal Antics
Fights over territory or mates between wild male sheep, called rams, are epic and sometimes last for hours. Two rams crash into each other noisily at high speed or rear up until one of them gives up.

MOUFLON
Ovis orientalis orientalis

SIZE: 66–198 pounds (30–90 kg)
HABITAT: Mountainous grassland, desert, woodland; central Asia
FOOD: Grasses, leaves, fruits

Mouflon are one of two ancestors of domestic sheep. Both males and females have horns that curl into almost complete circles. They are cautious animals with good senses that allow them to flee from predators.

BIGHORN SHEEP
Ovis canadensis

SIZE: 117–280 pounds (53–127 kg)
HABITAT: Alpine meadow, mountain slope, desert; western North America
FOOD: Grasses, herbs, shrubs

Relatives of goats, these sheep can navigate rocks on rough-bottomed hooves. Their senses of vision and balance are excellent. They bound over steep cliffs when they spot predators. Females (ewes) live with their babies (lambs) and one- and two-year-old offspring in groups of about 5 to 15, though larger groups are possible. Males live in smaller groups and join them for mating.

SNACK ATTACK
Sheep know how to find medicine for what ails them. When they are bothered by nematode parasites in their stomach, they eat more foods high in tannic acid, such as wild grapes and apples, which combats the invaders. When sheep have heartburn or are constipated, they change their diet to cope with those problems.

ANTELOPES

GRACEFUL LEAPING, PERMANENT HORNS, WASTEBASKET GROUP

"ANTELOPE" IS NOT AN OFFICIAL NAME; it's what's known as a wastebasket group—members of the Bovidae (cow) family that are not cows, sheep, goats, bison, or buffalo are called antelopes.

The 91 antelope species have many features in common: They all have an even number of toes on their hooves, are from Africa or Eurasia, and have adapted to many climates. Known for their graceful bodies, they are swift runners.

BLUE WILDEBEEST
Connochaetes taurinus

SIZE: 260–595 pounds (118–270 kg)
HABITAT: Plain, savanna, woodland; southern and eastern Africa
FOOD: Short grass melons, roots. High water demands

With its curvy sharp horns and stout hindquarters, the wildebeest (also called a gnu) looks frightening, but it is a gentle herbivore. Their calves are born right before they migrate every spring to find more grass to eat and join larger herds.

THOMSON'S GAZELLE
Eudorcas thomsonii

SIZE: male: 44–77 pounds (20–35 kg); female: 33–55 pounds (15–25 kg)
HABITAT: Savanna, grassland; Kenya, Tanzania, southern Sudan
FOOD: Fresh grasses, seeds, shrubs

The graceful gazelle will run, jump, and pronk to avoid predators; pronking is a move in which an animal stiffens as all four legs rise and then hit the ground at the same time. Cheetahs, which often prey on gazelles, are faster, but gazelles have greater stamina and are superior at turning. Thomson's gazelle has a black stripe on its side.

FUN FACT

Wildebeests, along with gazelles, zebras, and other mammals, migrate across Africa's Serengeti region every spring to find fresh grazing fields. Over 2 million animals create an awesome parade as they trek hundreds of miles seeking food and avoiding lions, crocodiles, and other predators.

IMPALA
Aepyceros melampus

SIZE: 99–132 pounds (45–60 kg)
HABITAT: Grassland, woodland, savanna near water; southern Africa
FOOD: Grass, shrubs, fruit, acacia pods

Impalas are fast runners and amazing jumpers—they can leap 30 feet (9 m) in a single jump; they sometimes jump over each other. Impalas have big eyes and ears, which produce excellent vision and hearing. The males have long, ridged horns. Female herd leaders watch for predators, then signal with sounds and body language. Red-billed oxpeckers often sit on impalas' backs and groom them.

About 100 years ago, hunters had reduced the pronghorn population on the Great Plains to about 13,000. After much activism by conservationists, President Herbert Hoover created a retreat in Nevada to protect them. Today, 2,500 pronghorns roam freely on the Sheldon National Wildlife Refuge's 572,896 acres.

PRONGHORN
Antilocapra americana

SIZE: 104–154 pounds (47–70 kg)
HABITAT: Grassland, brushland, desert; western and central North America
FOOD: Shrubs, grasses

Pronghorns look like antelopes, but are actually members of their own single-species family. Their horns have permanent bony cores, like antelopes, but with forked tops that they shed, like deer. They run very fast for long distances.

DEER ARE MEMBERS of the Cervidae family, which has about 50 members. They can adapt to a wide variety of climates, from tropical to polar. They are the only animals with antlers, the fastest growing tissue in the world. Primitive deer first appeared in Mongolia about 10 to 20 million years ago and expanded from there.

REEVE'S MUNTJAC

Muntiacus reevesi

SIZE: 24–62 pounds (11–28 kg)
HABITAT: Tropical and semitropical woodland; China, Taiwan
FOOD: Flowers, nuts, grains

This small deer looks and barks like a dog. It grows short antlers that it uses to push away predators. Native to China and Taiwan, it was brought to the United Kingdom, where there are now large populations. There are 12 species of muntjacs in different sizes and colors.

NORTH AMERICAN ELK

Cervus canadensis

SIZE: male: 705–730 pounds (320–331 kg); female: 496–531 pounds (225–241 kg)
HABITAT: Open prairie, mountain, temperate forest; United States and Canada
FOOD: Grasses, tree sprouts

Elk are known for their huge antlers, which grow on males during winter and then fall off. At first, antlers are soft and covered with a fuzzy substance called velvet. They later harden into bone. Elk males and females live in separate herds of up to 200 members. They mix during mating season when males make loud calls, spray urine, and fight to attract females.

MOOSE

Alces alces

SIZE: male: 794–1,323 pounds (360–600 kg); female: 595–882 pounds (270–400 kg)
HABITAT: Forest, wetland; northern North America, Russia, China
FOOD: Trees, shrubs, other plants

The largest member of the deer family and the tallest mammal in North America, moose have humped backs, thin legs, and big ears that they rotate for better hearing. Antlers (males only) can reach 6 feet (1.8 m) wide. Fur protects them from cold, but moose cannot tolerate heat. They are solitary, except during mating season.

FUN FACT

Once a year, female deer give birth to one to three fawns. They protect their offspring by hiding them in foliage. Young deer stay with their mothers for up to two years.

WHITE-TAILED DEER

Odocoileus virginianus

SIZE: 126–302 pounds (57–137 kg), with variations in subspecies
HABITAT: Forest, riverside, grassland; North, Central, and South America
FOOD: Leaves, twigs, berries, grass

There are white-tailed deer all over North America, possibly up to 15 million of them, and more deer now than at any other time. They graze at dusk and dawn and occasionally in daylight. In winter, male deer (bucks) grow elaborate, pointy antlers that they use to fight with other bucks over mates. After the mating season, the antlers fall off. Females (called does) care for their infants. When does leave to find food, the infants lay flat on the ground, camouflaging themselves in foliage.

CARIBOU

Caribou, also called reindeer, are known as symbols of nature and pullers of sleighs. They inhabit the northern region of North America and the landmass of Eurasia, and are well adapted to their snowy habitat. Hollow, flat hooves support the large animals on the snow and can double as small shovels for digging food. The hooves also make good paddles when crossing rivers. Healthy colonies of caribou are still found in the wild, but they are threatened by deforestation and climate change.

7 FACTS ABOUT THE CARIBOU

- ▶ Both male and female caribou have antlers
- ▶ Females shed antlers after having babies
- ▶ Calves join the herd right after birth
- ▶ Eats grass in summer, lichens in winter
- ▶ Weighs up to 700 pounds (318 kg)
- ▶ Can run 50 miles per hour (80 kph)
- ▶ Warns others of danger by releasing scent

ABOUT ME!

I'm a female caribou and I'm about to leave for my annual summer migration; the males and children from my herd will join me in a few weeks. I will walk with thousands of caribou, following well-worn tracks to the northern tundra. Once there, I'll feed on lush tundra grass all summer. When snow falls, I'll head back south. My round trip covers more than 1,600 miles (2,575 km).

PIGS HAVE A REPUTATION for being dirty. That's because they don't release heat through sweat, so they wallow in mud to cool off. But pigs are remarkably intelligent and social animals, though some wild kinds are quite vicious.

Pigs have large snouts with strong bones that are used to dig and root out food. They have four-toed hooves and sharp teeth that grow into tusks on wild species. These omnivores find nutritious food in almost any landscape and tolerate almost any habitat.

Pigs have large litters, and mother-child bonding is weaker than in many other mammals. Mothers sometimes kill some of their offspring, possibly to improve the chances of the rest surviving.

Pigs are members of the Suidae family, which consists of 17 living species. Fossils show that the earliest pigs appeared in Asia about 30 million years ago. Peccaries are in Tayassuidae family.

COMMON WARTHOG
Phacochoerus africanus

SIZE: male: 132–331 pounds (60–150 kg); female: 99–165 pounds (45–75 kg)
HABITAT: Grassland, savanna; central and southern Africa
FOOD: Grasses, fruits, roots, insects, carrion, lizards, small mammals

These herbivores use their snouts to dig for roots or bulbs. Their long tusks are sharp, but warthogs usually flee—they can run 30 miles (48 km) per hour—instead of fighting. The four large fat-filled warts on their heads are used for defense in fights with mates. They hide from predators and even sleep at night in abandoned aardvark dens. Mothers will aggressively defend young.

FOREST HOG
Hylochoerus meinertzhageni

SIZE: 397–606 pounds (180–275 kg)
HABITAT: Swamp, forest; Africa
FOOD: Grass, other plants, carrion

The largest member of the wild pig family is covered in sparse black hair that gets thinner as it ages. Forest hogs live in herds called sounders. Pregnant females leave the sounder before giving birth; when they return with piglets, all sounder members join in caring for them. They will even nurse each other's babies.

VISAYAN WARTY PIG
Sus cebifrons

SIZE: male: 77–88 pounds (35–40 kg); female: 44–66 pounds (20–30 kg)
HABITAT: Rain forest; Philippines
FOOD: Roots, fruits, cereal crops, small mammals

Three pairs of fatty warts on faces of male warty pigs may serve to protect them from the tusks of rival pigs. Bristly black hair hangs over their eyes. They play a role in their habitat's ecology by spreading seeds, but few of them are left.

DOMESTIC PIG
Sus domesticus

SIZE: 110–772 pounds (50–350 kg)
HABITAT: Farms; worldwide
FOOD: Fruits, seeds, roots, tubers

Pigs were domesticated as early as 10,000 years ago in the Near East. Early humans used pigs for meat, bones for tools, and skin for shields. They were brought to the new world by Spanish settlers. Today, there are more than 1 billion pigs alive at any one time. Domestic pigs build nests and share them with other pigs, sometimes huddling together for contact. They are intelligent and trainable.

BUSH PIG
Potamochoerus larvatus

SIZE: 119–254 pounds (54–115 kg)
HABITAT: Forest, swampland, woodland; southern Africa
FOOD: Roots, fruit, crops, carrion, invertebrates, small mammals

Bush pigs have manes of bristly hair from their heads to rear ends. Male bush pigs compete for females by butting heads and shoving at each other. Unlike most pigs, both parents take care of the young. The father drives his sons away from the herd when they are old enough to survive on their own.

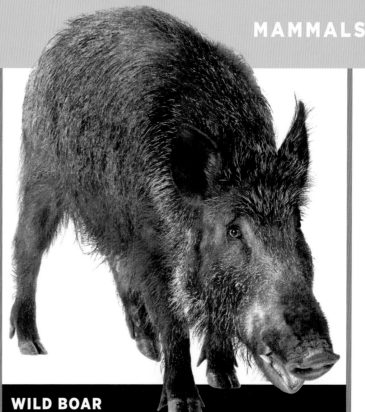

WILD BOAR
Sus scrofa

SIZE: 145-600 pounds (66-272 kg)
HABITAT: Moist forest, shrubland; worldwide, native to Eurasia, introduced elsewhere
FOOD: Fruits, seeds, roots, tubers, small vertebrates, invertebrates

Wild boars, the ancestors of domesticated pigs, have sharp teeth and tusks that sometimes wreak damage. Although they are mostly herbivores, they will eat almost anything they find, including living and dead animals. Females live in herds called sounders, with up to 100 (but typically 6–30) other boars. Females bear four to eight piglets in each litter; the piglets are dependent on their mothers for about six months.

HAIRY BABIRUSA
Babyrousa babyrussa

SIZE: 95–220 pounds (43–100 kg)
HABITAT: Tropical rain forest; Indonesia
FOOD: Leaves, roots, fruits, invertebrates

Hairy babirusas don't have the nose bones that most pigs have and use for digging, so they find most of their food in soft mud. They do have strong jaws that can crack nuts. Their meat is low in fat and regarded as a delicacy.

COLLARED PECCARY
Pecari tajacu

SIZE: 33–55 pounds (15–25 kg)
HABITAT: Desert, rain forest; South and Central America, Mexico, southwestern United States
FOOD: Roots, fruit, insects, cacti, fish, snakes

Collared peccaries are named for their collarlike mane. They're also called javelinas, for the sharp tusks which sharpen themselves as the jaws move. They have poor eyesight but smell and hear well. They mark their territories with a musky smell emitted from glands and communicate with a range of sounds.

Efforts are being made to save the pygmy hog, the world's tiniest pig; there are only a few hundred of them left in Assam in India. The Pygmy Hog Conservation Program (PHCP) is breeding captive pairs; six animals captured in 1996 have now multiplied to more than 75, and they have begun releasing young into the wild.

THERE ARE ABOUT 2,200 SPECIES in the Rodentia order: 42 percent of all mammal species are rodents. They live on every continent except Antarctica. They are very diverse; there are 33 different families of rodents.

All rodents have a single set of enamel-coated incisors that retain their chiseling ability throughout their lives. All rodents also lack canine teeth, the sharp teeth we see in carnivores. They use their sense of smell to find food, then use their teeth to gnaw through anything that might be covering it.

LESSER EGYPTIAN JERBOA
Jaculus jaculus

SIZE: **1.5–2.5 ounces (43–71 g)**
HABITAT: **Desert region; northern Africa, Middle East**
FOOD: **Seeds, insects, desert grasses**

Famous for their impressive leaping ability, desert jerboa have long, thin legs and a pointy face that's good for burrowing. Big eyes provide good vision at night or underground. They are built for jumping fast on their back legs. Rather than walk when they need to go slowly, they hop.

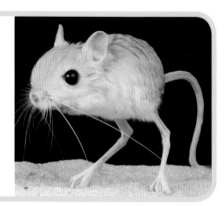

MALAGASY GIANT RAT
Hypogeomys antimena

SIZE: **2–3 pounds (1–1.5 kg)**
HABITAT: **Sandy coast, dry deciduous forest; Madagascar**
FOOD: **Fruit, seeds, leaves**

Malagasy rats can jump up to 3 feet (0.9 m) high but do so only when threatened. They are good burrowers, and they raise their young, hide from predators, and keep cool and dry in underground burrows. These rats mate for life but find new mates quickly if one dies. Their babies are born once a year. The entire range of this species is smaller than some cities.

BLACK-TAILED PRAIRIE DOG
Cynomys ludovicianus

SIZE: **1–3 pounds (0.5–1.5 kg)**
HABITAT: **Dry prairie, desert grassland; southern Canada, central United States, northern Mexico**
FOOD: **Grasses, herbs, invertebrates**

Stout, squirrel-like prairie dogs have one of the best-organized social systems of any animal. They live in super elaborate colonies of burrows (called towns) that have protected entrances and are divided into wards for families. Females bear one litter per year; sometimes, they nurse pups that are not their own. Females stay in the same town for life; males come and go. Town mates also share food.

HOUSE MOUSE
Mus musculus

SIZE: **0.5–1 ounce (14–28 g)**
HABITAT: **Indoors; originally central Asia, now worldwide**
FOOD: **Human food, seeds, invertebrates**

House mice live everywhere there is food, indoors and outdoors, though most populations are commensal with (dependent upon) humans. Indoor mice are bigger and darker in color. Mice can scamper straight up walls, walk on ropes, and squeeze into tiny spaces. They have very good senses of vision, smell, and hearing—and they can judge textures and movement with their whiskers. They build nests of shredded paper or fabric and give birth five to ten times a year, with four to eight babies in each litter.

Surprisingly Human

The faces of mice change according to what they are feeling; they have different expressions when they are frightened, hungry, or in pain. Experts believe that these varied expressions communicate information to other mice.

WE TEND TO THINK OF RODENTS as tiny creatures, though there are larger, more complex animals in the Rodentia order. Like small rodents, most large rodents have sleek bodies and long tails and are herbivores.

Some large rodents have developed sophisticated social and construction skills: beavers build dams, squirrels hide their food, and woodchucks burrow dens with many entrances. There are large rodents in every type of climate and habitat.

AMERICAN BEAVER
Castor canadensis

SIZE: 29–71 pounds (13–32 kg)
HABITAT: Stream, pond, lake; North America
FOOD: Bark and growing wood (cambium) of trees, leaves, twigs,

Beavers have two unique skills: felling large trees with their sharp front teeth and building amazing dams. They perform these feats to get access to food and to create still water for their homes, called lodges. The lodges are made of mud and sticks and have underwater entrances. Beavers mate for life and live with their families. Offspring come by the complicated engineering knowledge needed to build dams through instinct and by mimicking their parents.

NORTH AMERICAN PORCUPINE
Erethizon dorsatum

SIZE: 11–31 pounds (5–14 kg)
HABITAT: Temperate forest, tundra, desert; North America, Arctic Circle
FOOD: Nitrogen-rich plants, twigs, grasses, bark

Stout and slow, porcupines are tree-dwellers in the east, ground-huggers in the west. Their distinguishing characteristic is 30,000 barbed quills. Before using their quills, they will climb trees to escape predators, click their teeth, and emit warning scents. They don't shoot quills; they press them into attackers, then release quickly and escape.

WOODCHUCK
Marmota monax

SIZE: 4–13 pounds (2–6 kg)
HABITAT: Pasture, meadow near woodland; eastern United States, Canada
FOOD: Herbs, grass, leaves.

Woodchucks (also called groundhogs or whistlepigs) feed for two hours twice daily during midsummer, and only once a day in spring and fall. Though not social, they sometimes rub noses with other woodchucks. They growl and bark to defend their territory. Stocky and short, they sometimes stand upright to look taller. Great burrowers, woodchucks build underground dens with many entrances; they are a type of squirrel.

Animal Antics
Eastern gray squirrels can scamper up trees like many rodents, but they are one of very few mammals that can scamper down headfirst. They do this by gripping the trees with their back paws.

EASTERN GRAY SQUIRREL
Sciurus carolinensis

SIZE: 12–26 ounces (338–750 g)
HABITAT: Woodland, urban area; eastern United States, southern Canada, United Kingdom
FOOD: Seeds, nuts, acorns

Squirrels hide food in trees or underground in warm weather and return for it in winter. They communicate through sounds and by flicking their bushy tails. Gray squirrels keenly smell their hidden food and scents on females that are ready to mate. Females use twigs and straw to build nests, called dreys, in trees or inside of buildings, in which they give birth and raise young. They sometimes share dreys to keep warm.

THE ONLY FLYING MAMMALS, bats have many useful skills. They can locate prey by sending out high-pitched sounds that bounce back; this is called echolocation. They can roost, which is hanging upside down. Some eat fruit, others eat insects, frogs, flowers, and small rodents. A bat can eat 600 mosquitoes in an hour, which helps control pest populations.

They live in every climate, desert to rainforest, on every continent except Antarctica. Bat babies are born once a year; they are helpless at first, but their mothers quickly teach them to roost and forage.

More than 1,100 species of bats in the Chiroptera order are broken down into microbats and fruit bats. There are very few bat fossils because their skeletons are too fragile to survive, but there are teeth that show they existed 65 million years ago.

HOARY BAT
Lasiurus cinereus
SIZE: **0.7–1.2 ounces (20–35 g)**
HABITAT: **Wide range of habitats; North, Central, and South America**
FOOD: **Moths, other insects**

This large bat has dense brown-black fur edged in white; *hoary* means "frosted." Humans can hear their high-pitched calls, unlike most bat sounds. They are strong fliers and can be spotted soaring above trees for about five hours after sunset.

HAMMER-HEADED FRUIT BAT
Hypsignathus monstrosus
SIZE: male: 8–16 ounces (228–450 g); female: 7.7–13.3 ounces (218–377 g)
HABITAT: Mangrove, swamp, palm forest; central Africa
FOOD: Figs, mangos, bananas, guavas

This is the largest bat in Africa, with a wingspan of over 3 feet (0.9 m). Males and females of this species are different; only the male has the huge head, snout, and larynx that allow it to make very loud, honking sounds. Female faces look like foxes. When mating, females fly over groups of males and land on the one they choose.

PROBOSCIS BAT
Rhynchonycteris naso
SIZE: 0.13–0.14 ounce (3.8–3.9 g)
HABITAT: Tropical lowland; southeastern Mexico, Central America, northern South America
FOOD: Insects

Proboscis bats are nocturnal, but unlike most bats, they tolerate light. They often hang upside down in well-lit structures. They send out high-frequency calls to detect insects to eat. They usually forage near or over water; they are good at maneuvering to catch their insect prey.

TOWNSEND'S BIG-EARED BAT
Corynorhinus townsendii

SIZE: 0.18–0.5 ounce (5–14 g)
HABITAT: Pine forest, desert scrub, cave; western North America
FOOD: Moths, beetles, flies

One of 300 species of vesper bats that eat insects and feed in the evening (*vesper* means "evening"), Townsend's big-eared bats have enormous ears. When they roost, they curl their ears up like ram's horns, and when they fly, they expand and contract them. They roost in caves and abandoned mines.

CALIFORNIA LEAF-NOSE BAT
Macrotus californicus

SIZE: 0.4–0.8 ounce (12–22 g)
HABITAT: Hot desert, cave; United States, Mexico
FOOD: Moths, butterflies, crickets, grasshoppers, beetles

These tiny bats have leaf-shaped flaps on the front of their faces and extra-long ears. Their hearing is excellent; they can hear the footsteps of crickets. They also have the best eyesight of any bat, and hunt by sight. Good at hovering, they grab butterflies and other insects that sleep on the ground.

White-nose syndrome has killed millions of bats in North America, and some populations may not recover for generations. Bats that suffer from this syndrome develop a white fungus on their faces. The fungus causes the bats to use up precious energy, causing them to run out of energy before spring and die. Scientists recently isolated the fungus that causes it and seeks a cure. Project EduBat teaches citizens to recognize and report diseased animals.

Surprisingly Human

Female vampire bats are nice to one another. If one member of a female group has not managed to find blood to eat, a female that has had a good meal will regurgitate some for her hungry friend.

VAMPIRE BAT
Desmodus rotundus

SIZE: 0.5–2 ounces (14–57 g)
HABITAT: Arid and humid tropics and subtropics; Mexico, Central America, northern South America
FOOD: Blood of birds and mammals

There is only one item in the diet of vampire bats: blood. They get it by climbing on animals, use heat-sensing noses to find veins, and razor-sharp teeth to cut into them. This is the only bat species that hops, jumps, and walks on the ground. When on the ground they use a joint in each wing like front feet. Victims don't die; they barely hurt because the teeth are surgically sharp. Vampire bats live in colonies of 30 to 150 bats.

GREY-HEADED FLYING FOX

Named for its foxlike face, the grey-headed flying fox is actually a huge bat. It can't echolocate (find objects by bouncing sounds off them) like some other bats. Instead, it uses big eyes and a sharp sense of smell to navigate, forage, and keep track of children. Newborn flying fox babies can't fly; they cling to the fur on their mothers' bellies to get around. After three months, they learn to fly and forage with their mothers. They nurse until their wingspan is almost fully developed, which is when they can fly for long distances.

6 FACTS ABOUT THE GREY-HEADED FLYING FOX

- ▸ Lives on the eastern coast of Australia
- ▸ Has claws on first and second fingers
- ▸ Its enormous wingspan is more than 3 feet (1 m) long
- ▸ Eats fruit, nectar, pollen, and bark, especially eucalyptus and fig
- ▸ Communicates using more than 20 different sounds
- ▸ Predators include eagles, snakes, and crocodiles

ABOUT ME!

I'm a grey-headed flying fox mother. I live with my children in a camp with about 10,000 other flying foxes. The camp is in a gully filled with trees. My family stays in its territory, which is just one branch. I have a mate who defends the territory with strong scents and loud calls. During the day, we sleep and rest hanging upside down. At night, we fly up to 30 miles (50 km) looking for food.

MEMBERS OF THE LAGOMORPH ORDER, which includes 80 species, rabbits, hares, and pikas multiply rapidly by having large litters several times a year. Rabbits are born furless and with their eyes closed; hares are born with open eyes and fur.

Members of the Lagomorph order have two sets of incisors, but rather than side by side, one set is behind the other one. They are herbivores. They have strong back limbs that allow them to hop. Rabbits and hares tolerate all climates; pikas prefer cool weather.

EASTERN COTTONTAIL RABBIT
Sylvilagus floridanus

SIZE: 2–3 pounds (1–1.5 kg)
HABITAT: Woodland, prairie, swamp, even urban areas; southern Canada through northern South America
FOOD: Grasses, clover, woody plants

The most common rabbits, these fast-moving animals have gray-brown fur and the cotton-puff tail for which they are named. They can adapt to many habitats and breed impressively—females can have four (or more in areas without cold winters) litters of three to eight kits a year, but they are prey for many animals, and only about 15 percent survive their first year.

SNOWSHOE HARE
Lepus americanus

SIZE: **2–3 pounds (1–1.5 kg)**
HABITAT: **Forest, swamp, thicket; United States, Canada**
FOOD: **Leafy vegetation in summer, woody in winter**

The bottoms of this hare's feet are covered with thick, spiral hairs that help keep it from sinking in snow. In summer, its coat is brown, so it can hide in fields. In winter, its white coat provides good snow camouflage. Small ears conserve heat. Females bear up to four litters of up to eight kits (but usually two to four) a year.

Surprisingly Human

Pikas plan ahead in a sophisticated way. During summer, they prepare haystacks, spreading grasses and wildflowers in the sun to dry so they don't get moldy. They store them in dens to eat in winter.

BLACK-TAILED JACKRABBIT
Lepus californicus

SIZE: **2–7 pounds (1–3 kg)**
HABITAT: **Scrubland, prairie, farmland, dune; southwestern United States, Mexico**
FOOD: **Shrubs, grasses**

Actually hares and not rabbits, the jackrabbit has long, strong legs that enable jumping up to 10 feet (3 m) and running up to 40 miles per hour (64 kph); they evade predators by moving in zigzag patterns. Their large eyes are on the sides of their heads, so they have a broad range of vision. They can emit heat from their big ears. Jackrabbits don't burrow; they rest and give birth in shallow depressions.

AMERICAN PIKA
Ochotona princeps

SIZE: **4–6 ounces (115–170 g)**
HABITAT: **Cool, moist mountain. They require rocky slopes (called talus); western North America**
FOOD: **High-nutrition grasses and flowers**

American pikas have thick, dark fur that camouflages them against rocks; it keeps them warm, but they can't tolerate heat. Scientists consider them to be particularly vulnerable to climate change. Like all pikas, they make a high, shrill sound when alarmed, which is why they're also called "whistling hares."

ANTEATERS, ARMADILLOS, AND SLOTHS are all members of the Xenarthra superorder that developed in South America about 60 million years ago. Xenarthra means "strange joints"—these animals have special joints that allow them to dig and curl their bodies. Each has its own skill or special feature: the armadillo's tough armor, the anteater's long, bony snout, and the sloth's strong grip.

HOFFMAN'S TWO-TOED SLOTH
Choloepus didactylus

SIZE: 9–18 pounds (4–8 kg)
HABITAT: Rain forest; Central America, northern South America
FOOD: Leaves, buds, twigs, fruit

Sloths spend most of their time—including eating, sleeping, and giving birth—hanging upside down from tree branches. They only come down to the ground to poop or switch trees. They're some of the slowest creatures on Earth. They can grip branches extremely well and are good swimmers.

GROUND PANGOLIN
Smutsia temminckii

SIZE: 15–40 pounds (7–18 kg)
HABITAT: Savannah, woodland; eastern and southern Africa
FOOD: Ants, termites

Also called spiny anteaters (though they are not closely related to anteaters), pangolins are covered in leaf-shaped scales composed of fused hairs. They are toothless, but their incredible tongues—muscular, cone shaped, and sometimes as long as the rest of its body—poke into insect nests and slurp them up.

NINE-BANDED ARMADILLO
Dasypus novemcinctus

SIZE: 9–18 pounds (4–8 kg)
HABITAT: Temperate and tropical forest and scrub; United States, Mexico, Central and South America
FOOD: Insects, invertebrates

Nine-banded armadillos ingest ants and beetles by slurping them up. They're encased in a strong, flexible, bony armor that's covered in keratin (the material in fingernails), which makes them tough for predators to eat. Good swimmers, they can also hold their breath and walk across the bottoms of creeks. They build burrows with their long noses, but they are loners and do not share them except when mating.

GIANT ANTEATER
Myrmecophaga tridactyla

SIZE: 40–86 pounds (18–39 kg)
HABITAT: Grassland, woodland, rain forest; Mexico, Central and South America
FOOD: Ants, termites

The anteater has several unusual features. Its complicated snout holds a bone tube and an extra-long, sticky tongue. Its body is covered in thick skin and long hair that protect it from insect bites. It has sharp claws on its feet that can rip into anthills. Anteaters have poor vision, but a good sense of smell makes up for it. They have no teeth, but crush insects against the top of their mouth with their strong tongue. Anteaters don't make their own stomach acid, they use the acid in ants to help with digestion.

THESE BURROWING ANIMALS were once all considered to be in the same order, called Insectivora; they are now separated into five orders.

Little moles can dig 15 feet (5 m) an hour with their strong forearms, multi-jointed digits, and paddle-shaped paws. They can survive underground with very little oxygen. They can sense when earthworms, their main food, enter into their tunnel and then they paralyze them with the toxins in their saliva. Moles are members of the Talpidae family.

Shrews, elephant shrews, and tree shrews each belong to a different order. They all look like mice, but they have sharp, spiky teeth instead of the flatter incisors of mice. They also have more teeth than mice. Elephant shrews are also called jumping shrews for their ability to leap.

There are 17 species of hedgehogs, and all are covered in protective quills. Tenrecs look like hedgehogs, but they are in another order all together.

LONG-EARED HEDGEHOG
Hemiechinus auritus
SIZE: **10.5–18 ounces (300–500 g)**
HABITAT: **Arid desert and steppe; Middle East, central Asia**
FOOD: **Insects, small vertebrates, fruit**

One of the smallest hedgehogs, this burrowing animal curls into a ball with its spines facing outward to protect itself from predators. It forages for insects and even snakes every night, but can survive in a lab for up to ten weeks without food. Its large ears help keep it cool, like those of the fennec fox.

FUN FACT

Long-eared hedgehogs are not the only animals that evolved big ears to emit heat and keep cool in hot climates. Fennec foxes in Africa and black-tailed jackrabbits in North America—none of which are related to each other—have the same feature. Scientists use the term "convergent evolution" to describe how different animals adapt to the same problem in the same way.

COMMON SHREW
Sorex araneus
SIZE: **0.17–0.5 ounces (5–14 g)**
HABITAT: **Woodland, grassland, dune; Europe, northwest Asia**
FOOD: **Insects, slugs, snails, amphibians**

These tiny mammals eat constantly and consume up to 90 percent of their body weight every day; they rest for a few minutes between feedings. If they sleep too long they will starve to death. Their teeth have iron deposits, which makes them stronger and reddish. Each shrew keeps a territory about the size of a large building and defends it aggressively when invaded.

STAR-NOSED MOLE
Condylura cristata
SIZE: **1–3 ounces (28–85 g)**
HABITAT: **Wet lowland area; eastern North America**
FOOD: **Small invertebrates, aquatic insects**

Star-nosed moles are fairly ordinary except for the 22 pink tentacles around their noses. These appendages are sensory touch organs with over 25,000 tiny receptors; star-nosed moles use them to feel their way around dark burrows. It is the most sensitive skin on any mammal, about 20 times as sensitive as human fingers. Semi-aquatic, they build burrows with underwater openings and paddle in and out with their broad front paws. They are considered the fastest eaters in the mammal world, and can identify and eat potential food in less than a second.

EUROPEAN HEDGEHOG
Erinaceus europaeus

SIZE: 28–42 ounces (800–1,200 g)
HABITAT: Field, farmland, garden; western Europe
FOOD: Worms, slugs, insects, berries

The European hedgehog has very short legs that keep it just a few inches off the ground. It's covered in tightly packed spines; when threatened, a hedgehog curls into ball, protecting its bare face and underbelly. Hedgehogs live in shallow nests lined with foliage; several hedgehogs use each nest, but not at the same time.

GOLDEN-RUMPED ELEPHANT SHREW
Rhynchocyon chrysopygus

SIZE: 18–21 ounces (500–600 g)
HABITAT: Forest; Kenya
FOOD: Invertebrates, insects, spiders

Golden-rumped elephant shrews spend their days foraging with their long, flexible noses and running from eagles and snakes. To evade predators, they build several nests from leaves; at night, they choose one nest and sleep in it. They mate for life, but spend most of their time apart from one another.

Animal Antics
Hedgehogs "self-anoint." When they encounter a new animal or an unusual scent, they'll stop in their tracks, taste it, start foaming at the mouth, and spread the foamy saliva all over themselves. No one knows why.

TREE SHREW
Tupaia glis

SIZE: 5–7 ounces (140–198 g)
HABITAT: Tropical forest; southeastern Asia
FOOD: Arthropods, ants, fruit, leaves

Common tree shrews have pointy noses, bushy tails, and sharp claws that they use for climbing. Pairs mate for life; males build separate nests for parents and offspring. Mothers visit and nurse the young for just 15 minutes every two days.

LOWLAND STREAKED TENREC
Hemicentetes semispinosus

SIZE: 4–10 ounces (115–280 g)
HABITAT: Rain forest, agricultural land; Madagascar
FOOD: Earthworms, other invertebrates

Though they have spines like hedgehogs, tenrecs are in their own order. Streaked tenrecs build long burrows with latrines outside; sometimes, more than 20 tenrecs crowd into a burrow. Tenrecs push their spines into predators to defend themselves; they also communicate by rubbing the quills together, which makes a high-pitched noise.

EUROPEAN MOLE
Talpa europaea

SIZE: 2.5–4.5 ounces (71–128 g)
HABITAT: Woodland and pasture with deep soil; Europe, through Russia
FOOD: Invertebrates, especially worms

Moles have long, cylindrical bodies and flattened paws that are good for tunneling; their eyes are small because they live underground where it's dark. They dig elaborate, permanent tunnels, and males extend them when they look for mates underground.

WHALES ARE ENORMOUS, exceptionally intelligent, and communicative. As mammals, they need to breathe air, so they rise from the ocean to blow water and carbon dioxide from their lungs and take in oxygen through blowholes. Their bodies are covered in a thick layer of fat called blubber, which insulates them in the cold waters in which they swim.

Whales do not have good senses of smell or sight, but their hearing is superb. They locate prey through echolocation, sending out high-frequency sounds and following the objects off which the sounds bounce.

Whales are members of Cetacea, an order that includes at least 83 species of whales, porpoises, and dolphins. Experts believe that whales' ancestors were land animals, the same as hippopotamuses; after cetaceans returned to the sea about 50 million years ago, they lost their legs. Hippos are thought to be a bridge between their current order (Artiodactyla, even-toed hooved animals such as cows and camels) and whales. In fact, some scientists now consider whales and the even-toed hooved animals to be in the same order, which they call Cetartiodactyla.

HUMPBACK WHALE
Megaptera novaeangliae
SIZE: 48,501–79,366 pounds (22,000–36,000 kg)
HABITAT: Ocean; polar areas in summer to tropics in winter
FOOD: Krill, plankton, fish

Known for enchanting singing and graceful breaching, humpback whales migrate about 16,000 miles (25,700 km) every year, from polar feeding regions to subarctic breeding grounds. Hunting cooperatively, they dive and trap prey in bubbles of exhaled air. When humpback whales prepare to dive, they curl their backs into humps. Their flippers are the largest appendage on any animal.

Surprisingly Human
Whales, especially humpbacks, like to sing. All the whales in a pod know the same songs and repeat phrases from it; some of the songs go on for hours. The songs evolve and become longer over time. Whales may be singing to locate mates, or simply for enjoyment.

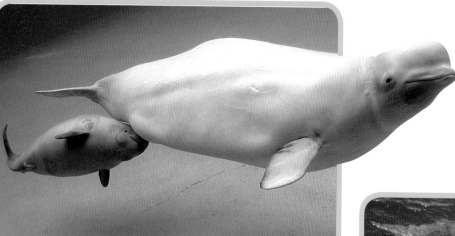

BELUGA WHALE
Delphinapterus leucas
SIZE: 1,102–3,307 pounds (500–1,500 kg)
HABITAT: Ocean, shallow bay in summer; Arctic waters around North America, Europe, Greenland
FOOD: Fish, invertebrates, worms

Beluga whales are called "sea canaries" for the many loud sounds they make. They have milky-white bodies and flexible necks that can turn their heads 90 degrees. They also move their lips and faces to form facial expressions. They live in small pods that may include up to 1,000 whales in the summer; they play, sing, and bounce out of the water together.

BLUE WHALE
Balaenoptera musculus
SIZE: up to 418,000 pounds (190,000 kg)
HABITAT: Ocean; all oceans except Arctic
FOOD: Krill

The blue whale is the largest animal that has ever lived. It can grow to 110 feet (33.5 m) long; that's the length of three school buses. (Most adult individuals are 80–90 feet (24–27 m).) Its tongue weighs as much as a rhinoceros; its heart is as big as a car. It can eat 8,000 pounds (3,629 kg) of krill—a tiny crustacean—in a day.

FUN FACT Hippos manufacture their own moisturizer. Their skin secretes an oily pink substance that keeps them from getting burned when they bask in the hot African sun. Some say it looks like they are sweating blood.

HIPPOPOTAMUS
Hippopotamus amphibius
SIZE: 1,444–7,055 pounds (655–3,200 kg)
HABITAT: Lake, river, swamp; eastern Africa
FOOD: Grasses

Hippopotamus means "river horse;" these huge land mammals spend up to 16 hours a day in water. Their eyes, ears, and nostrils are on the top of their heads so they can be almost completely submerged. They can't swim, but they can move well and hold their breath underwater. At night, they forage, eating up to 80 pounds (36 kg) of grass. Usually calm, they're dangerous when threatened.

SPERM WHALE
Physeter macrocephalus
SIZE: 77,161–110,231 pounds (35,000–50,000 kg)
HABITAT: Ocean; worldwide, though mostly in temperate and tropical regions
FOOD: Squid, octopus, fish

Sperm whales have enormous, squared-off heads and one of the largest mammal brains. Their heads are filled with sperm oil, a waxy substance that was sometimes harvested from dead whales and used for heating. One theory about the oil is that it may help the whales produce their echolocation calls. Sperm whales prefer warm water. They dive deep, and can stay underwater for over an hour; when they ascend, they will blow up to 70 times before they dive again.

BOWHEAD WHALE
Balaena mysticetus
SIZE: 132,277–220,462 pounds (60,000–100,000 kg)
HABITAT: Ocean; Arctic regions, including northern Atlantic and Pacific Oceans
FOOD: Crustaceans

Only the blue whale is larger than the bowhead. Named for their bow-shaped mouths, these huge animals are filter feeders. They swim with their mouth open, and water flows over a comblike bone called a baleen that's in the back of the mouth. This filter helps separate tiny crustaceans from water. Bowheads sometimes travel in groups of up to 14 whales that make a V-formation and filter feed together.

ORCA
Orcinus orca
SIZE: 12,125–19,842 pounds (5,500–9,000 kg)
HABITAT: Ocean; worldwide
FOOD: Marine mammals, fish, sea turtles, seabirds

Also known as killer whales, orcas are actually dolphins. They have striking black-and-white bodies, large fins, and rounded snouts. Orcas are voracious eaters and master hunters; they catch prey by stunning it with fins, chasing it until it tires, and jumping onto beaches. Some populations specialize in hunting certain foods, such as fish or seals; some scientists think these groups may evolve into different species. Orcas live in pods of females that develop unique calls and sounds; these pods hunt cooperatively and care for their young. Sometimes, pods join with other pods or loner orcas for even more efficient hunting.

GRACEFUL AND ACROBATIC as well as smart, dolphins have some of the biggest brain-to-body ratios in the animal world. They not only learn, they teach their offspring how to catch fish by stunning them with their tails, and how to use the squeaks and clicks that bounce off moving objects to locate prey (echolocation).

The dolphin's sleek and aerodynamic body gives it an advantage in catching favorite prey. Dolphins are found in warm waters, usually near the coast.

Porpoises have shorter, stouter bodies than dolphins, and their snouts are not as long. Porpoises don't have the curved mouths that make dolphins appear to be smiling, and they are not as talkative.

Sea cows (dugongs and manatees) are also aquatic mammals, but more closely related to elephants than dolphins. They are also very intelligent and can be trained.

WEST INDIAN MANATEE
Trichechus manatus

SIZE: 441–3,307 pounds (200–1,500 kg)
HABITAT: Warm coastal water; Caribbean Sea, Atlantic Ocean
FOOD: Sea grasses

Also called sea cows, manatees have flippers and propel themselves with their tails. They tolerate both fresh- and saltwater, but become stressed in cold water because their metabolism is slow. They're usually solitary, but mothers and offspring maintain contact for many years. They have good memories and can learn tasks like dolphins and seals do.

Surprisingly Human

Dolphins communicate with one another in ways similar to humans. Experts believe dolphins have a complex language and each sound is a word. Scientists are trying to recreate that language so that we can understand what dolphins are saying.

BOTTLENOSE DOLPHIN
Tursiops truncatus

SIZE: 573–1,102 pounds (260–500 kg)
HABITAT: Oceans; worldwide except for polar waters
FOOD: Eels, squid, shrimp, fish

These energetic animals are intelligent enough to learn complicated tricks for aquarium shows and to survive in their own environment. To find prey, they swim into schools of fish or follow commercial fishing vessels. Some say they are the most intelligent animals in the world. Bottlenose dolphins live in groups, sometimes numbering in the hundreds. They communicate and play constantly. They teach their calves survival skills and will come to the aid of injured dolphins.

DUGONG
Dugong dugon
SIZE: 507–882 pounds (230–400 kg)
HABITAT: Warm, shallow water; Indo-Pacific Ocean
FOOD: Sea grasses

Similar to the manatee and also called a sea cow, this is the only marine mammal that is strictly vegetarian. It has a very long digestive tract to handle plants. Sailors call them mermaids because of their long mammary glands.

SPINNER DOLPHIN
Stenella longirostris
SIZE: 121–165 pounds (55–75 kg)
HABITAT: Ocean; tropical and subtropical waters worldwide
FOOD: Squid, shrimp, fish

No one knows for certain why the spinner dolphins perform their amazing acrobatics, twisting in several (as many as 14) complete revolutions with each jump. Some theories include communication, throwing off parasites, or just enjoying themselves. They swim in large schools of several hundred and sometimes join with other dolphin species such as spotted dolphins. Mothers and offspring maintain their bonds for life.

COMMON PORPOISE
Phocoena phocoena
SIZE: 99–132 pounds (45–60 kg)
HABITAT: Ocean; polar and cool temperate waters of Northern Hemisphere
FOOD: Cephalopods, fish

Also called harbor porpoises because they are found in shallow harbor water, these animals come to the surface every 50 seconds to breathe. They are also found in estuaries and rivers; they tolerate both fresh- and saltwater. Shy and reclusive, they usually travel in pairs or small groups but sometimes join with other groups to feed on a rich source. Mothers take their calves to remote caves for nursing.

LONG-FINNED PILOT WHALE
Globicephala melas
SIZE: male: 4,000–8,000 pounds (1,814–3,628 kg); female: 2,000–4,000 pounds (907–1,814 kg)
HABITAT: Cold temperate water; Atlantic, Indo-Pacific, and Southern Oceans
FOOD: Fish, cephalopods

The long-finned pilot whale, which is actually a dolphin, has been called a pothead because its rounded head looks like a cooking pot. These large dolphins are very loyal to each other; if one is stranded, others in the pod will try to help and sometimes get stranded together. There are up to 100 of them in a pod.

Animal Antics Dolphins in western Australia have developed a technique to catch fish in shallow waters at the shoreline. They swim fast toward the shore, building up enough speed to glide onto the beach, right on top of their prey. Gliding on the water's surface in this way is called hydroplaning. After striking, the dolphins quickly turn back into the water to avoid being stranded on the sand.

AFRICAN WATERING HOLE

Massive to miniscule, herbivores or carnivores, predators and prey—
all visit this pond and the surrounding field and forest to find food,
to cool off, to clean up, and to drink.

Leopard

Hippopotamus

Vervet monkey

Treetop Safety
When they sense danger, monkeys head for the trees; they're fast and nimble climbers.

Scrub hare

Black rhinoceros

African lion

Too Big to Fall
Predators avoid this huge animal, it's too slow to outrun them, but it can kill with a crushing blow.

Zebra

Apex Predator
No animal attacks the king of the jungle. Its jaws are too powerful to brave.

Standing Tall

Gerenuks don't need water; they get moisture from leaves. They stand on two feet to reach upper branches.

Redbilled oxpecker

African elephant

Reticulated giraffe

Too Tall

Giraffes are at their most vulnerable when they bend over to drink; they can't rise and run fast enough, so sometimes one will stand guard.

Flight, not Fight

Its defenses are speed, agility, and stamina. It cannot fight the big cats—but it can outrun them.

Grant's gazelle

Rufous elephant shrew

Blending in

Their dark mottled fur makes these tiny creatures almost invisible as they race through wooded areas, foraging for insects.

ANIMAL PLANET L!VE

Check out the Animal Planet L!VE cam to see marvelous mammals in action by scanning this code or visiting animalplanet.timeincbooks.com/mammals.

Serval

Crocodile

83

Bluebird

Rainbow lorikeet

Bald eagle

Snowy owl

Mallard

Gentoo penguin

TOP TRAITS Birds have feathers, wings, and beaks. ▶Most have hollow, beaten feathers once or twice a year. ▶Some nonflyers, use as flippers for swimming. ▶Birds can be as short as 2 inches (5 cm) or as tall

BIRDS

lightweight bones that can support powerful wings. ▶ Most molt their wind-
like ostriches, have strong legs for running. ▶ Penguins have small wings they
as 8 feet (2.5 m). ▶ There are about 10,000 species of birds.

ALL ABOUT BIRDS

BIRDS ARE CLASSIFIED IN 28 DIFFERENT ORDERS and 203 families. Their aerial lifestyle requires enormous amounts of energy, so they stay close to large food supplies. Most birds operate like high-performance engines. Their superefficient respiratory systems pull oxygen from the air and push blood quickly through their bodies. Wings offer the amazing opportunity to fly—in most species—but birds have had to adapt to life without two extra grasping feet. Without two arms for expressive gestures, birds communicate through displays and songs. Their perching feet are specially adapted to their environments, enabling clinging to rock faces or to swaying grass. Their strong bills are adept at cracking nuts, pecking holes, and sometimes ripping flesh. Birds' wings may be suited for short flights from branch to branch. Or they may have 11-foot (3.4 m) wingspans that allow them to rise on air currents without a single flap.

EYES Birds' eyes are similar to humans' but proportionately much larger. Some birds of prey have eyes that are larger than humans' eyes.

BILL A bird's bill is made of an outer layer of keratin around sturdy internal bones. The keratin grows constantly, as it gets worn away through use.

FEET Species have different arrangements of their four toes, which they use for perching, swimming, snatching prey, or manipulating food.

EAR HOLES Birds don't have external ears; instead, they have specialized feathers that protect the ear openings but allow sound to enter.

BACKBONE All birds are vertebrates, but in most bird species the bones are hollow, with many struts (little connective rods) for support.

WINGS Feathers on a bird's wing are arranged in a streamlined airfoil shape, like the shape of a wing on a plane. Primary feathers attach to the outer wing, secondary feathers to the inner wing.

FEATHERS Each feather has a hollow central shaft and a series of parallel barbs that branch out of each side of the shaft.

SYRINX The vocal organ of a bird, the syrinx, sits at the end of the trachea. Muscles control airflow to produce sound.

HEART A bird's heart is larger in relation to its body size than any other vertebrate's.

LUNGS A bird's lung tissue is much denser than other vertebrates'. This, combined with heart size, gives a bird the most efficient respiratory system among all animals.

THESE FEET ARE MADE FOR...

PERCHING

SWIMMING

RUNNING

SNATCHING PREY

TORPOR

One strategy for surviving the cold or periods of low food availability is called torpor. A bird conserves energy by lowering its core body temperature, which lowers its heart rate. It becomes completely inactive and doesn't respond to most stimuli. When conditions improve, the bird can raise its temperature back to normal. Hummingbirds, nighthawks, and nightjars use this technique, as do many hibernating animals.

FLIGHT

Flight requires a light body and strong breast muscles to supply the power for lift. Hollow bones, a light bill, and a highly efficient digestive system help lighten a bird's load.

The long feathers of the wings and tail are referred to as the flight feathers. The shape and movement of these feathers create aerodynamic forces that enable flight. Lift is the force that gets a bird off the ground and keeps it in the air.

During lift, air travels faster over the wing than under it. This means that there is less air pressure above the wing than below it, allowing the bird to rise. Drag is the force that slows the air moving over the wing.

A bird can change the shape of its wings to slow down when landing, perhaps as it spots prey and starts a steep dive.

LIVE ACTION: AMERICAN GOLDEN PLOVER

It's late summer on the tundra breeding grounds. The American golden plover plucks larvae from the dirt, the last meal before its journey. It has gained 50 percent of its weight since the spring, enough energy to get it to South America. A group of 150 plovers takes off; there is safety in numbers. The wind is at their backs, and their long wings are perfect for fast flying. They sense Earth's magnetic fields, and they watch stars and patterns of sunlight to guide them thousands of miles across the Atlantic. Finally, they arrive in Argentina, where bugs are plenty and living is easy for a few months until spring.

MIGRATION

Some birds migrate, and most that do travel in large flocks. They may migrate from their winter habitats to summer breeding grounds, or they may be in search of food. Travel distances vary by species. Arctic terns make an annual round-trip of more than 20,000 miles (32,200 km) from their summer home in northern Canada to spend the winter in Antarctica. Whooping cranes travel more than 2,500 miles (4,000 km) from Canada to Texas. Other birds, such as blue jays, northern bobwhites, and killdeers, travel shorter distances. The seasonal migration of Canada geese is identified by a V-shaped flight formation.

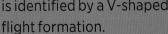

ALL ABOUT BIRDS

LIFE CYCLE

All birds reproduce by laying hard-shelled eggs. This reduces the amount of time females must carry young in their bodies, which would make it impossible to fly. Some species form monogamous bonds (each bird has only one mate) within breeding seasons, and some pair for life. About 13 percent of species nest in colonies. In a colony, anywhere from a few pairs to tens of thousands of pairs will build nests near one another. In about 300 species, helper birds aid pairs in raising young, a system called cooperative breeding. The newborn of waterbirds are often precocial, meaning that they are born with open eyes, downy feathers, and an ability to move about. Most songbird chicks are altricial, meaning that they hatch blind, bald, and helpless. Parents feed and protect offspring, but not for long. The quicker a chick can help itself, the better the whole family's chance for survival.

EGGS

CHICK

ADULT

HABITATS

Birds' ability to fly allows them to access many different habitats. Each species of bird is specially adapted to survive in a limited environment, based on the food it needs to eat and the resources it needs in order to breed. Species of birds may live in wetland, forest, grassland, or desert environments, at nearly every altitude. The emperor penguin is the only animal that remains on the Antarctic ice during winter. Pelagic birds, such as albatrosses, spend almost their entire lives at sea. They come ashore only to breed. Some species migrate in predictable patterns to make the best use of resources in different habitats.

WETLAND

FOREST

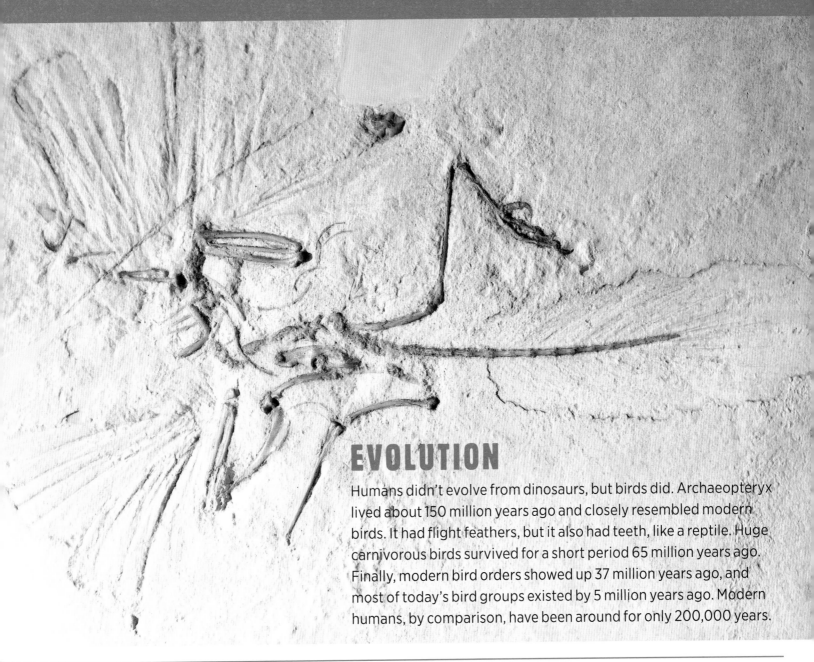

EVOLUTION

Humans didn't evolve from dinosaurs, but birds did. Archaeopteryx lived about 150 million years ago and closely resembled modern birds. It had flight feathers, but it also had teeth, like a reptile. Huge carnivorous birds survived for a short period 65 million years ago. Finally, modern bird orders showed up 37 million years ago, and most of today's bird groups existed by 5 million years ago. Modern humans, by comparison, have been around for only 200,000 years.

DESERT

GRASSLAND

ANTARCTIC

DUCKS, SWANS, AND GEESE all have flattened bills, streamlined bodies, and webbed feet for swimming. They live in a variety of aquatic habitats. Their feathers are waterproof, thanks to an intricate feather structure and a waxy substance spread while preening.

Some waterfowl feed by tipping up to reach their food in shallow water; others dive in deeper waters to catch small fish and invertebrates. Many have comblike lamellae on their bills that help them strain food.

Many waterfowl build well-hidden nests on the ground at the edges of wetlands, while others nest up in trees. Snakes, skunks, and gulls prey on eggs. Foxes, hawks, and owls also target nesting females and ducklings.

Most ducks can swim and feed themselves within hours of hatching, but up to 80 percent die within the first year. If they survive, many can live more than 20 years in the wild.

MAGPIE GOOSE
Anseranas semipalmata
SIZE: **1.5–3 feet long (0.5–0.9 m)**
HABITAT: **Pacific coastal area; Australia, New Guinea**
FOOD: **Swamp grass seeds, blades of dry grasses, bulbs of spike-rush**

Magpie geese are a unique family of birds, more closely related to a family of birds called screamers than they are to ducks. They will often breed in threes. Two females lay eggs on a floating platform of reeds made by a male goose. They are also the only species of waterfowl that feeds its young.

PLUMED WHISTLING DUCK
Dendrocygna eytoni
SIZE: **1.5–2 feet long (0.5–0.6 m)**
HABITAT: **Grassland and savanna near water; Australia, New Guinea**
FOOD: **Grasses, millet, rice, seeds, rushes**

During the day, these ducks gather with large numbers of waterfowl along lagoons and swamps to sleep and to preen. At night, they go long distances to feed on grasslands.

The North American Waterfowl Management Plan was developed in 1986 and focused on restoring waterfowl habitats. Since that time, many duck populations have increased substantially.

MANDARIN DUCK
Aix galericulata
SIZE: **1.5–2 feet long (0.5–0.6 m)**
HABITAT: **Forest, lake, pond; eastern Asia, eastern Siberia**
FOOD: **Water plants, rice, other grains**

Mandarin ducks put on funky courtship displays that involve a lot of shaking and bobbing. They can perch on branches with their long-clawed toes and nest as high as 30 feet up in a tree hole. Females line their nests with down feathers they pluck from their chests. Just a short time after the nestlings hatch, the mother calls to them from outside the nest. They launch out of the nest into a free fall and land unhurt.

BUFFLEHEAD
Bucephala albeola
SIZE: 1–1.5 feet long (0.3–0.5 m)
HABITAT: Lake and pond; North America
FOOD: Aquatic invertebrates, crustaceans, mollusks

Buffleheads dive underwater to grab aquatic insect larvae in freshwater habitats and arthropods and molluscs in saltwater. Female buffleheads use hollow tree cavities created by other birds as nests. They scout sites up to a year in advance. Young buffleheads are excellent swimmers and learn how to dive for food within the first few days of life.

SURF SCOTER
Melanitta perspicillata
SIZE: 1.5–2 feet long (0.5–0.6 m)
HABITAT: Lake, river, tundra, coastal water; North America, Oceania
FOOD: Insects, mollusks

While most diving ducks use their feet to propel themselves, the surf scoter uses its wings to swim in a dive. Its stout bill helps it yank shellfish from submerged rocks.

Many male ducks grow different plumage during breeding season. For about a month, they are completely flightless as their new feathers grow, which makes them vulnerable to predators. This process is called molting.

WHISTLING SWAN
Cygnus columbianus
SIZE: 4–5 feet long (1.2–1.5 m)
HABITAT: Lake, pond, stream; Arctic tundra, North America, northern Europe, southeastern Asia
FOOD: Aquatic plants, shellfish, insects, grain

Whistling swan families stick together. Males fight to protect their families and establish social dominance. The most dominant families, made up of both parents and their three to seven cygnets, obtain greater access to food and the safest areas for nests.
   They tip upside down in the water to feed, and they can be easily identified by their high-pitched yodeling call.

MUSCOVY DUCK
Cairina moschata
SIZE: 2–2.5 feet long (0.6–0.8 m)
HABITAT: Tropical pond and marsh; Mexico, Central and South America
FOOD: Grains, aquatic vegetation, fruits, nuts, small fish, insects, crabs

All domestic ducks are descendants of either mallards or Muscovys. These massive ducks roost in trees at night and build nests in tree holes. Males raise their crests in order to establish social dominance and to attract mates. Females protect nestlings for up to 70 days, teaching them how to eat, swim, and fend off enemies.

Surprisingly Human
Swans put their beaks together to kiss. They also mate for life. Divorce occurs in only 3 percent of pairs that breed successfully and 9 percent of pairs that breed unsuccessfully.

TURKEYS, GROUSE, CHICKENS, and related birds have strong legs and feet. Many sport colorful air sacs and ornamental feathers that are displayed during courtship.

They typically forage along the ground, scratching with their feet or beaks. During foraging, they store food at the base of the neck. Later, they rest and let the food travel to the stomach. Their powerful gizzards grind seeds and nuts.

Often, several families gather and form large winter flocks. As breeding season approaches, they begin to fight with each other. Many species have a mating system where males gather in a communal area, fight for dominance, and put on wild displays to attract a mate.

When startled, they seek cover in bushes. The smaller species such as quail are faster fliers, but the larger grouse are slower to take flight and escape a threat.

GUNNISON SAGE-GROUSE
Centrocercus minimus

SIZE: 1.5–2 feet (0.5–0.6 m)
HABITAT: Sagebrush-dominated habitat; southwestern Colorado, one county in southeastern Utah
FOOD: Sagebrush

This grouse was only described as a new species in 2000, making it the first new bird species in the United States since the 19th century. It is restricted to a tiny range and is considered to be endangered. It eats large amounts of sagebrush, which contains oils that kill microorganisms in the digestive tracts of most animals.

GREATER PRAIRIE CHICKEN
Tympanuchus cupido

SIZE: 1–1.5 feet long (0.3–0.5 m)
HABITAT: Prairie, cropland; southern Canada, midwestern United States
FOOD: Agricultural crops such as corn, soybeans, milo; small green leaves, seeds, insects

Just after sunrise, male greater prairie chickens can be seen shaking their wings, leaping, and dancing to attract the attention of females. During mating season, males make a booming sound with their inflated air sacs that can be heard a half mile away. They live within small areas of a hundred acres, but populations have declined rapidly as habitats get converted into cropland.

Animal Antics Male grouses put on some bizarre behaviors to woo the ladies. The greater sage-grouse scrapes its wings along short, bristly feathers on its inflated throat to create loud, rasping sounds.

CRESTED WOOD PARTRIDGE
Rollulus roulroul

SIZE: 1.5 feet long (0.3 m)
HABITAT: Evergreen forest, bamboo, lowland plain; southeastern Asia
FOOD: Fruits, seeds, large beetles, wood ants, small snails

These plump partridges have been known to follow wild pigs in order to feed on discarded fruit that they would be unable to eat whole. The young are fed by both mother and father.

CHUKAR
Alectoris chukar

SIZE: **1–1.5 feet long (0.3–0.5 m)**
HABITAT: **Dry and arid habitat; eastern Europe, China, Middle East**
FOOD: **Cheatgrass, wheat seeds**

The chukar, like other birds in the Phasianidae family, has a notch on the trailing edge of the wing where some flight feathers are unusually short. This gives the bird an explosive takeoff and makes it a strong and fast flier over short distances.

VULTURINE GUINEAFOWL
Acryllium vulturinum

SIZE: **2–2.5 feet long (0.6–0.8 m)**
HABITAT: **Dry savanna, scrubland; eastern Africa**
FOOD: **Seeds and leaves of grasses, herbs; berries, fruit**

The largest of all the guineafowl species, these baldheaded birds live in flocks of about 25, making soft, high-pitched calls. While they only fly about 100 yards and run rather than fly from danger, their population numbers more than one million. Females lay between four and eight eggs at a time.

OCELLATED TURKEY
Meleagris ocellata

SIZE: **2.5–4 feet long (0.8–1.2 m)**
HABITAT: **Tropical deciduous and evergreen forest; Yucatan Peninsula, Guatemala, Belize**
FOOD: **Seeds, nuts, berries, insects**

One of only two turkey species, the ocellated turkey lacks the fleshy beard of the wild turkey. It also has longer spurs and is much more colorful than its cousin. Males travel in groups and gobble and strut to impress females. When a female calls back, several males gather around her and display fanned tails, arched wings, and feather rattling. The female tends its young alone. They face threats from hunting and habitat loss.

The wild turkey now occupies all of its historic range, and then some, thanks to hunting regulations and reintroduction of the species into the wild. Conservationists also taught landowners "turkey-friendly" management techniques that would restore habitats and attract turkeys to their land.

TEMMINCK'S TRAGOPAN
Tragopan temminckii

SIZE: **2–2.5 feet long (0.6–0.8 m)**
HABITAT: **Evergreen and mixed forest; eastern Himalayan mountains**
FOOD: **Flowers, leaves, grass stalks, ferns, mosses, berries, seeds, insects**

Considered by many to be the most beautiful pheasant in the world, the courting male attracts the female by inflating its throat, raising its fleshy horns on its head, and fanning its tail as it dances.

THESE DIVERSE SHOREBIRDS have adaptations that allow them to make the most of marine environments. Their feathers are designed to withstand wear from rough weather. Most nest on the ground, but many have developed coloring and behaviors that make them almost invisible to predators.

Sandpipers and curlews sport long bills for reaching submerged prey and long toes that keep them from sinking into the ground. Gulls and terns dive or skim surface waters with their sharp bills to capture prey, then toss their catch into the air and swallow them whole. Auks, a group of birds that includes puffins, have muscular bodies, waterproof plumage, and wings designed to swim underwater in pursuit of prey.

Many of these birds return to the same breeding grounds and mates every year. Pairs often fiercely defend their nests and care for their young together.

TUFTED PUFFIN
Fratercula cirrhata

SIZE: 1–1.5 feet long (0.3–0.5 m)
HABITAT: Rocky coast, cliff face; western North America, Japan, northeastern Asia
FOOD: Anchovies and other small fish; squid, octopus, crabs, zooplankton, jellyfish

Tufted puffins are able to spend long periods at sea thanks to waterproof feathers and their ability to drink salt water and dive for fish. During breeding, they return to the shores where they were born. They prefer shorelines with steep, grassy slopes where they can build nests in burrows.

COMMON OYSTERCATCHER
Haematopus ostralegus

SIZE: 1–1.5 feet long (0.3–0.5 m)
HABITAT: Coastland, inland waterway; Britain, northern and western Europe
FOOD: Bivalves, worms, limpets, crabs

The oystercatcher's strong, flattened bill is shaped like a chisel. It uses it to hammer or pry open bivalve shells or to pull limpets and other shellfish from rocks.

Animal Antics
When tufted puffins fight each other, they spread their wings, open their mouths wide, stomp their feet, and wrestle. Crowds of birds gather around to watch the spectacle.

IVORY GULL
Pagophila eburnea

SIZE: 1–1.5 feet long (0.3–0.5 m)
HABITAT: Tundra; shorelines in Arctic regions, northern North America and Europe
FOOD: Small fish, small mammals, carrion, feces

Ivory gulls, like other gulls and terns, are opportunistic omnivores and will eat almost anything. They can swoop down and pluck small fish from surface waters, but will sometimes follow polar bears and human hunters to feed on scraps from their kills. They even consume polar bear excrement and seal placentas. Large breeding colonies nest on cliffs and broken icefields, in areas that are safe from predators and close to open water.

LONG-BILLED CURLEW
Numenius americanus

SIZE: 1.5–2 feet long (0.5–0.6 m)
HABITAT: Grassland, wetland, estuary; western North America, Mexico
FOOD: Insects, marine crustaceans, bottom-dwelling marine invertebrates

North America's largest shorebird, the long-billed curlew uses its downward-curved bill to catch shrimp and crabs living in crevices or earthworms in pastures. Pairs will incubate eggs together and aggressively guard over their nests, but the female leaves brood's care to her mate once the chicks are a few weeks old.

ELEGANT TERN
Sterna elegans

SIZE: 1–1.5 feet long (0.3–0.5 m)
HABITAT: Rocky shoreline, estuary, salt pond, lagoon; southern California, Mexico
FOOD: Fish (particularly northern anchovy), crustaceans

Over 90 percent of the world's elegant terns nest on Isla Rasa in the Gulf of California. Monogamous pairs are formed after elaborate courtship dances. The female scratches a shallow nest in the ground and lays a single egg, which hatches about 25 days later. Young terns are dependent on their parents for six months. Eventually, they learn to catch prey by plunging for shallow-water fish.

EURASIAN GOLDEN PLOVER
Pluvialis apricaria

SIZE: 10–11 inches long (25.4–28 cm)
HABITAT: Mossy tundra, marsh, bog; northern Europe, Asia
FOOD: Crustaceans, insects, worms, spiders, millipedes, snails, berries, seeds, grass

The plover will try to distract predators from its nest by pretending to be injured and limping away. While feeding, it trembles its foot on the ground to flush its prey into the open.

Auks are very vulnerable to oil spills, because petroleum ruins the bird's ability to insulate itself from the cold. The government and oil companies publicize rehabilitation of oil-soaked birds, but most of these birds don't survive after they're released into the wild.

STILT SANDPIPER
Calidris himantopus

SIZE: 8–9 inches long (20.3–22.9 cm)
HABITAT: Tundra, marshland; North and South America
FOOD: Insects, seeds

The stilt sandpiper feeds in freshwater or brackish marshes and shallow pools. It moves forward slowly and searches for prey, rapidly probing the water with its beak like a sewing machine. Monogamous pairs incubate their eggs together, and chicks are able to care for themselves within a couple weeks of hatching.

HOATZIN

Scientists tried to classify the unique, mystifying hoatzin with cuckoos, pheasants, pigeons, and turacos, but they eventually gave it its own order, Opisthocomiformes. It feeds almost entirely on marsh plants, and its digestive system acts just like a cow's. It "chews" the leaves, and then the food ferments in the massive crop—a pouch in the throat. As a result, the hoatzin smells like manure and has earned the nickname "stinkbird."

Young chicks have two claws at the wrist joint on each wing, causing some scientists to link the bird to the dinosaur *Archaeopteryx*. When an intruder spooks chicks, they jump into water below their nest until the danger is gone. Then they use their wing claws to climb out of the water and back to their nest.

10 FACTS ABOUT THE HOATZIN

- ▶ Has crop 50 times the size of stomach
- ▶ Rests on callus on chest that acts as tripod when belly is bloated
- ▶ Food takes 45 hours to pass
- ▶ Flocks in groups of 40 or more
- ▶ Adults hiss, hoot, and yelp at predators
- ▶ Is found mainly in Amazon and Orinoco River basins
- ▶ Both parents and older siblings help raise two to five young
- ▶ Has weak wing muscles and often crash-lands
- ▶ Becomes stressed by tourist visits; does poorly in captivity
- ▶ Capuchin monkeys consider its eggs delicacies

ABOUT ME!

I'm a hoatzin. I just love eating leaves. My buddies and I sit in trees and stuff our faces. We can strip an entire tree of its foliage. When we're done eating, our bellies are so full we can't even fly. We just sit around with our beaks hanging open and our wings drooping as we digest our massive meal.

MANY OF THESE WATERBIRDS spend much of their time at sea. They feed on fish, squid, and other aquatic animals, often by plunge-diving or snatching the prey from surface waters. Their bills may have hooked tips or serrated edges.

While some, like the albatross, may live lonely pelagic lives, they come ashore during breeding season to nest in large colonies. Most are monogamous, and lay only one or two eggs per breeding season. Couples often raise their young together, caring for offspring for longer periods than many other birds.

Their wings are designed to keep them aloft for hours or even days. They soar up and down air currents. However, they can be clumsy on land. Their takeoffs from land or water require a combination of heavy wing-beats, a strong thrust from their webbed feet, and some wind for lift.

GREAT FRIGATEBIRD
Fregata minor

SIZE: 3–3.5 feet long (0.9–1.5 m)
HABITAT: Tropical and sub-tropical waters; Indo-Pacific and Atlantic Oceans
FOOD: Flying fish, squid, jellyfish, scraps from fishing boats

Frigatebirds have the largest wing area to body mass ratio of any bird. Their scissor-shaped tail and angular wings allow them to make amazing aerial maneuvers. They can soar several days straight and may even sleep while aloft. The male frigatebird inflates its large, red throat pouch to attract a mate.

S N A C K ATTACK

The great frigatebird doesn't always have to catch its own meal. It's also a food thief! It will chase another bird until it drops or regurgitates its meal. With great agility, the frigatebird then snatches the food out of the air. This kind of thievery is called kleptoparasitism.

RED-TAILED TROPICBIRD
Phaethon rubricauda

SIZE: 2.5–3 feet long (0.8–0.9 m)
HABITAT: Islands in tropical waters; Indo-Pacific Ocean, southwest coast of Australia
FOOD: Flying fish, squid

Tropicbirds can remain at sea for long periods. They fly with rapid wing-beats, and then use their long wingspan to gain altitude on rising thermal air currents. Their wings are completely waterproof, allowing them to rest on the sea surface. To take off, they flap their powerful wings and thrust their webbed feet.

In the 1950s, cormorant populations were severely reduced by DDT and other pesticides. But once these chemicals were banned, populations recovered so well that fisherman now see these birds as competitors and fish farmers see them as thieves.

DALMATIAN PELICAN
Pelecanus crispus

SIZE: 5–6 feet long (1.5–1.8 m)
HABITAT: River delta, freshwater wetland, coastal lagoon; eastern Europe, east-central Asia, Middle East
FOOD: Eels, mullet, gobies, shrimps, worms, beetles, prawns, catfish, other small fish

This pelican sticks its head underwater in search of food. It uses its pouch like a net, to cover a larger area to catch more fish. It builds nests out of reeds, grass, and sticks, held together by droppings.

Surprisingly Human

The wandering albatross can fly thousands of miles without flapping its wings. It rides up and down air currents in a flight pattern called dynamic soaring. Scientists are now studying the bird's methods in order to build better gliders and drone airplanes.

WANDERING ALBATROSS
Diomedea exulans

SIZE: **3.5–4.5 feet long (1.1–1.4 m)**
HABITAT: **Savanna, grassland; subantarctic islands, open ocean in Southern Hemisphere**
FOOD: **Fish, squid**

The wandering albatross has the largest wingspan of any other bird, spanning up to 11 feet. It can live for 50 years and spends the majority of its life in flight. It returns to land only to mate, producing just one egg per breeding season. Couples mate for life and care for young together.

MASKED BOOBY
Sula dactylatra

SIZE: **2.5–3 feet long (0.8–0.9 cm)**
HABITAT: **Flat, treeless tropical islands; Atlantic and Pacific Oceans**
FOOD: **Fish, squid**

The masked booby lays two eggs, but the first chick to hatch always pushes the second out of the nest. The parents do not protect the ejected chick, and so predators quickly swoop in to eat it.

AUSTRALIAN PELICAN
Pelecanus conspicillatus

SIZE: **5–6 feet long (1.5–1.8 m)**
HABITAT: **Coastal inlet, shoreline, lake, swamp; Australia, Indonesia, Papua New Guinea**
FOOD: **Fish, insects, small crustaceans; sometimes small birds, reptiles, amphibians**

The Australian pelican has the longest bill of any bird. It has a hooked tip and a fleshy pink throat pouch that turns dark blue and red during courtship. The pelican catches fish by diving or by swimming on the water's surface with its bill open. Pelicans often feed in flocks of nearly 2,000 individuals. Dozens of chicks gather together in pods. Adults can spot offspring in the crowd and feed only their own chicks.

RED-FOOTED BOOBY
Sula sula

SIZE: **2–2.5 feet long (0.6–0.8 m)**
HABITAT: **Tropical and sub-tropical waters, forest; worldwide**
FOOD: **Fish**

The red-footed booby has strong wings for flying, but takeoffs can be difficult. If it doesn't have enough wind, it runs and flaps its wings for a short distance to get liftoff. It glides just above the water, then plunges like a torpedo to catch prey with its serrated bill.

CRANES AND RELATIVES

THESE LONG-LEGGED, LONG-NECKED birds fly with their necks stretched and their legs straight out behind them. They are among the tallest flying birds. They have long, thin bills. Their large, round wings have feathers that form a bustle when folded at their sides.

Cranes, and relatives including crake, rails, coots, and bustards, are generally opportunistic omnivores, taking whatever food is available. Species with northern breeding grounds migrate long distances, sometimes thousands of miles, to wintering grounds. All of these species face threats from loss of habitat.

While rails, crakes, and coots vary in whether they mate for life, cranes mostly do. They are also well known for their spectacular courtship dances. Rails, crakes, and coots build cup- or dome-shaped nests on the ground or over water, while cranes usually build large platforms on the ground, surrounded by a moat of water.

WHOOPING CRANE
Grus americana

SIZE: 4–5.5 feet long (1.2–1.7 m)
HABITAT: Wetland near large bodies of water; Canada, midwestern United States, Florida
FOOD: Plant tubers and grains, blue crabs, wolfberry fruits, clams, acorns, snails, grasshoppers, mice, voles, snakes

The whooping crane is the tallest North American bird and also one of the most endangered. In 1941, only 15 birds were left, but today 600 live in captivity or in the wild.

These birds form pairs around age two or three and mate for life. Like other cranes, during courtship, they dance by bowing, hopping, wing flapping, and calling in unison. After hatching, the young reach independence at nine months.

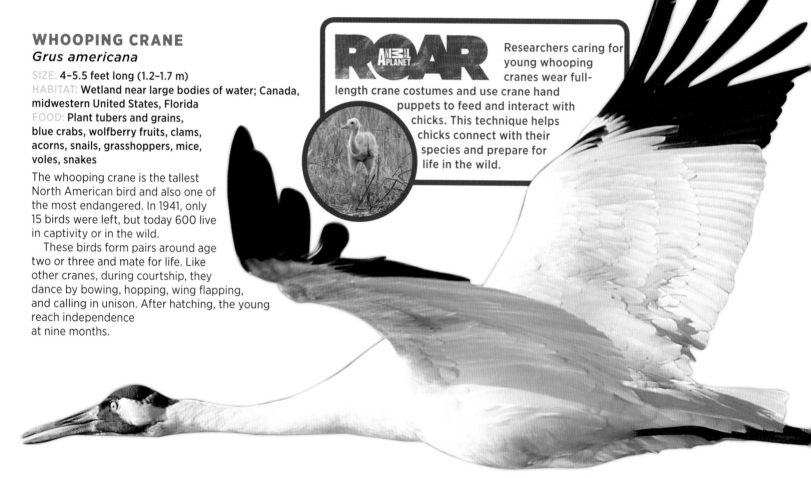

ROAR Researchers caring for young whooping cranes wear full-length crane costumes and use crane hand puppets to feed and interact with chicks. This technique helps chicks connect with their species and prepare for life in the wild.

GRAY-WINGED TRUMPETER
Psophia crepitans

SIZE: 1–1.5 feet long (0.3–0.5 m)
HABITAT: Tropical rain forest; northern Amazon basin, Guiana Shield of South America
FOOD: Insects, fallen fruit, occasionally small reptiles

Like cranes, trumpeters strut and dance in noisy courtship displays. Their name refers to the booming sound they make. As troops of monkeys travel the trees above, trumpeters follow and forage the forest floor for dropped fruit and nuts. They nest in tree holes and lay two to four eggs.

Surprisingly Human

Cranes don't just dance as a courtship behavior. Sometimes, one crane just gets excited and breaks out dancing, and then the rest of the flock can't help themselves and they all join in. It makes for a wild show!

KORI BUSTARD
Ardeotis kori

SIZE: 3.5–4 feet long (1.1–1.2 m)
HABITAT: Open grassland, semi-desert; eastern and southern sub-Saharan Africa
FOOD: Grasshoppers, dung beetles, small reptiles, rodents, seeds, roots and wild melons

The Kori bustard is one of the world's heaviest flying birds. It has a very deep, booming voice and barks when it is alarmed. During courtship, males strut with their chests puffed and crests and tail feathers raised. Females tend the nests and brood alone.

SIBERIAN CRANE
Grus leucogeranus

SIZE: 3.5–4 feet long (1.1–1.2 m)
HABITAT: Bog, marsh, wetland; lowland tundra regions of Russia, southern Asia
FOOD: Primarily aquatic tubers, but also insects, small mammals, snails, worms, fish, cranberries

Siberian cranes use their serrated bills to dig roots and tubers out of wetland ponds. They face serious threats from habitat loss on their winter grounds. The massive Three Gorges Dam on the Yangtze River in China will likely hurt populations, and the war in Afghanistan has also affected migrating cranes.

GREY-CROWNED CRANE
Balearica regulorum

SIZE: 3.5–4 feet (0.9–1.2 m)
HABITAT: Wetland, open grassland; eastern and southern Africa
FOOD: Insects, lizards, amphibians, fish, grasses, seeds

Grey-crowned cranes eat a variety of foods, which helps them adapt to a variety of habitats. However, as people dam and drain wetlands for agricultural development, these birds struggle to survive with less and less suitable nesting habitat. When foraging, they stomp heavily upon the ground to frighten and catch insects.

SANDHILL CRANE
Grus canadensis

SIZE: 3–4 feet long (0.9–1.2 m)
HABITAT: Freshwater marsh or bog, grassland; North America, northeastern Siberia
FOOD: Tubers, seeds, berries; small animals, including insects, worms, snakes, mice

Sandhill cranes make up 80 percent of the world's cranes. Every March, up to 600,000 of them gather at an 80-mile stretch of the Platte River in Nebraska, just as they have for thousands of years. There, they plump up on leftover grain in empty cornfields, then continue on their migration north to their subarctic nesting grounds.

KING RAIL
Rallus elegans

SIZE: 1–1.5 feet long (0.3–0.5 m)
HABITAT: Rice field, marsh; midwestern and eastern United States
FOOD: Crustaceans, fish, insects, plants, seeds

The saying "thin as a rail" originated with this bird, whose narrow body allows it to slip through reeds and cattails. Well-camouflaged, they use distinctive calls to find each other.

THESE WADING BIRDS usually have long necks, legs, and bills, and short, rounded tails. Some, like the bitterns, are secretive and stealthy, while others, like the snowy egret, stand out.

Most of these birds eat only live prey. The bills of herons, egrets, and bitterns are designed to spear or grasp prey; ibises use curved bills to dig through mud. Most storks feed mainly on fish, but pretty much any small animal is on the menu. Storks' bills are very sensitive, allowing them to feel for prey in the water.

Most species live in coastal and inland wetlands. They build nests in reed beds and high up in trees, where they lay small clutches of two to seven eggs. Males often put on courtship displays that include stretching its neck to show off plumage. They also circle and chase potential mates.

MARABOU STORK
Leptoptilos crumeniferus

SIZE: 3.5–5 feet long (1.1–1.5 m)
HABITAT: Open savanna, swamp, river margin, lake shore; sub-Saharan Africa
FOOD: Carrion; live prey including reptiles, amphibians, insects, small mammals and birds

The marabou stork features a nearly featherless head, perfect for feeding on carrion or foraging in muddy waters. It has adapted well to human encroachment, scavenging around dumps, slaughterhouses, and fishing villages for scraps; waiting on the outskirts of urban areas in hopes of being offered food, it will get testy if refused. It walks awkwardly on land, but soars elegantly through the air.

AFRICAN SPOONBILL
Platalea alba

SIZE: 2.5–3 feet long (0.8–0.9 m)
HABITAT: Shallow inland water; central and southern Africa
FOOD: Small fish, aquatic invertebrates

Spoonbills feed by walking and swinging their bills through the water from side to side. They feed in groups and nest in colonies with other species, usually in groups of up to 20 pairs, and sometimes as many as 250 pairs. They roost in trees or reeds along shallow bodies of water.

SHOEBILL STORK
Balaeniceps rex

SIZE: 3.5–4.5 feet long (1.1–1.4 m)
HABITAT: Swamp, flooded marsh; central tropical and eastern Africa
FOOD: Fish (especially African lungfish), amphibians, rats, young waterfowl, young crocodiles

This prehistoric-looking bird lives a solitary life in remote marshlands. It feeds at night and will ambush its prey, crushing it and piercing it instantly with its hooked bill. Young stand after two and a half months and hunt after three and a half.

YELLOW BITTERN
Ixobrychus sinensis

SIZE: 1–1.5 feet long (0.3–0.5 m)
HABITAT: Freshwater wetland; eastern and southern Asia
FOOD: Small fish, frogs, invertebrates

This well-camouflaged bird hunts from vegetated cover, killing its prey by striking and shaking it. When breeding, males hunch and puff their throats. Both parents protect nests in reed beds.

Animal Antics
Bitterns will stand completely still and stick their bills straight up in the air. With their cryptic coloring and thin sharp beak, they blend in with the grasses and reeds.

YELLOW-CROWNED NIGHT HERON
Nycticorax violaceus

SIZE: 2–2.5 feet long (0.6–0.8 m)

HABITAT: Wetland, coastal water, swamp; eastern United States, Central America, northern South America, Caribbean

FOOD: Crustaceans, fish, terrestrial arthropods, lizards, small snakes, small mammals

True to its name, this heron is nocturnal. It stalks its prey alone, along shorelines. It strikes and seizes prey with its bill. It swallows its small catches whole and bashes, spears, or shakes larger prey into pieces. Pairs will bond as they build shallow stick nests up to four feet wide in trees up to 60 feet high.

SACRED IBIS
Threskiornis aethiopicus

SIZE: 2–2.5 feet long (0.6–0.8 m)

HABITAT: Tropical and temperate river, stream, coastline; sub-Saharan Africa, southeast Iraq

FOOD: Insects, worms, bird and reptile eggs, crustaceans, frogs, lizards, small mammals, carrion

The sacred ibis can live for more than 20 years. It forages in groups of up to 20, probing the mud with its long bill to capture prey. It also chases moving prey by running with its wings half open. Certain populations will migrate to breeding grounds, flying in a V formation.

SNOWY EGRET
Egretta thula

SIZE: 1.5–2 feet long (0.5–0.6 m)

HABITAT: Salt-marsh pool, tidal channel, shallow bay; North, Central, and South America

FOOD: Fish, crustaceans, insects, small amphibians, reptiles, mammals

Snowy egrets are known for their frantic feeding behaviors. They prefer shallow waters, where they can be seen flying low and stabbing their head down to grab fish. They also flick their wings or shuffle their feet to startle and flush out prey. During breeding season, they develop wispy plumes on their head, neck, back, and breast. Various types of herons nest together in dense colonies.

GREAT BLUE HERON

The great blue heron is a majestic sight. It glides above the water with slow, deep wingbeats, its necked tucked in an S shape and its legs trailing behind it. It stands like a statue in the shallows, scanning for prey, then strikes like lightning to snatch a fish or a frog or even a gopher. It impales larger fish with its daggerlike bill, sometimes shaking them apart before gulping them down. Look for great blue herons in saltwater and freshwater habitats, sometimes poised atop floating kelp. At breeding colonies, they perform nest relief ceremonies in which the birds erect their plumes and clapper their bill tips before trading places on the nests.

ABOUT ME!

I'm a great blue heron. Standing around in fishy waters takes a toll on my gorgeous feathers. My middle toe has a fringed claw that I use to comb my chest. As I do, pieces of my fine feathers crumble into a powder, which I use to wash away fish slime. When I'm done preening, I look—and smell—much better.

8 FACTS ABOUT THE GREAT BLUE HERON

- ▸ Breeding colony is called heronry
- ▸ Heronries may have several hundred pairs
- ▸ Builds stick nests in trees, on bushes, or on ground
- ▸ Forages alone
- ▸ Aggressively defends territory
- ▸ Approaches intruders—animal or human—with bill straight up and wings out
- ▸ Has specially shaped neck vertebrae that allow it to tuck head or strike at prey
- ▸ Has eyes specialized for night vision

ONLY FIVE SPECIES OF LOONS exist worldwide, and they occur only in the Northern Hemisphere. They are almost all aquatic birds. Their bones are very dense, which helps them dive after prey. They are strong swimmers, but they can only push themselves along on their bellies while on land.

Grebes share many of the same traits as loons, but they are actually unrelated. Their bodies are good for swimming. Like loons, their legs are at the tail of their bodies. However, grebes' toes are lobed rather than webbed. Their legs trail behind them as they fly, acting like rudders.

Surprisingly Human

Loons and grebe parents have to teach their hatchlings how to swim. Hatchlings ride on their parents' backs. The adults dive and leave their young bobbing. Then they resurface a few feet away, forcing the young chicks to swim to them, much like many human parents do with their kids.

GREAT CRESTED GREBE
Podiceps cristatus

SIZE: 1.5–2 feet long (0.5–0.6 m)
HABITAT: Fresh and brackish water; Europe, central Asia, Africa, Australia, New Zealand
FOOD: Fish, insects, invertebrate larvae

Great crested grebes put on elaborate courtship displays. Pairs raise the feathers on their heads and swim to each other holding weeds in their bills. They rise up in the water, breast to breast, and turn their heads side to side. They build hidden nests out of reeds. Usually mothers lay four eggs, and young become independent by 79 days old.

BLACK-THROATED LOON
Gavia arctica

SIZE: 2–2.5 feet long (0.6–0.8 m)
HABITAT: Tundra lake, open ocean; northern Canada, Alaska, Pacific coast of United States and Asia
FOOD: Small fish, other aquatic insects and animals

The black-throated loon, like other loons and grebes, cannot take off from land and needs an open stretch of 100 to 150 feet of water to get airborne. It has well-developed air sacs that allow it to pursue prey underwater for a whole minute or more.

RED-THROATED LOON
Gavia stellata

SIZE: 1–2.5 feet long (0.3–0.8 m)
HABITAT: Lake, pond, river, coast; worldwide throughout Northern Hemisphere
FOOD: Fish, aquatic insects, mollusks, crustaceans

The red-throated loon migrates in flocks. An expert swimmer, it dives for prey with wings tucked, pumping its webbed feet to reach depths of 200 feet. Loons call to each other with a gurgling yodel. Its feathers are mostly gray during winter, but it gets beautiful striped plumage during breeding season. Males and females dip their bills, splash, and dive into the water during courtship. Males battle violently for territory. Couples tend their nests together.

SNACK ATTACK

Fish bones can be dangerous, even for birds that feed on fish! Grebes swallow feathers to trap bones and protect their stomachs. Then they regurgitate the feathers to dislodge the bones. Their digestive systems aren't strong enough to crush the bones in the fish they eat.

RATITES

THE RATITE FAMILY INCLUDES OSTRICHES, rheas, kiwi, emus, tinamous, and cassowaries. While kiwis are about the size of a chicken, ostriches can stand more than 8 feet tall. Most ratites have three toes, but ostriches have only two. These birds have underdeveloped wings. Their sternums lack a keel, where flight muscles would be connected. Their feathers don't have vanes, giving them silky bustles rather than stiff feathers. Their legs are very strong. All of these features render them flightless. Most ratites have communal nests, and members of a flock share incubation duties.

GREAT SPOTTED KIWI
Apteryx haastii

SIZE: **1–1.5 feet tall (0.3–0.5 m)**
HABITAT: **Grassland, forest, scrub-covered coastal pasture; South Island of New Zealand**
FOOD: **Insects, snails, spiders, earthworms, crayfish, fallen fruits, berries**

The great spotted kiwi is the national symbol of New Zealand. External nostrils on the tip of its beak, unique only to kiwi birds, give it a highly developed sense of smell. They live in dens that are close to 10 feet long. Their large feet have fleshy footpads, allowing them to walk silently.

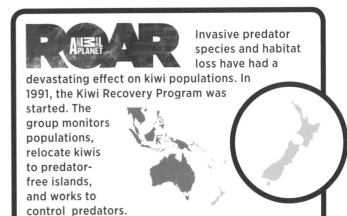

ROAR Invasive predator species and habitat loss have had a devastating effect on kiwi populations. In 1991, the Kiwi Recovery Program was started. The group monitors populations, relocate kiwis to predator-free islands, and works to control predators.

SOUTHERN CASSOWARY
Casuarius casuarius

SIZE: **3.5–6 feet long (1.1–1.8 m)**
HABITAT: **Rain forest, savanna, forested swamp; Australia, New Guinea**
FOOD: **Fruit**

The southern cassowary uses its helmet of tough skin to push through thick vegetation in the rain forest. While not as tall as an emu, it weighs more. It has razor sharp talons and a bad reputation for reacting violently when startled.

EMU
Dromaius novaehollandiae

SIZE: **5–6 feet tall (1.5–1.8 m)**
HABITAT: Grassland, wooded savanna, dry forest, semi-desert; Australia
FOOD: Fruits, shoots, seeds, insects, small animals, droppings

Emus are the second tallest bird in the world. The male incubates the female's eggs alone, and goes without food for two months until they hatch. Chicks can find food after a few days, but adults guard them until they're five months. They can travel hundreds of miles when food is scarce.

OSTRICH
Struthio camelus

SIZE: **5.5–8 feet tall (1.7–2.5 m)**
HABITAT: **Semi-arid plain, open woodland, savanna; Africa, southern Australia**
FOOD: **Roots, seeds, leaves; sometimes insects, small animals**

Ostriches are the tallest, fastest-running, and heaviest birds, weighing up to 325 pounds. They have the biggest eyes of any land animal. During courtship, the male drops to the ground, spreads his wings, and sways from side to side. He scratches a nest in the ground, and one or several females—or "hens"—will lay her eggs in it. They fight ferociously to protect their brood. One good kick from their powerful legs can kill a lion.

FUN FACT Contrary to popular belief, ostriches do not bury their heads in the sand. But when scared, they lie low and press their whole bodies to the ground. The head and neck plumage blends with sandy soil, making their heads appear buried.

PARROTS

DEFT CLIMBERS, SOCIAL, NON-MIGRATORY

PARROTS HAVE A LARGE HEAD, short neck, and short legs. Most have green plumage that acts as camouflage. Their zygodactyl feet, with the first and fourth toe pointed backwards, allow them to nimbly handle food and climb with great agility. They have sharp, curved beaks and strong jaw muscles.

Parrots flock in large numbers. Most species mate for life. Couples build nests together, often in tree cavities. Few species migrate, but flocks fly daily between foraging and roosting sites. Larger species lay one to three eggs, while smaller species lay up to 11.

This family contains 360 species and dates back 40 million years. Little is known about life spans in the wild, but smaller parrots live 20 to 30 years in captivity, and larger ones can live to 100.

HYACINTH MACAW
Anodorhynchus hyacinthinus

SIZE: **3–3.5 feet long (0.9–1.1 m)**
HABITAT: **Savanna, grassland, palm stand; Central and South America**
FOOD: **Nuts from native palms, such as acuri and bocaiuva palms**

The hyacinth macaw can reach more than three feet in length, making it the longest parrot in the world. It uses its massive beak to crack palm nuts. Sometimes, it feeds on palm nuts that have passed through the digestive tracts of cows. Highly social, these macaws are most often found in pairs. Unfortunately, their gentle personalities have made them a target for the pet industry. In the 1980s, more than 10,000 of them were captured.

SENEGAL PARROT
Poicephalus senegalus

SIZE: **8–10 inches long (20.3–25.4 cm)**
HABITAT: **Savanna, woodland; western Africa**
FOOD: **Fruit, seeds, grain, locust beans, young tree buds**

This small, quiet bird bonds well with humans, making it a popular pet. In the wild, the female incubates its two to four eggs while the male delivers food and guards the nest. Despite the capture and export of more than 400,000 Senegal parrots from 1993 to 2004, populations in Africa remain healthy.

Surprisingly Human

Some species of parrots are capable of mimicking and even understanding human speech. The African grey parrot is considered the best talker and the most intelligent of all. Its reasoning ability surpasses that of three-year-old humans.

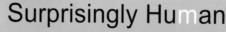

SUN CONURE
Aratinga solstitialis

SIZE: 11–12 inches long (28–30.5 cm)
HABITAT: Semi-deciduous forest, wooded savanna, scrubland; northern South America
FOOD: Ripe fruits, buds, and flowers

Trapping of this stunning bird has made it one of the rarest parrots in South America. They flock in groups of 30 or more, in areas where food is abundant. They use their hooked beak to climb trees with great agility, display a natural curiosity about their surroundings, and are particularly loud given their size.

SALMON-CRESTED COCKATOO
Cacatua moluccensis

SIZE: 1.5–2 feet long (0.5 – 0.6 m)
HABITAT: Lowland rain forest; southern Moluccan Islands of Indonesia
FOOD: Seeds, nuts, fruits, berries, insects, larvae

This cockatoo's beauty could cost the whole species its existence, as it is a very popular pet. They feast on coconuts, chewing through the husk to get to the milk and pulp inside, much to farmers' dismay.

KEA
Nestor notabilis

SIZE: 1–1.5 feet long (0.3–0.5 m)
HABITAT: High-altitude forest, wooded valley, alpine basin; South Island of New Zealand
FOOD: Seeds, flowers, insects, mountain flax, young birds, carrion

Keas get their name from their loud shrill of keee-aa. Playful and curious, they have been known to investigate and destroy human equipment. When food is scarce, they will steal chicks from other bird species' nests, feed on carrion, and even attack live sheep!

RED-AND-GREEN MACAW
Ara chloroptera

SIZE: 3–3.5 feet long (0.9–1.1 m)
HABITAT: Forest, woodland; northern and central South America
FOOD: Fruits, seeds

These are the second longest parrots. Like other macaws in certain regions of the Amazon, they are known to feed on clay along cliffs. Scientists aren't sure why they do this, but some wonder whether it helps them neutralize the toxins present in their other foods.

RAINBOW LORIKEET
Trichoglossus haematodus

SIZE: 10–12 inches long (25.4–30.5 cm)
HABITAT: Rain forest, woodland, well-treed urban area; Australia
FOOD: Fruit, pollen, nectar

These noisy and colorful parrots will occasionally mob people, screeching and biting as they try to get food. They travel in pairs and small flocks up to about 20 birds, but they can roost in much larger flocks.

Many species of parrots are becoming increasingly endangered. The World Parrot Trust (parrots.org) offers ways to get involved and help save the wild parrots around the world.

OWLS

UNLIKE OTHER BIRDS OF PREY, owls have forward-facing eyes and an outer toe that can rotate backward. There are two families of owls: typical owls and barn owls. Barn owls have narrow skulls and lack the ear-tufts of most typical owls.

Owls are carnivorous. Most hunt at night, relying on a combination of sight and sound. Asymmetrical ear openings help them detect sounds more precisely. They also bob their heads to estimate distances.

Owls' eyes do not move in their sockets, but they can rotate their heads 270 degrees. It's a feat made possible by having more vertebrae in their neck, giving them the flexibility to turn their head almost all the way around.

Owls usually nest in cavities in trees, buildings, or cliffs. Mostly monogamous, they lay one to three eggs at a time.

BARN OWL
Tyto alba

SIZE: 1–1.5 feet long (0.3–0.5 m)
HABITAT: Grassland, desert, marsh, agricultural field; worldwide
FOOD: Small mammals

The pale, ghostly barn owl produces long, eerie screeches. Typical of owls, it has asymmetrical ears, but it also has movable earflaps, giving it the most acute hearing of any animal. Barn owls are more adaptable in nesting, but agriculture restricts roosts and perches for hunting. They mostly hunt at night, but will hunt during the day to feed a hungry brood. Modified flight feathers give them silent flight.

EURASIAN SCOPS OWL
Otus scops

SIZE: 6.5–8 inches (16–20 cm)
HABITAT: Woodland; southern Europe, Asia, sub-Saharan Africa
FOOD: Insects, earthworms, spiders, small birds, reptiles, amphibians, mammals

The common scops owl's gray, mottled plumage camouflages it almost completely when perched in a tree. During the day, it tucks its wings close, lowers down its ear-tufts, and closes its eyes. If it is approached by a predator, it will stretch and sway to look like a branch. It hunts at night, mostly for insects.

Surprisingly Human

Some male owls will entice a female by calling, offering her food, and leading her to his nest. He continues calling to her as he walks into the nesting cavity, to show her how well he can provide for their brood.

BOREAL OWL
Aegolius funereus

SIZE: 8.5–11 inches long (21.6–28 cm)
HABITAT: Boreal and subalpine forest; Alaska, Canada, northern Eurasia
FOOD: Small mammals, birds, insects

The female boreal owl is much larger than the male. Females incubate their five eggs, while males deliver food to their mates and brood. They don't defend hunting territory, but will defend the nest.

Logging has destroyed habitats for owl nest sites, but conservationists have tried to build nest boxes for them. The efforts have helped several species rebound, including the boreal owl.

ELF OWL
Micrathene whitneyi

SIZE: 5–5.5 inches long (12.7–14 cm)
HABITAT: Desert, canyon forest, evergreen woodland; southwestern United States, Mexico
FOOD: Insects, small mammals, reptiles

The smallest owl in the world, the elf owl waits for insects from a perch and strikes in a straight line. It will pluck off dangerous stingers and sometimes store prey for later.

PEL'S FISHING-OWL
Scotopelia peli

SIZE: 1.5–2 feet long (0.5–0.6 m)
HABITAT: Forest, woodland, edge of river, swamp, lake, estuary; Africa
FOOD: Fish up to 4.5 pounds, frogs, crabs, freshwater mussels, large insects, small crocodiles

Pel's fishing-owl is specially adapted to catching fish. Its legs and toes lack feathers that would otherwise get wet while hunting. Spiky scales cover its toes and help it grip slippery fish. It lacks the muffling on its flight feathers, because fish can't hear it coming anyway.

LONG-EARED OWL
Asio otus

SIZE: 1–1.5 feet long (0.3–0.5 m)
HABITAT: Dense vegetation and forest close to grassland; North America, Europe, Asia
FOOD: Small mammals (especially voles), sometimes birds

The long-eared owl is mostly solitary, but will roost in groups of up to 20. It hunts in complete darkness, zigzagging silently above a meadow and listening for the most subtle movement. It swoops down and kills with one bite to the back of the skull, and then swallows its victim whole.

BURROWING OWL
Athene cunicularia

SIZE: 8.5–11 inches long (21.6–28 cm)
HABITAT: Grassland, treeless plain, savanna, desert; North and South America
FOOD: Beetles, moths, caterpillars, spiders, small birds, rats, mice

The burrowing owl is the only owl to nest underground. It moves into holes made by other animals or digs its own with its beak. It piles dung around the entrance to bait dung beetles, which it eats. It will chase prey on foot or dive down from a perch.

SPOTTED OWL
Strix occidentalis

SIZE: 1–1.5 feet long (0.3–0.5 m)
HABITAT: Rocky canyon, old-growth forest, lowland forest; western North America
FOOD: Small mammals, birds

One of the largest owls in North America, the spotted owl prefers old-growth forests. It hunts at night and only in its own territory. When prey population is abundant, owls nest closer together. When it's scarce, they need more space for hunting and nest further apart. They are considered an "indicator species" because their presence indicates that the forest population is healthy. Spotted owls are heavily affected by the clear-cutting of forests.

SNACK

Owls have an amazing digestive system. They swallow prey whole. Then their digestive system crushes the fur, feathers, and bones into a pellet, which the owl regurgitates eight hours later. You can buy owl pellets from biological supply stores and see what owls had for dinner.

ATTACK

HAWKS, EAGLES, AND FALCONS are diurnal, meaning they hunt during the day. Their eyesight is up to eight times better than humans. They have strong legs and sharp talons for capturing and killing their prey and hooked beaks for tearing flesh. Wingspans measure from two feet to more than six feet.

Some species don't migrate, but other species journey in groups and always by day. This may explain why most other bird species migrate by night.

Females are generally larger than males. Both sexes of eagles and hawks build stick nests lined with vegetation. Falcons do not build nests, but simply lay eggs on perches.

Raptors usually lay two to five eggs. During the 1940s and '50s, heavy use of the pesticide DDT killed many birds. It thinned eggshells and concentrated in prey, which poisoned many raptors. After DDT was banned, populations rebounded.

ROAR
ANIMAL PLANET

The Morley Nelson Snake River Birds of Prey National Conservation Area in Idaho was established to provide a protected habitat for eagles, falcons, hawks, and owls.

Surprisingly Human

When golden eagle chicks have to poop, they face the center of the nest and back up to poop off the side—but often don't quite make it. So parents line the nest with vegetation that they can easily clean up.

EGYPTIAN VULTURE
Neophron percnopterus

SIZE: 2–2.5 feet long (0.6–0.8 m)
HABITAT: Steppe, desert, pasture, cereal field; southern Europe, central Asia, Africa
FOOD: Carrion, rotting fruits and vegetables, excrement

The Egyptian vulture will eat anything dead, injured, or dying. It also eats eggs. In a rare example of tool use among birds, it will throw rocks to crack the shell. They soar better than they flap and do best when launched from a high perch in an updraft. Pairs perform talon grappling during courtship. Both parents incubate the eggs, defend the nest, and bring food to nestlings.

GOLDEN EAGLE
Aquila chrysaetos

SIZE: 2–3.5 feet long (0.6–1.1 m)
HABITAT: Mountainous area, pine-oak forest; worldwide throughout Northern Hemisphere
FOOD: Small mammals, including hares, rabbits, young foxes, rodents; gamebirds, carrion

The largest predatory bird in North America, the golden eagle's wingspan stretches more than six feet. Pairs perform plunging and looping acrobatics during courtship, and mate for life. Their nests can weigh hundreds of pounds. They lay two eggs. In lean years, the younger, weaker chick may die and then be eaten by the older sibling. They hunt while soaring, but sometimes fly low and ambush prey. They can live up to 32 years.

PEREGRINE FALCON
Falco peregrinus

SIZE: 1–2 feet long (0.3–0.6 m)
HABITAT: Tundra, desert, wetland, grassland, forest; worldwide except Antarctica
FOOD: Birds, small mammals, insects, reptiles, fish

The fastest animal in the world, the peregrine can reach speeds of 200 miles per hour in a dive. In a maneuver called a "stoop," it tucks its wings and plummets in an aerodynamic teardrop, swinging its talons out for a devastating strike. Only 20 percent of attacks end in a kill, and pigeons can outrun a peregrine.

FUN FACT

Humans have been using falcons to hunt since 2200 BC. Falconers care for the birds and train them to hunt prey, deliver their catch, and return to captivity!

SAKER FALCON
Falco cherrug

SIZE: 1–2 feet long (0.3–0.6 m)
HABITAT: Forest steppe, desert steppe, arid montane area; eastern Europe, Asia
FOOD: Small mammals, birds

The saker falcon is extremely agile and fast when it hunts close to the ground. It can dive at speeds of 200 miles per hour and engage in surprise attacks. Males put on spectacular aerial displays to attract a mate. They will perform "bowing" gestures to communicate with one another.

CRESTED CARACARA
Caracara cheriway

SIZE: 1.5–2 feet long (0.5–0.6 m)
HABITAT: Pastureland, semi-desert; Central and South America, Texas, Arizona, Florida
FOOD: Insects; small and occasionally large vertebrates, including fish, reptiles, amphibians, birds, mammals; eggs; carrion

The crested caracara has long legs especially adapted to walking. It scavenges at dawn, tearing off bits of meat and placing them in a pile to carry back to its nest. It also forages for small animals from the ground, making it less visible than other raptors.

SECRETARY BIRD
Sagittarius serpentarius

SIZE: 55 inches (138 cm)
HABITAT: Savanna, grassland, semi-desert, lightly wooded area; sub-Saharan Africa
FOOD: arthropods, small mammals, young birds, eggs, amphibians, reptiles

Known as "Africa's marching eagle," the secretary bird can cover 18 miles on foot in a day. It stamps on its prey, which sometimes includes highly venomous snakes, and swallows it whole.

OSPREY
Pandion haliaetus

SIZE: 1.5–2 feet long (0.5–0.6 m)
HABITAT: Marsh, lake, river, swamp bog; worldwide except Antarctica
FOOD: Fish, small mammals, injured birds, reptiles, amphibians, crustaceans

Also called the "fish hawk," the osprey has a reversible outer toe and barbed pads on its feet to help it catch fish while in flight. It plunges head and feet first as it strikes, sometimes becoming completely submerged. Ospreys use a variety of tall structures for nesting, including cacti, rock towers, and manmade platforms.

AFRICAN FISH EAGLE

The African fish eagle perches majestically on a high branch. Its evocative, ringing cry, weeah kyoh koh koh, is a familiar sound at watersides throughout sub-Saharan Africa. It watches the water from on high and swoops down once prey is spotted. Gliding low over the water, it swings its feet down at the last moment to snatch a fish at the surface. Like the osprey, the African fish eagle has barbs on its talons for grasping a slippery catch. Unlike the osprey, it does not enter the water as it strikes. It occasionally eats small mammals or young waterbirds, and, though rarely, will feed on carrion when food is scarce.

7 FACTS ABOUT THE AFRICAN FISH EAGLE

▸ Catches fish in only one out of eight attempts
▸ Spends less than ten minutes hunting each day
▸ Carries fish away from body to protect eyes
▸ Pairs interlock talons in midair and perform whirling falls
▸ Uses same nest year after year
▸ Nests can measure 6 feet (1.8 m) across and 4 feet (1.2 m) deep
▸ Can live 12 to 24 years in the wild

ABOUT ME!

I'm an African fish eagle, and I love performing duets with my mate. She and I throw our heads back and let our voices ring out. My voice is mellower but higher pitched than hers. Sometimes we fly together, climbing higher and higher. We fly around in tight circles, calling to each other the whole time.

THE SMALLEST OF ALL BIRDS, hummingbirds have tiny bodies and long, slim bills. Their tongues stretch beyond the tips of their bills. Hummingbirds are such great pollinators that certain plants have developed adaptations that discourage other insects and benefit hummingbirds.

Their wings produce a hum as they beat 40 to 80 times per second. They fly at speeds of up to 60 miles per hour. Hummingbirds need more oxygen than any living animal.

Their lungs are specially adapted to allow 500 breaths per second. While flying, their heart beats 1,250 times per minute.

Swifts are closely related to hummingbirds because their feet are very weak and they share similar wing structures. They have long distal bones to make fast wing movements. The most aerial of all birds, swifts can capture food, bathe, and even spend the night in the air while migrating.

CHIMNEY SWIFT
Chaetura pelagica

SIZE: 4.5–6 inches long (1.4–15.2 cm)
HABITAT: Lowland evergreen forest, humid forest, savanna; North and South America
FOOD: Flying insects

Chimney swifts fly almost constantly, stopping only to roost in groups at night or to nest. They bathe by slapping the surface of water, then shaking off as they fly away. These birds cannot perch. Their long claws only allow them to cling to vertical surfaces. Before Europeans settled North America and brought chimneys, these swifts nested in caves and cliff faces and hollow trees.

As chimneys fall into disuse across North America, chimney swift populations have declined by 50 percent over the past 40 years. Boy Scout troops have helped by building artificial towers that have become homes for dozens of swifts.

Surprisingly Human

Sometimes an unmated swift will help a pair care for its young. It takes a village to raise a child, even for swifts!

BLUE-THROATED HUMMINGBIRD
Lampornis clemenciae

SIZE: 4.5–5.5 inches long (11.4–14 cm)
HABITAT: Pine-oak forest, stream, mountain canyon; Central America, southwestern United States
FOOD: Nectar, small arthropods

The blue-throated hummingbird is three times heavier than the ruby-throated. It beats its wings much more slowly, but still manages 23 beats per second. The male does not perform aerial displays. Instead, it uses several calls to defend its territory and attract mates. The female makes a series of short flights during courtship.

RUFOUS HUMMINGBIRD
Selasphorus rufus

SIZE: 3–3.5 inches long (7.6–8.9 cm)
HABITAT: Spruce-fir and pine-oak forest, riverside shrub, mountain meadow; western North America
FOOD: Insects, nectar

The rufous hummingbird is well known for defending flowers and feeders, going after hummingbirds three times its size. It will also lap up sap from tree holes dug by woodpeckers, known as "sapsucker wells." Courting males sometimes perform a series of figure eights for a female.

RUFOUS-TAILED HUMMINGBIRD
Amazilia tzacatl

SIZE: 3–4.5 inches long (7.6–11.4 cm)
HABITAT: Second-growth forest, coffee plantation; Central America, northern South America
FOOD: Nectar, small insects

This hummingbird is extremely territorial and will dive at other hummingbirds that trespass on its foraging area. Like most hummingbird species, it lowers its heartbeat dramatically at night and on cold days to conserve energy. This is called a torpor state. The pattern of the male's song is intentionally rhythmic.

BEE HUMMINGBIRD
Mellisuga helenae

SIZE: 2–2.5 inches long (5.1–6.4 cm)
HABITAT: Woodland, swampland, forest edge; Cuba, Isla de la Juventud
FOOD: Nectar, tiny insects

The bee hummingbird is the smallest living bird in the world. During elaborate courtship displays, its wing beats can increase to 200 beats per second. They often adorn their nest with lichen.

WHITE-THROATED SWIFT
Aeronautes saxatalis

SIZE: 6–6.5 inches long (15.2–16.5 cm)
HABITAT: Canyon, cliff, forest; western United States, southwestern Canada
FOOD: Flying insects

This highly social bird can be seen rushing into a communal roost at dusk, charging at a slender crevice. When courting, a male and female will grasp each other in the air and free fall for over 500 feet, separating just above the ground to fly back up to the canyon wall.

RUBY-THROATED HUMMINGBIRD
Archilochus colubris

SIZE: 3–3.5 inches long (7.6–8.9 cm)
HABITAT: Deciduous and pine forest, garden, orchard; North and Central America
FOOD: Nectar, insects

The ruby-throated hummingbird feeds on the nectar of orange and red flowers, visiting up to 2,000 flowers each day. They also catch flying insects or pluck them off spider webs.

During courtship, males show off by flying 50 feet up, then diving at top speed and pulling up at the last second. Females make nests out of spider silk, lichen, and vegetation. During migration, they fly 500 miles nonstop over the Gulf of Mexico.

RELATIVES OF THIS GROUP include jacamars, puffbirds, barbets, honeyguides, toucans, and woodpeckers. These birds are all tree dwellers. Most have two toes pointing forward and two behind. They also share similarities in the structure of breastbone and palate.

Woodpeckers creep up tree trunks and drill into wood to find food and excavate nest holes. They have a vertical posture, rounded wings, a chisel-shaped bill, and an undulating flight pattern. They have very thick skulls, adapted to withstand the shock of continual pecking.

Although toucan bills look heavy, they are actually lightweight. The inside is reinforced with lightweight networks made of bone. Toothlike edges help them catch and grasp food. Toucans are born blind and with very short beaks. On their heels, they have special pads that protect them from the bottoms of their nests.

COLLARED ARACARI
Pteroglossus torquatus

SIZE: 1–1.5 feet long (0.3–0.5 m)
HABITAT: Woody lowland forest, humid rain forest; Mexico, northern South America
FOOD: Fledgling birds, insects, eggs, dry fruit

Collared aracaris fly using rapid beats of their wings and make springy jumps to move along a branch. They are monogamous and cooperative breeders. Five to six adults care for nestlings together, bringing food and guarding them. Offspring from previous clutches will help parents take care of siblings. Up to six adults and fledglings will roost in a woodpecker hole, sleeping with their tails folded over their backs.

Surprisingly Human

Acorn woodpeckers keep a close watch over their stores. One group member protects the supply from thieves, frequently making screechy waka-waka calls. As acorns dry out, group members move the shrunken nuts to smaller holes.

ACORN WOODPECKER
Melanerpes formicivorus

SIZE: 7.5–9 inches long (19.1–22.9 cm)
HABITAT: Pine-oak woodland; western United States, Central and South America
FOOD: Acorns, sap, fruit, nectar, seeds, insects (especially flying ants)

These unusual woodpeckers live in groups of a dozen or more. They work together to store thousands of acorns each year by jamming them into holes dug out of trees or wooden structures. One tree can have 50,000 holes, each of which is filled every autumn. Males and females raise young in a single nest. Offspring stay with parents for several years and help raise more young.

RUFOUS-TAILED JACAMAR
Galbula ruficauda

SIZE: 7.5–10 inches (19.1–25.4 cm)
HABITAT: Tropical lowland evergreen forest edge; Central and South America
FOOD: Flying insects

Rufous-tailed jacamars hunt flying insects such as butterflies, dragonflies, and wasps. They sally out to catch prey, and then beat large catches against a perch and remove wings before eating.

CHANNEL-BILLED TOUCAN
Ramphastos vitellinus

SIZE: 1.5–2 feet long (0.5–0.6 m)
HABITAT: Lowland forest, swamp forest; northern and central South America, Amazonian Brazil
FOOD: Fruit, insects, eggs, small reptiles, frogs

Large toucans are either "croakers" or "yelpers." The channel-billed toucan is the most widespread croaker. It forages in the treetops in humid forest, dining on fruit, and also nestlings and eggs of smaller birds, frogs, and roosting bats. It faces threats from deforestation for cattle farming and soy production.

GREATER HONEYGUIDE
Indicator indicator

SIZE: 8–8.5 inches long (20.3–21.6 cm)
HABITAT: Savanna, shrubland, forest edge, riverside, orchard; sub-Saharan Africa
FOOD: Wax, waxworms, insects, spiders, fruits

Greater honeyguides call and flare their tail feathers to attract the attention of humans, honey badgers, or baboons, in order to get help. They lead the stronger species to hidden beehives in the hope that they will crack open the hive and expose wax stores and larvae for an easy feast.

SAFFRON TOUCANET
Pteroglossus bailloni

SIZE: 1–1.5 feet long (0.3–0.5 m)
HABITAT: Subtropical forest; southeast Brazil, eastern and central Paraguay, northeast Argentina
FOOD: Figs, palm fruits

Saffron toucanets creep around treetops in pairs or small groups searching for fruits such as figs and palm fruits. During courtship, the male sings to and feeds the female. Breeding pairs build nests in old woodpecker holes. They face threats from the illegal cage-bird trade, hunting, and habitat loss.

YELLOW-BELLIED SAPSUCKER
Sphyrapicus varius

SIZE: 8–9 inches (20.3–22.9 cm)
HABITAT: Evergreen-deciduous forest, tropical woodland; North and Central America
FOOD: Beetles, ants, moths, dragonflies, fruits, berries, sap

Yellow-bellied sapsuckers drill tidy rows of holes from which they lap up leaking sap and eat any trapped insects with a specialized, brush-tipped tongue. They feed mostly during the day.

Animal Antics
Yellow-bellied sapsuckers—and other woodpeckers—will hammer on metal gutters and signs to signal their territory to other birds. The birds apparently suffer no harmful effects from whacking their heads against the metal.

121

KEEL-BILLED TOUCAN

This social bird is best known for its oversize bill, which can grow to one-third the size of its 20-inch (50.8 cm) body. Yet the bill is quite light because it is made of protein and supported by hollow bones. The keel-billed toucan travels around treetops in flocks of 6 to 12 birds, searching for fruit. Its short broad wings make distance flying difficult, so while searching for food it prefers to hop from limb to limb on its zygodactyl feet (two toes facing forward and two facing back). It plucks fruit from trees, flips it into the air, crushes it and swallows it whole. Sometimes it tosses fruit to its buddies. It regurgitates larger seeds and passes smaller seeds in its poop, which makes it a helpful seed disperser and gives it a symbiotic relationship with plants in its habitat.

7 FACTS ABOUT THE KEEL-BILLED TOUCAN

- ▶ Is found in tropical rain forests in Central America
- ▶ Is crepuscular (meaning most active at dawn and dusk)
- ▶ Will duel other toucans using bills
- ▶ Bony bill is covered with keratin, just like your fingernails
- ▶ Croaks sound just like a tree frog's—krrrrrk!
- ▶ Eats primarily fruit, also eggs or fledglings of other birds, insects, small lizards, and tree frogs
- ▶ Defends fruit trees with threat displays

ABOUT ME!

I'm a keel-billed toucan. At night, I sleep with my flock. A group of us packs together in one woodpecker hole to roost for the night. We fold up our tails over our backs and tuck our beaks beneath our wings to make room for one another. We are squeezed together tightly. I feel safe with my friends.

PIGEONS AND DOVES

PIGEONS ARE THE LARGER SPECIES and doves the smaller within the Columbidae family. They are plump birds with short legs, short necks, and small heads. They have short, slender bills with nostrils in a bumpy mound.

They store food in a large crop, a part of their digestive system. Their muscular gizzards grind food. Unique among birds, they can immerse their bill and suck up large amounts of water quickly. These systems allow the birds to forage or drink in areas where predators pose a risk. Strong wing muscles make them powerful and agile fliers. When alarmed, they burst into flight.

Males strut, bow, and puff their breasts to attract a mate. They lay one to two eggs, which both parents incubate in a flimsy nest. They feed hatchlings crop milk, which is secreted from the crop. Flamingos are the only other birds to produce milk like this.

INCA DOVE
Columbina inca

SIZE: 6.5–9 inches long (16.5–22.9 cm)
HABITAT: Residential area, thorn forest, savanna; southwestern United States, Mexico, Central America
FOOD: Seeds from grains, weeds, and grasses

The Inca dove spends its day sunning, roosting, and foraging on the ground. Couples preen each other. Males gather one stick at a time for the nest and deliver it by standing on the female's back. The female takes it and arranges the nest. They build their nests in high perches, safe from predators.

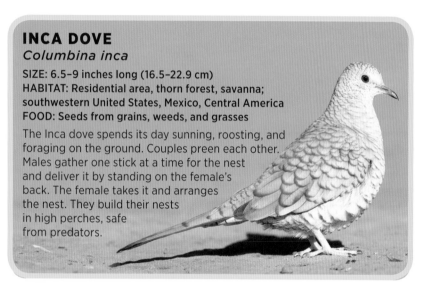

Animal Antics During cold weather, Inca doves will stand on each other's backs in a pyramid several tiers high. Every few minutes, they tumble down and rotate positions, to make sure everybody gets a chance to get warm.

SUPERB FRUIT DOVE
Ptilinopus superbus

SIZE: 8–9 inches long (20.3–22.9 cm)
HABITAT: Rain forest; New Guinea, Australia, Solomon Islands, Sulawesi of Indonesia
FOOD: Fruits, berries

This dove lives almost entirely in trees, feeding on fruit. They are one of the most important seed dispersers in Australia's forests. They build flimsy nests nearly 100 feet off the ground. The female will incubate eggs during the night, and the male during the day.

MOURNING DOVE
Zenaida macroura

SIZE: 9–13 inches long (22.9–33 cm)
HABITAT: Savanna, agricultural field, desert; North and Central America, Caribbean
FOOD: Seeds

The mourning dove was named for the soft, sad coo-oo sound that unpaired males will repeat over and over. During courtship, males fly up from a perch with noisy, clapping wing beats, and then descend in gliding circle. They feed mostly on seeds, but will occasionally feed on snails to glean calcium from its shell. Although 70 million mourning doves are shot annually, its population remains stable.

ROCK DOVE (OR COMMON PIGEON)
Columba livia

SIZE: 11.5–12.5 inches long (29.2–31.8 cm)
HABITAT: Urban area, farmland, rocky cliff; worldwide
FOOD: Seeds

Wild rock doves nest along seaside cliffs. They are well known for their ability to find their way home even after being blindfolded and released from a great distance. They orient themselves by using the position of the sun, earth's magnetic field, and possibly odors, low-frequency sounds, and polarized light. They fly as fast as 50 miles per hour and can cover 600 miles in a day.

NAMAQUA DOVE
Oena capensis

SIZE: 8–8.5 inches long (20.3–21.6 cm)
HABITAT: Savanna, grassland, agricultural land; sub-Saharan Africa, Arabian Peninsula
FOOD: Small grass seeds, invertebrates

The female namaqua lacks the bright bill and black mask of the male namaqua. They are usually seen in pairs, but several hundred will flock together at watering holes. Some populations migrate seasonally, depending on rainfall. Eggs are incubated for two weeks, and chicks fledge at 16 days old.

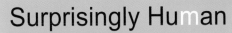

Surprisingly Human

During World War I, 100,000 homing pigeons were used to carry messages. The pigeons often flew through heavy artillery fire, sometimes sustaining serious injuries, yet they managed a 95 percent success rate for deliveries.

VICTORIA CROWNED PIGEON
Goura victoria

SIZE: 2–2.5 feet long (0.6–0.8 m)
HABITAT: Swamp, dry lowland forest; Oceania
FOOD: Fallen fruit (particularly figs), seeds, insects

The largest pigeon in the world, the Victoria crowned pigeon can be identified by its crest of lacy feathers. They forage on the forest floor in groups of two to ten and roost at night in bushes and trees. They are monogamous and generally mate for life. Unfortunately, their striking plumage and large size make them a target for hunters.

NICOBAR PIGEON
Caloenas nicobarica

SIZE: 1–1.5 feet long (0.3–0.5 m)
HABITAT: Remote inlet with forest vegetation, lowland rain forest; Oceania
FOOD: Seeds, buds, fruits, and grains

The Nicobar pigeon is the closest living relative to the dodo. It breeds in dense colonies on small, wooded islands and nearby mainland. Because it has been isolated from natural predators, it has developed bright, beautiful plumage.

KINGFISHERS ARE THICKSET BIRDS with big heads, short necks, and small, weak feet. Their outer and middle front toes are partially joined, a characteristic known as syndactyly. They have striking plumage and long, sharp bills perfect for catching prey.

While some live near water, others live far and hunt terrestrial prey. Most species live solitary lives when they're not breeding, and most are monogamous and mate for life. A courting male will chase a female through the air, and then offer her a fish.

Couples excavate nests in tree holes, termite mounds, and unlined burrows in banks of rivers. They lay two to eight eggs, one to two times per year. Both sexes incubate the eggs.

Unlike some birds, kingfishers do not clean their nests. Soon after hatching, the nest is littered with discarded food and excrement.

PIED KINGFISHER
Ceryle rudis

SIZE: 10–12 inches long (25.4–30.5 cm)
HABITAT: Stream, lake, river, estuary; sub-Saharan Africa, Middle East, southern Asia
FOOD: Fish, insects, frogs, tadpoles and mollusks

The pied kingfisher is the largest bird capable of hovering in midair. It's so good at hovering that it doesn't need woodland nearby for a perch. It is one of the most common kingfishers in the world, and in some areas it has benefited from damming and fish farming.

BELTED KINGFISHER
Megaceryle alcyon

SIZE: 11–14 inches long (28–35.6 cm)
HABITAT: Coastal and inland aquatic habitat; North and Central America, West Indies, northern South America
FOOD: Fish

Once a belted kingfisher spots its prey, it hovers briefly before diving into the water. It pinches its target in its beak, then twists its body and flies back out of the water. Back at its perch, it whacks its prey on a branch and swallows it whole. A breeding pair excavates its nest together. They will dig for up to ten days to create a tunnel 2 inches wide and 3 to 10 feet long.

INDIAN ROLLER
Coracias benghalensis

SIZE: 10–11 inches long (25.4–28 cm)
HABITAT: Open cultivated area, deciduous forest; tropical Asia, Indian subcontinent, Iraq, Saudi Arabia
FOOD: Insects (especially beetles, crickets, grasshoppers), amphibians

The Indian roller's striking deep purple wings, bright blue bottom, and blue band on the tail become visible in flight. It acquired its name from the aerial acrobatics it performs during courtship. It hunts from a perch, dropping down to snatch prey and then returning immediately. It only dives into water to bathe.

Surprisingly Human

Belted kingfishers teach their young to fish by dropping dead prey into the water for retrieval. But the fishing lessons can be dangerous; young birds sometimes drown.

ROAR

Common kingfishers are indicator species, which means they let us know about the state of our ecosystem. They are found in areas where fresh water is clean and healthy.

COMMON KINGFISHER
Alcedo atthis

SIZE: 6.5–8 inches long (26–20.3 cm)
HABITAT: Shore of lake, pond, stream, wetland; Eurasia, North Africa
FOOD: Fish, invertebrates

Although they are iconic birds in England, common kingfishers are rarely seen. Females can be distinguished from males by the red base of their bill. Populations fluctuate after severe winters, because they cannot fish when there is ice.

BLUE-WINGED KOOKABURRA
Dacelo leachii

SIZE: 1–1.5 feet long (0.3–0.5 m)
HABITAT: Savanna woodland, forest, swamp; northern Australia, southern New Guinea
FOOD: Insects, snakes, lizards, small birds, small mammals, invertebrates, frogs

The blue-winged kookaburra is a famous snake hunter with a maniacal cackle. It carefully snatches a snake behind the head and bashes it against a branch or rock to kill it. Several helper birds—often offspring from the previous breeding season—will assist a pair in caring for the young. Kookaburra chicks are aggressive for food in their first week and may kill the youngest hatchling.

GREEN WOOD HOOPOE
Phoeniculus purpureus

SIZE: 1–1.5 feet long (0.3–0.5 m)
HABITAT: Forest, woodland, suburban garden; sub-Saharan Africa
FOOD: Insects

A relative to the kingfisher, green wood hoopoes feed mostly on insects found on the ground, on termite mounds, or on tree trunks. Honeyguides often parasitize their nests, laying eggs that the wood hoopoes raise as their own.

EUROPEAN BEE-EATER
Merops apiaster

SIZE: 11–12 inches long (28–30.5 cm)
HABITAT: Forest, savanna, shrubland; southern Europe, sub-Saharan Africa, India
FOOD: Honeybees, dragonflies, other flying insects

True to its name, this bird feeds on honeybees. It sallies out from a perch to catch its prey. When it returns, it crushes the insect's head to kill it, then wipes the abdomen to shed the sting. Parents feed their young for a while, because catching flying insects is a tough skill to learn.

CUCKOOS AND TURACOS

THE CUCULIDAE FAMILY includes cuckoos, roadrunners, and anis. They are slender birds with long, curved bills and zygodactyl feet. Tails measure at least half of their full length. Turacos and birds of paradise are not closely related, but share some traits.

Certain species of cuckoos are known for laying eggs in other birds' nests. A short nestling period gives young cuckoos an advantage over their host parents' offspring.

Cuckoos are one of the few birds that eat hairy caterpillars. They'll eat as many as 100 in one sitting. The hairs form pellets in their stomachs that are later regurgitated.

These birds typically lay two to six eggs in a clutch, but parasitic species can lay more than 25 eggs per year. While some birds forage at a slow pace, roadrunners and certain cuckoos will pounce on prey with great speed.

DIDERIC CUCKOO
Chrysococcyx caprius

SIZE: 7–8 inches long (17.8–20.3 cm)
HABITAT: Forest edge, savanna, woodland, semi-arid shrubland; sub-Saharan Africa
FOOD: Invertebrates, eggs of its host

The dideric cuckoo is a brood parasite, meaning it lays its eggs in other birds' nests, who then raise the chicks as their own. When a potential host leaves the nest, it flies in and throws out any existing eggs or carries them to a nearby perch to eat them. Then it lays its egg in the nest. Although it is often chased by the host birds, it manages to lay three to five eggs a day.

SMOOTH-BILLED ANI
Crotophaga ani

SIZE: 1–1.5 feet long (0.3–0.5 m)
HABITAT: Forest clearing, plantation, garden; Florida, Caribbean, Central and South America
FOOD: Insects, other arthropods, lizards, frogs, fruit

Smooth-billed anis live in groups of up to five breeding pairs, along with juvenile offspring. They lay their eggs in a communal nest, and all the group members care for the young. Laying females bury other females' clutches with twigs and leaves, and only the top layer hatches. While a group forages, one member will sit on a high perch and watch for danger.

BLUE BIRD OF PARADISE
Paradisaea rudolphi

SIZE: 11–12 inches long (28–30.5 cm)
HABITAT: Tropical and subtropical moist forest; Papua New Guinea
FOOD: Mostly fruit

The blue bird of paradise has a lek mating system. Males compete for attention by hanging upside down from a tree and spreading their fine plumage while making almost unnatural humming calls. It faces threats from habitat loss as well as hunting for its beautiful feathers.

GUIRA CUCKOO
Guira guira

SIZE: 11–13 inches long (28–33 cm)
HABITAT: Dry mixed-scrub savanna and woodland; eastern Brazil, northern Argentina
FOOD: Frogs, eggs, large arthropods, small mammals

This highly social bird congregates in flocks of up to 20 individuals. It breeds communally, with several females laying up to 20 eggs in a single nest. However, only a quarter of the eggs survive to fledging. The remainder are destroyed or killed as hatchlings by competing adults.

LIVINGSTONE'S TURACO
Tauraco livingstonii

SIZE: 1–1.5 feet long (0.3–0.5 m)
HABITAT: Humid montane and coastal forest area; southeastern Africa
FOOD: Fruits, leaves, buds, flowers, small insects, snails, slugs

Livingstone's turaco is a member of the green turaco species. The feathers of most birds use structural coloration. However, turaco feathers have a copper-containing pigment called turacoverdin that creates the green coloration. This is one of the only truly green pigments found in birds.

Animal Antics The greater roadrunner is one of the only animals known to attack rattlesnakes, often hunting in pairs. One bird distracts the snake while the other pecks or grabs its head.

GREATER ROADRUNNER
Geococcyx californianus

SIZE: 1.5–2 feet long (0.5–0.6 m)
HABITAT: Desert, grassland, open woodland, coastal sage scrub; southwestern United States, northern Mexico
FOOD: Insects, scorpions, lizards, snakes, rodents, birds

The greater roadrunner has been clocked at 26 miles per hour, the fastest running speed for a flying bird. They use their sturdy tail for steering, braking, and balancing. Nests are made from sticks, grass, feathers, and sometimes snakeskin or cow manure. Both parents incubate the eggs and feed the chicks. Weaker or sickly chicks are sometimes eaten or fed to the older, stronger siblings.

TYRANT FLYCATCHERS

PASSERIFORMES (SONGBIRDS) is the largest order of birds. This order is broken into two groups: the suboscines and the oscines. Tyrant flycatchers are suboscines, which differ from oscines in that they do not learn their songs.

These small to medium-size perching birds have large heads, broad bills, short legs, and pointed wings. They mainly eat insects. Certain species are experts at hawking, where they fly out, catch insects, and return to a perch. Others forage near the ground.

Both sexes can be territorial, especially during breeding. Their name refers to their tyrannical attacks on intruders. Eastern kingbirds will even ride on the backs of hawks or crows, pecking them with their bills.

Females build nests with a variety of materials in the fork of a bush or tree with heavy foliage. Flycatchers live in a wide variety of habitats. North American species migrate south for winter.

GREAT KISKADEE
Pitangus sulphuratus

SIZE: 8–10 inches long (20.3–25.4 cm)
HABITAT: Second-growth woodland, savanna; southern United States, Central and South America
FOOD: Insects, small reptiles

The boisterous great kiskadees were named for their brash kis-ka-dee call. These versatile hunters will hawk for flying insects, glean insects off foliage, and even pluck small fish and tadpoles from the water. They also eat fruit and sometimes handouts from people.

Both sexes work together to build a nest, complete with a domed roof. They will bravely chase larger animals that try to eat their young, such as monkeys, raptors, and snakes.

Surprisingly Human

The great kiskadee's black mask works just like the eye-black that athletes wear under their eyes. This adaptation reduces glare and helps them hunt in bright light.

SHORT-TAILED PYGMY TYRANT
Myiornis ecaudatus

SIZE: 2–3 inches long (5.1–7.6 cm)
HABITAT: Humid forest, open woodland; northern and central South America
FOOD: Insects

The smallest passerine on earth, this bird has no tail and mechanical-looking flight. It is often mistaken for a beetle while flying. It hovers around plants and gleans insects from beneath leaves. Its call is a high-pitched squeak that sounds more like a cricket's.

ACADIAN FLYCATCHER
Empidonax virescens

SIZE: 5–6 inches long (12.7–15.2 cm)
HABITAT: Deciduous and lowland tropical forest; eastern United States, Central and South America
FOOD: Mosquitoes, flies, insect larvae, small moths, flying ants, small beetles, spiders

Acadian flycatchers are expert hawkers and gleaners who can hover and even fly backward! They build hammock- or cuplike nests in forks of trees and shrubs, often over water. Nests are woven with fine plant maters, held together with spider silk and concealed with hanging plant debris.

SCISSOR-TAILED FLYCATCHER
Tyrannus forficatus

SIZE: 11–15 inches long (28–38.1 cm)
HABITAT: Open scrubby country; central southern United States
FOOD: Insects

The long tail helps these agile fliers make sharp turns as they snatch bugs in midair. They will swallow small prey while in flight, but beat large prey against a perch before eating them. Before migration, scissor-tails gather in groups of up to 1,000. Males arrive at breeding grounds before females to establish territories. The female builds a cup nest using a wide variety of plant materials.

The scissor-tailed flycatcher builds its nests with many artificial materials, including string, cloth, paper, and carpet fuzz. One study in an urban area in Texas found that human products made up 30 percent of many nests' weight.

HAMMOND'S FLYCATCHER
Empidonax hammondii

SIZE: 4.5–5.5 inches (11.4–14 cm)
HABITAT: Mountain forest, closed canopy forest; western United States, Canada
FOOD: Ants, flying insects

The males of this species make a pip sound, while females call with peek. Their songs are made up of see-wit, bzurrp, and bzeep. Birders identify them by their song, because they live high in trees and are rarely seen. They sit and wait for prey, and attack in a flash.

YELLOW-BELLIED FLYCATCHER
Empidonax flaviventris

SIZE: 5–6 inches long (12.7–15.2 cm)
HABITAT: Evergreen and dense tropical forest; North and Central America
FOOD: Insects, fruit

Little is known about the yellow-bellied flycatcher's behavior—except that it is very secretive. It hides under shrubs on the forest floor and keeps pretty quiet, even during breeding season. They hawk from low perches. Bristles on their beaks called rictal bristles aid them in eating insects off of plants.

VERMILLION FLYCATCHER
Pyrocephalus rubinus

SIZE: 5–5.5 inches long (12.7–14 cm)
HABITAT: Woodland near river, desert scrub, savanna, agricultural land; southwestern United States, Mexico, Central and northern South America
FOOD: Flies, butterflies, moths, grasshoppers, beetles, termites, bees, spiders

Males have more bold red plumage than females. During the breeding season, the male fluffs his feathers. He flaps furiously, rising 100 feet, then drops down—all while serenading a female.

The only population of vermilion flycatchers facing decline is in the Galapagos Islands. While the islands are famous for their biodiversity, the birds are now threatened by the tourists they attract.

SONGBIRDS

MUSICAL SINGERS, EXCELLENT PERCHING GRIP

THESE SONGBIRDS—MEMBERS of the Passeriformes order, also known as perching birds—are distinct from other passerines in that they learn their songs. Their songs sound like music, as opposed to a single note repeated in a pattern. There are thousands of birds in the songbird family, more than all other bird families put together.

Most have strong feet for perching and climbing. They require a lot of high-energy food for their active lifestyle.

They keep busy all day, building nests, foraging for food, and protecting young.

Males sing more than females, to establish territories and attract a mate. They often have individual calls between pairs or with offspring. They also sound alarm calls.

They're vulnerable to many predators. While some birds live up to 15 years, most face a 50/50 chance of surviving each year. The average life span is six years.

BANANAQUIT
Coereba flaveola

SIZE: 4–5 inches long (10.2–12.7 cm)
HABITAT: Open field, garden, park; Central and South America, Caribbean, Florida
FOOD: Nectar, small insects, spiders

Bananaquits feed on flowers, which help transfer pollen to other plants. However, they also cut small slits at the base of a flower to drink its nectar, but never contact and distribute the pollen. Thus, this technique is called nectar-robbing. Their wheezy, buzzy song is a familiar sound on Caribbean islands.

AMERICAN ROBIN
Turdus migratorius

SIZE: 9–11 inches long (22.9–28 cm)
HABITAT: Town, pasture, tundra, deciduous woodland, pine forest; North America
FOOD: Earthworms, insects, berries

People celebrate the arrival of spring when an American robin visits their yard, but the birds were nearby all winter. They simply spent more time in trees and less time in the open. Robins eat earthworms in the morning and fruit later in the day. Robin roosts can contain a quarter million birds during winter. In summer, females sleep at their nests and males gather at roosts.

BLACK-AND-WHITE WARBLER
Mniotilta varia

SIZE: 4.5–5.5 inches long (11.4–14 cm)
HABITAT: Deciduous, cloud, and low evergreen forest; North, Central, and South America
FOOD: Insects

Black-and-white warblers use their extra-long hind claw and strong legs to creep around the bark of trees in search of hidden insects. Year-round, they fight with chickadees, nuthatches, and sometimes other warblers to defend their territories. They build cup-shaped nests at the bases of trees.

JAPANESE WHITE-EYE
Zosterops japonicus

SIZE: 4–4.5 inches long (10.2–11.4 cm)
HABITAT: Second-growth forest, scrub, garden; eastern and southeastern Asia, Hawaii
FOOD: Fruit, insects, nectar

These tiny birds eat massive amounts of pest insects and larvae, usually hanging in awkward positions as they forage. They were introduced to Hawaii as a form of pest control, but also brought diseases that hurt native bird species. People often keep them as pets, because they are social and easy to tame.

AMERICAN GOLDFINCH
Carduelis tristis

SIZE: 4.5–5 inches long (11.4–12.7 cm)
HABITAT: Meadow, bushy field, suburban yard, coastal area; North America
FOOD: Seeds, grains, nuts

These acrobatic little birds balance on thistles and dandelions as they pluck seeds. They bounce in flight. Pairs have matching calls, perhaps to distinguish each other in a crowd.

CACTUS WREN
Campylorhynchus brunneicapillus

SIZE: 7–9 inches long (17.8–22.9 cm)
HABITAT: Arid desert, shrubland; southwestern United States, Mexico
FOOD: Insects, seeds, fruits, small reptiles, frogs

To survive the desert heat, cactus wrens move to shady areas and decrease activity during the hottest part of the day. They keep their flight close to the ground. They nest in prickly cactuses to defend against predators. They also aggressively defend territory, sometimes destroying intruder birds' nests.

NORTHERN MOCKINGBIRD
Mimus polyglottos

SIZE: 8–10 long inches (20.3–25.4 cm)
HABITAT: Forest edge, open land at low elevation, city park, brushy desert; North America
FOOD: insects and fruits

These birds like to sing from a conspicuous perch—all day and night, especially during a full moon. Most nocturnal singers are unmated males. Mockingbirds learn new songs throughout their lives, and an adult male may know more than 200. They feed on the ground, occasionally flashing their wings to flush out insects. During courtship, the male jumps off a perch mid-song, flaps its wings, and parachutes back. Males often make several nests for females.

FUN FACT

In the 1800s, people enjoyed mockingbird songs so much that they kept them as cage birds. People captured so many birds that mockingbirds were nearly wiped out in the wild on the East Coast.

A male songbird sings to attract a mate and protect his territory. The rapid expansion of urban areas threatens songbirds in many places. Some have adapted their mating calls to the late-night hours, when cities are quieter.

BALI MYNAH

Unfortunately, this bird's beauty has also been its downfall. Historically, its range was already quite small, but once it was discovered in 1910, it became a popular pet and trade took a toll on its population. By 1990, only 15 individuals remained, and by 2001, there were 6. Organizations have worked to save the Bali mynah from extinction. But one effort to release 39 birds into the wild was thwarted when the birds were stolen. In 2004, the Friends of the National Parks Foundation transformed three islands off the coast of Bali into a bird sanctuary. Residents agreed to help protect the birds, and now the sanctuary is home to at least 100 Bali mynahs.

8 FACTS ABOUT THE BALI MYNAH

- ▶ Is national bird of Bali, province of Indonesia
- ▶ Feeds on seeds, small fruits, and insects
- ▶ Nests in abandoned woodpecker holes
- ▶ Calls creer when taking off
- ▶ Calls tschick tschick tschick as an alarm
- ▶ 1,000 individuals live in captivity
- ▶ Lays two or three pale blue eggs; usually, only one survives
- ▶ Parents feed chicks for up to seven weeks after leaving the nest

ABOUT ME!

I'm a Bali mynah. People say I'm the most beautiful bird in the world. I like to perch on the backs of cattle. The cattle don't mind, because I help them out. I forage for yummy insects to eat, and then the insects don't bite the cattle.

NIGHTHAWKS AND NIGHTJARS look similar to owls or small hawks, but differ in their horizontal stance, short legs, and weak feet. Species make their presence known by their commanding calls.

Both bird species have small bills that open wide. Nightjars have stiff rictal bristles that act as a net for catching insects while flying. Nighthawks are mostly crepuscular, meaning they are active during twilight hours. Nightjars have larger eyes to help them feed at night.

The two also differ in their hunting techniques. Nightjars perch on the ground and fly up to capture insects, while nighthawks fly over treetops, catching insects as they go.

OILBIRD
Steatornis caripensis
SIZE: 1.5–2 feet long (0.3–0.5 m)
HABITAT: Forest and woodland with caves; northern South America
FOOD: Fruits of the oil palm, tropical laurels

Oilbirds roost in caves and use echolocation to navigate in the dark. They use smell to locate food and will forage more than 70 miles away from the cave, sometimes foraging over several nights.

WHIP-POOR-WILL
Caprimulgus vociferus
SIZE: 8.5–10 inches long (21.6–25.4 cm)
HABITAT: Deciduous and tropical forest, pine-oak woodland; North and Central America
FOOD: Flying insects

This bird was named for its emphatic three-tone call that it chants through the night. Strictly nocturnal, they perch close to the ground and fly almost straight up to attack passing insects. The whip-poor-will nests with the moon's cycle. Eggs hatch about ten days before a full moon, providing plenty of light for catching food. Both males and females care for the brood.

COMMON NIGHTHAWK
Chordeiles minor
SIZE: 8.5–9.5 inches long (21.6–24.1 cm)
HABITAT: Coastal dune, savanna, sagebrush plain; North, Central, and South America
FOOD: Insects

The male common nighthawk performs dramatic display flights to impress females and ward off intruders. Just a few feet above the ground, he flexes his wings downward to peel out of his dive, which vibrates his primary feathers and creates a booming sound. Nighthawks forage at dusk and dawn, and in cloudy weather. They locate prey by sight, possibly with the help of a structure in their eyes that reflects light back to the retina.

FUN FACT Nighthawks and nightjars are commonly known as "goatsuckers." People used to believe that they would fly into barns at night and drink goats' milk.

ROAR Common nighthawks were once, well, common in New Hampshire, where they built nests on flat gravel-topped roofs. Changes in construction may have contributed to their decline in the state. Project Nighthawk is a NH Audubon initiative that places gravel "nest patches" on rooftops to attract the birds back to the area.

ANTBIRDS, ANTPITTAS, GNATEATERS, and other related species are suboscine passerines that live in the American tropics. They are small birds with rounded wings and strong legs. They have a stout bill with a hooked or notched tip. Their front toes are partly joined at the base.

Sometimes 50 species of antbirds will flock together, creating a pecking order at an insect feast. The largest, most dominant species position themselves at the center of the ant swarm, where the insects are most abundant. The smaller species forage in less-productive areas and compete with each other for the scattering prey.

CHESTNUT-CROWNED GNATEATER
Conopophaga castaneiceps

SIZE: 5–7 inches long (12.7–17.8 cm)
HABITAT: Upper tropical and lower subtropical rain forest; Colombia, Ecuador, Peru
FOOD: Arthropods

The chestnut-crowned gnateater sings only in the predawn hours and at dusk. It gleans its food from foliage. It will strike prey on the ground, but quickly returns to its perch. It spends little time on the ground, but also rarely travels more than a few feet up into the understory.

GIANT ANTPITTA
Grallaria gigantea

SIZE: 9.5–11 inches long (24.1–28 cm)
HABITAT: Humid montane forest, cloud forest, swamp; Colombia, Ecuador
FOOD: Large beetles, slugs, grubs

This secretive bird can be spotted in the rain forest pounding its beak into the soil in search of earthworms. It forages from just before dawn until just after dusk. Males and females build a cup nest with dry sticks lined with moss and dry grass. When a predator is near, it freezes and flees only if it has no other choice.

CINEREOUS ANTSHRIKE
Thamnomanes caesius

SIZE: 5.5–6 inches (12.7–15.2 cm)
HABITAT: Evergreen lowland forest, flooded forest; Amazonia, coastal Brazil
FOOD: Insects

The sharp, rattling call of the cinereous antshrike can be heard over the murmuring sounds of other species in the Amazonian understory. It perches with a vertical, upright posture. When it spots prey, it flies to catch it midair or on foliage, and then returns to its perch. It often chases insects as they are flushed from hiding spots.

SNACK ATTACK

When antbirds follow ants to an insect feast, they're not alone. Several species of butterflies trail the antbirds. Droppings are usually unpredictable sources of food, but the butterflies can easily follow the predictable path as the birds pursue their prey.

THESE MEDIUM-SIZE TO LARGE birds have strong toes and rounded wings. They have strong, slightly curved bills and dense nasal bristles. They live in most terrestrial habitats, on every continent except Antarctica.

While technically songbirds, none has a pretty song. Some live year-round in extended family groups, but all species will gather in roosts outside the breeding season. One bird stands guard in a group and sounds an alarm when it spots predators. Depending on the call, the other birds hide, fly away, or form a mob to chase away the predator with angry calls.

Jays prefer insects, nuts, and large seeds. Crows and ravens are opportunistic scavengers and frequent trash sites. All crows and jays store extra food and can remember thousands of locations.

BLACK-BILLED MAGPIE
Pica hudsonia

SIZE: **1.5–2 feet long (0.5–0.6 m)**
HABITAT: **Open wooded area and shrubland near water; western North America**
FOOD: **Insects, insect larva, eggs and hatchlings of songbirds, fruit, grain, small mammals, carrion**

Black-billed magpies walk with a swagger. They'll land on large mammals, like buffalo, and pick ticks off of them. After spreading and quivering their feathers during courtship, they form monogamous pairs. Females spend up to 40 days building bulky nests surrounded by a dome of sticks, up to 3 feet in diameter.

COMMON RAVEN
Corvus corax

SIZE: **2–2.5 feet long (0.6–0.8 cm)**
HABITAT: **Tundra, seacoast, riverbank, mountain forest, plain, desert, scrubby woodland; Northern Hemisphere**
FOOD: **Eggs and nestlings of other birds, rodents, grains, worms, insects, carrion**

These confident and curious birds strut and hop as they forage and find spots to hide food. During breeding season, they put on elaborate dances of chases, dives, and rolls. Less social than crows, they are usually seen alone or in pairs, except at food sources like landfills. Yet, teams of ravens will work together to catch prey too large for one bird. Researchers have found that common ravens are capable of using insight to solve problems.

GREEN JAY
Cyanocorax yncas

SIZE: **11–11.5 inches long (28–29.2 cm)**
HABITAT: **Open woodland, mesquite thicket; southern Texas, Central and South America**
FOOD: **Arthropods, vertebrates, seeds, fruit**

Some green jay flocks consist of a breeding pair, and the current and previous year's offspring. The one-year-olds defend the territory. Once the nestlings have fledged, the older birds are ejected.

AMERICAN CROW
Corvus brachyrhynchos

SIZE: 1.5–2 feet long (0.5–0.6 m)
HABITAT: Field, open woodland, forest, grassland; North America
FOOD: Insects, seeds, grains, nuts, eggs, small birds, small mammals, amphibians, reptiles, carrion, terrestrial arthropods, mollusks, terrestrial worms

These large black birds with their familiar caw caw have adapted extremely well to the presence of humans. They eat almost anything and are talented thieves, stealing fish from river otters and food from dog bowls. Helper birds assist a pair with raising young. They gather in massive roosts, sometimes with tens of thousands of birds.

BLUE JAY
Cyanocitta cristata

SIZE: 10–12 inches (25.4–30.5 cm)
HABITAT: Deciduous forest; southern Canada, eastern United States
FOOD: Fruits, seeds, nuts, insects, mice, frogs, eggs and nestlings of other birds

The blue jay often mimics the calls of hawks in order to scare other animals from a food source. Several days before a brood fledges, some nestlings will wander away from the nest. If someone finds an abandoned baby jay, it can be returned near the nest, and the parents will resume feeding it.

Surprisingly Human

When one magpie discovers a dead magpie, it calls loudly to attract others. Up to forty birds will gather around the body, raucously chattering. The funeral will last 10 to 15 minutes before the birds fly off silently.

COMMON GREEN MAGPIE
Cissa chinensis

SIZE: 1–1.5 feet long (0.3–0.5 m)
HABITAT: Tropical and subtropical evergreen and mixed deciduous forest; southern Asia
FOOD: Beetles, crickets, mantises, small frogs, snakes, lizards

Green magpies tend to hide under green vegetation. Their green plumage is produced by two factors: a special feather structure that reflects blue light and yellow carotenoids that come from the bird's diet. Remember, yellow and blue make green! But too much time in the sun and a lack of carotenoids will turn their feathers turquoise.

WESTERN SCRUB-JAY
Aphelocoma californica

SIZE: 11–12 inches long (28–30.5 cm)
HABITAT: Scrub, brush, chaparral, pine-oak forest; western North America
FOOD: Acorns, fruit, grains, vegetables, insects, small birds and their eggs, and small amphibians and reptiles

Western scrub-jays have developed specialized bills depending on food choice and habitat. Jays in areas with oak trees have deep, hooked bills for cracking nuts. Those near piñon pine trees have a more pointed bill to penetrate piñon cones. They store seeds in the ground for later use, hiding them under rocks or on top of telephone poles.

PENGUINS

PENGUINS ARE FLIGHTLESS BIRDS that live most of their lives in the water and raise their young on land. Their streamlined bodies are highly adapted to marine life, with wings that act as powerful flippers. Their black backs and white bellies help to camouflage them from predators.

They live almost exclusively in the southern hemisphere. Larger penguin species live in colder climates where their body mass helps them survive harsh winters. They mostly feed on krill, a shrimplike crustacean, as well as fish and squid.

Most species are highly social, feeding and nesting in groups. During the breeding season, thousands may gather in nesting grounds. They lay one to two eggs. When young penguins are old enough, they gather in groups called crèches while parents forage for food. Each penguin has a distinct call, allowing parents to find their chicks.

ROYAL PENGUIN
Eudyptes schlegeli
SIZE: 2–2.5 feet tall (0.6–0.8 m)
HABITAT: Tundra; Macquarie Island
FOOD: krill, fish, and squid

Royal penguins spend most of the year in the waters around Macquarie Island, which sits halfway between Australia and Antarctica. Males come ashore two weeks before females in order to build their nests. During courtship, males swing their heads up and down and call to the females. The female lays two eggs; only the second gets incubated as the first egg is much smaller and often pushed from the nest. They may form large colonies of up to 500,000 birds.

GENTOO PENGUIN
Pygoscelis papua
SIZE: 2–3 feet tall (0.6–0.9 m)
HABITAT: Tussock grass, gravel beach, dry moraine; Southern Hemisphere between 45 and 65 degrees south latitude
FOOD: Atlantic krill, other crustaceans, fish, cephalopods, polychaetes

With its strong flippers, the gentoo penguin is capable of diving up to 600 feet in search of prey. They have a variety of calls, including a trumpet sound they release as they throw their heads back. Pairs form loyal bonds and often return to the same nest site each year.

Animal Antics Sheep farmers love when gentoo penguins come to nest. The penguins' droppings fertilize the ground, resulting in lush grass the next year.

ROCKHOPPER PENGUIN
Eudyptes chrysocome
SIZE: 1.5–2 feet tall (0.5–0.6 m)
HABITAT: Tussock grass, rocky shoreline near freshwater; islands in the South Atlantic, Indian, and Pacific Oceans
FOOD: Krill, crustaceans, squid, octopus, fish

The rockhopper waterproofs its feathers by spreading a waxy substance secreted from above its tail. Over the past 60 years, the population has declined by 90 percent due to many factors.

R🐾AR ANIMAL PLANET

Sadly, climate change is causing a rapid reduction of Antarctic sea ice, the emperor penguin's breeding habitat. It is doubtful that the species can adapt fast enough to survive such a drastic change. Scientists predict that populations will decline 95 percent by 2100.

YELLOW-EYED PENGUIN
Megadyptes antipodes

SIZE: **1.5–2.5 feet tall (0.5–0.8 m)**
HABITAT: **Coastal scrub forest; southern New Zealand**
FOOD: **Fish, mostly species from the seafloor**

Yellow-eyed penguins are not especially sociable. They nest far from each other in the forest. Females lay two eggs, and the monogamous mates take turns feeding and protecting their young. They spend most of their time on land, entering the water only to hunt at the edge of the continental shelf.

GALAPAGOS PENGUIN
Spheniscus mendiculus

SIZE: **1.5–2 feet tall (0.5–0.6 m)**
HABITAT: **Volcanic deposit; Galapagos Islands**
FOOD: **Krill, crustaceans, squid, fish**

The Galapagos penguin stands with its flippers outstretched in order to stay cool in the warmth of its habitat. It also pants, seeks shade, and hunches to shade its feet. Pairs build lifelong bonds through mutual preening and bill tapping, and breed quickly during times of food abundance. Fewer than 2,000 individuals remain.

LITTLE PENGUIN
Eudyptula minor

SIZE: **11.5–12 inches tall (29.2–30.5 cm)**
HABITAT: **Rocky coastline, coastal savanna; New Zealand, Tasmania, southern Australia**
FOOD: **Krill, crustaceans, squid, fish**

Though they're the smallest penguin species, little penguins can be very aggressive. They stand with their flippers out, staring and braying at an intruder. If an intruder doesn't take the hint, they lunge forward to peck, bite, and slap it with its flippers until it retreats. During courtship, mates bray and march in circles together around the nest.

EMPEROR PENGUIN
Aptenodytes forsteri

SIZE: **3.5–4 feet tall (1.1–1.2 m)**
HABITAT: **Stable sea ice; Antarctica**
FOOD: **Fish, squid, krill**

After a female lays her egg on top of her feet, she immediately transfers the egg to her mate's feet and he covers it with a fold of skin to start incubation. The female leaves to feed at sea, while the male incubates the egg throughout Antarctica's harsh winter. In order to survive, 5,000 male penguins huddle in large colonies. Chicks hatch nine weeks later, as the female returns. The male then leaves to feed until the chicks are large enough and need the care of both parents.

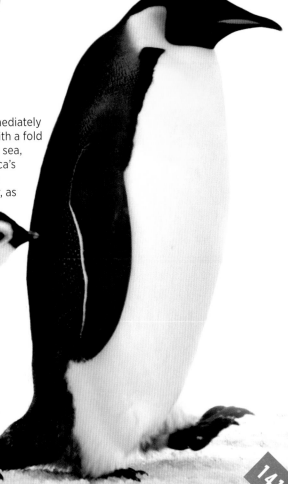

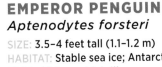

RAIN FOREST

The rain forest provides food for birds at every height—insects crawling along the floor, fruits growing in the canopy, or a clueless sloth lazing about in the trees. This lush habitat is found in Latin America, Southeast Asia, the Pacific Islands, and western Africa.

Black backed kingfisher

Violet sabrewing hummingbird

Black panther

Curl-crested aracari

Red bird of paradise

Lychee shield bug

Fine Feathers
The scale crested pygmy tyrant raises the little crown of feathers on its head to attract mates and to appear larger when threatened.

Black and yellow broadbill

Night Life
The common potoo blends in perfectly perched on a small log during the day, but at night it pops open its huge orange eyes to search for insects.

Golden beetle

Strike From Above
Harpy eagles nimbly fly through thick foliage to snatch sloths and howler monkeys right off branches. Their 4-inch-long (10.2 cm) rear talons are as large as a grizzly bear's claw.

Sloth

Fruit Looper
The great blue turaco, the biggest of the turacos, lives in the mid-canopy layer, munching on fruits, leaves, and buds.

King vulture

Panther chameleon

Macaw

Follow the Leader
The gray-winged trumpeter follows marching ants and feasts on insects flushed out by the invading army. It also enjoys fruits that have fallen to the floor.

Bright tree frog

ANIMAL PLANET L!VE

Check out the Animal Planet L!VE cam to see breathtaking birds in action by scanning this code or visiting animalplanet.timeincbooks.com/birds.

143

Birds capture our imaginations with their vivid colors, funky shapes, and awe-inspiring flight maneuvers. Check out these interesting birds.

DUCKS, SWANS, GEESE

AMERICAN BLACK DUCK
Anas rubripes

AUSTRALIAN SHELDUCK
Tadorna tadornoides

BAR-HEADED GOOSE
Anser indicus

BARNACLE GOOSE
Branta leucopsis

BLACK-NECKED SWAN
Cygnus melancoryphus

CANADA GOOSE
Branta canadensis

CANVASBACK DUCK
Aythya valisneria

CHINESE GOOSE
Anser cygnoides

COMMON MERGANSER
Mergus merganser

EGYPTIAN GOOSE
Alopochen aegyptiaca

EURASIAN WIDGEON
Anas penelope

GREYLAG GOOSE
Anser anser

HARLEQUIN DUCK
Histrionicus histrionicus

* African gray parrot

* Satyr tragopan

HOODED MERGANSER
Lophodytes cucullatus

LESSER SCAUP
Aythya affinis

MUTE SWAN
Cygnus olor

NORTHERN PINTAIL DUCK
Anas acuta

NORTHERN SCREAMER
Chauna chavaria

NORTHERN SHOVELER
Anas clypeata

RED-BREASTED GOOSE
Branta ruficollis

SMEW
Mergellus abellus

SNOW GOOSE
Anser caerulescens

SOUTHERN SCREAMER
Chauna torquata

SPECKLED TEAL
Anas flavirostris

WHITE-WINGED SCOTER
Melanitta fusca

TURKEYS, GROUSE

BEARDED WOOD PARTRIDGE
Dendrortryx barbatus

BLACK FRANCOLIN
Francolinus francolinus

BLUE-THROATED PIPING GUAN
Pipile cumanensis

CRESTED GUINEAFOWL
Guttera pucherani

DOMESTIC CHICKEN
Gallus gallus domesticus

DOUBLE-BANDED SAND GROUSE
Pterocles bicintus

GAMBEL'S QUAIL
Callipepla gambelii

LADY AMHERST'S PHEASANT
Chrysolophus amherstiae

MALEO SCRUB FOWL
Macrocephalon maleo

MALLEEFOWL
Leipoa ocellata

NORTHERN BOBWHITE QUAIL
Colinus virginianus

PLAIN CHACHALACA
Ortalis vetula

RED JUNGLEFOWL
Gallus gallus

RING-NECKED PHEASANT
Phasianus colchicus

RUFFED GROUSE
Bonasa unbellus

SPRUCE GROUSE
Falcipennis canadensis

TEMMINCK'S TRAGOPAN
Tragopan temminkii

WATTLED CURASSOW
Crax globulosa

WILD TURKEY
Meleagris gallopavo

WILLOW PTARMIGAN
Lagopus lagopus

GULLS, SANDPIPER

ANCIENT MURRELET
Synthliboramphus antiquus

ARCTIC TERN
Sterna paradisaea

AUSTRALIAN PRATINCOLE
Stiltia Isabella

BLACK GUILLEMOT
Cepphus grylle
Black oystercatcher
Haematopus bachmani

BLACK SKIMMER
Rynchops niger

* Black swan

BLACK TURNSTONE
Arenaria melanocephala

BLACK-BELLIED PLOVER
Pluvialis squatarola

BROWN SKUA
Catharacta antarctica

BURCHELL'S COURSER
Cursorius rufus

CALIFORNIA GULL
Larus calinfornicus

CASSIN'S AUKLET
Ptychoramphus aleuticus

COMMON GUILLEMOT
Uria aalge

EURASIAN STONE CURLEW
Burhinus oedicnemus

GREATER YELLOWLEGS
Tringa melanoleuca

HAWAIIAN STILT
Himantopus mexicanus knudseni

HERRING GULL
Larus argenttus

INCA TERN
Larosterna inca

KILLDEER
Charadrius vociferus

LEAST SANDSNIPE
Thinocorus rumicivorus

LONG-TAILED JAEGER
Stercorarius longicaudus

MARBLED AUK
Brachyramphus marmoratus

MASKED LAPWING
Vanellus miles

NORTHERN JACANA
Jacana spinosa

* Gouldian finch

PAINTED SNIPE
Rostratula australis

PHEASANT-TAILED JACANA
Hydrophasianus chirurgus

PIED AVOCET
Recurvirostra avosetta

PLAINS WANDERER
Pedionomus torquatus

RING-BILLED GULL
Larus delawarensis

RINGED PLOVER
Charadrius hiaticula

RUDDY TURNSTONE
Arenaria interpres

SANDERLING
Calidris alba

SEMIPALMATED SANDPIPER
Calidris pusilla

SNOWY PLOVER
Charadrius nivosus

SNOWY SHEATHBILL
Chionis albus

SOUTHERN LAPWING
Vanellus chilensis

SPOTTED SANDSNIPER
Actitis macularia

WATTLED JACANA
Jacana jacana

WESTERN GULL
Larus occidentalis

PELICANS, ALBATROSSES

ANHINGA
Anhinga anhinga

BLUE-FOOTED BOOBY
Sula nebouxii

BROWN PELICAN
Pelecanus occidentalis

BULLER'S ALBATROSS
Thalassarche bulleri

CORY'S SHEARWATER
Calonectris diomedea

GALAPAGOS CORMORANT
Phalacrocorax harrisi

HAMERKOP
Scopus umbretta

MAGELLANIC DIVING PETREL
Pelecanoides magellani

MAGNIFICENT FRIGATEBIRD
Fregata magnificens

NORTHERN FULMAR
Fulmarus glacialis

NORTHERN GANNET
Morus bassanus

ORIENTAL DARTER
Anhinga melanogaster

PELAGIC CORMORANT
Phalacrocorax pelagicus

POLYNESIAN STORM PETREL
Nesofregetta fuliginosa

RED-BILLED TROPICBIRD
Phaeton aethereus

ROYAL ALBATROSS
Diomedea epomophora

SNOW PETREL
Pagodroma nivea

WHITE AMERICAN PELICAN
Pelecanus erythrorhynchos

WHITE-BREASTED CORMORANT
Phalacrocorax carbo ssp. lucidus

* Resplendent quetzal

CRANES

AMERICAN COOT
Fulica americana

LIMPKIN
Aramus guarauna

MASKED FINFOOT
Heliopais personatus

RED-CROWNED CRANE
Grus japonensis

SUBDESERT MESITE
Monias benschi

SUNBITTERN
Eurypyga helias

HERONS, STORKS, IBISES

AMERICAN BITTERN
Botaurus lentiginosus

BLACK-CROWNED NIGHT HERON
Nycticorax nycticorax

BOAT-BILLED HERON
Cochlearius cochlearius

CATTLE EGRET
Bubulcus ibis

GRAY HERON
Ardea cinerea

GREAT EGRET
Ardea alba

MADAGASCAR CRESTED IBIS
Lophotibis cristata

* Red-winged blackbird

PAINTED STORK
Mycteria leucocephala

REDDISH EGRET
Egretta rufescens

ROSEATE SPOONBILL
Platalea ajaja

SADDLEBILL STORK
Ephippiorhychus senegalensis

SCARLET IBIS
Eudocimus ruber

STRIATED HERON
Butorides striatus

WHITE IBIS
Eudocimus albus

WOOD STORK
Mycteria americana

LOONS, GREBES

COMMON LOON
Gavia immer

YELLOW-BILLED DIVER LOON
Gavia adamsii

RATITES

BROWN KIWI
Apteryx australis

GREATER RHEA
Rhea americana

NORTH ISLAND BROWN KIWI
Apteryx mantelli

* Greater flamingo

* Wood duck

RED-THROATED LOON
Gavia stellata

SLATY-BREASTED TINAMOU
Crypturellus boucardi

PARROTS

BROWN-THROATED PARAKEET
Aratinga pertinax

BLUE AND YELLOW MACAW
Ara ararauna

BUDGERIGAR
Melopsittacus undulatus

COCKATIEL
Nymphicus hollandicus

CUBAN PARROT
Amazona leucocephala

ECLECTUS PARROT
Eclectus roratus

FISCHER'S LOVEBIRD
Agapornis fischeri

GALAH
Eolophus roseicapillus

PINK COCKATOO
Cactua leadbeateri

PUERTO RICAN AMAZON PARROT
Amazona vittata

RED-FAN PARROT
Deroptyus accipitrinus

ROSE-RINGED PARAKEET
Psittacula krameri

SCARLET MACAW
Ara macao

SULFUR-CRESTED COCKATOO
Cacatua galerita

SUN CONURE
Aratinga solstitialis

THICK-BILLED PARROT
Rhynchopsitta pachyrhyncha

VIOLET-NECKED LORY
Eos squamata

OWLS

BARRED OWL
Strix varia

EURASIAN EAGLE OWL
Bubo bubo

GREAT HORNED OWL
Bubo virginianus

* Northern cardinal

INDIAN EAGLE OWL
Bubo bengalensis

MOTTLED OWL
Strix virgata

NORTHERN HAWK OWL
Surnia ulula

SOUTHERN BOOBOOK
Ninax novaseelandiae

SOUTHERN WHITE-FACED OWL
Ptilopsis granti

SPECTACLED OWL
Pulsatrix perspicillata

TAWNY OWL
Strix aluca

BIRDS OF PREY

ANDEAN CONDOR
Vultur gryphus

BATELEUR EAGLE
Terathopius ecaudatus

COMMON BLACK HAWK
Buteogallus anthracinus

COMMON KESTREL
Falco tinnunculus

COMMON TURKEY VULTURE
Cathartes aura

GALAPAGOS HAWK
Buteo galapagoensis

HARPY EAGLE
Harpia harpyja

KING VULTURE
Sarcoramphus papa

LAPPET-FACED VULTURE
Torgos tracheliotos

LESSER KESTREL
Falco naumanni

MERLIN
Falco columbarius

NORTHERN GOSHAWK
Accipiter gentilis

RED-LEGGED SERIEMA
Cariama cristata

* Tawny frogmouth

RED-TAILED HAWK
Buteo jamaicensis

ROADSIDE HAWK
Buteo magnirostris

SOUTHERN CRESTED CARACARA
Caracara plancus

TAWNY EAGLE
Aquila rapax

WHITE-BACKED VULTURE
Gyps africanus

HUMMINGBIRDS, SWIFTS

ALLEN'S HUMMINGBIRD
Selasphorus sasin

CALLIOPE HUMMINGBIRD
Stellula calliope

BARN SWALLOW
Hirundo rustica

CLIFF SWALLOW
Petrochelidon pyrrhonota

COMMON SWIFT
Apus apus

COSTA'S HUMMINGBIRD
Calypte costae

FORK-TAILED SWIFT
Apus pacificus

OLIVE-BACKED SUNBIRD
Cinnyris jugularis

SCARLET HAWAIIAN HONEYCREEPER
Vestaria coccinea

SUNBIRD
Aethopyga duyvenbodei

TREE SWALLOW
Tachycineta bicolor

PIGEONS, DOVES

AFRICAN COLLARED DOVE
Streptopelia roseogrisea

BAND-TAILED PIGEON
Columba fasciata

BLACK-NAPED FRUIT DOVE
Ptilinopus melanospilus

COMMON GROUND DOVE
Columbina passerina

DOMESTIC DOVE
Streptopelia risoria

WHITE-CROWNED PIGEON
Columba leucocephala

WHITE-NAPED PIGEON
Columba albinucha

WHITE-TIPPED DOVE
Leptotila verreauxi

WOOD PIGEON
Columba palumbus

KINGFISHERS, HORNBILLS

AFRICAN PYGMY KINGFISHER
Ceyx pictus

AMAZON KINGFISHER
Chloroceryle amazon

CARMINE BEE-EATER
Merops nubicus

* Spectacled eider

DOLLARBIRD
Eurystomus orientalis

GRAY-HEADED KINGFISHER
Halcyon leucocephala

GREAT INDIAN HORNBILL
Buceros bicornis

JAMAICAN TODY
Todus todus

LAUGHING KOOKABURRA
Dacelo novaeguineae

LILAC-BREASTED ROLLER
Coracias caudatus

LILAC KINGFISHER
Cittura cyanotis

NORTHERN GROUND HORNBILL
Bucorvus abyssinicus

RAINBOW BEE-EATER
Merops ornatus

RED-BILLED HORNBILL
Tockus erythrorhynchus

SOUTHERN YELLOW-BILLED HORNBILL
Tockus leucomelas

WHITE-THROATED KINGFISHER
Halcyon smyrnensis

WREATHED HORNBILL
Aceros undulatus

* Common hoopoe

CUCKOOS, TURACOS

COMMON CUCKOO
Cuclus canarus

GRAY TURACO
Corythaixoides concolor

GREAT BLUE TURACO
Corythaeola cristata

LADY ROSS'S TURACO
Musophaga rossae

RAGGIANA BIRD OF PARADISE
Paradisaea raggiana

RED BIRD OF PARADISE
Paradisaea rubra

RESPLENDENT TROGON
Pharomachrus mocinno

SATIN BOWERBIRD
Ptilonorhynchus violaceus

SPECKLED MOUSEBIRD
Colius striatus

STRIPED CUCKOO
Tapera naevia

SUPERB LYREBIRD
Menura novaehollandiae

WHITE-BELLIED GO-AWAY BIRD
Corythaixoides leucogaste

WHITEHEAD'S TROGON
Harpactes whiteheadi

YELLOW-BILLED CUCKOO
Coccyzus americanus

* Atlantic puffin

TYRANT FLYCATCHERS

BLACK-THROATED TODY-TYRANT
Hemitriccus granadensis

EASTERN KINGBIRD
Tyrannus tyrannus

FORK-TAILED FLYCATCHER
Tyrannus savana

GREAT SHRIKE-TYRANT
Agriornis lividus

MANY-COLORED RUSH TYRANT
Tachuris rubrigastra

OLIVE-SIDED FLYCATCHER
Contopus cooperi

ROYAL FLYCATCHER
Onychorhynchus coronatus

* California condor

RUSSET-WINGED SPADEBILL
Platyrinchus leucoryphus

WHITE-CRESTED ELAENIA
Elaenia albiceps

SONGBIRDS

ALTAMIRA ORIOLE
Icterus gularis

AMERICAN DIPPER
Cinclus mexicanus

ANDEAN COCK-OF-THE-ROCK
Rupicola peruvianus

ANTILLEAN EUPHONIA
Euphonia musica

AUSTRALIAN GOLDEN WHISTLER
Pachycephala pectoralis

BALTIMORE ORIOLE
Icterus galbula

BARE-FACED BULBUL
Pycnonotus hualon

BEARDED REEDLING
Panurus biarmicus

BLACK-CAPPED CHICKADEE
Parus atricapillus

BLACK-STRIPED WOODCREEPER
Xiphorhynchus lachrymosus

* Indian peafowl

Radiated tortoise

Emerald tree boa (juvenile)

Borneo anglehead

Green pit viper

American alligator

TOP TRAITS Reptiles are living relatives of long-extinct dinosaurs. others shed all in one piece, like taking off a coat. ▶ Reptiles are cold-blooded, ▶ Most species lay eggs, but boas and pythons give birth to live young. ▶ Some,

REPTILES

Thorny devil

▶ Reptiles have scales and periodically shed their skin. Some shed in flakes and meaning they can't create their own body heat. They bask in the sun to stay warm. like snakes, don't have eyelids. ▶ There are more than 10,000 species of reptiles.

ALL ABOUT REPTILES

THERE ARE SIX GROUPS of reptiles: snakes, lizards, turtles and tortoises, crocodiles, worm lizards, and a tiny group called tuatara that includes just two species. The appearances and behaviors of the animals in these groups are widely varied, but they do share characteristics that make them all reptiles. For instance, they all have scaly, watertight skin; most reproduce by laying eggs; they breathe using lungs; and, at some point in their histories, they all had four limbs—even snakes. Plus, all reptiles are ectothermic, or cold-blooded, meaning that their body temperatures are dependent on their environments—which is why turtles by a pond can be found basking in the sun on a cool spring day and later, in summer, cooling off in the water on a hot day.

TAIL Most reptiles have tails that are useful for defense and balance. Some are prehensile— they can be used for grasping a tree branch, for instance.

HABITATS

Reptiles live in every part of the world except for very cold regions; being ectothermic makes it impossible to live in areas that are cold year round. Reptiles thrive in hot, wet places like rain forests and hot, dry places such as deserts. Though they have to breathe air like humans do, reptiles such as sea turtles, sea snakes, and crocodiles can spend most of their lives in water.

LIFE CYCLE

Nearly all reptiles lay eggs. Most reptile eggshells are not hard like a chicken's eggshell is, but soft and leathery like a thin orange peel. Some species of snake give birth to live young. Reptiles are almost all absentee parents—they abandon their eggs and let the baby reptiles grow up by themselves. Crocodiles are the exception: They sometimes carry babies in their huge mouths. But baby snakes are usually on their own. They use special egg teeth to crack through their shells to hatch and must seek prey immediately. Baby sea turtles have to get out of their eggs, dig out of the sand the eggs were in, and try to make it to the ocean safely.

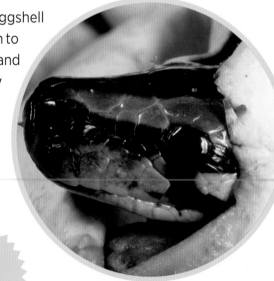

Surprisingly Human

Crocodiles are good mothers. They guard the nest, help the babies hatch, and carry them to the water in their mouths.

The spectacle is a special scale that protects a snake's eye.

GROWING

MOLTING A snake molts, or sheds its skin, as it grows. This can happen several times over its life.

SHEDDING A turtle's shell is part of its body, so it can't molt to grow. Instead, it sheds scale-like scutes to make room for larger ones growing underneath.

SKIN Reptiles have dry, scaly, watertight skin. They are not slimy.

BACKBONE All reptiles are vertebrates; that is, they have backbones made of individual bones called vertebrae.

EAR HOLES Many reptiles do not have external ears but still have excellent hearing through holes on the sides of their heads where sound enters. Thin membranes stretch across the openings— sometimes close enough to the outside to see.

CLAWS Claws help lizards climb and help carnivorous species hold down prey.

FEEDING HABITS

Most reptiles are carnivores and eat other animals. Tortoises and some species of lizards are herbivores that eat just plants. Most turtles are omnivores that eat insects, rotting flesh, snails, or small fish, but also eat vegetation, especially when they are older.

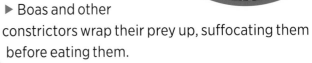

▶ Snakes like vipers and elapids bite their prey, injecting venom with their fangs. When it is paralyzed or dead, the snake swallows the animal whole.

▶ Boas and other constrictors wrap their prey up, suffocating them before eating them.

▶ Crocodiles and alligators use their speed and sharp teeth to grab prey and pull it underwater to drown it before tearing off hunks of flesh to eat.

▶ Tortoises have no teeth, and use their beaks and strong jaws to cut and eat plants.

▶ Snapping turtles use their beaks to eat animals such as fish, lizards, or anything they can overpower.

EYES Does it have eyelids? It might be a lizard. No eyelids? It's probably a snake.

149

ALL ABOUT REPTILES

SENSES

Reptiles have fascinating ways of getting the information they need to survive. Snakes and many lizards, such as the Komodo, smell with their tongues and have an organ (or two) in their heads to process complex chemical signals. Many reptiles don't have ears at all, or have only the ear parts that allow them to hear a short range of sounds or sense vibrations. Some lizards, crocs, and turtles have more traditional senses, like tongues that taste and ears that hear. While most snakes do not see well, some lizards have excellent vision—some can even turn their eyes in different directions at once. Some snakes have a bonus sense: They use pits in their heads to detect changes in heat.

JACOBSON'S ORGAN This internal tool helps snakes and lizards take in scent information—chemicals in the air—which aids them in hunting and avoiding predators. This is called chemoreception.

Heat pits

HEAT PITS Some snakes have heat pits that allow them to sense the slightest change in temperature, which tells them how close and how big a predator or prey is. This is called thermoreception.

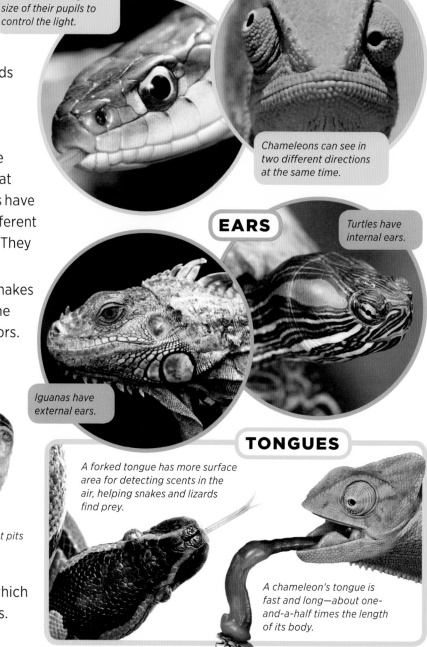

EYES

Snakes can change the size of their pupils to control the light.

Chameleons can see in two different directions at the same time.

EARS

Turtles have internal ears.

Iguanas have external ears.

TONGUES

A forked tongue has more surface area for detecting scents in the air, helping snakes and lizards find prey.

A chameleon's tongue is fast and long—about one-and-a-half times the length of its body.

LIVE ACTION: KOMODO DRAGON

The Komodo dragon smells the dead water buffalo from a distance—3 miles away. The lizard's forked yellow tongue darts out partway, then again the whole way a few seconds later, gathering scent molecules from the air. As the animal approaches, it sees a cloud of flies buzzing near the rotting flesh. Objects standing still are hard for the Komodo to see, since it doesn't have cones in its retinas. Distance vision is more important for a stealth hunter like the Komodo.

ECTOTHERMIA

Ectothermic (cold-blooded) animals can't produce their own body heat, so they find sunny areas or shady places, warm rocks or cool ones, and warm or cool water to maintain steady temperatures. Endothermic (warm-blooded) animals, such as mammals and birds, have fat, fur, feathers, and other body coverings that insulate them from cold. Reptiles don't have these features, but they also don't need to eat as often—endothermic animals need to eat to fuel their warmth-producing bodies.

EVOLUTION

Today's reptiles are descendants of the mighty dinosaurs. Turtles and crocodiles and lizards all had ancestors that lived in the time of the dinosaurs, more than 300 million years ago. About 150 million years ago, some lizards starting living underground—possibly to avoid predators, to escape from too-cold or too-hot conditions, or because food sources were found there. Over time, some reptiles evolved without legs, which weren't needed for slithering underground. After a great extinction of the huge dinosaurs about 65 million years ago, smaller reptiles survived. Why did they live while the dinosaurs perished? It might have been because they were better adapted to living in the cold, because they needed to eat less frequently than the huge dinosaurs did, or because they could live either on land or in freshwater. Some scientists even think it might have been because ancient small reptiles were smarter than dinosaurs.

SUPER CROC *Sarcosuchus imperator*, an ancient relative of the crocodile, lived about 110 million years ago. This giant reptile was about 40 feet (about 12 m) long and weighed about 20,000 pounds.

VIPERS

WHEN MOST PEOPLE think of snakes, they think of vipers. Though some vipers do bite humans when they are threatened or provoked, they do not seek out people for food. But vipers are indeed fierce predators of their chosen prey—they eat widely from a menu of just about any animal they can catch, from other snakes to rodents, birds, and small mammals.

As members of the same family, vipers have several traits in common. A viper has a triangular-shaped head, and hollow fangs that fold back into the head. Vipers also have a unique style of reproduction: Nearly all viper species give birth to live young, whereas many other snakes lay eggs.

There are about 225 species of vipers, living mostly in the Southern Hemisphere and nearly all in warm climates.

COPPERHEAD
Agkistrodon contortrix

SIZE: 2–3 feet long (0.6–0.9 m)
HABITAT: Forest, woodland, desert; eastern and midwestern United States, northern Mexico
FOOD: Rodents, reptiles, amphibians, large insects

These snakes sometimes hibernate in communal dens, but they hunt alone. They bite large prey, release it while the venom goes to work, and then swallow it whole. Juveniles wiggle their tails to lure small lizards or frogs within striking distance.

Surprisingly Human

Human hair and rattlesnake buttons are made of the same substance—a fibrous protein called keratin. Keratin is durable, waterproof, and fast growing, making it the perfect material for protecting heads and tails.

EYELASH PALM PIT VIPER
Bothriechis schlegelii

SIZE: 2–3 feet long (0.6–0.9 m)
HABITAT: Rain forest; Central America
FOOD: Lizards, rodents, amphibians

Some of these cool-looking snakes can be bright yellow, green, brown or gold. Their most famous features are the high ridges on their foreheads. Pit vipers get their name from the heat pit organs on their faces that let them sense temperature changes that can signal nearby prey.

EASTERN DIAMONDBACK RATTLESNAKE
Crotalus adamanteus

SIZE: 5.5–8 feet long (1.7–2.4 m)
HABITAT: Woodland; southeastern United States
FOOD: Small mammals, birds, other snakes

Long, thick, and dangerous, this is the largest venomous snake in the United States. Like other rattlers, the Eastern diamondback has a tail that ends in a hard, flexible rattle. The rattle is made up of several segments, called buttons, which knock together when shaken to make the rattle sound. The snake shakes it to warn off predators. Its scale pattern forms diamond shapes, which helps it blend into forest floors, where rabbits are a favorite prey.

GABOON VIPER
Bitis rhinoceros

SIZE: 4–5 feet long (1.2–1.5 m)
HABITAT: Rain forest, woodland; western Africa
FOOD: Mostly rodents, but also other snakes

A pattern of multicolored scales and a triangular head similar in shape to a leaf let this predator hide and wait for prey to come by. This snake is a record breaker: It has the longest fangs in the snake world (about 2 inches (5 cm)), and it produces the largest volume of venom of any known snake. An adult female gives birth to as many as 30 or more live young every two to three years.

SIDEWINDER
Crotalus cerastes

SIZE: 1.5–2.75 feet long (0.46–0.84 m)
HABITAT: Desert; western and southwestern United States, northern Mexico
FOOD: Rodents, lizards, birds

The sidewinder is named for its method of locomotion (movement), which allows it to keep most of its body off the hot sand when it moves through its desert environment. It can be found resting in cooler, shaded places during the hottest hours of the day.

WESTERN DIAMONDBACK RATTLESNAKE
Crotalus atrox

SIZE: 3–5 feet long (0.9–1.5 m)
HABITAT: Desert, plain, forest, rocky areas; southwestern United States, northern Mexico
FOOD: Rodents, lizards, birds, other small animals

The western diamondback snake has a distinctive diamond-shaped pattern on its back, and the thick body common to rattlesnakes. As with all rattlesnakes, each time it sheds its skin, a new button is added to its rattle.

COTTONMOUTH
Agkistrodon piscivorus

SIZE: 2.5–6 feet long (0.8–1.8 m)
HABITAT: Swamp, wetland; southern United States
FOOD: Amphibians, fish, small mammals

This viper gets its name from the inside of its mouth, which is bright white. It opens wide to show off this feature when threatened. It's also known as the water moccasin, as it spends most of its time living in freshwater seeking animals that live in the water or nearby it.

BOAS AND PYTHONS

BOAS AND PYTHONS are recognized by their body shape. They are all cylindrical, thick, and powerful-looking. Boas and pythons kill by constricting, or squeezing, prey. They coil their long bodies around a victim several times and then flex their muscles. This squeezing makes it impossible for the prey to breathe and it suffocates; the snake then eats the prey whole. Other types of snakes use constriction, but these two types of snake are especially known for the practice.

The 12 known species of pythons live only in Australia, Asia, and Africa, and some adjacent islands. More than 40 species of boas live around the world. There are only small differences in some body parts between the two families. Boas give birth to live young, while pythons lay eggs. Both are at home in tropical rainforest environments. Boas and pythons are among the largest types of snakes in the world.

RETICULATED PYTHON
Python reticulatus

SIZE: **10–30 feet long (3–9 m)**
HABITAT: **Rain forest; southeastern Asia**
FOOD: **Mammals, birds**

This is not the heaviest known species of snake, but it is considered the longest. The reticulated python is more slender than an anaconda. Like other pythons, it uses its powerful body to coil around prey. The word reticulated means webbed or netlike, which describes its scale pattern.

BURMESE PYTHON
Python bivittatus

SIZE: **12–19 feet long (3.7–5.7 m)**
HABITAT: **Rain forest; southeastern Asia**
FOOD: **Mammals, birds, reptiles**

This heavy, thick snake is among the largest. The pattern of large blotches on its brownish skin help it blend into a forest environment, both near water and in trees. Like most very large snakes, it doesn't have to eat often. A large meal can hold a Burmese python for several weeks or longer.

GREEN TREE PYTHON
Morelia viridis

SIZE: **5–6 feet long (1.5–1.8 m)**
HABITAT: **Tropical rain forest; New Guinea, Indonesia, Australia**
FOOD: **Small mammals, birds, reptiles**

A bright green color helps adults of this species hide among the foliage of their rain forest habitat as they await prey. Juveniles, however, can be bright yellow or orange. Living primarily in trees, the green tree python uses its tail like a hand, gripping onto a branch while its body shoots out to strike prey—mostly birds and small mammals.

EMERALD TREE BOA
Corallus caninus

SIZE: **5–6 feet long (1.5.–1.8 m)**
HABITAT: **Forest, rain forest; South America**
FOOD: **Mammals, birds, lizards**

This boa has a unique sensory organ for perceiving prey: heat pits. Detecting heat through these organs on the head, an emerald tree boa can discern the approach of warm-blooded animals such as small mammals or birds. Once it has captured prey, it will usually hang upside down in a tree while swallowing.

KENYAN SAND BOA
Gongylophis colubrinus

SIZE: **2–3 feet long (0.6–0.9 m)**
HABITAT: **Sandy soil, scrubland; northern and western Africa**
FOOD: **Small mammals**

These snakes spend most of their time in desert burrows made in soft sand or soil, only emerging to dart out and strike at small mammal prey. They are more brightly colored than most boas, with yellow or orange scales.

BALL PYTHON
Python regius

SIZE: **3–5 feet long (0.9–1.5 m)**
HABITAT: **Grasslands, woodlands; Africa**
FOOD: **Small mammals, reptiles**

Also called the royal python, this is one of the most popular snake pets. This species is mellow and doesn't seem to mind living in a well-kept cage and being fed small rodents.

RAINBOW BOA
Epicrates cenchria

SIZE: **3–5 feet long (0.9–1.5 m)**
HABITAT: **Rain forest, woodlands; southern Central America, northern South America**
FOOD: **Small mammals**

This boa gets its name from its skin, which has a blotchy pattern but also scales that seem to change color depending on the angle of light. It lives throughout northern South America and southern Central America. Subspecies in the rainbow boa's range have a variety of scale patterns and colors, including orange, red, black, and brown.

GREEN ANACONDA
Eunectes murinus

SIZE: **10–30 feet long (3–7.6 m)**
HABITAT: **Rainforest near water; South America**
FOOD: **mammals, birds, reptiles**

The anaconda is the heaviest snake in the world, weighing more than 500 pounds (227 kg). It is one of the longest, too, though some individual pythons have been found that are longer than even very long anacondas. The green anaconda eats the largest prey we know of and has been seen eating deer and crocodiles, using its massive body to encircle, suffocate, and swallow.

FUN FACT

Anacondas are among the largest snakes in the world . . . and among the slowest. Their huge bodies are hard to move on land, so many spend most of their time in the water.

155

COLUBRIDS

THE SNAKE WORLD'S BIGGEST FAMILY

COLUBRIDS ARE THE LARGEST family of snakes in the world, with more than 2,000 species. While most snake families are organized by common body shape or internal body parts, colubrids are less easily classified; they are generally grouped together because they don't fit in with any other family.

Colubrids come in just about every size, shape, and color, though many are slim and slender. The majority are not dangerous to humans, but the boomslang and a couple of others can be deadly. There are colubrids that eat eggs, insects, small mammals, fish, and other snakes. They live in just about every habitat on Earth and on every continent except Antarctica. If you've ever seen a snake near you, chances are it was in this family.

GREEN WHIPSNAKE
Hierophis viridiflavus

SIZE: **5 feet long (1.5 m)**
HABITAT: **Woodland, scrubland; western, central, and southern Europe**
FOOD: **Eggs, reptiles**

Found in most countries of southern Europe, the whipsnake gets its name from its long, very thin shape. Whipsnakes live mostly in trees but will head to the ground to slide through leaf litter looking for nests. A subspecies in Italy is dark black.

COMMON KINGSNAKE
Lampropeltis getula

SIZE: **2–6 feet long (0.6–1.5 m)**
HABITAT: **Anywhere not aquatic; eastern and southern United States, northern Mexico**
FOOD: **Reptiles, small mammals**

Found throughout the United States, kingsnakes are nonvenomous. Each subspecies has a very different scale pattern, from long bands to thin stripes and from very dark to very bright coloration.

PARADISE FLYING SNAKE
Chrysopelea paradisi

SIZE: **2–4 feet long (0.6–1.2 m)**
HABITAT: **Rain forest; southeastern Asia**
FOOD: **Small mammals, reptiles**

No wings, but they can fly . . . in a way. The paradise flying snake can flatten its body to let it glide from tree to tree. Gravity does most of the work, but these snakes become aerodynamic enough to choose where they land.

CORN SNAKE
Elaphe guttata

SIZE: **3–6 feet long (0.9–1.8 m)**
HABITAT: **Woodland, grassland; eastern and southern United States**
FOOD: **Small mammals, birds**

A type of ratsnake, the corn snake is seen widely in the southern United States. Harmless to people, it's a very popular species to keep as a pet. It can be orange or brown in the wild, but breeders have created hundreds of "morphs," or alternate color patterns. Thus, pet cornsnakes can be black, white, yellow, red, or even albino.

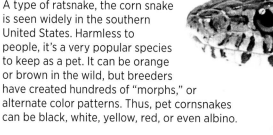

SNACK ATTACK

Snakes often have to eat things larger than themselves. In most species, the jaw bones can spread much wider than those of other animals. The bones are attached by a stretchy ligament to the skull. Snakes eat their prey headfirst so that the prey's limbs fold back as they are swallowed.

WESTERN HOGNOSE
Heterodon nasicus

SIZE: 1–2 feet long (0.3–0.6 m)
HABITAT: Sandy areas; southern Canada, central United States, northern Mexico
FOOD: Reptiles, amphibians, small mammals

The dark and light brown scale pattern of the hognose might call to mind a rattlesnake, but unlike rattlesnakes this species is harmless to humans. It gets its name from the upturned snout that it uses to search through soil or forest floors for prey. It lives on the plains stretching below the Rocky Mountains.

 **FUN FACT** Scales covering its skin help a snake move and provide protection both from the elements and predators.

BOOMSLANG
Dispholidus typus

SIZE: 4–5 feet long (1.2–1.5 m)
HABITAT: Forest; central and southern Africa
FOOD: Birds, reptiles

Thanks to venom injected through small fangs in the back of its mouth, the boomslang is one of the very few colubrids that can be deadly to humans. Bites are rare but they do happen, especially when these tree-loving snakes come down to rest in areas of western Africa where people are present.

NORTHERN WATER SNAKE
Nerodia sipedon

SIZE: 2–5 feet long (0.6–1.5 m)
HABITAT: Rivers, streams, marshes; southern Ontario, northeastern and midwestern United States
FOOD: Amphibians, fish, reptiles

As their name implies, water snakes spend most of their life in the water. They are reptiles, so they need to surface to breathe air, but they swim swiftly after prey. If they are grabbed by a predator, they let out a stinky goo from their glands in hopes that the smell will drive away the threat.

ELAPIDS

WITH SHARP FANGS and, in many cases, deadly venom, elapids are among the most famous and dangerous snakes in the world. Cobras, coral snakes, mambas, and kraits are some of the members of this family.

Elapids all have fangs that are fixed to their upper jaws. That is, their fangs, unlike those of vipers, do not fold back when they close their mouths. Elapids use these fangs when they strike quickly and inject venom into their prey, which includes several varieties of small animals. Most elapids live in the Southern Hemisphere, though a few species can be found north of the Equator. In Australia, there are no vipers; elapids are the only fanged snakes that live there. Sea snakes are also part of this family, having adapted ways of swimming for their supper.

KING BROWNSNAKE
Pseudechis australis

SIZE: **5–9 feet long (1.5–2.7 m)**
HABITAT: **Forest, desert, grassland; Australia**
FOOD: **Mammals, reptiles, birds**

Found throughout Australia, brownsnakes can be deadly to humans. They also can act like cobras, raising up and flattening their head and upper body. The amount of venom they can release is much greater than what many other snakes can.

KING COBRA
Ophiophagus hannah

SIZE: **10–18 feet long (3–5.5 m)**
HABITAT: **Forest; India, southeastern Asia**
FOOD: **Snakes**

At up to 18 feet (5.5 m), the king cobra is the longest venomous snake in the world. Its home in the deep forest, however, makes human bites rare. King cobras pair up to create a nest, with both male and female protecting the eggs. The cobra's famous defensive move comes from flattening out a hood of skin. This makes the upper part of the body look wider as it rises up from the ground.

YELLOW-BELLIED SEA SNAKE
Pelamis platurus

SIZE: **3–5 feet long (0.9–1.5 m)**
HABITAT: **Ocean waters; coastal regions of eastern Africa, Arabian Peninsula, India, southeastern Asia, Baja California**
FOOD: **Fish**

This animal is perfectly adapted to spending its whole life in saltwater: Its tail is like a paddle, special glands remove salt from its body, and its scales prevent sea parasites from attaching to it. Very venomous, it lives in warm oceans, where its bright coloring warns predators of its deadly venom.

 Conservation scientists are concerned about fishermen taking too many sea snakes out of oceans near Thailand. The snakes are sold for use in restaurants and for folk medicine. If the snakes become too popular, they might be overfished and unable to reproduce fast enough.

DEATH ADDER
Acanthophis praelongus

SIZE: 1–2 feet long (0.3–0.6 m)
HABITAT: Scrub brush; Australia, New Guinea and western Indonesia
FOOD: Amphibians, snakes, small mammals

Lying in wait in the brush, the death adder twitches its tail to look like a tasty worm. When hungry prey comes to eat, the adder strikes. They are most active at night.

BLACK MAMBA
Dendroaspis polylepis

SIZE: 7–14 feet long (2.1–4.3 m)
HABITAT: Grassland; southern and eastern Africa
FOOD: Small mammals, birds

One of the most deadly snakes in Africa, the mamba's bite can result in death in less than an hour. The "black" in its name comes from the inside of its mouth, which it shows off when threatened. Black mambas are equally at home on the ground and in trees.

COASTAL TAIPAN
Oxyuranus scutellatus

SIZE: 5–6.5 feet long (1.5–2 m)
HABITAT: Low brush and woodlands; northern and eastern Australia, New Guinea
FOOD: Rodents

Found only in northern and eastern Australia and southern New Guinea, this snake has some of the deadliest venom in the world. Experts consider it one of the deadliest land-dwelling snakes. It strikes once and injects the venom, then waits nearby while its prey dies, which is usually very quickly. It does not often attack humans, but will defend itself if provoked.

BANDED KRAIT
Bungarus fasciatus

SIZE: 5–7 feet long (1.5–2.1 m)
HABITAT: Grassland near water; northeastern India, southern China, southeastern Asia
FOOD: Snakes, small mammals

This snake's most striking feature is its shape. A high spinal ridge makes its body almost triangular, as opposed to the tubelike shape of most snakes. It usually lives near water, but does not hunt or swim in it. Its bite can be deadly to humans as well as to the snakes and rodents it hunts.

MOZAMBIQUE SPITTING COBRA

The Mozambique spitting cobra is an elapid, a family of venomous snakes that includes coral snakes, kraits, and mambas. It is native to Africa. With fixed fangs at the front of the mouth, it bites prey to inject poisonous venom. When threatened, it shoots venom from holes in the front of the fangs.

ABOUT ME!

I am a spitting cobra. If you get too close, I can use my muscles to spread the ribs in my neck to form a hood. This is a warning sign called a defensive display. What it means is: Back off!

6 FACTS ABOUT THE MOZAMBIQUE SPITTING COBRA

- ▶ Is one of the smallest cobra species at 4 feet (1.2 m) long
- ▶ Shoots venom up to 8 feet (2.4 m) away
- ▶ Venom can cause blindness
- ▶ Eats amphibians, small birds, rodents, and other snakes
- ▶ Can raise itself up more than half its body length
- ▶ Female lays up to 20 eggs a year

SMALL SNAKE FAMILIES

SOME SNAKE FAMILIES include species that few of us will ever see. They either don't come out in daylight hours or else live in remote, inaccessible locations. Interestingly, these reclusive creatures are rarely harmful to humans.

Pipe snakes get their name from their cylindrical shape. They live most of their lives underground. Shield-tailed snakes are so called because of the way their tails are shaped; some species use them as plugs when they go into underground dens. Sunbeam snakes are one of the smallest snake families. Difficult to find in their native habitat of the Central American rain forest, they are worth the search for their sparkling skin. File snakes take their name from their raspy scales. Finally, blind snakes—another small snake family—live underground, where their poor eyesight isn't a problem.

BANANA BOA
Ungaliophis continentalis

SIZE: **1.5–2 feet long (0.5–0.6 m)**
HABITAT: **Forest floor; Mexico, Guatemala, Honduras**
FOOD: **Reptiles, amphibians**

Wood snakes used to be part of the boa family. Slight differences in how their lungs were formed moved into their own family, *Tropidophiidae*. There are about two dozen species, most living in the Caribbean or northern South America. This species got its name from stowing away in fruit shipments in the early 20th century.

SOUTH AMERICAN PIPE SNAKE
Anilius scytale

SIZE: **2–3 feet long (0.6–0.9 m)**
HABITAT: **Forest floor, underground; northern South America**
FOOD: **Snakes, lizards, insects**

Three separate families are called pipe snakes, approximately 15 species all together. Some live in Southeast Asia, others in China, and this species in South America. *Scytale* is the only species in its family, making it a rare example of a "monotypic" species. They can be confused with deadly coral snakes, which have similar colors.

GRAY'S EARTH SNAKE
Uropeltis melanogaster

SIZE: **4–10 inches long (10–25 cm)**
HABITAT: **Underground in forest; Sri Lanka**
FOOD: **Insects, snails, eggs**

Shield-tailed snakes take their name from their back ends. The 50 species in this family have a variety of shields, spines, plates, or scales on their tails. They all live underground and have pointed heads to help them burrow into the ground and find insects and worms to eat. Their tails can be used to defend themselves against predators coming up from behind. They are found exclusively in Sri Lanka.

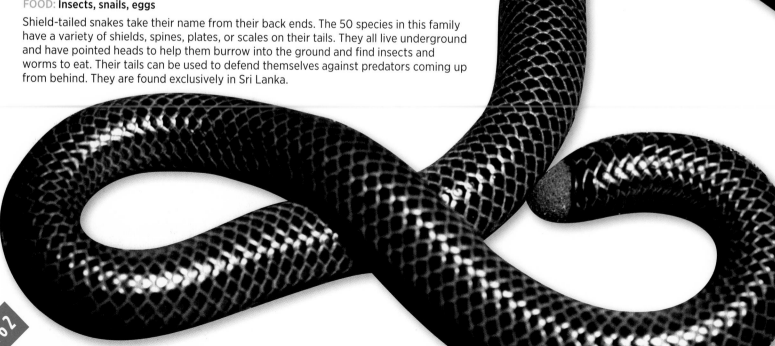

SUNBEAM SNAKE
Xenopeltis unicolor

SIZE: 3–4 feet long (0.9–1.2 m)
HABITAT: Forest, grassland;
Mexico, Central America
FOOD: Lizards, eggs, rodents

The three species of the sunbeam snake family—there are two in Asia and one in Central America—used to be part of the boas. Like boas, sunbeams squeeze their prey. They also use their heads to dig up eggs or nesting lizards. Their shimmering, shiny scales reflect light in rainbow patterns. Young sunbeams have a band of white scales beneath their heads.

LITTLE FILE SNAKE
Acrochordus granulatus

SIZE: 2–3.5 feet long (0.6–1.1 m)
HABITAT: Freshwater swamp or marsh; coastal regions of southeastern Asia, Indonesia, northern Australia
FOOD: Fish, amphibians

File snakes spend nearly their entire lives in the water; they actually have a hard time moving on land. There are only three species. Two prefer saltwater, while the little file snake lives in freshwater. All live in Southeast Asia. Their raspy, bumpy skin gives them their name. Some can be as long as 8 feet.

ROUND ISLAND BOA
Casarea dussumieri

SIZE: 5 feet long (1.5 m)
HABITAT: Scrubland; Round Island (Indian Ocean)
FOOD: Lizards

This very rare family might have only one remaining species living on a tiny island off Madagascar. Once part of the boa family, they are now classified as their own family, thanks to their unique two-part jaw.

BRAHMINY BLIND SNAKE
Ramphotyphlops braminus

SIZE: 6–7 inches long (15–18 cm)
HABITAT: Underground; Australia, southern Asia, Arabian Peninsula, Sub-Saharan Africa, Central America, Florida, Hawaii
FOOD: Insects

Blind snakes are not completely blind, but nearly so. Living their lives underground, their eyes have adapted to see only shades of light, if anything at all. In some of the 200-plus blind snake species, the "eye" is nothing more than a single dark scale.

FUN FACT

The Brahminy blind snake is one of few parthenogenetic reptiles, meaning they can reproduce without both a male and a female. Females can lay eggs that will produce babies, without having mated with a male.

BIG LIZARDS

DRAGONS WALK THE EARTH

MORE THAN 6,000 SPECIES of lizards skitter and lumber around in habitats around the globe. Like other reptiles, they are cold-blooded and have scaly skin. Unlike snakes, they don't shed their skins whole, but instead patches peel off as they grow. Unlike snakes, lizards have legs and eyelids. Lizards come in a rainbow of colors. In the case of chameleons, those colors can all appear in one animal.

Larger lizards eat any animals they can catch; the bigger they are, the bigger their prey. Lizards can be less than an inch long, or more than 10 feet. Here are some examples of the largest lizards.

Surprisingly Human

Does your face get red when you get angry or embarrassed? Chameleons also change color based on how they feel. These "color shows" are used to scare off rivals and communicate with other chameleons.

PARSON'S CHAMELEON
Calumma parsonii

SIZE: 1.5–2.5 feet long (0.5–0.8 m)
HABITAT: Forest; Madagascar
FOOD: Insects

An adult Parson's chameleon is about the size of a house cat. It has two horns on its nose, fused toes that make its feet look a bit like mittens, and a long tail that it can use like a hand to wrap around a tree limb for balance. Its large eyes move independently, and it can see 360 degrees around.

MARINE IGUANA
Amblyrhynchus cristatus

SIZE: 2–3.5 feet long (0.6–1 m)
HABITAT: Rocky ocean shores; Galapagos Islands
FOOD: Algae

The marine iguana is one of several subspecies of iguanas that can swim and dive. They only live on the Galapagos Islands off the coast of Ecuador. Marine iguanas have tails that help them steer as they swim with webbed claws. They also have glands that spew out salt they absorb from seawater.

KOMODO DRAGON
Varanus komodoensis

SIZE: 8–10 feet (2.4–3 m)
HABITAT: Scrubland; Lesser Sunda region of Indonesia
FOOD: Mammals, reptiles

Though it lives on only a few islands in Indonesia, this lizard is famous around the world. It is the largest lizard, weighing as much as 200 pounds (90 kg), and can take down deer, large water buffalo, or even humans. As if its sharp teeth were not enough, its saliva is a kind of poison that can paralyze its prey. Komodo dragons also eat carrion, or dead and rotting animals.

LITTLE LIZARDS CUTE BUT NOT CUDDLY

SMALLER TYPES OF LIZARDS have the same traits as their larger relatives: scaled skin, four legs, and cold blood. They will chase down prey including insects, snails, and fish. Smaller lizards might also be prey themselves, so they have developed some good defensive moves. Many smaller lizards can let their own tail break off to escape the clutches of a predator. In most cases, a small tail will grow back.

GREEN ANOLE
Anolis carolinensis

SIZE: 1.5–3 inches long (4–8 cm)
HABITAT: Garden, woodland; southeastern United States
FOOD: Insects

These little guys like to show off. When threatened or when fighting a male for a mate, green anoles spread out the skin around their necks. They can also inflate a neck pouch called a dewlap and do "push-ups" as a power display, too. Also called the Carolina anole, they live in the southeastern United States.

EMERALD SKINK
Lamprolepis smaragdina

SIZE: 4 inches long (10 cm)
HABITAT: Trees; eastern Indonesia, Philippines, Taiwan
FOOD: Insects, plants

With its long legs and wide-spread "fingers" on each foot, skinks are built to live in trees. They only head to the ground to lay their eggs. Skinks in general have more tubular bodies than other lizards. Like some other lizards, they can drop their tails if a predator grabs hold.

Animal Antics
Autotomy is what scientists call it when a lizard loses its tail on purpose. When a predator seizes the tail, weak points called "fracture planes" between or across vertebrae make it possible for the lizard to break away and leave the tail behind. The tail will keep wiggling for a few moments even after the lizard has detached it from its body. This can distract a predator long enough for the lizard to escape.

TWO-LEGGED WORM LIZARD
Bipes biporus

SIZE: 6–9 inches long (15–23 cm)
HABITAT: Desert; Baja California
FOOD: Insects, earthworms

This is an example of a small branch of reptiles known as amphisbaenians. It's also called the Mexican mole lizard or, in Spanish, *ajolote*. They live mostly underground, using their two limbs to dig tunnels.

AGAMA LIZARD
Agama agama

SIZE: 5–11 inches long (13–30 cm)
HABITAT: Rocky areas; eastern Africa
FOOD: Insects

Don't depend on color alone to identify this agama lizard that lives in West Africa. At night, when it's cool and the lizard is at rest, it is gray or light brown. Like all reptiles, it needs sunlight to warm up. When it does, its body turns blue and red or even turquoise. Females might turn green or yellow, too. Agamas don't control this color change as chameleons do, however.

TOKAY GECKO

This brightly spotted lizard makes a squeaking call when looking for a mate or signaling danger. The call sounds to some people like "TOH-kay, TOH-kay." The tokay gecko lives in the tropical rain forests of Southeast Asia, mostly in trees and on cliffs, eating a diet of insects. It is the largest gecko living in Asia, growing to about 1 foot (0.3 m) long, and the second-largest gecko in the world. Its range has been reduced by development and urbanization.

ABOUT ME!

I'm a tokay gecko. I like to eat insects. I live with a family of humans and help them by eating any insects that come into the house. They let me roam around, in the same way some families let pet cats hunt for mice.

6 FACTS ABOUT THE TOKAY GECKO

▸ Toes spread wide to help with climbing
▸ Ridges on bottom of feet help grip surfaces
▸ Eats mostly insects, but can also eat small mammals, birds, and reptiles
▸ Some can change skin color slightly to blend in
▸ Hisses when threatened and opens mouth wide to look scary
▸ Parents stay with eggs until they hatch

FEW CREATURES on Earth have changed so little since prehistoric times as crocodiles and alligators. Other than their size—today's 23 species are smaller than their ancient relatives—crocs and gators are almost the same as they were tens of millions of years ago.

Both crocodiles and alligators spend most of their lives in water, though as reptiles they need to breathe air. Long rows of sharp teeth aligned in cone-shaped snouts are used to grab prey that is sometimes larger than they are—and, yes, that can include humans. Hard, tough, waterproof outer skins are covered with scales. Unlike many other reptiles, after crocodile eggs hatch, the parents stay around to help the babies.

The differences between crocodiles and alligators are seen in their snouts: Crocodiles have longer, pointed heads, while alligators' mouths are more rounded.

SALTWATER CROCODILE
Crocodylus porosus

SIZE: **10–20 feet long (3–6 m)**
HABITAT: **Watery areas, lakes, rivers, near-shore ocean; northern Australia, eastern India, southeastern Asia**
FOOD: **Any animal**

The largest crocodile species, the saltwater croc is also one of the deadliest. These crocs have captured and devoured humans many times. Fast and an excellent swimmer, it's at the top of food web across its habitat, which ranges from Australia through Southeast Asia. When threatened, it may grunt or hiss.

GANGES GHARIAL
Gavialis gangeticus

SIZE: **13–23 feet long (4–7 m)**
HABITAT: **Large rivers; India, Nepal**
FOOD: **Fish, small mammals**

Fast disappearing from its home in India and neighboring countries, the gharial is a fish-catching machine. It has a very long, narrow snout packed with teeth for snatching fish in mid-swim. Males have a bulb of flesh on the end of their snouts called a ghara.

AMERICAN ALLIGATOR
Alligator mississippiensis

SIZE: **9–14 feet long (2.7–4.3 m)**
HABITAT: **Swamps, lakes; southeastern United States**
FOOD: **Reptiles, birds, mammals**

Alligators live in the hot and humid Southeast, and they can't sweat off their heat. Instead, they lie with mouths open, cooling their insides. They are patient hunters, able to float almost motionlessly for hours while waiting for their prey to come near. Once hunted in the wild for their skin, which was then used to make luggage and clothing, today wild alligators are protected. There are alligator farms where animals are raised for meat and skins.

CUBAN CROCODILE
Crocodylus rhombifer

SIZE: 10–11.5 feet long (3–3.5 m)
HABITAT: Swamps and rivers; Cuba
FOOD: Fish, reptiles, amphibians

This species has the smallest range of any croc, living only in the southern swamps of Cuba. In fact, it almost became extinct in the 1960s; conservation efforts have saved it. These crocs are yellow and green and have high, bony ridges behind their eyes.

NILE CROCODILE
Crocodylus niloticus

SIZE: 11.5–17 feet long (3.5–5.2 m)
HABITAT: Rivers, lakes, swamps; Sub-Saharan Africa, Nile River Valley
FOOD: Fish, amphibians, reptiles, birds

Strong and fast with powerful jaws, the Nile croc has no real enemies in its world, which includes most of central Africa. It can take down wildebeests, buffalo, and even lions that come to the edge of a watering hole. The croc waits stealthily and then sprints out to grab unsuspecting prey. Due to loss of habitat, there are no more Nile crocodiles in the Nile River itself.

MUGGER CROCODILE
Crocodylus palustris

SIZE: 13–16 feet long (4–4.9 m)
HABITAT: Freshwater lakes, rivers; India, Pakistan, Sri Lanka
FOOD: Fish, reptiles, mammals

A wide, flat snout makes this croc look more like a gator. The name derives from a Hindi word that means "water monster." They prefer freshwater but sometimes swim in saltwater lagoons.

ROAR

Nearly one in five reptile species is in danger of extinction. The Orinoco crocodile, which lives in Columbia and Venezuela, was thought to be down to 250 left on Earth. Conservation efforts by people in Venezuela have resulted in more than 5,000 eggs being hatched and the hatchlings being released into their river habitat.

CHINESE ALLIGATOR
Alligator sinensis

SIZE: 5–6 feet long (1.5–1.8 m)
HABITAT: River; coastal regions of eastern China
FOOD: Fish, reptiles, small mammals

Living only on a small stretch of China's Yangtze River, this is the world's rarest alligator. Conservation efforts in China and the United States are trying to help it come back in numbers.

TURTLES AND TORTOISES

TURTLES AND TORTOISES are easy to spot. They carry a hard shell around on their backs. When they are threatened or when it's time for them to sleep, they can pull their legs, heads, and necks into this shell. More than 270 species of turtle and tortoise crawl slowly across Earth. Their eggs are encased in thick, leathery shells.

In general, turtles are aquatic, living in or near water. Smaller turtles live in rivers, streams, and ponds. Larger turtles swim the ocean using feet that have adapted as flippers. They will eat plants, fish, or other sea creatures. Tortoises usually only live on land. With a few exceptions, they are herbivores, which means they depend on plants for food.

GALÁPAGOS TORTOISE
Chelonoidis nigra

SIZE: Up to 4 feet long (1.2 m)
HABITAT: Volcanic rocks, scrubland; Galápagos Islands
FOOD: Plants

The tortoises that live on the isolated Galápagos Islands off Ecuador are the longest-living animals on Earth. They easily exceed 100 years each, and some have lived to 175 years or more. On each island, a subspecies has adapted to feed on that island's plants.

INDIAN STAR TORTOISE
Geochelone elegans

SIZE: 6–12 inches long (15–30 cm)
HABITAT: Dry, desert areas; western and southeastern India, southeastern Pakistan, Sri Lanka
FOOD: Plants

This tortoise's shell looks like a mountain range. Each large scute, or section, rises up to form a striped cone. The stripes form the stars for which it is named.

COMMON SNAPPING TURTLE
Chelydra serpentina

SIZE: 8–16 inches long (20–40 cm)
HABITAT: Ponds, lakes, streams; southern Canada, United States
FOOD: Fish, amphibians, reptiles

People wading in areas where snapping turtles live should watch out for these slow-moving predators. They have powerful jaws that can snap tree limbs . . . or fingers and toes. They use those jaws to catch fish, frogs, and anything small enough to swallow. Snapping turtles live in many types of wild, watery areas throughout eastern North America as well as Central America.

HAWKSBILL SEA TURTLE
Eretmochelys imbricata

SIZE: 2–3 feet long (0.6–0.9 m)
HABITAT: Ocean; tropical waters of Atlantic, Pacific, and Indian Oceans
FOOD: Sponges, reptiles

The hawksbill stands apart from other sea turtles. Its distinctive, sharp beak is the source of its name. On land, it moves using only two flippers at a time, rather than all four as many other species do. Though found throughout the world, each animal moves within a small area as compared to other species.

Turtle conservation efforts are going on around the world. In the United States, some young sea turtles that swim north in the summer get stranded in Cape Cod Bay as the season—and water—turn cold. Rescue groups take sea turtles that get stranded back to Florida. The sea turtles fly first class on Coast Guard airplanes.

Cape Cod

Florida

Range of Kemp's ridley turtle

EASTERN BOX TURTLE
Terrapene carolina

SIZE: 4–9 inches long (10–23 cm)
HABITAT: Marsh, woodland, pasture; eastern United States, Mexico
FOOD: Plants, insects, snails

Many turtles can pull themselves into their shell. The box turtle does it one better. Its plastron (the bottom half of the shell) has a hinged plate that shuts over its head to create a complete "box." With their attractive markings, box turtles are also popular pets.

RIVER COOTER
Pseudemys concinna

SIZE: 9–12 inches long (23–30 cm)
HABITAT: Ponds, rivers, streams; eastern, southeastern, and central United States
FOOD: Plants

Cooter is a slang word for "turtle" in the southern United States. River cooters can often be spotted basking on rocks or logs alongside streams and ponds. They are very comfortable swimming and will move around looking for waterside grasses (and possibly other animals) to eat.

SPINY SOFTSHELL TURTLE
Apalone spinifera

SIZE: 5–19 inches long (13–48 cm)
HABITAT: Freshwater; southern Canada, central United States, northern Mexico
FOOD: Crustaceans, insects, fish

When it's not basking in the sun, the spiny softshell turtle is underwater waiting for prey to swim by. It is one of the largest freshwater turtles found in North America

LEOPARD TORTOISE
Stigmochelys pardalis

SIZE: 1–2.3 feet long (0.3–0.7 m)
HABITAT: Savanna and woodland; eastern and southern Africa
FOOD: Plants

Happy to live alone and munch grass all day long, the leopard tortoise gets its name from the patterns on its shell. The yellow-and-black design breaks up more and more as the turtle ages and the shell grows, so each animal looks slightly different. Thanks to their thick shells and size, leopard tortoises can have very long lives, sometimes more than 100 years.

LEATHERBACK SEA TURTLE

The leatherback sea turtle is a true world traveler. Scientists have tracked some of these long-distance swimmers and found that they have made journeys of more than 3,000 miles (4,800 km)—across whole ocean basins and back again. Their migration route includes stops at feeding, mating, and nesting sites. Tracking large groups of turtles may help guide boat traffic away from heavily traveled routes, which could save turtles from harm.

Leatherbacks are the largest turtle species in the world, ranging from 4–7 feet (1.2–2.1 m) long and weighing 600-2,000 pounds (300-900 kg). A leatherback does not have a hard shell. Its back is covered, as its name indicates, by a thin, leathery skin.

8 FACTS ABOUT THE LEATHERBACK SEA TURTLE

- ▸ Has flippers instead of feet
- ▸ Eats jellyfish
- ▸ Is threatened by plastic bags, which can be mistaken for prey
- ▸ Is the only reptile that can thrive in water as cold as 40 degrees Fahrenheit (4°C)
- ▸ Can dive as deep as 3,300 feet (1,000 m)
- ▸ Temperature of egg in nest determines a baby's sex
- ▸ Can't retract its head and feet into its shell
- ▸ Streamlined shape helps it glide through water

ABOUT ME!

I'm a leatherback sea turtle hatchling. That means I was just hatched out of my egg. My brothers and sisters and I were born on this beach. We use our flippers to push ourselves toward the ocean, where we will spend the rest of our lives.

IN THE DESERT

Desert inhabitants are well-suited to survive their habitat, where extreme temperatures and dry, arid conditions may make food and water scarce.

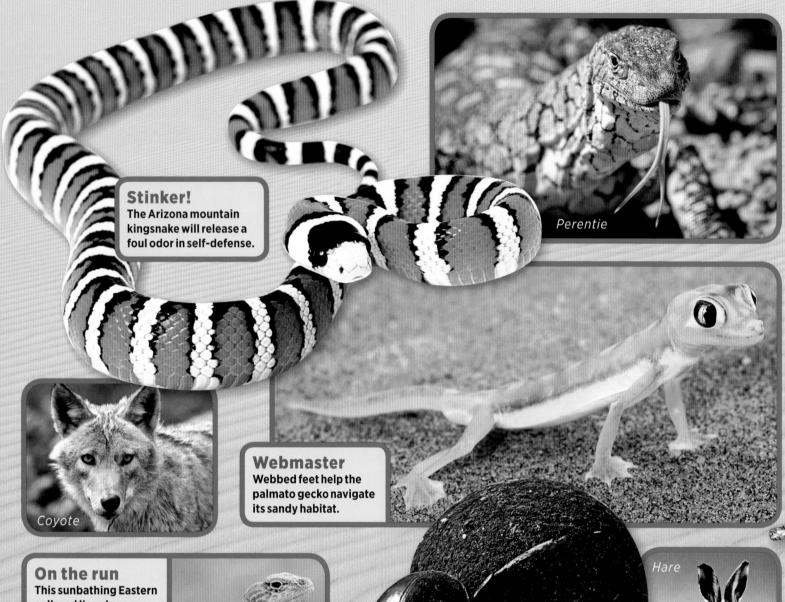

Stinker!
The Arizona mountain kingsnake will release a foul odor in self-defense.

Perentie

Coyote

Webmaster
Webbed feet help the palmato gecko navigate its sandy habitat.

On the run
This sunbathing Eastern collared lizard can run on its two back legs to make a fast escape.

Hare

Dung beetle

Goulds monitor

Quick change
The skin of the desert iguana darkens to absorb heat when the air cools down, and turns white to reflect the sun's rays and keep cool when it's hot.

Blue-tongued lizard

Arizona longnose snake

Smooth knob-tailed gecko

Frilled lizard

Nine-banded armadillo

Coming through! Pronghorns race through the desert at up to 53 mph (86 kph).

Down under Desert tortoises spend almost all their time underground to survive extreme desert temperatures.

Mojave rattlesnake

Gila monster

ANIMAL PLANET L!VE

Check out the Animal Planet L!VE cam to see remarkable reptiles in action by scanning this code or visiting animalplanet.timeincbooks.com/reptiles.

175

MORE REPTILES

There are more than 10,000 known reptile species in the world. Here are some interesting ones to learn more about.

* *Alligator snapping turtle*

VIPERS

ADDER
Vipera berus

BUSHMASTER
Lachesis muta

CANTIL
Agkistrodon bilineatus

GREEN PIT VIPER
Trimeresurus albolabris

HAIRY BUSH VIPER
Atheris hispida

HOG-NOSED PIT VIPER
Porthidium nasutum

HORNED VIPER
Cerastes cerastes

MATILDA'S HORNED VIPER
Atheris matildae

PIGMY RATTLESNAKE
Sistrurus miliarius

PRAIRIE RATTLESNAKE
Crotalus viridis

PUFF ADDER
Bitis arietans

* *Eastern tiger snake*

RHINOCEROS VIPER
Bitis nasicornis

SPIDER-TAILED VIPER
Pseudocerastes urarachnoides

SPINY-HEADED SEA SNAKE
Acalyptophis peronii

TIMBER RATTLESNAKE
Crotalus horridus

WAGLER'S PIT VIPER
Tropidolaemus wagleri

BOAS AND PYTHONS

AFRICAN ROCK PYTHON
Python sebae

AMETHYST PYTHON
Morelia amethistina

BLOOD PYTHON
Python curtus

BOA CONSTRICTOR
Boa constrictor

CAICOS ISLANDS DWARF BOA
Tropidophis greenwayi

CARPET PYTHON
Morelia spilota

CHILDREN'S PYTHON
Antaresia childreni

COOK'S TREE BOA
Corallus cookii

* *Eastern coral snake*

FALSE WATER COBRA
Hydrodynastes gigas

HOG ISLAND BOA
Boa constrictor imperator

INDIAN PYTHON
Python molurus

MONOCLED COBRA
Naja kaouthia

PYGMY PYTHON
Antaresia perthensis

ROSY BOA
Charina trivirgata

RUBBER BOA
Charina bottae

YELLOW ANACONDA
Eunectes notaeus

COLUBRIDS

AESCULAPIAN SNAKE
Elaphe longissima

AURORA HOUSE SNAKE
Lamprophis aurora

BANDED SAND SNAKE
Chilomeniscus stramineus

BLUE RACER
Coluber constrictor

BLUNTHEAD TREE SNAKE
Imantodes cenchoa

BROWN BANDED WATER SNAKE
Helicops angulatus

CALIFORNIA RED-SIDED GARTER SNAKE
Thamnophis sirtalis infernalis

COACHWHIP SNAKE
Masticophis flagellum

COMMON BRONZEBACK SNAKE
Ophidiocephalus taeniatus

COMMON GARTER SNAKE
Thamnophia sirtalis

DARK GREEN WHIPSNAKE
Coluber viridiflavus

EASTERN BLACK NECK GARTER SNAKE
Thamnophis cyrtopsis ocellatus

EGG-EATING SNAKE
Dasypeltis scaber

GOLDEN FLYING SNAKE
Chrysopelea ornata

GOPHER SNAKE
Pituophis catenifer

GRASS SNAKE
Natrix natrix

GREEN CAT SNAKE
Boiga cyanea

GREEN VINE SNAKE
Oxybelis fulgidus

HONDURAN MILK SNAKE
Lampropeltis triangulum hondurensis

* *Speckled rattlesnake*

INDIAN EGG-EATING SNAKE
Elachistodon westermanni

INDIGO SNAKE
Drymarchon couperi

KOPSTEIN'S BRONZEBACK
Dendrelaphis kopsteini

LONG-NOSED SNAKE
Rhinocheilus lecontei

MALAGASY LEAF-NOSED SNAKE
Langaha madagascariensis

MANGROVE SNAKE
Boiga dendrophila

MEXICAN VINE SNAKE
Oxybelis aeneus

MILKSNAKE
Lampropeltis triangulum

MOLE SNAKE
Pseudaspis cana

MONTANE SLUG-EATING SNAKE
Pareas vertebralis

MONTPELLIER SNAKE
Malpolon monspessulanus

PYGMY WOLF SNAKE
Lycophidion pygmaeum

* *Black caiman*

RAT SNAKE
Elaphe obsoleta

RED-TAILED GREEN RATSNAKE
Gonyosoma oxycephalum

RHINOCEROS RAT SNAKE
Rhynchophis boulengeri

RINGNECK SNAKE
Diadophis punctatus

SCARLET KINGSNAKE
Lampropeltis elapsoides

SCHOKARI SAND RACER
Psammophis schokari

SINALOAN MILK SNAKE
Lampropeltis triangulum sinaloae

SIX-LINED RACERUNNER
Cnemidophorus sexlineatus

ST. LUCIA RACER
Liophis ornatus

WESTERN BROWN SNAKE
Psuedonaja nuchalis

YELLOW-HEADED CALICO SNAKE
Oxyrhopus formosus

ELAPIDS

BANDED SEA KRAIT
Laticauda colubrina

BLUE-LIPPED SEA KRAIT
Laticauda laticaudata

CHAPPELL ISLAND TIGER SNAKE
Notechis ater serventyi

COMMON DEATH ADDER
Acanthophis antarcticus

EASTERN GREEN MAMBA
Dendroaspis angusticeps

INLAND TAIPAN
Oxyuranus microlepidotus

NORTHERN DEATH ADDER
Acanthopis praelongus

OLIVE SEA SNAKE
Aipysurus laevis

RENNELL ISLAND SEA KRAIT
Laticauda crockeri

ROUGH-SCALED SEA SNAKE
Hydrophis donaldi

TAIPAN
Oxyuranus scutellatus

TURTLE-HEADED SEA SNAKE
Emydocephalus annulatus

BIG LIZARDS

AMBOINA SAIL-FINNED LIZARD
Hydrosaurus amboinensis

BASILISK LIZARD
Basiliscus vittatus

BLACK SPINY TAIL IGUANA
Ctenosaura similis

BLUE-CRESTED LIZARD
Calotes mystaceus

BROWN PRICKLENAPE
Acanthosaura lepidogaster

CHINESE WATER DRAGON
Physignathus cocincinus

CHUCKWALLA
Sauromalus ater

COMMON FLYING DRAGON
Draco volans

COMMON GREEN IGUANA
Iguana iguana

COMMON TEGU
Tupinambis teguixin

FIJI BANDED IGUANA
Brachylophus fasciatus

FLYING LIZARD
Draco spilonotus

GOULD'S GOANNA
Varanus gouldii

GRAND CAYMAN IGUANA
Cyclura lewisi

GREEN BASILISK
Basiliscus plumifrons

HELMETED IGUANA
Corytophanes cristatus

LAND IGUANA
Conolophus subcristatus

LESSER ANTILLEAN IGUANA
Iguana delicatissima

MEXICAN BEADED LIZARD
Heloderma horridum

PINK IGUANA
Conolophus marthae

RHINOCEROS IGUANA
Cyclura cornuta

ROUGH-SCALED PLATED LIZARD
Gerrhosaurus major

SAILFIN LIZARD
Hydrosaurus amboinensis

TEXAS HORNED LIZARD
Phrynosoma cornutum

YELLOW-BACKED SPINY LIZARD
Ctenosaura flavidorsalis

* *Banded sea krait*

LITTLE LIZARDS

ALLIGATOR LIZARD
Elgaria multicarinata

AMERICAN LEGLESS LIZARD
Anniella grinnelli

ARMADILLO LIZARD
Cordylus cataphractus

ARGENTINE BLACK TEGU
Tupinambis merianae

BLOTCHED BLUE-TONGUE LIZARD
Tiliqua nigrolutea

BLUE-TAILED SKINK
Cryptoblepharus egeriae

BROADLEY'S FLAT LIZARD
Platysaurus broadleyi

BROWN ANOLE
Analis sagrei

CALIFORNIA LEGLESS LIZARD
Anniella pulchra

CHANGEABLE LIZARD
Calotes versicolor

COMMON CHAMELEON
Chamaeleo chamaeleon

COMMON GARDEN SKINK
Lampropholis guichenoti

COMMON WALL LIZARD
Podarcis muralis

COMMON HOUSE GECKO
Hemidactylus frenatus

CUBAN NIGHT ANOLE
Anolis equestris

EVEN-FINGERED GECKO
Alsophylax pipiens

EUROPEAN GLASS LIZARD
Pseudopus apodus

EUROPEAN WORM LIZARD
Blanus cinereus

FENCE LIZARD
Sceloporus undulatus

* *Cape cobra*

THESE 15 REPTILES ARE DEADLY TO HUMANS ✳

✳ *Cantor's giant softshell turtle*

FIVE-LINED SKINK
Plestiodon fasciatus

FLAP NECKED CHAMELEON
Chamaeleon dilepis

FLORIDA WORM LIZARD
Rhineura floridana

GIANT AMEIVA
Ameiva ameiva

GOLD DUST DAY GECKO
Phelsuma laticauda

GREAT PLAINS SKINK
Plestiodon obseletus

GREEN LIZARD
Lacerta viridis

HORNED LEAF CHAMELEON
Brookesia superciliaris

IBIZA WALL LIZARD
Podarcis pityusensis

JACKSON'S CHAMELEON
Chamaeleo jacksonii

KUHL'S FLYING GECKO
Ptychozoon kuhli

LAVA LIZARD
Microlophus albemarlensis

LEAF-TAILED GECKO
Uroplatus fimbriatus

LEOPARD GECKO
Eublepharis macularius

LEOPARD LIZARD
Gambelia sila

LESSER CHAMELEON
Furcifer minor

MADAGASCAN CHAMELEON
Furcifer labordi

✳ *Eastern brown snake*

MADAGASCAR DAY GECKO
Phellsuma madgascariensis

MADREAN ALLIGATOR LIZARD
Elgaria kingii

MWANZA FLAT-HEADED ROCK AGAMA
Agama mwanzae

NEW MEXICO WHIPTAIL LIZARD
Cnemidophorus neomexicanus

NORTH AFRICAN SPINY-TAILED LIZARD
Uromastyx acanthinura

NORTHERN ALLIGATOR LIZARD
Elgaria coerulea

OTAGO SKINK
Oligosoma otagense

PRICKLENAPE LIZARD
Acanthosaura capra

SAND SKINK
Neoseps reynoldsi

SOLOMON ISLANDS SKINK
Corucia zebrata

SOUTHERN ALLIGATOR LIZARD
Elgaria multicarinata

SPINY-TAILED GECKO
Strophurus spinigerus

SPOTTED SKINK
Niveoscincus ocellatus

STANDING'S DAY GECKO
Phelsuma standingi

STRIPED DAY GECKO
Phelsuma lineata

TEXAS ALLIGATOR LIZARD
Gerrhonotus liocephalus

TEXAS BANDED GECKO
Coleonyx brevis

UNION ISLAND GECKO
Gonatodes daudini

VEILED CHAMELEON
Chamaeleo calyptratus

VIVAPAROUS LIZARD
Lacerta vivipara

WEB-FOOTED GECKO
Pachydactylus rangei

YELLOW-THROATED PLATED LIZARD
Gerrhosaurus flavigularis

ZEBRA-TAILED LIZARD
Callisaurus draconoides

✳ *Carpet viper*

SMALL SNAKE FAMILIES

ARAFURA FILE SNAKE
Acrochordus arafurae

BARBADOS THREADSNAKE
Leptotyphlops carlae

COFFEE WORM SNAKE
Amerotyphlops tenuis

CUBAN WOOD SNAKE
Tropidophis mealnurus

JAVAN WART SNAKE
Acrochordus javanicus

KUKRI SNAKE
Oligodon arnensis

LARGE SHIELD-TAILED SNAKE
Pseudotyphlops phillippinus

RED-TAILED PIPE SNAKE
Cylindrophis ruffus

TEXAS BLIND SNAKE
Leptotyphlops dulcis

WESTERN SLENDER BLIND SNAKE
Leptotyphlops humilis

CROCODILES AND ALLIGATORS

AFRICAN DWARF CROCODILE
Osteolaemus tetraspis

AFRICAN SLENDER-SNOUTED CROCODILE
Crocodylus cataphractus

AMERICAN CROCODILE
Crocodylus acutus

COMMON CAIMAN
Caiman crocodilus

DWARF CAIMAN
Paleosuchus palpebrosus

FALSE GHARIAL
Tomistoma schlegelii

PHILLIPINES CROCODILE
Crocodylus mindorensis

SIAMESE CROCODILE
Crocodylus siamensis

SLENDER-SNOUTED CROCODILE
Mecistops cataphractus

SMOOTH-FRONTED CAIMAN
Paleosuchus trigonatus

YACARE CAIMAN
Caiman yacare

TURTLES AND TORTOISES

AFRICAN HELMETED TURTLE
Pelomedusa subrufa

AFRICAN SPURRED TORTOISE
Geochelone sulcata

ALDABRA GIANT TORTOISE
Disochelys dussumieri

✳ *Mexican beaded lizard*

✳ *Indian cobra*

BELL'S HINGE-BACK TORTOISE
Kinixys belliana

AMERICAN RED-BELLIED TURTLE
Pseudemys rubriventris

ASIAN FOREST TORTOISE
Manouria emys

BIG-HEADED TURTLE
Platysternon megacephalum

BLACK-BREASTED LEAF TURTLE
Geoemyda spengleri

BOG TURTLE
Glyptemys muhlenbergii

BROWN TORTOISE
Manouria emys

CENTRAL AMERICAN WOOD TURTLE
Rhinoclemmys pulcherrima

COMMON SLIDER
Trachemys scripta

COMMON SNAKE-NECKED TURTLE
Chelodina longicollis

DIAMONDBACK TERRAPIN
Malaclemys terrapin

EASTERN MUD TURTLE
Kinosternon subrubrum

ELOGATED TORTOISE
Indotestudo elongata

EUROPEAN POND TURTLE
Emys orbicularis

FALSE MAP TURTLE
Graptemys pseudogeographica

✳ *Common lancehead*

FLATBACK SEA TURTLE
Natator depressus

FLORIDA SOFTSHELL TURTLE
Apalone ferox

FOREST HINGE-BACK TORTOISE
Kinixys erosa

GIANT SNAKE-NECKED TURTLE
Cheldonia expansa

GIANT SOUTH AMERICAN RIVER TURTLE
Podocnemis expansa

GOPHER TORTOISE
Gopherus polyphemus

GREEN SEA TURTLE
Chelonia mydas

HERMANN'S TORTOISE
Testudo hermanni

FOREST HINGE-BACK TORTOISE
Kinixys erosa

HOME'S HINGE-BACK TORTOISE
Kinixys homeana

KEMP'S RIDLEY SEA TURTLE
Lepidochelys kempii

LOGGERHEAD SEA TURTLE
Caretta caretta

MADAGASCAN BIG-HEADED TURTLE
Erymnochelys madagascariensis

NORTH AMERICAN WOOD TURTLE
Clemmys insculpta

OLIVE RIDLEY SEA TURTLE
Lepidochelys olivacea

PAINTED TURTLE
Chrysemys picta

RADIATED TORTOISE
Astrochelys radiata

RED-BELLIED SHIRT-NECKED TURTLE
Emydura subglubosa

RED-EARED TERRAPIN
Trachemys scripta elegans

RED-FOOTED TORTOISE
Chelonoidis carbonaria

PIG-NOSED TURTLE
Carettochelys insculpata

RUSSIAN TORTOISE
Testudo horsfieldi

✳ *Russell's viper*

SMOOTH SOFTSHELL TURTLE
Apalone mutica

SPUR-THIGHED TORTOISE
Testudo graeca

BURMESE STAR TORTOISE
Geochelone platynota

STINKPOT TURTLE
Sternotherus odoratus

SOUTH AMERICAN YELLOW-FOOTED TORTOISE
Chelonoidis denticulate

SOUTHEAST ASIAN BOX TURTLE
Cuora amboinensis

YELLOW MUD TURTLE
Kinosternon flavescens

YELLOW-SPOTTED AMAZON RIVER TURTLE
Podocnemis unifilis

TUATARA

BROTHERS ISLAND TUATARA
Sphenodon guntheri

NORTHERN TUATARA
Sphenodon punctatus

AMPHISBAENANS

GHANA WORM LIZARD
Cynisca kraussi

PUERTO RICAN DUSKY AMPHISBAENA
Amphisbaena hyporissor

RED WORM LIZARD
Amphisbaena alba

SLOW WORM
Anguis fragilis

SPECKLED WORM LIZARD
Amphisbaena fulginosa

✳ *Malayan water monitor*

177

Green frog

Sonoran desert toad

Mountain lake frog

Spotted salamander

Golden sedge frog

TOP TRAITS The word *amphibian* means "two lives," because these because of the food they eat. ▶ Amphibians often have the ability to change climate change. ▶ A small class of animals, amphibians include about 5,000 types

AMPHIBIANS

American green tree frog

animals typically live both on land and in water. ▶Many amphibians are toxic
their color. ▶Amphibians are sensitive to environmental changes, including
of frogs and toads, a few hundred salamanders and newts, and 170 caecilians.

ALL ABOUT AMPHIBIANS

THE AMPHIBIAN CLASS IS divided into three groups: frogs and toads, salamanders and newts, and caecilians. All are cold-blooded (relying on the temperature of their surroundings to regulate body temperature), so they share a preference for warmer climates. They also have in common a connection to the water—the place where most amphibians return every year to spawn (and where some spend their entire lives), and an essential element to their survival. Each group has unique traits and talents, too. For instance, many salamanders can detach their tails to escape predators, and grow new ones to replace them. Caecilians are excellent burrowers, with heads specially evolved for digging through dirt and for protecting mouths and eyes underground. Frogs and toads are perhaps the most dramatic example of that extraordinary amphibian experience: metamorphosis.

LIFE CYCLE

Most amphibians start life as larvae or tadpoles in water, move to land as adults, then return to the water to reproduce. During the larval stage, dramatic changes occur for many species. These changes coincide with changes in the animals' biology. For instance, anurans metamorphose from swimming tadpoles with gills into adult frogs and toads that can hop or walk on land and breathe air.

Among the thousands of species that make up the amphibian class, there are many, many exceptions to this life cycle, which is closely associated with frogs. Some frogs lay their eggs on land. Some carry their tadpoles inside their vocal sacs or on their backs. And a few seem to give birth to live young that look just like smaller versions of themselves. Many amphibians breathe through gills in those earliest days, then switch to lungs as they mature. Others keep gills all their lives, and still others lack both gills and lungs, getting all the oxygen they need through their skin.

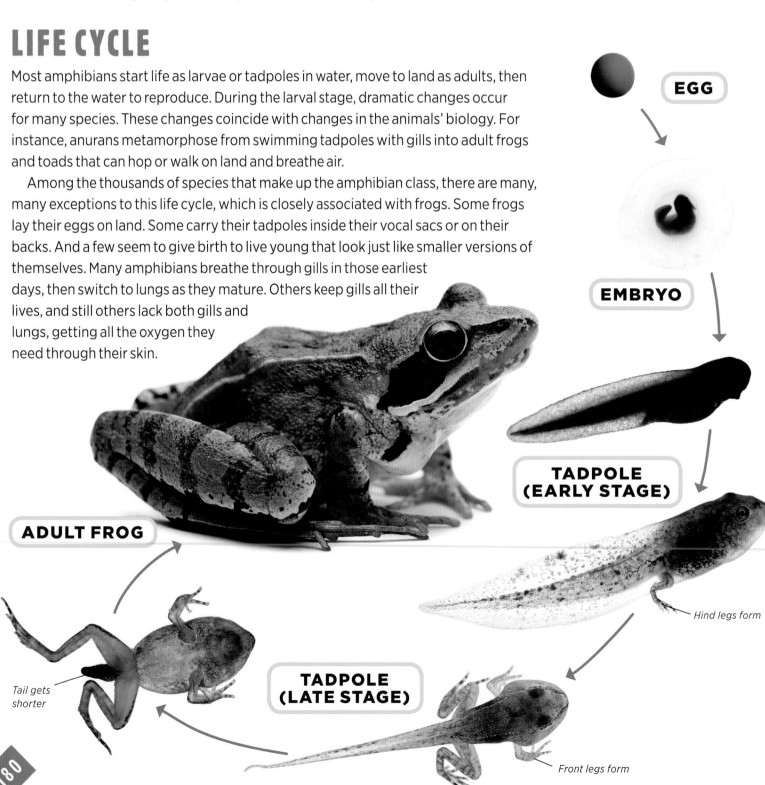

EGG

EMBRYO

TADPOLE (EARLY STAGE)

Hind legs form

ADULT FROG

Tail gets shorter

TADPOLE (LATE STAGE)

Front legs form

HABITATS

Because their permeable skin lets air and water pass through, frogs, toads, and caecilians are very sensitive to the environment. In many cases, species have evolved in tune with a specific habitat, usually a wet or humid tropical or temperate climate near a consistent water source. When that habitat alters—through pollution, forest density, or climate change—it can have a dramatic impact on the amphibians within it. Even changes in humidity can be devastating to amphibians such as the Kihansi spray toad, which depended on the spray from one specific waterfall. When the waterway was dammed and the spray was reduced, the frog became extinct in the wild. Because relationships like this are so delicate, the worldwide amphibian population is in decline. Ecosystem conservation efforts are key to protecting remaining amphibian habitats. Some are already damaged or lost forever.

American toad

INDICATOR SPECIES

With their permeable skin, amphibians are especially sensitive to climate change. Even tiny differences in water levels, temperature, and acidity can have big effects on frogs, toads, and salamanders. By paying close attention to these "indicator species," scientists are able to detect changes in the environment sooner than they could do otherwise. For instance, parasite populations may grow faster in an environment that has been polluted by chemicals, or where the climate has warmed—or both. Some scientists think this might be the case in ponds where the American toad is suffering from more mutations—such as growing extra limbs—than would normally be expected.

LIVE ACTION: *TRICOLOR POISON DART FROG*

The tricolor poison dart frog chases an ant away from its eggs. Until the eggs hatch, this is the job of the frog parents: Keep away pests, clean away fungi, and keep the eggs moist until tadpoles emerge. The eggs hatch! The male tricolor poison dart frog carries the tadpoles on his back to the pond close by. Now his parental duties are complete. But the mother's job has just started. She brings her tadpoles food as they begin their metamorphosis. In the water, they develop lungs, legs, and larger mouths. Tails and gills begin to fall away. After 12 weeks, the adult frogs hop onto land to begin the reproductive process again.

ALL ABOUT AMPHIBIANS

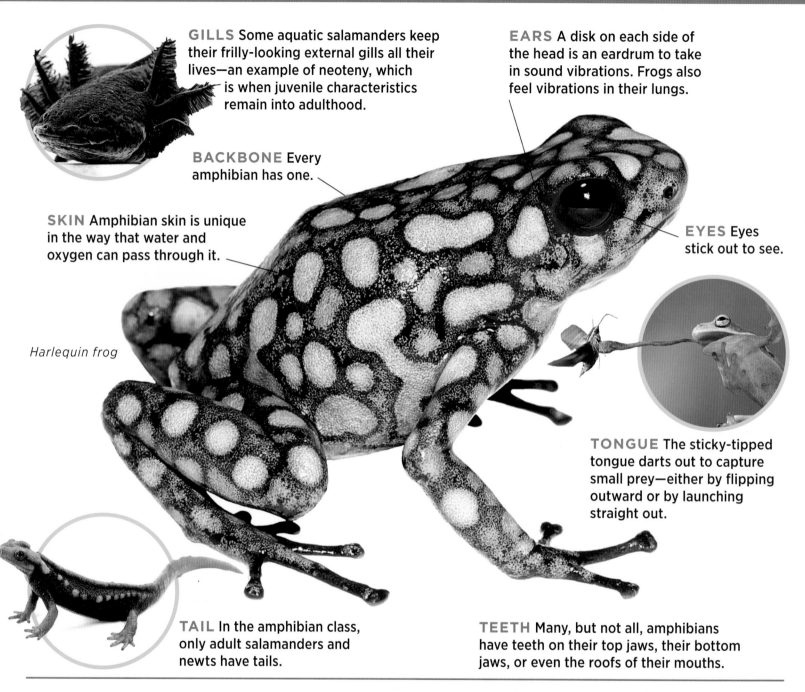

GILLS Some aquatic salamanders keep their frilly-looking external gills all their lives—an example of neoteny, which is when juvenile characteristics remain into adulthood.

EARS A disk on each side of the head is an eardrum to take in sound vibrations. Frogs also feel vibrations in their lungs.

BACKBONE Every amphibian has one.

SKIN Amphibian skin is unique in the way that water and oxygen can pass through it.

EYES Eyes stick out to see.

Harlequin frog

TONGUE The sticky-tipped tongue darts out to capture small prey—either by flipping outward or by launching straight out.

TAIL In the amphibian class, only adult salamanders and newts have tails.

TEETH Many, but not all, amphibians have teeth on their top jaws, their bottom jaws, or even the roofs of their mouths.

SENSES

An amphibian's use of its senses depends on its habitat. Amphibians that live in water may use lateral line organs to sense movement in the water, like a fish would. On land, excellent vision helps detect predators, and the position of the eyes—protruding above the head—helps many frogs see sideways and even backward. In land- and tree-dwelling frogs, a very keen sense of hearing helps tell the difference between the mating calls of different species. In some other amphibians, such as caecilians, which spend much of their time burrowing in the dirt, the eyes are shielded behind a layer of skin and even bone. A caecilian relies instead on information taken in by two small feelers or antennae.

Eastern banjo frog burrowing in sand

EVOLUTION

According to fossil record, the oldest amphibian ancestor, the temnospondyl, lived about 340 million years ago. Like long fish with feet, temnospondyls looked a lot like giant salamanders, but they could have sounded like modern frogs: They were the first animals to use sound (and hearing) to locate mates. They probably moved a bit slowly and awkwardly, but they thrived as the first predators of their kind, growing more diverse and larger—up to 15 feet long (4.6 m) or more. By around 250 million years ago, the lissamphibian group appeared, and amphibians as we know them today were born. Some modern amphibians look similar to their long-ago ancestors (although without the tails and boomerang-shaped heads that marked some early species). Others have changed dramatically to live in different environments, developing unique ways to cope with the world they live in: for mobility, they developed leg strength; for camouflage, colors and patterns; for extreme weather, the ability to burrow underground or even partially freeze until warmer weather returns.

Eryops, a primitive amphibian

FEEDING HABITS

Most adult amphibians are carnivores—they eat other animals. Burrowing caecilians thrive on earthworms, small salamanders eat insects and other arthropods, and large salamanders eat small vertebrates including birds and mammals. Frogs look for prey that fit in their mouths and that they can swallow whole.

THEY ARE THE CLASSIC AMPHIBIAN: As hatchlings from their jellylike eggs, most frogs begin as tiny, water-dwelling tadpoles. Then they undergo a dramatic transformation as they grow legs, shed tails, and transition from gills to lungs, thus taking their adult form.

Since they are cold blooded, frogs' body temperature changes depending on the temperature around them. In colder climates, many species hibernate rather than face weather that would make it hard to function.

They require less food than warm-blooded animals, so they can exist even where food (usually insects, but sometimes also other frogs, small snakes, and even mice) is scarce. That's part of why these adaptable animals are so widespread across the earth—thousands of species in all—appearing nearly everywhere except Antarctica and the open ocean, and in a wondrous variety of colors, shapes, and sizes.

AMERICAN BULLFROG
Lithobates catesbeianus

SIZE: **3.5–6 inches long (8.9–15.2 cm)**
HABITAT: **Lake, pond, river, bog; North America**
FOOD: **Insects, rodents, reptiles, birds, invertebrates, algae**

The American bullfrog is North America's largest species of frog. Its name is derived from the male's deep, booming croak that resembles the sound of a male cow or bull. They are nocturnal and can often be heard bellowing throughout the night.

BLUE POISON DART FROG
D. tinctorius "azureus"

SIZE: **1–2 inches long (2.5–5.1 cm)**
HABITAT: **Rain forest; Central and South America**
FOOD: **Ants, termites, centipedes, beetles**

Unlike many frogs, toxic species like this one sleep at night and keep busy by hunting and defending their territory during the day—all the better for predators to see the striking colors that warn: You won't like the taste of me! Just a touch of the poisonous secretions on its skin can kill many small animals.

EMERALD GLASS FROG
Espadarana prosoblepon

SIZE: **1–1.5 inches long (2.5–3.8 cm)**
HABITAT: **River, rain forest; Central America**
FOOD: **Insects**

Wondering what this frog had for dinner? Just take a look inside its transparent belly. Despite their glasslike appearance, these frogs are surprisingly tough: When males fight over territory, they wrestle while suspended from a tree. The battle—which may last up to an hour—ends when the loser drops to the ground, lying flat to acknowledge defeat before hopping away from the victor's turf.

Animal Antics

Not all frogs have tongues—but in those that do, the tongue is usually attached to the front of the mouth. It flips out to grab prey, then folds back in.

TOMATO FROG
Dyscophus antongilii
SIZE: 2.5–4 inches long (6.4–10.2 cm)
HABITAT: Leafy or disturbed ground near lake and stream; northeastern Madagascar
FOOD: Insects

It's not hard to see where this frog gets its name: Tomato frogs are round, red, and shiny—a warning to predators. A sticky white mucus secreted from the skin acts like glue, gumming up the eyes and nose of its attackers. Tomato frogs are ambush predators. They hide among the leaves on the ground, waiting for prey to come within range.

RED-EYED TREE FROG
Agalychnis callidryas
SIZE: 1.5–3 inches long (3.8–7.6 cm)
HABITAT: Tropical rain forest; Mexico, Central America, Colombia
FOOD: Insects

The red-eyed tree frog is known for its striking colors. While sleeping, it tucks in its legs and closes its eyes so its green back blends with the tree leaves. If a predator does come near, the flash of color as the frog opens its eyes and hops away may startle the hunter.

AMAZON BLUE MILK FROG
Trachycephalus resinifictrix
SIZE: 2.5–4 inches long (6.4–10.2 cm)
HABITAT: Rain forest canopy; northern South America
FOOD: Insects, small anthropods

The irises of this frog's eyes demonstrate the variety that makes the species so unique. Also known for the toxic milky secretions it uses to ward off predators, the milk frog has a unique way of feeding their young: The male fertilizes one batch of eggs, then has another female lay eggs—unfertilized—to feed the tadpoles.

AFRICAN CLAWED FROG
Xenopus laevis
SIZE: 2–5 inches long (5.1–12.7 cm)
HABITAT: Pond, river; sub-Saharan Africa
FOOD: Scavenged food, including living or dead animals and organic waste

This scavenger will eat pretty much anything it can find. It has no tongue and no teeth. Instead, it relies on the sharp claws of its hind feet to tear food into small pieces, which it pushes into its mouth with its front feet. It relies on touch, smell, and vibrations to sense its surroundings.

FUN FACT

The eyeballs of many frogs do double-duty: They not only have excellent perception for color and depth, but also can descend into the head while the frog is swallowing to help push food along.

TOADS

SHORT, STOUT, TOOTHLESS, AND TOXIC

WHAT'S THE DIFFERENCE BETWEEN a frog and a toad? Not much, actually. Both are anurans—tailless amphibians—with similar ways of hunting, eating, and breeding. The names "frog" and "toad" were originally used to distinguish just a few species of anurans from one another. As thousands of new species were discovered, they were grouped largely by which of those originals they most resembled.

Telling a frog from a toad is not an exact science. Usually, though, it's possible to spot a toad by its rougher, drier skin, shorter legs, and stouter body. While most frogs have teeth, toads don't. Toads also (typically) don't hop as well or as far as frogs do, and they produce toxins to defend against predators. There is another thing frogs and toads have in common: amazing diversity.

SMOOTH-SIDED TOAD
Bufo guttatus

SIZE: 5–10 inches long (12.7–25.4 cm)
HABITAT: Tropical forest, freshwater marsh; South America
FOOD: Insects, invertebrates, small mammals

Part of the group known as "true toads," this species has the classic toad features like a stocky body, short legs, and no teeth or nails. Its speckled brown color works as camouflage, making it tough to spot among leaf matter on the forest floor. The toxins on its skin can cause heart failure in predators.

CANE TOAD
Rhinella marina

SIZE: 4–6 inches long (10.2–15.2 cm)
HABITAT: Tropical forest; southern United States, Central America, northern South America
FOOD: Insects, snails, plants

This big eater will consume just about anything: living animals, dead animals, plants, and even pet food left outside homes. This is one reason it has thrived as a species; another is the white, milky poison that oozes from its back. When under attack, the toad puffs up its body and stands on its legs to look bigger—but if that doesn't work, it just stays still and waits for the poison to do its work.

MEXICAN BURROWING TOAD
Rhinophrynus dorsalis

SIZE: 3–3.5 inches long (7.6–8.9 cm)
HABITAT: Underground burrow; Texas, Mexico, Central America, Costa Rica
FOOD: Termites, ants

Using its stout head and the shovel-like parts of its front feet, this toad digs its way underground, where it lives most of its life. There it feeds on termites with its short tongue, which it sticks straight out like an anteater. It comes out to breed, laying eggs in puddles after a heavy rain.

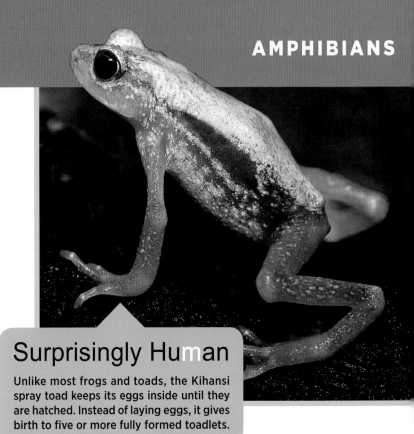

HARLEQUIN TOAD
Atelopus varius

SIZE: **1–1.5 inches long (2.5–3.8 cm)**
HABITAT: **Tropical forest; Central and South America**
FOOD: **Insects**

Like toxic frogs, this toad warns predators of its dangerous poison with bright colors and eye-catching patterns. It uses its eye-catching design to attract mates, drawing attention by moving body and hands. Colors vary toad to toad: they may be bright pink or other colors such as yellow, orange, or green.

Surprisingly Human

Unlike most frogs and toads, the Kihansi spray toad keeps its eggs inside until they are hatched. Instead of laying eggs, it gives birth to five or more fully formed toadlets.

GOLDEN TOAD
Bufo periglenes

SIZE: 1.5–2.5 inches long (3.8–6.4 cm)
HABITAT: Cloud forest; Costa Rica
FOOD: Unknown; most likely small invertebrates

The golden toad was first discovered in the 1960s in Costa Rica, and has only been spotted on a single hill. The male of the species has golden-orange coloring; females are much darker—olive green or nearly black. Neither has been seen in decades, and the species is now thought to be extinct.

MIDWIFE TOAD
Alytes obstetricans

SIZE: **1.5–2 inches long (3.8–5.1 cm)**
HABITAT: **Temperate forest, stone wall, river, pond; Europe, northwestern Africa**
FOOD: **Insects**

The males of this species carry strings of eggs on their backs, protecting their offspring until they are ready to hatch. Then they enter the water so the tadpoles can swim out.

SURINAM TOAD
Pipa pipa

SIZE: **4–5 inches long (10.2–12.7 cm)**
HABITAT: **Tropical forest, swamp, freshwater marsh; South America**
FOOD: **Worms, insects, fish, crustaceans**

This flat toad is an unusual breeder: During fertilization, eggs are pressed onto the female's back, which then grows a protective skin over them. In their pockets, they can safely mature until they are ready to emerge as froglets.

The aggressive chytrid fungus threatens amphibian species the world over, and has already brought many to extinction. Scientists are now studying ways to contain the fungus, including medicating water by amphibian habitats.

187

ORIENTAL FIRE-BELLIED TOAD

With its ordinary-looking green-and-black back, the fire-bellied toad blends right in with its forest habitat—as long as it remains crouched on the forest floor or resting on the bed of its favorite stream. But when under threat, it stretches its front legs and arches its back to show off the colors on its belly. The bright red-and-black pattern on its underside is a signal to predators of toxic secretions on its skin. Sometimes it even flips over completely, to send an extraclear message: This toad is not for eating! This trick may be one reason why it is such a successful species in its native Asia, living up to 20 years in the wild.

ABOUT ME!

I am a male Oriental fire-bellied toad. During mating season, I make a barking croak to let females know I'm nearby. But if my croak brings a predator close, I'll flip over to show that I am definitely not a tasty meal.

7 FACTS ABOUT THE ORIENTAL FIRE-BELLIED TOAD

▸ Lays up to 300 eggs
▸ Male's mating call sounds like dog's barking
▸ Has white belly when young
▸ Eggs hang from plant stems
▸ Can hibernate on land or in water
▸ Has bumpy, warty back
▸ Has triangular-shaped pupils

A SALAMANDER MAY LOOK like a lizard, but it is every bit an amphibian. Most species have a life cycle that begins in the water and continues on land, followed by adulthood either in water, on land, or in trees. Permeable skin lets air and water in, and sometimes lets toxic or distasteful fluids out to protect against predators.

Some salamanders skip the middle stage of metamorphosis, and some keep traits of the juvenile even as adults. Gills, for instance, may remain throughout the life cycle, or may close up in species that breathe with lungs or through their skin.

All salamanders feature a hardworking tail, which helps them swim, climb, or reproduce, and stores important nutrients. It can slash against predators and even detach if caught—a new tail will grow in its place within a few weeks.

MUDPUPPY
Necturus maculosus

SIZE: 7.5–13 inches long (19.1–33 cm)
HABITAT: River, pond, stream; Canada, United States
FOOD: Crayfish, insect larvae, small fish, eggs, worms, other amphibians

Mudpuppies are designed for an aquatic life, with flattened, fin-edged tails and external gills. In the rivers and streams where they are found, mudpuppies may be found walking along the streambed. When predators are near, they hide under rocks or logs until the danger passes. Underground caves provide protection for their eggs, which are stuck to the ceiling by the female to hatch in the spring.

 FUN FACT Fire salamanders like to shelter in damp logs. When, in days past, people placed those logs onto a fire, the salamanders could be seen running out of the flames.

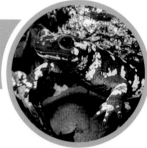

AXOLOTL
Ambystoma mexicanum

SIZE: 9–12 inches long (22.9–30.5 cm)
HABITAT: Lake; near Mexico City
FOOD: Mollusks, worms, insect larvae, fish, crustaceans

This Mexican species is a close relative of the tiger salamander—but unlike its cousin, the axolotl does not complete its metamorphosis. Instead, it retains its gills and a dorsal fin. The feathery rakers that stick out from the gills add surface area to gather more oxygen. They are most easily seen on the pale-colored juveniles.

RED SALAMANDER
Pseudotriton ruber

SIZE: 4–7 inches long (10.2–17.8 cm)
HABITAT: Under rock, log, leaf litter near stream; eastern United States
FOOD: Worms, insects, spiders

After hatching, members of this species remain in the larval stage for two to three years before becoming full adults. As adults, they can wander far from their watery birthplace and have offspring of their own.

TIGER SALAMANDER
Ambystoma tigrinum

SIZE: 7–13 inches long (17.8–33 cm)
HABITAT: Near pond, lake; North America
FOOD: Insects, worms, frogs

This salamander is named for its striped markings, but some adults display spots instead. It is the world's largest salamander on land, reaching lengths of over a foot. During the daytime, tiger salamanders sleep in underground burrows near bodies of water, emerging at night to hunt.

RED-BACKED SALAMANDER
Plethodon cinereus

SIZE: 2–4 inches long (5.1–10.2 cm)
HABITAT: Moist area beneath rock, log, leaf litter; United States, Canada
FOOD: Mites, spiders, insects, centipedes, earthworms, flies, beetles, snails

This land-dwelling, lungless salamander breathes through its skin. It has to remain in moisture; thus, it can only climb trees after a rainfall. Otherwise it hunts close to the ground, amid fallen leaves or under rocks and logs—wherever the conditions are damp. Territorial like most salamanders, it marks its home area with scent and droppings.

THREE-LINED SALAMANDER
Eurycea guttolineata

SIZE: 4–6.5 inches long (10.2–16.5 cm)
HABITAT: Temperate forest, river, swamp; southeastern United States
FOOD: Insects, spiders, slugs, other invertebrates

The long tail of this North American species is close to two-thirds of its body length. When threatened, the salamander may lift the tail up in a defensive posture. The three-lined salamander will migrate in the wild, moving uphill in times of heavy rain and downhill in drier weather.

FIRE SALAMANDER
Salamandra algira

SIZE: 7–9.5 inches long (17.8–24.1 cm)
HABITAT: Oak and pine forest; Europe
FOOD: Insects, earthworms, spiders, slugs, small frogs

Bright colors on the fire salamander's body mean one thing to predators: poison! Its back contains a line of glands that give off a toxic substance. The fire salamander lives on land, where its relatively long legs help it move about. It only returns to water to give birth to live young. It is the only salamander to do this—all other species lay eggs.

In Japan, the giant salamander is considered a national treasure. In the waterways where it lives, special recesses have been constructed to mimic the burrows where it likes to breed, and the law forbids feeding or handling giant salamanders without special permission.

OLM

The first known reference to an olm is in a book published in the year 1689, at which time many thought it was a baby dragon. It's not hard to see why! With its transparent skin, colorful external gills, long body, and habit of living in caves, the olm certainly bears a resemblance to a mythical creature. But not only is the olm real—it is a celebrated animal in some parts of the world. Olms are considered a national treasure in Slovenia, where tourists can take an "Olm Tour" at Postojna Cave.

6 FACTS ABOUT THE OLM

- ▶ **Can live without eating food for ten years**
- ▶ **Is sightless but can sense light**
- ▶ **Lives its entire life in water**
- ▶ **Swallows its prey whole**
- ▶ **Takes up to 25 days to lay its eggs**
- ▶ **Can live as deep as 985 feet (300 m) underground**

ABOUT ME!

I am an olm. I am unique among amphibians. I live my whole life underwater in dark caves. I don't have eyes that see, but I don't need them. And I'm white or a pinkish beige because there's no need for skin color camouflage where I live.

A SUBGROUP OF SALAMANDERS, newts share the usual salamander traits: long bodies, four equal-length legs, and the ability to breathe in water or on land. However, their skin is drier and rough instead of slimy. Newts are also an impressive example of the salamander's ability to re-grow lost limbs: Many can re-grow not just tails and legs, but also eyes, jaws, backbones, intestines, and even hearts. Among aquatic species, many newts also have feathery external gills that give them a striking appearance.

GREAT CRESTED NEWT
Triturus cristatus

SIZE: 4–5.5 inches long (10.2–14 cm)
HABITAT: Wooded area; Great Britain, northern Europe
FOOD: Tadpoles, froglets, snails, other newts

As a newt, this dramatic-looking species has rougher skin than other salamanders. It lives on land, returning to water only to breed. There the female lays hundreds of eggs in a careful and time-consuming process: About three per day are laid and then individually wrapped in underwater leaves for protection.

EASTERN RED-SPOTTED NEWT
Notophthalmus viridescens

SIZE: 2.5–5.5 inches long (6.4–14 cm)
HABITAT: Body of water in forest; eastern North America
FOOD: Small invertebrates

This unique species takes on a new name during its juvenile stage: "red eft." The rough-skinned eft emerges from the water to live for one to several years on land. When its development is complete, the adult red-spotted newt returns to the water to breed. If they feel they are in danger of a predator, they secrete a toxic substance for protection.

EMPEROR NEWT
Tylototriton shanjing

SIZE: 4.5–6 inches long (11.4–15.2 cm)
HABITAT: Pond in subtropical forest; China
FOOD: Earthworms, crickets, other invertebrates

When under threat, the venomous emperor newt can poke its rib bones through the colorful spots on its back, then use them to stab and inject poison into predators.

CALIFORNIA NEWT
Taricha torosa

SIZE: 5–8 inches long (12.7–20.3 cm)
HABITAT: Wet forest, grassland; coastal mountains of California
FOOD: Worms, snails, slugs, other invertebrates, newt larvae

The rough, red-brown skin on the back of the California newt turns slimy black in breeding males. Like other land-dwelling salamanders, California newts migrate to water to lay eggs. Scientists believe each community returns to the pool where it was born—a journey that can take several weeks. When predators are near, California newt parents can send chemical signals that tell their larvae to hide.

CAECILIANS NO FEET, SHY

CAECILIANS ARE THE LEAST WELL-KNOWN of the amphibian class. In fact, if you saw a caecilian in the wild, you might assume it was a snake or an earthworm. It's easy to understand the confusion. After all, most caecilian species spend almost all their lives hidden away in underground burrows.

When they do come out long enough to be spotted and studied, they prove to be creatures of contradiction: They are classified as tetrapodal—four footed—but have no feet at all. They have eyes, but have so little need of them that the sockets are often covered over with skin or even bone. Scientists have identified around 120 species so far, but there is still a lot to learn about these mysterious animals.

CAYENNE CAECILIAN
Typhlonectes compressicauda

SIZE: 1–2 feet long (0.3–0.6 m)
HABITAT: Bank of stream and river; South America
FOOD: Shrimp, insect larvae, small fish

This social caecilian lives in group burrows. A flattened body and raised, fin-like ridge on its back help it swim in the waterways of the Amazon, where it hunts its small prey. To deter predators, the Cayenne caecilian secretes a toxic substance from its back. Conditions are more hospitable inside its body, where offspring nibble on the female's nutrient-rich insides as they prepare for birth.

RINGED CAECILIAN
Siphonops annulatus

SIZE: 11–17 inches long (28–43.2 cm)
HABITAT: Tropical and subtropical forest, savanna; South America
FOOD: Worms, termites, other invertebrates

The rings that show clearly on this amphibian are a feature common to all caecilians. They are actually inside the body, attached to the backbone. As with other caecilians, the skin that sheathes these rings can excrete a toxic substance to defend against predators. In their earliest days, a ringed caecilian's offspring feed off of her skin—tearing away a layer in a seven-minute feeding frenzy. The skin grows back within a few days so the process can repeat.

Surprisingly Human

Unlike their egg-spawning relatives, female Cayenne caecilians are pregnant for eight months—nearly as long as humans—before giving birth to live young.

GABOON CAECILIAN
Geotrypetes seraphini

SIZE: 8–15 inches long (20.3–38.1 cm)
HABITAT: Underground burrow in forest, farm, wetland; western Africa
FOOD: Earthworms, other invertebrates

The Gaboon caecilian is blind and limbless, but it is not defenseless. It has sharp teeth, which it uses to either bite repeatedly or grab prey with its jaws and pull it into its underground burrow. It can twist its body rapidly to complete the task of killing its food before eating it.

SNACK ATTACK

Caecilians may not be able to see their prey, but they have another trait that helps them catch things to eat. They have a mouthful of needle-sharp teeth that curve inward, useful for grasping prey. They aren't for chewing, though: termites, worms, snakes, frogs, and other prey are swallowed whole.

AT THE FRESHWATER

Amphibians need moist conditions to survive and thrive, so ponds are an ideal habitat for them. A great variety of species either lives in this freshwater habitat or goes there to breed.

Common toad

Alpine newt

Mallard duck

European grass frog

Breathtaking
Lungless salamanders breathe through their skin, which needs to be moist to absorb oxygen.

Moving along
The northern leopard frog leaves the comfort of its pond habitat to forage for food in grassy areas.

Grotto salamander

Vocal performance
The male spring peeper uses its vocal sac to make loud peeping noises. A group of peepers sounds like a loud chorus.

Pacman frog

Laos warty newt

Snapping turtle

POND

Hiding out
Spotted salamanders are nighttime hunters. They burrow under fallen leaves, logs, and mossy tree trunks to rest during the day.

Eastern American toad

Crocodile newt

European green toad

Hour glass tree frog

Dragonflies
Emperor dragonflies visit ponds to breed. The female deposits eggs into the water, where they hatch into nymphs.

Arroyo toad

Brrrr!
Wood frogs survive being partially frozen in subfreezing northern winters. They thaw out in the spring.

Construction
Beavers build dams with mud, stones, and sticks. Some cause flooding, but beaver dams also help keep water clean.

There are more than 5,000 known amphibian species in the world. Here are some interesting ones to learn more about.

FROGS

AMAMI TIP-NOSED FROG
Odorrana amamiensis

AMERICAN BULLFROG
Rana catesbeiana

ASIAN HORNED FROG
Megophrys montana

AUSTRALIAN GREEN TREE FROG
Litoria caerulea

BARKING TREE FROG
Hyla gratiosa

BEAUTIFUL TORRENT FROG
Amolops formosus

BLUE-SIDED TREE FROG
Agalychnis annae

BOOROOLONG FROG
Litoria booroolongensis

BRIMLEY'S CHORUS FROG
Pseudacris brimleyi

BROWN NEW ZEALAND FROG
Litoria ewingii

CARBINE FROG
Mixophyes carbinensis

CHACOAN BURROWING FROG
Chacophrys pierottii

CHINESE TREE FROG
Hyla chinensis

CINNAMON-BELLIED REED FROG
Hyperolius cinnamomeventris

COASTAL TAILED FROG
Ascaphus truei

COLUMBIAN SPOTTED FROG
Rana luteiventris

COMMON COQUÍ
Eleutherodactylus coqui

COMMON PARSLEY FROG
Pelodytes punctatus

COPE'S GRAY TREE FROG
Hyla chrysoscelis

CRAWFISH FROG
Rana areolata

CROWNED FOREST FROG
Astylosternus diadematus

CRUCIFIX FROG
Notaden bennettii

CUBAN TREE FROG
Osteopilus septentrionalis

CUYABA DWARF FROG
Eupemphix nattereri

DAINTY GREEN TREE FROG
Litoria gracilenta

DELICATE SPINY REED FROG
Afrixalus delicatus

DESERT FROG
Crinia deserticola

DORIS SWANSON'S POISON DART FROG
Ranitomeya dorisswansoni

DRING'S HORNED FROG
Xenophrys dringi

EASTERN BANJO FROG
Limnodynastes dumerilii

EASTERN NARROW-MOUTHED FROG
Gastrophryne carolinensis

EMERALD FOREST FROG
Hylorina sylvatica

✳ *Rough-skinned newt*

✳ *Red-backed poison dart frog*

EUROPEAN FROG
Rana temporaria

EUROPEAN TREE FROG
Hyla arborea

FLEA-FROG
Brachycephalus didactylus

FLORIDA BOG FROG
Rana okaloosae

GIANT BULLFROG
Limnodynastes interioris

GIANT STUMP-TOED FROG
Stumpffia grandis

GLIDING LEAF FROG
Agalychnis saltator

GOLDEN BANANA FROG
Afrixalus aureus

GOLFODULCEAN POISON FROG
Phyllobates vittatus

GOLIATH FROG
Conraua goliath

GRAY TREE FROG
Hyla versicolor

GREEN AND BLACK POISON DART FROG
Dendrobates auratus

GREEN AND GOLDEN BELL FROG
Litoria aurea

GREEN FROG
Rana clamitans

GREEN TREE FROG
Hyla cinerea

GUIANA SHIELD FROG
Adelophryne gutturosa

HAMILTON'S FROG
Leiopelma hamiltoni

HARLEQUIN FLYING FROG
Rhacophorus pardalis

HARLEQUIN POISON DART FROG
Dendrobates histrionicus

HORNED MARSUPIAL FROG
Gastrotheca cornuta

HOURGLASS TREE FROG
Dendropsophus ebraccatus

IVORY COAST WARTY FROG
Acanthixalus sonjae

JAPANESE FLYING FROG
Rhacophorus arboreus

JAPANESE TREE FROG
Hyla japonica

JAVAN GLIDING FROG
Rhacophorus reinwardtii

JAVAN HORNED FROG
Megophrys montana

KNYSNA SPINY REED FROG
Afrixalus knysnae

LAKE TITICACA FROG
Telmatobius coleus

LARUT TORRENT FROG
Amolops larutensis

LEAF GREEN TREE FROG
Litoria phyllochroa

LEMON YELLOW TREE FROG
Hyla savignyi

LIMOSA HARLEQUIN FROG
Atelopus limosus

LONG-NOSED FROG
Megophrys nasuta

MADAGASCAR JUMPING FROG
Aglyptodactylus madagascariensis

MALABAR FLYING FROG
Phacophorus malabaricus

✳ *Fowler's toad*

MALAYSIAN PAINTED FROG
Kaloula pulchra

MARBLED FROG
Limnodynastes convexiusculus

MARSUPIAL FROG
Assa darlingtoni

MEXICAN WHITE-LIPPED FROG
Leptodactylus fragilis

MISFIT TREE FROG
Agalychnis saltator

MONTE IBERIA ELEUTH FROG
Eleutherodactylus iberia

MOUNTAIN CHICKEN FROG
Leptodactylus fallax

MOUNTAIN CHORUS FROG
Pseudacris brachyphona

MOUNTAIN TREE FROG
Hyla eximia

MOUNTAIN YELLOW-LEGGED FROG
Rana muscosa

MUSTACHED FROG
Leptodactylus mystacinus

NORTHERN CORROBOREE FROG
Pseudophryne pengilleyi

NORTHERN LEOPARD FROG
Rana pipiens

NORTHERN RED-LEGGED FROG
Rana aurora

ORANGE-BELLIED FROG
Geocrinia vitellina

ORNATE NARROW-MOUTHED FROG
Microhyla ornata

PACIFIC CHORUS FROG
Pseudacris regilla

PAINTED FROG
Discoglossus pictus

PEPPER FROG
Leptodactylus labyrinthicus

PICKEREL FROG
Rana palustris

PINE BARRENS TREE FROG
Hyla andersonii

RED-BANDED POISON DART FROG
Oophaga lehmanni

RIO ROCKET FROG
Allobates olfersioides

ROBBER FROG
Craugastor omiltemanus

ROCKY MOUNTAIN TAILED FROG
Ascaphus montanus

SAHARA FROG
Rana saharica

SARDINIAN TREE FROG
Hyla sarda

SEYCHELLES FROG
Sooglossus gardineri

✳ *Phantasmal poison frog*

SHOVEL-NOSED FROG
Hemisus marmoratus

SOLOMON ISLANDS HORNED FROG
Ceratobatrachus guentheri

SPOTTED NURSE FROG
Allobates algorei

SOUTH AMERICAN HORNED FROG
Ceratophrys cornuta

SOUTHERN CORROBOREE FROG
Pseudophryne corroboree

SPOTTED CHORUS FROG
Pseudacris clarkii

SPOTTED GRASS FROG
Limnodynastes tasmaniensis

SPOTTED SNOUT-BURROWER
Hemisus guttatus

SQUIRREL TREE FROG
Hyla squirella

STRECKER'S CHORUS FROG
Pseudacris streckeri

STRIPED SPINY REED FROG
Afrixalus dorsalis

✳ *Green toad*

SUNSET FROG
Spicospina flammocaerulea

WESTERN BULLFROG
Limnodynastes dorsalis

TURTLE FROG
Myobatrachus gouldii

TUSKED FROG
Adelotus brevis

WHITE-BELLIED FROG
Geocrinia alba

YELLOW-HEADED POISON FROG
Dendrobates leucomelas

YELLOW-SPOTTED BELL FROG
Litoria castanea

YUCATAN SHOVEL-HEADED TREE FROG
Tiprion petasatus

✳ *Long-tailed salamander*

TOADS

AFRICAN COMMON TOAD
Amietophrynus gutturalis

AFRICAN TREE TOAD
Nectophryne afra

AMERICAN DISCOGLOSSOID TOAD
Ascaphus truei

ARROYO TOAD
Anaxyrus californicus

BEDDOME'S TOAD
Duttaphrynus beddomii

BOREAL TOAD
Anaxyrus boreas

BOULENGER'S STUBFOOT TOAD
Atelopus boulengeri

BLACK-SPECTACLED TOAD
Duttaphrynus melanostictus

CARABAYA STUBFOOT TOAD
Atelopus erythropus

CLOUD FOREST STUBFOOT TOAD
Atelopus sorianoi

COMMON SPADEFOOT TOAD
Neobatrachus sudelli

CRESTED TOAD
Bufo divergens

DEAD-LEAF TOAD
Amietophrynus brauni

EASTERN LEOPARD TOAD
Amietophrynus pardalis

ELEGANT NARROWMOUTH TOAD
Gastrophryne elegans

EUROPEAN GREEN TOAD
Bufo viridis

✳ *Asiatic toad*

✳ *Splash-backed poison dart frog*

* *Spotted-tail cave salamander*

FLAT-BACKED TOAD
Amietophrynus maculates

FOUR-DIGIT TOAD
Didynamipus sjostedti

GREAT PLAINS TOAD
Anaxyrus cognatus

HELMETED WATER TOAD
Caudiverbera caudiverbera

HIMALAYAN TOAD
Bufo himalayanus

HOUSTON TOAD
Bufo houstonensis

KADAMAIAN STREAM TOAD
Ansonia hanitschi

LARGE TOADLET
Pseudophryne major

LICHUAN BELL TOAD
Bombina lichuanensis

MALAYAN TREE TOAD
Pedostibes hosii

MALCOLM'S ETHIOPIA TOAD
Altiphrynoides malcolmi

MAURITANIAN TOAD
Amietophrynus mauritanicus

MEXICAN ARROYO TOAD
Anaxyrus californicus

NILE DELTA TOAD
Amietophrynus kassasii

NORTHERN SPADEFOOT TOAD
Notaden melanoscaphus

PETERS' TOADLET
Leptodactylus petersii

SEUDO FOREST TOAD
Nectophrynoides pseudotornieri

PUERTO RICAN CRESTED TOAD
Peltophryne lemur

* *Kokoe poison frog*

REDNOSE STUBFOOT TOAD
Atelopus oxyrhynchus

RED-SPOTTED TOAD
Anaxyrus punctatus

SAND TOAD
Vandijkophrynus angusticeps

SPINY-FINGERED HORNED TOAD
Xenophrys spinata

SPINY SLENDER TOAD
Ansonia spinulifer

QUITO STUBFOOT TOAD
Atelopus ignescens

WHITE-LIPPED SLENDER TOAD
Ansonia albomaculata

WOODHOUSE'S TOAD
Anaxyrus woodhousii

WYOMING TOAD
Anaxyrus baxteri

YOSEMITE TOAD
Anaxyrus canorus

SALAMANDERS

ALPINE STREAM SALAMANDER
Batrachuperus tibetanus

APPALACHIAN SALAMANDER
Plethodon jordani

BLUE RIDGE TWO-LINED SALAMANDER
Eurycea wilderae

BLUE-SPOTTED SALAMANDER
Ambystoma laterale

CALIFORNIA GIANT SALAMANDER
Dicamptodon ensatus

CHINESE GIANT SALAMANDER
Andrias davidianus

COPE'S GIANT SALAMANDER
Dicamptodon copei

DWARF SIREN
Pseudobranchus striatus

DWARF WATERDOG
Necturus punctatus

FISCHER'S LONG-TAILED CLAWED SALAMANDER
Onychodactylus fischeri

FLATWOODS SALAMANDER
Ambystoma cingulatum

FORMOSAN SALAMANDER
Hynobius formosanus

FOUR-TOED SALAMANDER
Hamidactylium scutatum

GREATER SIREN
Siren lacertina

GOLD-STRIPED SALAMANDER
Chioglossa lusitanica

GULF COAST WATERDOG
Necturus beyeri

IDAHO GIANT SALAMANDER
Dicamptodon aterrimus

JAPANESE CLAWED SALAMANDER
Onychodactylus japonicus

JAPANESE GIANT SALAMANDER
Andrias japonicus

JEFFERSON'S SALAMANDER
Ambystoma jeffersonianum

* *Eastern spadefoot toad*

JORDAN'S SALAMANDER
Plethodon jordani

LONGDONG STREAM SALAMANDER
Batrachuperus longdongensis

LONG-TAILED SALAMANDER
Erycea longicauda

LONG-TOED SALAMANDER
Ambystoma macrodactylum

MARBLED SALAMANDER
Ambystoma opacum

MOLE SALAMANDER
Ambystoma taploideum

NEUSE RIVER WATERDOG
Necturus lewisi

NORTHWESTERN SALAMANDER
Ambystoma gracile

OKI SALAMANDER
Hynobiusokiensis

OLYMPIC TORRENT SALAMANDER
Rhyacotriton olympicus

ONE-TOED AMPHIUMA
Amphiuma pholeter

PACIFIC GIANT SALAMANDER
Dicamptodon tenebrosus

RETICULATED FLATWOODS SALAMANDER
Ambystoma bishopi

RIO GRANDE LESSER SIREN
Siren intermedia

SALVIN'S MUSHROOMTONGUE SALAMANDER
Bolitoglossa salvini

SIBERIAN SALAMANDER
Salamadrella keyserlingii

SLIMY SALAMANDER
Plethodon glutinosus

SONAN'S SALAMANDER
Hynobius sonani

SPOTTED SALAMANDER
Ambystoma maculatum

* *Dyeing poison dart frog*

* *Striped poison dart frog*

THREE-TOED AMPHIUMA
Amphiuma tridactylum

TOKYO SALAMANDER
Hynobius tokyoensis

TWO-TOED AMPHIUMA
Amphiuma means

WESTERN CHINESE MOUNTAIN SALAMANDER
Batrachuperus pinchonii

NEWTS

ALGERIAN RIBBED NEWT
Pleurodeles nebulosus

ANDERSON'S CROCODILE NEWT
Echinotriton andersoni

AZERBAIJAN NEWT
Neurergus crocatus

BLACK KNOBBY NEWT
Tylototriton asperrimus

BLACK-SPOTTED NEWT
Notophthalmus meridionalis

CARPATHIAN NEWT
Lissotriton montandoni

CHINHAI SPINY NEWT
Echinotriton chinhaiensis

COAST RANGE NEWT
Taricha torosa

DAYANG NEWT
Ichthyophis monochrous

EASTERN NEWT
Notophthalmus viridescens

FIRE-BELLIED NEWT
Cynops cyanurus

IBERIAN NEWT
Lissotriton boscai

ITALIAN NEWT
Lissotriton italicus

* *Red-headed poison dart frog*

KURDISTAN NEWT
Neuregus microspilotus

MARBLED NEWT
Triturus marmoratus

PALMATE NEWT
Lissotriton helveticus

REDBELLY NEWT
Taricha rivularis

* *Long-toed salamander*

ROUGHSKIN NEWT
Taricha granulosa

SHARP-RIBBED NEWT
Pleurodeles waltl

SMOOTH NEWT
Lissotriton vulgaris

SOUTHERN BANDED NEWT
Ommatotriton vittatus

SPOTLESS STOUT NEWT
Pachytriton labiatus

SPOT-TAILED WARTY NEWT
Paramesotriton caudopunctatus

STRIPED NEWT
Notophthalmus perstriatus

SWORD-TAILED NEWT
Cynops ensicauda

YUNNAN LAKE NEWT
Cynops wolterstorffi

CAECILIANS

ARMORED CAECILIAN
Caecilia armata

BANDED CAECILIAN
Scolecomorphus vittatus

BEARDED CAECILIAN
Caecilia tentaculata

* *Boettger's caecilian*

BLACK CAECILIAN
Ichthyophis monochrous

BOKERMANN'S CAECILIAN
Caecilia bokermanni

CHANGAMWE CAECILIAN
Boulengerula changamwensis

ELONGATED CAECILIAN
Ichthyophis elongatus

FALSE ANGEL'S CAECILIAN
Geotrypetes pseudoangeli

* *Giant leaf frog*

GOA CAECILIAN
Gegeneophis goaensis

KHUMHZI STRIPED ICHTHYOPHIS
Ichthyophis khumhzi

LA BONITA CAECILIAN
Caecilia orientalis

LAKE TANGANYIKA CAECILIAN
Scolecomorphus kirkii

MARBLED CAECILIAN
Epicrionops marmoratus

MEXICAN CAECILIAN
Dermophis mexicanus

MOUNT OKU CAECILIAN
Crotaphatrema lamottei

NORMANDIA CAECILIAN
Caecilia crassisquama

REINHARDT'S CAECILIAN
Mimosiphonops reinhardti

* *Black-legged dart frog*

RIO LITA CAECILIAN
Caecilia nigricans

SAGALLA CAECILIAN
Boulengerula niedeni

SHARP-NOSED CAECILIAN
Hypogeophis rostratus

TWO-COLORED CAECILIAN
Epicrionops bicolor

WHITEBELLY CAECILIAN
Caecilia albiventris

WHITE-HEADED CAECILIAN
Caecilia leucocephala

YELLOW-SPOTTED CAECILIAN
Caecilia flavopunctata

Jewel grouper

Honeycomb toby

Hairy frogfish

Ranchu lionhead goldfish

Longhorn cowfish

TOP TRAITS There are more species of fish than all the other vertebrates combined. in the water, a fish can suffocate. ▶ Some species of fish keep the cold-blooded creatures were the first vertebrates to evolve from invertebrates, more than

FISH

Blue marlin

▶ Most fish have swim bladders that help keep them buoyant. ▶ If there isn't sufficient oxygen eggs they lay in their mouths until the eggs hatch. ▶ Sharks cannot swim backward. ▶ These 500 million years ago. ▶ There are more than 27,500 species of fish.

ALL ABOUT FISH

THERE ARE THREE MAIN FISH GROUPS. Jawless fish, such as lampreys, are an ancient type of fish that are now mostly extinct. Cartilaginous fish have skeletons made of flexible cartilage and include sharks, rays, and skates. The largest group, bony fish, consists of fish with skeletons of bone. This group is further divided into two subgroups: ray-finned fish and lobe-finned fish.

Amazingly diverse, fish vary greatly in appearance and behavior. They range in size from the tiniest reef fish—a member of the carp family called *Paedocypris progenetica*—to the giant whale shark, a fish as long as a school bus. Some are fearsome predators, while others feed on plankton. Many reproduce by laying eggs, but certain sharks and rays give birth to live young. Almost all fish breathe through gills and have fins and scales. And every fish on Earth has one thing in common: They all live in water.

LIFE CYCLE

Most fish lay eggs that hatch into larvae. Some species release thousands, even millions, of eggs. Perhaps only a few will survive to become adults. These fish swim off after laying their eggs, leaving the larvae to fend for themselves. Other species, such as the triggerfish, produce fewer eggs but stay to look after them, keeping the eggs clean and guarding them from predators. Some sharks and rays grow eggs inside their bodies and give birth to live young. Once born, the young swim away.

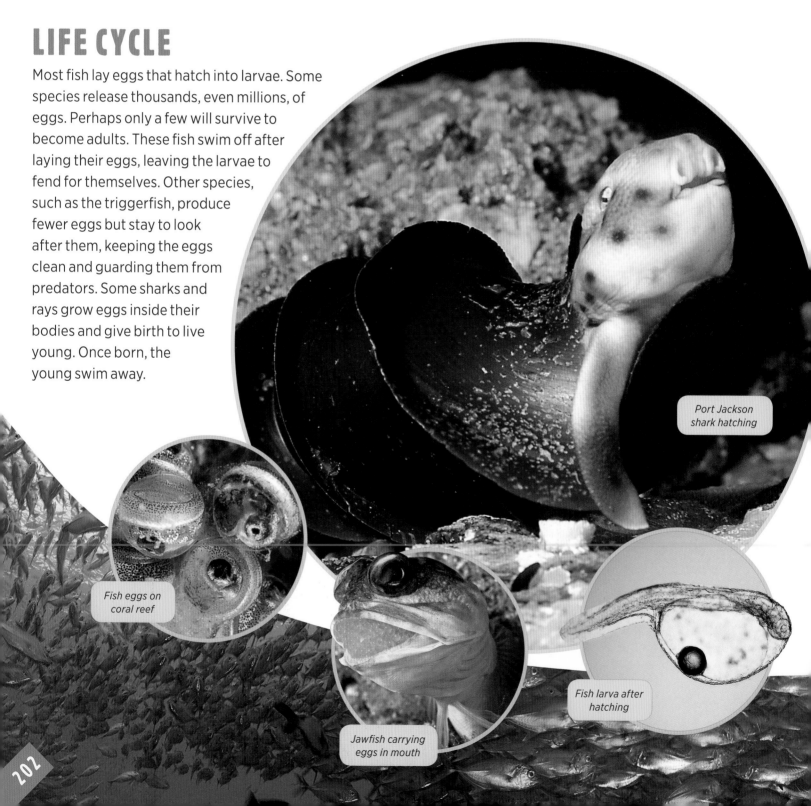

Port Jackson shark hatching

Fish eggs on coral reef

Jawfish carrying eggs in mouth

Fish larva after hatching

TAIL Connected to the spine, the tail fin is used to propel the fish through water.

SCALES Most fish are covered with overlapping plates called scales. They help protect the fish from injury.

BACKBONE Every fish is a vertebrate; it has a backbone and an internal skeleton. The skeleton of a bony fish is made up of bone and cartilage. Sharks and rays have skeletons made of cartilage.

GILLS

BREATHING UNDERWATER

All animals need to take in oxygen and expel carbon dioxide. Air-breathing animals do this through their lungs. Fish use their gills, fleshy organs on either side of the head, to take oxygen out of the water. Fish "breathe" in water as it flows past their gills, and the oxygen in the water seeps into the gill membranes and then into the blood. Carbon dioxide seeps out the same way. Certain fish, such as lungfish, have both gills and lungs, allowing them to spend a short amount of time on land.

SWIM BLADDER Many bony fish have gas-filled swim bladders, which help keep them buoyant.

NARES These holes are similar to nostrils and are used only for smelling.

EYES Fish use their eyesight to find food and escape predators.

FINS Fins help a fish swim. Depending on its location on the fish, a fin can be used for balance, for moving forward, for turning, or for braking.

LOCOMOTION

A fish's body has evolved to make swimming as efficient as possible. From flattened fish to streamlined sharks, fish are built to slip smoothly through the water. Most fish swim by bending their flexible bodies from side to side, using their tails to propel themselves forward. Eels swim similarly to how snakes move: by undulating their bodies through the water in wavelike movements.

A bony fish has a balloonlike bag of air called a swim bladder to help keep it afloat. By increasing or decreasing the amount of air in the bladder, a fish can rise or descend as it swims. Sharks don't have swim bladders, which is why they need to always keep moving. If they stop, they will sink.

JUMPING

UNDULATING

TWISTING

USING AIR

ALL ABOUT FISH

FEEDING HABITS

The answer to the question "What's for dinner?" depends on the fish. Some, such as certain reef fish, are plant eaters, scraping algae off rocks or nibbling on sea grasses. Other fish are predators, lying in wait for dinner to swim by or actively going after other fish, crustaceans, and mollusks. A number of sharks, perhaps the fiercest predators in the sea, consume marine mammals as well, hunting sea lions and seals. Some of the biggest sharks, such as the whale shark, are filter feeders that sieve plankton through their gills. Then there are fish that eat both plants and other animals. A piranha is an example of an omnivorous fish that will eat almost anything in its path: river plants, insects, snails, fish, birds, and even mammals that are unlucky enough to tumble into the water.

Squid

Seagrass

Sealion

BEHAVIOR

Fish have developed clever ways to stay safe and defend themselves against predators in their eat-or-be-eaten environments. Camouflage is an effective method for many fish, especially bottom dwellers. By disguising themselves in the same colors and patterns as their surroundings, fish can "hide" in the open with little fear. Many fish that swim in coral reefs have evolved to have spines or other sharp body parts that serve as weapons. The porcupine fish is such a fish. When threatened, it pumps water into its body, and as it inflates, its long spines stick out. Other fish sport venomous barbs. Anchovies, herring, and many other species of small fish find safety in numbers. Traveling in a large school made up of hundreds makes it difficult for a predator to pick out an individual fish.

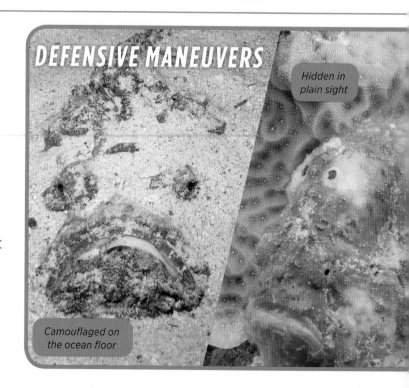

DEFENSIVE MANEUVERS

Hidden in plain sight

Camouflaged on the ocean floor

SENSES

Life underwater is different than on land, and a fish's extraordinary senses are well suited to its watery environment. Besides being able to see, smell, taste, and hear, fish have the remarkable ability to pick up even the slightest movements. Running along each side of a fish's body just beneath its skin is its lateral line, a fluid-filled tube. Sensory cells inside the tube allow the fish to detect vibrations, helping it find prey and avoid enemies.

Most fish have a keen sense of vision—useful in murky waters—and many can see in color. Predatory fish, such as sharks, have an especially accurate sense of smell. Sharks can also detect electric signals, helping them locate prey. Sensory spots on a shark's snout, called ampullae of Lorenzini, can pick up even weak electrical signals from other animals.

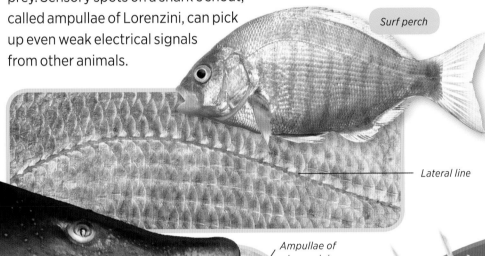

Surf perch

Lateral line

Ampullae of Lorenzini

Sand tiger shark

LIVE ACTION: FISH TALE

A barracuda swims in the warm waters of a tropical reef. It's on the lookout for tasty prey. Spying a small brownish porcupine fish slowly swimming near an underwater cave, it zooms in for the kill. The little fish spots the barracuda heading its way and starts gulping water. Its elastic skin stretches as the fish drinks, and, like a beach ball, it immediately inflates so that 2-inch-long (5 cm) spines poke out and cover its body. The barracuda quickly takes off, deciding that it doesn't want to tangle with this prickly opponent.

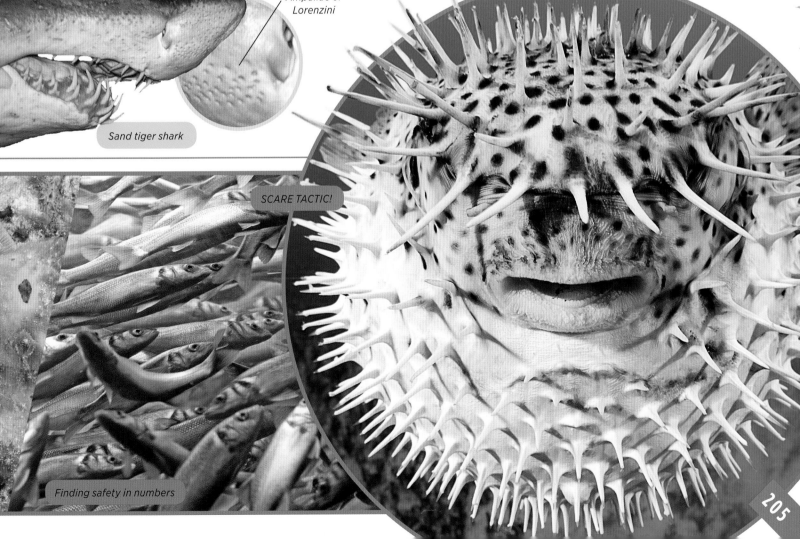

SCARE TACTIC!

Finding safety in numbers

FEARSOME PREDATORS, SHARKS are at or near the top of the ocean's food web. Most species prey on fish, mollusks, invertebrates, marine mammals, and even other sharks. Others, like the bulky whale shark, exist almost entirely on tiny plankton.

All sharks have a skeleton made of cartilage, a firm but flexible tissue, and have a thick skin covered with tooth-like scales that are rough to the touch. Unlike their bony fish cousins, sharks lack gas-filled swim bladders. This means to avoid sinking, sharks must swim constantly.

While 70 percent of sharks give birth to live young, the rest lay eggs. All female sharks give birth to fully formed young that are able to fend for themselves.

Sharks are found in all the world's oceans, and a few, such as the bull shark, can also survive in fresh water. There are about 500 species of sharks.

VELVET BELLY LANTERN SHARK
Etmopterus spinax

SIZE: **1.5–2 feet long (0.5–0.6 m)**
HABITAT: **Eastern Atlantic Ocean and Mediterranean Sea**
FOOD: **Crustaceans, squid, small fish**

One of the smallest species of shark, this is a deep-sea dweller that has adapted to its extreme environment. The large-eyed shark is bioluminescent; its belly is covered with light-producing organs called photophores. These organs allow the shark to find other velvet-belly lantern sharks. By staying together in schools, the sharks increase their chances of survival.

TIGER SHARK
Galeocerdo cuvier

SIZE: **10.5–18 feet long (3.2–5.5 m)**
HABITAT: **Tropical and temperate waters worldwide**
FOOD: **Fish, turtles, birds, marine animals**

There's almost nothing this huge shark won't eat. A voracious predator, the tiger shark dines on small sharks, marine mammals, sea turtles, and all manner of fish. The stomach contents of some sharks have included nonedible objects, such as license plates and car tires. No wonder it's known as the "trash can of the sea."

OCEANIC WHITETIP SHARK
Carcharhinus longimanus

SIZE: **7–13 feet long (2.1–4 m)**
HABITAT: **Deep ocean waters worldwide**
FOOD: **Fish, stingrays, sea turtles, sea birds, squid, crustaceans, carrion**

Although they typically swim in waters far away from coasts, these slow-moving, aggressive sharks are responsible for a large number of fatal attacks. The danger comes to people stranded in the open ocean. Due to overfishing for its fin, which is considered a delicacy in Asia, the oceanic whitetip shark is considered at risk for extinction.

FISH

GREAT WHITE SHARK
Carcharodon carcharias
SIZE: 13–21 feet long (4–6.4 m)
HABITAT: Oceans worldwide, except polar waters
FOOD: Fish, birds, turtles, marine mammals

A powerful hunting machine, the great white shark seeks fish, penguins, porpoises, seals, and sea lions to eat. It usually attacks its prey from underneath, swimming so fast that its torpedo-shaped body can leave the water completely. Great whites' 300 razor-sharp teeth are arranged in rows and can cut through the toughest flesh.

 The University of Florida Museum of Natural History keeps track of shark attacks. The data makes clear which species—shark or human—faces the greater danger. In a ten-year period, sharks killed 51 people. Over that same time, almost 80 million sharks were killed by people.

BULL SHARK
Carcharhinus leucas
SIZE: 7–11.5 feet long (2.1–3.5 m)
HABITAT: Coastal waters and freshwater rivers and lakes worldwide
FOOD: Fish, other sharks, marine and terrestrial mammals, birds, sea turtles

Unlike most sharks, the bull shark can swim in both saltwater and freshwater. With its blunt snout and stout body, it resembles a bull. Like its namesake, the bull shark butts its prey with its head. The blow disorients the prey and gives the bull shark the opportunity to move in and devour its meal.

SPOTTED WOBBEGONG
Orectolobus maculatus
SIZE: 5–6 feet long (1.5–1.8 m)
HABITAT: Temperate to tropical waters in the western Pacific Ocean
FOOD: Fish, octopuses, crabs, lobsters

A species of carpet shark, the spotted wobbegong is a sluggish bottom dweller that waits for prey. A master of camouflage, it has a flattened body and tassels around its mouth that help it blend with the sea floor.

WHALE SHARK
Rhincodon typus
SIZE: 40–65 feet long (12.2–19.8 m)
HABITAT: Tropical and temperate waters worldwide
FOOD: Plankton, small fish

The largest fish in the ocean, the whale shark is the size of a school bus. Despite its girth, this shark doesn't feast on large prey. It's a filter feeder, sucking huge amounts of water into its mouth and pumping it back out again through its gills. Plankton and small fish are trapped and then swallowed. Everything about the whale shark is huge, including its mouth, which is roomy enough to fit a person inside.

 **FUN FACT** Shark teeth are arranged in rows. When a shark loses a tooth, another one moves in from the backup rows to take its place.

207

SCALLOPED HAMMERHEAD SHARK

Like all nine species of hammerhead, the scalloped hammerhead shark has a uniquely shaped head. This species gets its name from the three indentations at the front of its head. Scientists speculate that the hammerhead shark's wide head helps with finding prey. With eyes spaced far apart, the hammerhead has a visual range greater than most other sharks'. All sharks have special sensors called ampullae of Lorenzini located on their snouts. Because a hammerhead's snout is so broad, it has more of these sensors. The sensors help a hammerhead shark detect the electrical field of one of its favorite prey—a stingray buried in the sandy ocean floor.

7 FACTS ABOUT THE SCALLOPED HAMMERHEAD SHARK

- ▸ Eats fish, cephalopods, crustaceans, and rays
- ▸ Swims in tropical and warm waters
- ▸ Gives birth to live young
- ▸ Produces large litters of up to 30 pups
- ▸ Juveniles swim in large schools
- ▸ Lives more than 30 years
- ▸ Has few natural predators

ABOUT ME!

I'm a scalloped hammerhead shark. I may swim in the deep ocean most of the time, but I also take in the rays and get a tan. When I hang out in shallow water, my skin is exposed to bright sunlight, and it darkens.

RAYS AND SKATES

RAYS AND SKATES ARE SIMILAR to sharks in that they too have boneless skeletons made of cartilage. Their flattened shapes and wide pectoral fins make them easy to distinguish from the torpedo-like bodies of most sharks, though.

The major difference between rays and skates is that rays give birth to live young, while skates lay their eggs in hard cases. Rays are usually larger than skates and have long, whiplike tails.

Although a few species of rays reside in lakes and rivers, most rays and skates live in tropical or temperate seas and oceans. Many are bottom dwellers that are camouflaged to blend in with their surroundings.

Both rays and skates are predators that feed on shellfish and mollusks, although some species eat fish as well. About 500 species of rays and skates exist.

LARGETOOTH SAWFISH
Pristis microdon

SIZE: **16.5–23 feet long (5–7 m)**
HABITAT: **Shallow coastal and freshwaters; offshore eastern Africa, Philippines, Vietnam, Australia**
FOOD: **Fish, crustaceans, mollusks**

With a snout that resembles a chainsaw blade, the sawfish is a type of ray. A sawfish uses its long, flat snout to dig out prey on the ocean floor. Its snout is also a weapon against predators, batting away sharks and other enemies. The largetooth sawfish has between 14 and 23 teeth to a side.

Animal Antics
Some stingrays visit "cleaning stations" where small fish such as wrasses eat parasites and bacteria off the larger fish. In this way, the wrasses get food to eat and the bigger fish get their teeth cleaned.

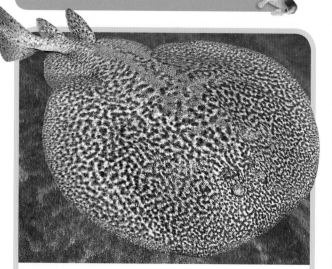

MARBLED ELECTRIC RAY
Torpedo marmorata

SIZE: **1.5–2 feet long (0.5–0.6 m)**
HABITAT: **Seagrass, rocky reefs; eastern Atlantic Ocean, Mediterranean Sea**
FOOD: **Small fish**

Zap! The marbled electric ray kills its prey with a powerful shock. After ambushing its victim, the ray wraps itself around the fish and delivers an electric shock from electric organs located in its fins. These organs produce a charge up to 200 volts that either stun or kill the fish.

BLUE-SPOTTED STINGRAY
Taeniura lymma

SIZE: 1–2.5 feet long (0.3–0.8 m)
HABITAT: Sea floor near coral reefs of western Australia and southern Africa
FOOD: Mollusks, crabs, shrimp, worms

Dotted with bright blue spots, this ray's coloration serves as a warning to predators that it is venomous. Its long tail comes equipped with two sharp, venomous spikes at the end, which it uses to strike at enemies.

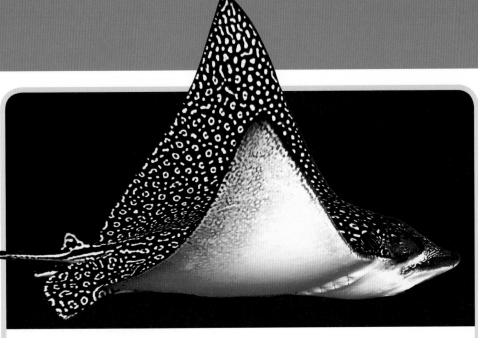

SPOTTED EAGLE RAY
Aetobatus narinari

SIZE: **6–10.5 feet wide (1.8–3.2 m)**
HABITAT: **Tropical waters worldwide**
FOOD: **Clams, oysters, shrimp, octopus, squid, sea urchins, bony fish**

Agile swimmers, these striking rays flap their large fins and appear to "fly" through the water. Although usually solitary, these rays do gather in open water in schools of 100 or more individuals. Bottom feeders, they use their upturned snouts to dig in the mud for crustaceans.

GIANT MANTA RAY
Manta birostris

SIZE: **26–29.5 feet wide (7.9–9 m)**
HABITAT: **Tropical waters worldwide**
FOOD: **Plankton, small fish**

These mostly solitary creatures, the largest of all the rays, are found in tropical seas. Unlike most rays, they prefer to swim near the surface and to stay close to land. Despite their huge size, manta rays are filter feeders and feast on plankton and small fish. Graceful and acrobatic, these gentle giants swim by flapping their wing-shaped fins and have been known to leap out of the water.

AUSTRALIAN THORNBACK SKATE
Dentiraja lemprieri

SIZE: **1.5–2 feet long (0.5–0.6 m)**
HABITAT: **Shallow coastal waters; offshore southern Australia, Tasmania, New South Wales**
FOOD: **Crabs, shrimp, small fish**

Native to Australia, this bottom dweller protects itself from unwanted predators with the many thorns that cover its back and tail. Its thorns do have one drawback: the creatures often become tangled in commercial fishing nets.

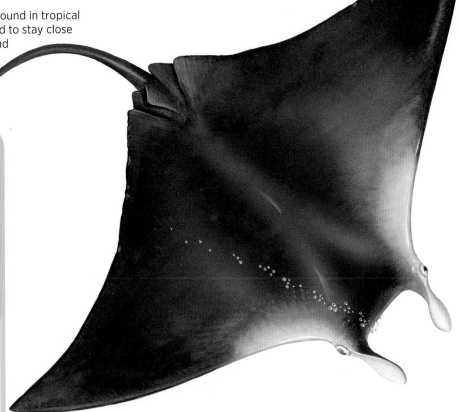

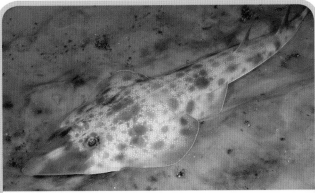

ATLANTIC GUITARFISH
Rhinobatos lentiginosus

SIZE: **2–2.5 feet long (0.6–0.8 cm)**
HABITAT: **Coastal waters; offshore regions of southeastern United States and south to Central America**
FOOD: **Mollusks, crabs**

Although this fish belongs to the ray family, it swims like a shark, using its thick tail to propel itself forward. The guitarfish often buries itself in sand, blending in with the ocean floor. This ray gets its name from its elongated body, which resembles a guitar.

RESEMBLING SNAKES MORE THAN FISH, eels have long, narrow bodies and fewer fins than other fish. Their cylindrical bodies allow them to swim in shallow water and even glide on land, if needed. Most eels do not have scales and instead are covered in thick mucus.

Eels have a unique method of reproducing, one that separates them from other bony fish. Their eggs hatch into transparent larvae that drift in the ocean waters, feeding on plankton. The larvae are leaf shaped and look very different from adult eels. The larvae mature into young eels called elvers and after several years into adults.

There are about 800 species of eels found in rivers and seas all over the world. As predators, they hunt small fish, shellfish, mollusks, and sea urchins.

STARRY MORAY EEL
Gymnothorax nudivomer

SIZE: **5–6 feet long (1.5–1.8 m)**
HABITAT: **Coral reefs; Indo-Pacific Ocean, Red Sea**
FOOD: **Fish**

Ambush predators, moray eels, like the starry moray eel, wait in reef holes for fish to swim past them. When one does, this eel strikes out like a snake and grabs its prey. This slimy eel's skin is covered in toxic mucus, making it unappetizing to predators.

SLENDER SNIPE EEL
Nemichthys scolopaceus

SIZE: **4–5 feet long (1.2–1.5 m)**
HABITAT: **Temperate and tropical waters worldwide**
FOOD: **Shrimp**

Although it can grow 5 feet (1.5 m) long, the slender snipe eel weighs only a few ounces (grams). With its birdlike beak this deep-sea dweller drifts through the water feeding on shrimp. Not much is known about this eel, as it is rarely caught.

FUN FACT
Because young eels look very different from adults, for a long time people mistook them for a different species.

GULPER EEL
Saccopharynx ampullaceus

SIZE: 5–6.5 feet long (1.5–2 m)
HABITAT: Deep sea; eastern Atlantic Ocean
FOOD: Fish, crustaceans, octopus, squid

When its enormous jaws are wide open, the gulper eel can swallow fish as large as itself. It helps that this deep-sea eel has a stomach that stretches to accommodate prey. Gulper eels are well adapted to the ocean depths where they reside. Rather than waste energy chasing down scarce prey, the eel waits for dinner to come to it, using a glowing light at the end of its tail as a lure.

THE 338 SPECIES THAT MAKE UP this group all have rigid bodies encased in body rings, not scales. Most species have tube-shaped snouts which they use to suck in small crustaceans such as brine shrimp. Champion camouflagers, they frequently change their color to match their surroundings.

What sets off these fish from other animals is their unique method of reproducing. The female lays her eggs in the male's pouch, where they remain until hatching. The fully formed young, newly released, swim off and immediately start feeding.

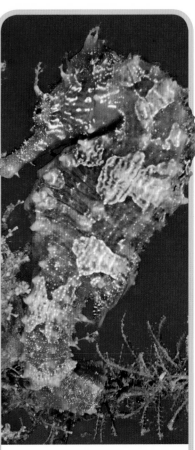

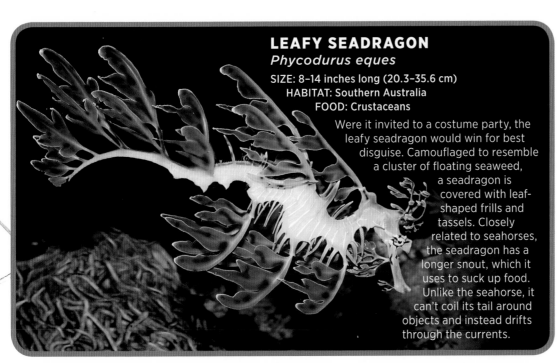

LEAFY SEADRAGON
Phycodurus eques

SIZE: 8–14 inches long (20.3–35.6 cm)
HABITAT: Southern Australia
FOOD: Crustaceans

Were it invited to a costume party, the leafy seadragon would win for best disguise. Camouflaged to resemble a cluster of floating seaweed, a seadragon is covered with leaf-shaped frills and tassels. Closely related to seahorses, the seadragon has a longer snout, which it uses to suck up food. Unlike the seahorse, it can't coil its tail around objects and instead drifts through the currents.

Animal Antics
Seahorses hardly gallop. These poor swimmers are the slowest fish in the sea. They have four fins which they flap quickly, but they don't build up much speed. The dwarf seahorse swims 0.001 mile per hour.

ROAR
Seahorses are taken from the sea and left to dry on sandy beaches. Their carcasses are then sold as souvenirs to tourists. You can help seahorses by not buying these cruel trinkets.

LINED SEAHORSE
Hippocampus erectus

SIZE: 5–7 inches long (12.7–17.8 cm)
HABITAT: Atlantic Ocean
FOOD: Crustaceans, brine shrimp

Like all seahorses, the lined seahorse has sharp eyesight, which it uses to locate prey, usually tiny crustaceans and brine shrimp. Its eyes move independently of each other, allowing them to look forward and backward simultaneously. The males of this species are larger than females and have longer tails.

SHORT-SNOUTED SEAHORSE
Hippocampus hippocampus

SIZE: 3–6 inches long (7.6–15.2 cm)
HABITAT: Mediterranean Sea, northeastern Atlantic Ocean
FOOD: Brine shrimp

This seahorse's snout is shorter than other species, measuring less than a third of its head length. That doesn't keep this voracious feeder from sucking up thousands of brine shrimp a day. Like all seahorses, the male is the one to give birth to his offspring. The female lays her eggs in the male's pouch and he carries them until they develop into fully formed seahorses. The process of giving birth can sometimes last up to two days.

RIBBON EEL

A member of the moray eel family, the ribbon eel is a brilliantly colored fish. It doesn't start out that way, though. A juvenile is jet black with a yellow dorsal fin. As it matures, the fish undergoes a remarkable color change. Its body turns bright blue and the mouth area becomes yellow. But that isn't the only change this long, slender fish will experience. Ribbon eels start life as males. After they reach about 4.5 feet (1.4 m) in length, ribbon eels again turn color—all yellow—and become egg-laying females.

7 FACTS ABOUT THE RIBBON EEL

- ▶ Lives in coral reefs
- ▶ Hides in sand, mud, and reef crevices
- ▶ Is found throughout Indian and Pacific Oceans
- ▶ Hunts small fish
- ▶ Is the only species in genus *Rhinomuraena*
- ▶ Scientists once believed juveniles and adults to be separate species
- ▶ Lives 30 years or more in wild

ABOUT ME!

I'm a young ribbon eel, and I'm facing a lot of changes. Right now, I'm a male with a black body and a yellow stripe down my back. When I get older, I'll turn bright blue. Once I reach my full size, I'll become an all-yellow female and will be able to lay eggs. I lead a very colorful life!

ANGLERFISH FAMILY

THE STRANGE-LOOKING FISH that make up this family share a similar method of hunting. They catch their prey, usually other fish, by luring them with a rod attached to their huge heads. The rod is actually a long spine of the dorsal fin at the tip of which is a fleshy organ.

There are more than 200 species of anglerfish. Some live in shallow waters or coral reefs and are camouflaged to resemble their surroundings. Deep-sea anglerfish are usually black with luminous lures that help them catch prey in the pitch-black waters.

Most anglerfish release their eggs into the water and allow them to drift off in the current. A few species, though, lay fewer eggs but watch over them until they hatch.

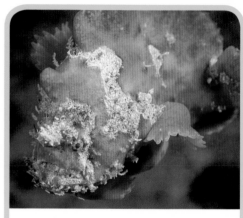

PSYCHEDELIC ANGLERFISH
Histiophryne psychedelica

SIZE: **3–6 inches long (7.6–15.2 cm)**
HABITAT: **Indonesian waters, western Pacific Ocean**
FOOD: **Small fish, shrimp**

A swirl of contrasting colors, this recently discovered species of frogfish gets around by "hopping" on the sea floor. It uses its leglike fins to push off and, shooting water from its gills, propels itself forward. Unlike most anglerfish, its dorsal spine is too small to be effective in luring prey.

SMOOTH ANGLERFISH
Phyllophryne scortea

SIZE: **4 inches long (10.2 cm)**
HABITAT: **Southern and western Australia**
FOOD: **Gobies**

Most female anglerfishes lay their eggs and swim away. The smooth anglerfish is unusual in that it guards over its eggs. Curving their body and tail, they create a pocket for the eggs and stay huddled over them until they hatch.

ANGLER
Lophius piscatorius

SIZE: **6.5 feet long (2 m)**
HABITAT: **Sand and muddy bottoms on the continental shelf and continental slope; Baltic Sea, North Sea, Mediterranean Sea, Black Sea, eastern Atlantic Ocean**
FOOD: **Fish, seabirds**

Buried in sand on the ocean floor or lurking in seaweed, the greenish-brown angler blends in with its environment, making it hard to spot. On the front of its huge head, above its gaping mouth, is its secret weapon: an elongated dorsal spine with a fleshy lure at the end. As the angler lies in wait, it flicks the lure to entice prey to come closer. When an unsuspecting fish approaches, the angler attacks.

SARGASSUM FISH
Histrio histrio

SIZE: 7.5–8 inches long (19–20.3 cm)
HABITAT: Tropical and temperate waters; western Atlantic Ocean, western Pacific Ocean, Indian Ocean
FOOD: Small fish, shrimp

This crafty fish makes its home among rafts of floating sargassum seaweed. Covered in leafy skin tassels the same color and pattern as seaweed, it is practically invisible to both prey and predators. Its pectoral fins are shaped like legs, which the fish uses to scramble about the rafts.

WARTY FROGFISH
Antennarius maculatus
SIZE: 6 inches long (15.2 cm)
HABITAT: Coral reefs; Indo-Pacific Ocean, Red Sea
FOOD: Fish

Covered with wart-like bumps all over its body, the warty frogfish is a poor swimmer. It lives in shallow waters and coral reefs, "walking" along the seafloor on its angled fins. Like other frogfish, it uses its lure to attract prey, which occasionally includes other warty frogfish. Its mouth stretches to allow it to swallow prey.

HUMPBACK BLACK DEVIL
Melanocetus johnsonii
SIZE: 1–7 inches long (2.5–17.8 cm)
HABITAT: Tropical to temperate oceans worldwide
FOOD: Crustaceans, small fish

This anglerfish loves to swim in deep, tropical ocean waters. This species is sexually dimorphic, meaning that the females appear to be much different than the male. For instance, females can grow to be six times larger than the males, and they have a "fishing rod" growing from their head that ends in a blob of light.

Surprisingly Human
Fishermen use many kinds of lures to attract fish. Some even add scent to lures to coax fish. Batfish have a similar technique. This member of the angler family secretes an odor that entices prey to come closer.

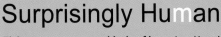

SNACK ATTACK

The enormous mouths of many species of anglerfish are filled with long, sharp teeth that curve inward. Even when its mouth is open, the teeth do a good job of trapping fish inside the anglerfish's mouth.

SALMON, TROUT, AND CHAR are members of the same family of fish, numbering about 300 species in all. These medium- to large-size fish have lengthy bodies and range in color from the silver-gray sheen of a Coho salmon to the multi-hues of a rainbow trout. Predators, they mainly hunt other fish, though some species will also feed on insects, crustaceans, amphibians, and even birds.

On of the most extraordinary features of these fish is their life cycle. Salmon, trout, and char are born in freshwater with most migrating to the sea when they mature. When they are ready to reproduce, these migratory fish return to the waters of their birth. Once home, the female lays her eggs and the male fertilizes them. Many species die soon after reproducing. Their decomposing bodies supply nourishment to the young that later hatch.

SOCKEYE SALMON
Oncorhynchus nerka

SIZE: **2–2.5 feet long (0.6–0.8 m)**
HABITAT: **Northern Pacific Ocean and adjacent rivers**
FOOD: **Plankton**

Like its cousin the Atlantic salmon, the sockeye salmon spends most of its life at sea, returning to the river in which it was born only to breed. As they make their journey home, sockeyes turn a distinctive bright red, and the males develop a humped back and hooked jaws. Not long after spawning, both males and females die.

COHO SALMON
Oncorhynchus kisutch

SIZE: **2–3 feet long (0.6–0.9 m)**
HABITAT: **Northern Pacific Ocean**
FOOD: **Plankton, insects, small fish**

Like sockeye salmon, Coho salmon turn red when swimming upstream to their place of birth. When she arrives, the female digs a nest, called a red, in the gravel of the riverbed and lays about 100 eggs.

RAINBOW TROUT
Oncorhynchus mykiss

SIZE: **1–4 feet long (0.3–1.2 m)**
HABITAT: **Rivers and lakes of North America**
FOOD: **Insects, crustaceans, small fish**

These torpedo-shaped fish are bullets in the water, whether in freshwater streams or out in the ocean. Some rainbow trout will spend their lives in freshwater, while others, known as steelhead trout will migrate to sea, returning only to spawn. The lifestyle choices of adult trout are reflected in their appearance. Freshwater rainbow trout are a multicolored fish, while steelhead trout are silver. Rainbow trout are a popular game fish.

APACHE TROUT
Oncorhynchus apache

SIZE: **1–1.5 feet long (0.3–0.5 m)**
HABITAT: **High elevation streams; Arizona, Gila River basin**
FOOD: **Insects, plankton, small fish**

Apache trout are found in the cool headwaters of streams high in the White Mountains of Arizona. When non-native trout were introduced into its habitat, the competition led to this yellow-bellied fish's decline.

Animal Antics
Some species of salmon can migrate as far as 3,000 miles (4,828 km) to reproduce. That's about the same distance you would travel to get from the east to the west coast in the United States.

WHITE-SPOTTED CHAR
Salvelinus leucomaenis

SIZE: **4 feet long (1.2 m)**
HABITAT: **Pacific Ocean and adjoining rivers in Japan**
FOOD: **Fish, insects**

This big fish begins life in a cool river, where it lives until it is big enough to survive the open waters. It heads to the sea at about two years of age, returning to the river to spawn once it is four years old. A hungry predator, this large bony fish is a carnivore. It's a popular game fish in Japan.

BROOK TROUT
Salvelinus fontinalis

SIZE: **1–2.5 feet long (0.3–0.8 m)**
HABITAT: **Eastern North American rivers and streams**
FOOD: **Worms, leeches, mollusks, minnows, crayfish, amphibians, insects**

Most brook trout live exclusively in streams, creeks, and lakes, the colder the better. There they tend to hide under large rocks and wait for prey. Some, however, migrate to the sea. Known as salters, these salmon venture just a few miles out and stay at sea for a short period of time.

ATLANTIC SALMON
Salmo salar

SIZE: **2.5–5 feet long (0.8–1.5 m)**
HABITAT: **North Atlantic Ocean and adjoining rivers**
FOOD: **Squid, fish, shrimp**

Strong and powerful, the Atlantic salmon has a sleek, streamlined body designed for long-distance swimming. These salmon start their lives in a river, making their way downriver and out to sea when they still small. As adults they migrate to the open ocean, staying there for several years. When they are ready to breed, they make the long journey back to the birthplace, struggling upriver against the current and leaping over waterfalls to reach their spawning grounds.

THIS GROUP OF FISH CONTAINS about 8,000 species, the vast majority of them living in freshwater. They can be found on all the continents except Antarctica. Members of this diverse group include the familiar goldfish and other carps, as well as bottom-dwelling catfish and fierce piranhas. All share a common feature: their inner ear and their swim bladder are connected, giving these fish excellent hearing.

Such a diverse group of fish naturally have a wide range of eating habits. Some carp are herbivores, consuming only plant matter, while many catfish are omnivores that scavenge for plants, invertebrates, fish, and fish eggs. Piranhas are voracious predators, devouring fish and other prey.

While most members of this large group are less than 12 inches (30 cm) in length, some, such as certain species of catfish, are monstrously large and can weigh well over 200 pounds (90 kg). These species females reproduce by laying eggs, and the newly hatched young are miniature versions of their parents.

ELECTRIC EEL
Electrophorus electricus

SIZE: **6.5–8 feet long (2–2.4 m)**
HABITAT: **Streams and ponds in South America**
FOOD: **Invertebrates, fish, small mammals**

Despite their name, electric eels are not eels. They are actually members of the catfish family. These predatory river fish produce electric currents that they use to locate and stun prey and to protect themselves from predators. They can deliver a 600-volt blast of electricity—strong enough to knock a full-grown man to the ground.

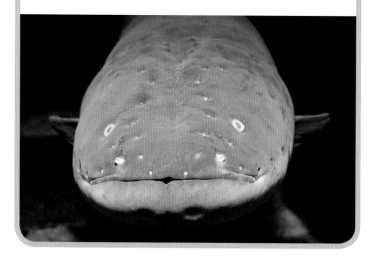

CHANNEL CATFISH
Ictalurus punctatus

SIZE: **1–4 feet long (0.3–1.2 m)**
HABITAT: **Lower Canada, midwestern United States**
FOOD: **Fish, crustaceans, insects**

Channel catfish are found at the bottom of streams, rivers, ponds, lakes, and reservoirs. The males of this species are caring parents—for fish. When it is time to breed, the male builds a next at the bottom of the river. After the female lays her eggs there, the male fertilizes the eggs and then chases the female away. Otherwise she may eat them. The male guards the eggs until they hatch.

GOLDFISH
Carassius auratus

SIZE: **8.5–16 inches long (21.6–41 cm)**
HABITAT: **Native to eastern Asia**
FOOD: **Crustaceans, insects, plants**

In the wild goldfish are usually not reddish gold in color but a greenish brown. A member of the carp family, goldfish are now mainly domesticated and come in a variety of colors, shapes, and sizes. Initially bred in China, where this freshwater species originated, goldfish can live long lives, reaching 30 years of age.

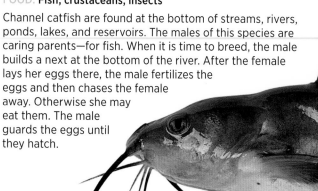

RED-BELLIED PIRANHA
Pygocentrus nattereri

SIZE: 0.5–1 foot long (15.2–30.5 cm)
HABITAT: Rivers and lakes of South America
FOOD: Insects, fish, crustaceans, worms, carrion

Red-bellied piranhas are fearsome predators. While most piranhas are harmless herbivores, this species comes equipped with razor-sharp teeth and powerful jaws. Most of the time, they prefer to eat fish around their size. But during the dry season, when water levels get low, they can become particularly dangerous. Hunting in large schools of 100 or more individuals, they will attack prey much larger than themselves.

GLASS CATFISH
Kryptopterus bicirrhis

SIZE: 4–6 inches long (10.2–15.2 cm)
HABITAT: Rivers of southeast Asia
FOOD: Insect larvae

These tiny, transparent catfish, native to southeast Asia, travel in schools, and unlike most catfish are not bottom feeders. Their transparent bodies let light pass through them, making them practically invisible to predators.

 The Mekong giant catfish is in danger of extinction due to overfishing. Another threat to this giant fish are the dams scheduled to be built on the Mekong River. Damming the river would prevent the fish from returning to their breeding grounds to lay eggs.

MEKONG GIANT CATFISH
Pangasianodon gigas

SIZE: 8–10 feet long (2.4–3 m)
HABITAT: Mekong River of southeast Asia
FOOD: Plants, algae

The world's largest freshwater fish, this monster of a catfish can grow as long as 10 feet (3 m). Although it is so large, this gentle giant is an herbivore that feeds on the plants and algae found in the Mekong River. Due to overfishing, the Mekong giant catfish is threatened with extinction, and it is estimated that there are only a few hundred of these creatures left.

GLOWLIGHT TETRA
Hemigrammus erythrozonus

SIZE: 1.5–2 inches long (3.8–5.1 cm)
HABITAT: Tropical rivers of South America
FOOD: Insect larvae

A peaceful schooling fish native to South America, the glowlight tetra is a popular choice for aquariums. A glowing red line runs along the side of its body.

As its name suggests, the upside-down catfish, an African species, swims upside-down. This usual habit allows the fish to easily eat insects that have landed on the water's surface.

SNACK ATTACK

PERCIFORMES

LONG, ROUND, FINS WITH SPINES

FORTY PERCENT OF ALL BONY FISH are classified as perciformes, making them the largest and most diverse order of fish. About 9,500 fish species are part of this group, and they live in a variety of habitats all over the world, from fast-running mountain streams to brackish estuaries to the open ocean. Most have spines, and for this reason they are known as spiny-ray fish.

While many of these fish are carnivores, devouring fish, mollusks, crustaceans, and insects found in their environment, others are plant eaters. All reproduce by laying eggs. Some, like the banded sunfish, tend to their eggs, guarding them from predators. Many perciformes are consumed by humans as food, while other species frequently show up in aquariums.

Suction disk

COMMON REMORA
Remora remora
SIZE: 1.5–2.5 feet long (0.5–0.8 m)
HABITAT: Tropical and subtropical waters worldwide
FOOD: Plankton, parasites, food scraps from host

A more accurate name for this fish is sharksucker. Remoras attach themselves to sharks and other sea creatures, such as rays, whales, and turtles, by latching on with a suction disc on the top of their heads that is really a modified fin. Thus attached, remoras can then travel with its host, eating leftovers from the host's meals. In return, the remoras rid their hosts of parasites.

Surprisingly Human

People often band together to fight a common enemy. Certain fish in the perciformes order act this way, too. Butterflyfish, for instance, work together to drive away bigger fish, such as moray eels. This behavior is known as mobbing.

LONGNOSE BUTTERFLYFISH
Forcipiger longirostris
SIZE: 7–8.5 inches long (17.8–21.5 cm)
HABITAT: Indo-Pacific Ocean
FOOD: Worms, crustaceans

The butterfly fish has a snout that is about one third of its body length. It uses its extra-long snout like a tool to extract worms and crustaceans from their homes in coral reefs.

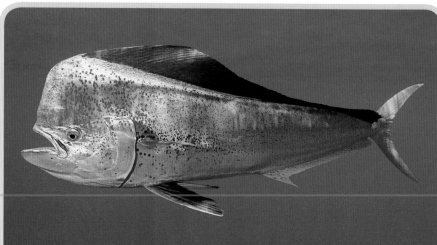

DOLPHINFISH
Coryphaena hippurus
SIZE: 3–6.5 feet long (0.9–2 m)
HABITAT: Tropical, subtropical, temperate waters worldwide
FOOD: Fish, crabs, octopuses, squid

Despite their name, dolphinfish are not related to dolphins, which are mammals. These large, shimmering fish are fast and agile predators, able to outrace most prey, including flying fish, one of their favorite meals. Dolphinfish often hunt in pairs or in small groups, using their excellent vision to track down prey.

ATLANTIC BLUEFIN TUNA
Thunnus thynnus

SIZE: **6.5–8 feet long (2–2.4 m)**
HABITAT: **Northern and central Atlantic Ocean, Mediterranean Sea**
FOOD: **Fish, squid, crustaceans**

A migratory fish, this hefty tuna travels long distances and can cross the Atlantic Ocean in less than two months. Weighing up to 550 pounds (250 kg), they are constantly on the hunt for food. With the sharpest vision of any fish, they gorge on schools of herring and mackerel. Atlantic bluefin tuna are also an important food fish.

ATLANTIC SAILFISH
Istiophorus albicans

SIZE: **5.5–11 feet long (1.7–3.4 m)**
HABITAT: **Temperate and tropical Atlantic Ocean, Mediterranean Sea**
FOOD: **Fish, octopuses, squid, crustaceans**

The speediest fish in the ocean is the sailfish. At its fastest, it can reach speeds of 68 miles (110 km) per hour. Like another member of this family, the swordfish, the Atlantic sailfish has an extended upper jaw that resembles a spear. The sailfish uses its spear as a weapon, using it to stun and maim its prey.

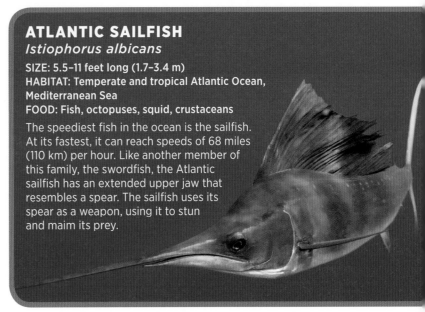

GREAT BARRACUDA
Sphyraena barracuda

SIZE: **6–6.5 feet long (1.8–2 m)**
HABITAT: **Tropical and subtropical waters worldwide**
FOOD: **Fish, octopuses, shrimp**

Nicknamed "the tiger of the sea," the great barracuda is an aggressive hunter. These daytime predators have notably keen eyesight and are especially attracted to anything that shines, like a fish's silvery scales. When prey is spotted, the long, narrow fish can accelerate quickly, reaching speeds over 30 miles (48 km) per hour in just a few seconds. Small fish are swallowed in one gulp, while larger prey fall victim to the barracuda's razor-sharp teeth.

ATLANTIC MACKEREL
Scomber scombrus

SIZE: **1.5–2 feet long (0.5–0.6 m)**
HABITAT: **Temperate waters of northern Atlantic Ocean, Mediterranean Sea, Black Sea**
FOOD: **Fish, crustaceans**

Fast-swimming schools of Atlantic mackerel feed closer to the shore for most of the year, eating small fish and tiny crustaceans. During the winter they migrate to deeper water and eat little. A commercial fish, Atlantic mackerel have a strong taste.

CLOWNFISH

Sea anemones are stinging animals that attach themselves to rocks in coral reefs and wait for passing fish to swim by. When one does, an anemone reaches out and ensnares the prey in its venomous tentacles. It may seem surprising, then, that one fish, the clownfish, makes its home among these tentacles. This small, colorful fish is covered in a coating of mucus that protects it from the anemone's sting. The living arrangements are advantageous to both sides. The clownfish has a safe refuge from predators, and it dines on leftovers from the anemone's meals. By peeping out from the tentacles, the brightly colored clownfish may lure other fish to come close, allowing the anemone to grab its dinner. The clownfish also eats dead tentacles and removes any parasites that linger on the anemone. Thus, the relationship between the two is symbiotic, or mutually beneficial.

6 FACTS ABOUT THE CLOWNFISH

▸ Is a slow swimmer
▸ There are 28 known species
▸ Can be up to 4.3 inches (11 cm) long
▸ Lives in shallow waters around reefs
▸ All are born male; some later become female and have babies
▸ Can live an average of 6 to 8 years in the wild

ABOUT ME!

I'm a clownfish, and I like to introduce myself to my sea anemone host before I move in. First I touch the anemone's tentacles with different parts of my body; then I perform a wiggle dance that lets us get used to each other.

THIS FAMILY OF BOTTOM DWELLERS is found throughout the word in shallow, mostly marine, waters. All 1,326 members of this group are equipped with spines, which in most species are venomous. The slightest pressure releases the venom, and the sting is extremely painful and in some cases can be fatal. Scorpionfish and sculpins don't use their spines to hunt, though; they are strictly for self-defense.

Well camouflaged with fleshy, warty skin and mottled coloring that matches their rocky sea homes, these large-headed fish feed primarily on crustaceans and small fish. Most species lay their eggs in clumps under rocks, while some travel near the surface of the water to give birth to live young. The unique "rays" at the base of the sculpin's pectoral fin help it grip to the ocean floor to avoid being swept away by violent currents.

SPOTTED SCORPIONFISH
Scorpaena plumieri

SIZE: 1–1.5 feet long (0.3–0.5 m)
HABITAT: Western Atlantic Ocean
FOOD: Crustaceans, small fish

The fleshy plumes over its eyes and mottled skin flaps all over its body help to conceal this venomous scorpionfish as it lies motionless on the rocky seabed. Whenever it feels threatened, it spreads its pectoral fins and displays black-and-white spots that resemble the eyes of a much bigger creature, scaring off any potential predators.

FUN FACT! Because they remain motionless for much of the time, scorpionfish are often covered in parasites. Many of these bottom dwellers can shed their skin to get rid of these pests.

Surprisingly Human

On the sports field, referees wear striped shirts so they can be seen easily by players. Lionfish also want to be noticed. Their contrasting stripes serve as a warning to predators to keep their distance from sharp spines.

RED LIONFISH
Pterois volitans

SIZE: 1–1.5 feet long (0.3–0.5 m)
HABITAT: Indo-Pacific Ocean
FOOD: Fish, shrimp

This beautiful fish with its long, flowing fins and striking red stripes is not to be messed with. Along its fins are sharp, venomous spines that, while rarely fatal to people, are nevertheless painful. The lionfish, also known as turkey fish or dragon fish, uses its spines as protection against predators rather than to hunt.

ESTUARINE STONEFISH
Synanceia horrida

SIZE: 1–2 feet long (0.3–0.6 m)
HABITAT: Indo-Pacific Ocean
FOOD: Small fish, shrimp, crustaceans

Although this sluggish stonefish remains motionless for long periods on the floors of estuaries and coral reefs, it can quickly open its mouth to swallow prey. Similar to the reef stonefish, this species has eyes higher up on its mottled, rust-brown head.

DUSKY FLATHEAD
Platycephalus fuscus

SIZE: **1.5–4 feet long (0.5–1.2 m)**
HABITAT: **Western Pacific Ocean**
FOOD: **Small fish, prawns**

Found in Australian waters, the dusky flathead is a crafty hunter, hiding its body in the sand and waiting for prey. Because its eyes are on the top of its head, the flathead is able to spot any fish that swims above it. Its body is perfectly matched to its sandy habitat, so its prey is unaware of the danger until it is too late.

EUROPEAN BULLHEAD
Cottus gobio

SIZE: **2.5–3 inches long (6.4–7.6 cm)**
HABITAT: **Freshwater streams, rivers, and lakes in Europe**
FOOD: **Insects, crustaceans, other invertebrates**

This freshwater fish is widely distributed in the cold and medium-sized rivers of Europe. However, they are sometimes found on gravel or rocky shores along the Baltic coast. Similar to other fish in the bullhead family, males are attentive parents, guarding the nest for the four weeks it takes the eggs to hatch.

FRILLFIN TURKEYHEAD
Pterois mombasae

SIZE: **6–8 inches long (15.2–20.3 cm)**
HABITAT: **Indo-Pacific Ocean**
FOOD: **Crustaceans, small fish**

This species of lionfish is found in tropical water of both the Indian and Pacific Oceans. Like other members of its family, its spines are venomous and are used to defend itself from predators.

REEF STONEFISH
Synanceia verrucosa

SIZE: **1–1.5 feet long (0.3–0.5 m)**
HABITAT: **Indo-Pacific Ocean, Red Sea**
FOOD: **Fish, shrimp**

With its numerous warty lumps and mottled coloration, the reef stonefish is cleverly camouflaged to resemble a lone rock at the bottom of tropical reefs. Poor swimmers, these fish lie in wait for passing fish. Along its back the stonefish is armed with long spines, each of which is attached to a sac of venom. If an unsuspecting predator touches the stonefish, it releases its venom.

PUFFERS AND FILEFISH

SOME OF THE MOST BIZARRE-LOOKING fish in the sea are in this family. Unlike the streamlined bodies of the typical fish, the approximately 350 members of the puffer family range from round and spiny to boxy to flat as a pancake. They also come in a variety of weights and sizes, from tiny fish no longer than your finger to the ocean sunfish, the world's heaviest bony fish.

Found in temperate and tropical marine waters worldwide, most species are slow moving and poor swimmers. To compensate for a lack of speed, these fish make it hard for predators to eat them. All species have either sharp spines, tough, leathery skin, or are poisonous to eat.

Puffers lay their eggs in the water, where they float until hatching. Other members of this family make nests for their eggs and guard over them until they hatch.

SPOTTED TRUNKFISH
Ostracion meleagris
SIZE: 8–10 inches long (20.3–25.4 cm)
HABITAT: Indo-Pacific Ocean
FOOD: Mollusks, algae, sea cucumbers, sea urchins, marine plants

Trunkfish are also called boxfish, and one glance at their boxy shape tells you why. These tropical fish don't have scales. Instead they protected by hard, bony plates that act as armor. These rigid plates means the spotted trunkfish isn't able to bend its body. Its inflexibility combined with its shape makes this fish a poor swimmer.

SCRAWLED COWFISH
Acanthostracion quadricornis
SIZE: 1–1.5 feet long (0.3–0.5 m)
HABITAT: Western Atlantic Ocean
FOOD: Anemones, sponges, tunicates, crustaceans, marine vegetation

A close relative of boxfish and triggerfish, the scrawled cowfish has bright blue markings over its body, making it a popular aquarium fish. It is also a popular and tasty food fish in Caribbean cuisine.

LONGSPINED PORCUPINEFISH
Diodon holocanthus
SIZE: 1–1.5 feet long (0.3–0.5 m)
HABITAT: Atlantic, Pacific, and Indian Oceans
FOOD: Sea urchins, mollusks, crabs

When this fish feels threatened, it begins a drastic transformation. Sucking water into its body, its stretchy stomach blows up like a balloon. Its many spines pop up and stick out. Now several times its original size, this prickly ball deters most predators. Despite its unusual defense, the porcupinefish prefers to hide in crevices during the day, coming out at night to feed.

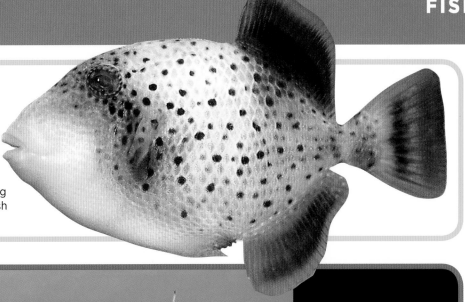

TITAN TRIGGERFISH
Balistoides viridescens

SIZE: **2–2.5 feet long (0.6–0.8 m) long**
HABITAT: **Indo-Pacific Ocean, Red Sea**
FOOD: **Shellfish, crustaceans, sea urchins**

The largest of the triggerfish is a protective parent that guards its nest of eggs aggressively. They will charge and bite any intruder than enters their territory, including divers. This fish is also known as the mustache triggerfish due to the dark band above its lips.

SCRAWLED FILEFISH
Aluterus scriptus

SIZE: **2 feet (0.6 m)**
HABITAT: **Coral reefs and lagoons; Atlantic, Pacific, and Indian Oceans**
FOOD: **Jellyfish, crustaceans, algae**

The scrawled filefish lives in tropical waters around the world. Camouflage helps it evade predators, but it has another maneuver as well. The scrawled filefish will wedge itself into a crevice and extend its spines, lodging itself firmly in place. This makes it difficult for a predator to latch on.

CLOWN TRIGGERFISH
Balistoides conspicillum

SIZE: **1–1.5 feet long (0.3–0.5 m)**
HABITAT: **Indo-Pacific Ocean**
FOOD: **Mollusks, crustaceans, sea urchins**

An attractive fish with striking black-and-white markings, the clown triggerfish is aggressive and will defend its territory. In the wild they are shy and solitary, but will bite if approached.

WHITE-SPOTTED PUFFER
Arothron hispidus

SIZE: **1–1.5 feet long (0.3–0.5 m)**
HABITAT: **Indo-Pacific Ocean**
FOOD: **algae, mollusks, sponges, corals, crustaceans**

Like all pufferfish, the white-spotted puffer can swell to several times its usual size by swallowing large amounts of water. These fish are also poisonous to eat, producing tetrodotoxin, which is more deadly than cyanide. A small amount can kill a person in less than 30 minutes.

SNACK ATTACK

Pufferfish have four strong teeth that grow together in their small, beak-shaped mouths. With their powerful jaws, they use these teeth to crack open clams, crabs, and other types of shellfish.

PACIFIC HAGFISH

The hagfish is a jawless fish with ancient roots. A fossil of a hagfish that dates from 300 million years ago looks very similar to today's hagfish. Like other hagfish species, the Pacific hagfish has an unusual defense. When threatened, it produces copious amounts of slime from glands lining its body. This makes the hagfish so slippery that most predators can't grasp it. To rid itself of the slime, the wormlike hagfish will tie its long body into a knot and slide the knot up and down, scraping away the mucus as it goes.

8 FACTS ABOUT THE PACIFIC HAGFISH

- ▶ Has soft, scaleless skin
- ▶ Breathes through nose and skin
- ▶ Is jawless and boneless
- ▶ Has skull but no spine
- ▶ Can be up to 18 inches (46 cm) long
- ▶ Is almost blind
- ▶ Is found in cold ocean waters
- ▶ Is one of 76 species of hagfish

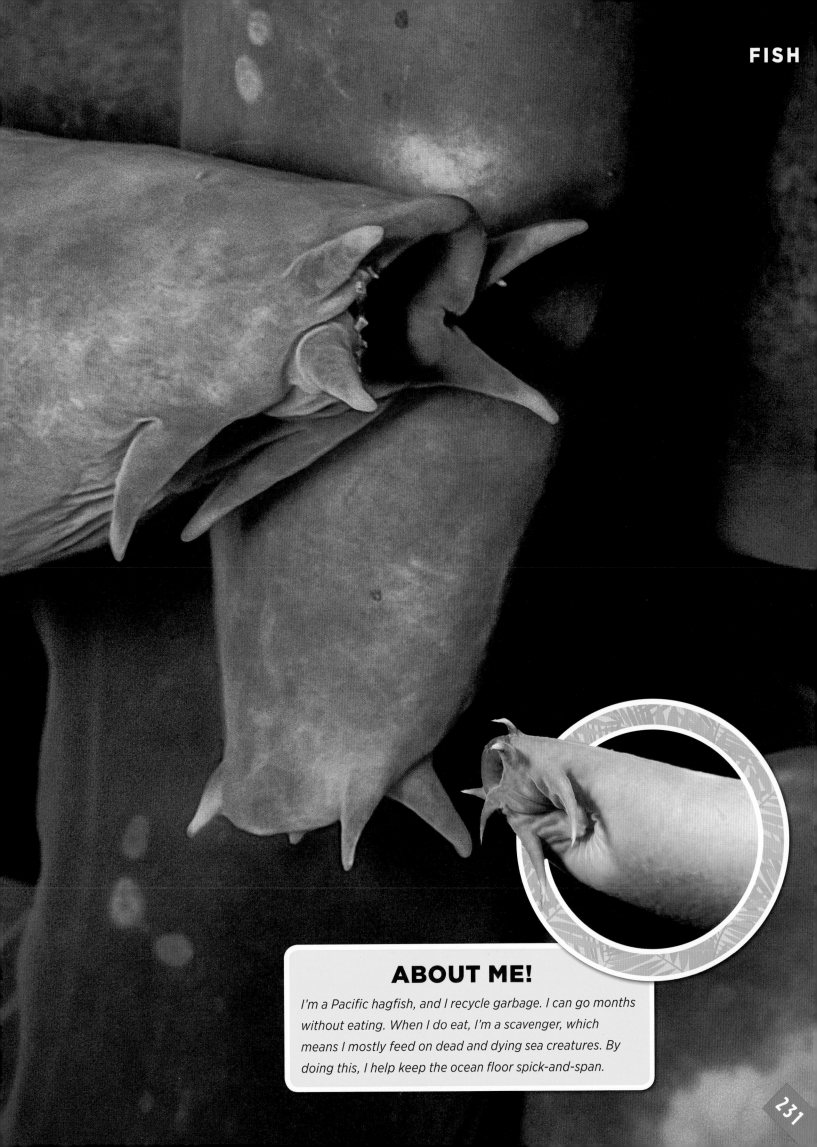

ABOUT ME!

I'm a Pacific hagfish, and I recycle garbage. I can go months without eating. When I do eat, I'm a scavenger, which means I mostly feed on dead and dying sea creatures. By doing this, I help keep the ocean floor spick-and-span.

AT THE CORAL REEF

Coral reefs are home to a complex community of fish and sea life.
They thrive in warm water, and are endangered by pollution.

Cleaning station

When a moray eel needs its teeth cleaned, a hungry shrimp helps out. It's like having a living toothbrush.

Mandarinfish

Red devil cichlid

Bluecheek butterflyfish

Emperor angelfish

Daddy day care

Seahorse daddies have an unusual job—they carry the eggs until the babies are born.

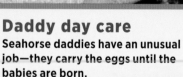

Hingebeak shrimp

Recycling

Parrot fish grind up coral to extract nutrients, then excrete it as sand.

Blacktip shark

Starfish

Zoanthid coral

Pumping water
Jellyfish don't have legs. They move by pumping their bells up and down.

Back off!
They may look pretty, but surgeonfish spines are venomous.

Regal angelfish

Yellow tang

Comet

Super swimmers
Sea turtles spend most of their lives in the ocean, and their flippers make them powerful swimmers.

Spotted cardinal fish

ANIMAL PLANET L!VE
Check out the Animal Planet L!VE cam to see fascinating fish in action by scanning this code or visiting animalplanet.timeincbooks.com/fish.

Commerson's frogfish

There are more than 27,500 known fish species in the world. Here are some interesting ones to learn more about.

SHARKS

ANGULAR ROUGH SHARK
Oxynotus centrina
ARABIAN CARPET SHARK
Chiloscyllium arabicum
ATLANTIC ANGEL SHARK
Squatina dumeril
BASKING SHARK
Cetorhinus maximus

* *Gold goby*

BIGNOSE SHARK
Carcharhinus altimus
BLACKFIN GHOST SHARK
Hydrolagus lemurs
BLACKNOSE SHARK
Carcharhinus acronotus
BLACKTAIL REEF SHARK
Carcharhinus amblyrhynchos
BLACKTIP REEF SHARK
Carcharhinus melanopterus
BLUE SHARK
Prionace glauca
BLUNTNOSE SIXGILL SHARK
Hexanchus griseus
BONNETHEAD SHARK
Sphyrna tiburo
BORNEO CATSHARK
Apristurus platyrhynchus
BRAMBLE SHARK
Echinorhinus brucus
BROADNOSE SEVENGILL SHARK
Notorynchus cepedianus
COMMON SMOOTHHOUND
Mustelus mustelus
CROCODILE SHARK
Pseudocarcharias kamoharai
FRILLED SHARK
Chlamydoselachus anguineus
GALAPAGOS BULLHEAD SHARK
Heterodontus quoyi
GALAPAGOS SHARK
Carcharhinus galapagensis
HORN SHARK
Heterodontus francisci
ICELANDIC CATSHARK
Apristurus laurussonii
LEOPARD SHARK
Triakis semifasciata
LONGNOSE SAWSHARK
Pristiophorus cirratus
LONGNOSE VELVET DOGFISH
Centroscymnus crepidater

* *Pygmy seahorse*

NURSE SHARK
Ginglymostoma cirratum
PACIFIC ANGEL SHARK
Squatina californica
PORBEAGLE SHARK
Lamna nasus
PRICKLY SHARK
Echinorhinus cookie
ROUGHTAIL CATSHARK
Galeus area
SANDBAR SHARK
Carcharhinus plumbeus
SHARPNOSE SEVENGILL SHARK
Heptranchias perlo
SHORTFIN MAKO SHARK
Isurus oxyrinchus
SILVERTIP SHARK
Carcharhinus albimarginatus
SMOOTH HAMMERHEAD
Sphyrna zygaena
SPINED PYGMY SHARK
Squaliolus laticaudus

* *Oyster toadfish*

SPINNER SHARK
Carcharhinus brevipinna
SPINY DOGFISH
Squalus acanthias
STRIPED CATSHARK
Poroderma africanum
THRESHER SHARK
Alopias vulpinus
TOPE SHARK
Galeorhinus galeus
WHITE-SPOTTED BAMBOOSHARK
Chiloscyllium plagiosum
WHITE-TIP REEF SHARK
Triaenodon obesus
ZEBRA SHARK
Stegostoma fasciatum

RAYS AND SKATES

AFRICAN RAY
Raja Africana
AUSTRALIAN BUTTERFLY RAY
Gymnura australis
BIG SKATE
Raja binoculata
BLONDE RAY
Raja brachyuran
CALIFORNIA SKATE
Raja inorata
COMMON STINGRAY
Dasyatis pastinaca
COWNOSE RAY
Rhinoptera bonasus
DEEPWATER STINGRAY
Plesiobatis daviesi
JAPANESE BUTTERFLY RAY
Gymnura japonica
KUHL'S STINGRAY
Neotrygon kuhlii
LESSER DEVIL RAY
Mobula hypostoma
LONGNOSE SKATE
Raja rhina
LONG-NOSED SKATE
Dipturus oxyrinchus
LONG-TAILED BUTTERFLY RAY
Gymnura poecilura
MEDITERRANEAN STARRY RAY
Raja asterias
OCELLATE RIVER STINGRAY
Potamotrygon motoro
PORCUPINE RIVER STINGRAY
Potamotrygon histrix
RIBBONTAIL STINGRAY
Taeniura lymma
SMOOTH BUTTERFLY RAY
Gymnura micrura

SPECKLED RAY
Raja polystigma
SPINY BUTTERFLY RAY
Gymnura altavela
SPOTTED RAY
Raja montagui
SYDNEY SKATE
Dipturus australis
THORNBACK RAY
Raja clavata
UNDULATE RAY
Raja undulate
WEDGENOSE SKATE
Dipturus whitleyi
YELLOW STINGRAY
Urobatis jamaicensis

EELS

ABYSSAL CUTTHROAT EEL
Meadia abyssalis
ASIAN SWAMP EEL
Monopterus albus
AVOCET SNIPE EEL
Avocettina infans
BROWN GARDEN EEL
Heteroconger longissimus
DEATH-BANDED SNAKE EEL
Ophichthus frontalis
EUROPEAN EEL
Anguilla Anguilla
GREEN MORAY EEL
Gymnothorax funebris
GREY CUTTHROAT EEL
Synaphobranchus affinis
JAVA SPAGHETTI EEL
Moringua javanica
KEEL TAIL NEEDLEFISH
Platybelone argalus spp. argalus
LEOPARD-SKINNED GARDEN EEL
Gorgasia sillneri
LESSER SPINY EEL
Macrognathus aculeatus
LITTLE CONGER EEL
Gnathophis habenatus
MALABAR SPINY EEL
Macrognathus guentheri
MARBLED SWAMP EEL
Synbranchus marmoratus
PELICAN EEL
Eurypharynx pelecanoides
RINGED SNAKE EEL
Myrichthys colubrinus
RUSTY SPAGHETTI EEL
Moringua ferruginea
SNOWFLAKE MORAY EEL
Echidna nebulosa
SPOTTED MORAY EEL
Gymnothorax moringa
SWOLLEN-HEADED CONGER EEL
Bassanago bulbiceps
TAIWANESE MORAY EEL
Gymnothorax taiwanensis
WHITE RIBBON EEL
Pseudechidna brummeri
ZEBRA MORAY EEL
Gymnomuraena zebra

ANGLERFISH FAMILY

BANDED ARCHERFISH
Toxotes jaculatrix
KROYER'S DEEP SEA ANGLER FISH
Ceratias holboelli
ORBICULAR BATFISH
Platax orbicularis

* *Sargassum fish*

* *Peacock flounder*

SLOANE'S VIPERFISH
Chauliodus sloani
SOFT LEAFVENT ANGLER
Haplophryne mollis
SPOTTED ARCHERFISH
Toxotes chatareus

SALMON FAMILY

BROWN TROUT
Salmo trutta spp. trutta
CHINOOK SALMON
Oncorhynchus tshwaytscha
CHUM SALMON
Oncorhynchus keta
GOLDEN TROUT
Oncorhynchus aguabonita
MASU SALMON
Oncorhynchus masou
PINK SALMON
Oncorhynchus gorbuscha
TAIMEN
Hucho taimen

CATFISH, CARP, AND OTHERS

AFRICAN CATFISH
Clarias gariepinus
AFRICAN GLASS CATFISH
Pareutropius debauwi
ALMORA LOACH
Botia almorhae
BIGHEAD CARP
Hypophthalmichthys noblis

* *Spotted scorpionfish*

BLACKSTRIPE TOPMINNOW
Fundulus notatus
COMMON EUROPEAN CARP
Cyprinus carpio
CRUCIAN CARP
Carassius carassius
DESERT SUCKER
Catostomus clarkia
GIANT RIVER CATFISH
Sperata seenghala
GOLDEN TOPMINNOW
Fundulus chrysotus
GRASS CARP
Ctenopharyngodon idella
HOVEN'S CARP
Leptobarbus hoevenii
JONKLAAS'S LOACH
Lepidocephalichthys jonklaasi
LONGNOSE SUCKER
Catostomus catostomus spp. catostomus
MOTTLED LOACH
Acanthocobitis botia
PHILIPPINE CATFISH
Clarias batrachus
PORTHOLE CATFISH
Dianema longibarbis
RED-TAILED CATFISH
Phractocephalus hemioliopterus
STERBA'S CORYDORAS CATFISH
Corydoras sterbai
TORRENT SUCKER
Thoburnia rhothoeca
TWIG CATFISH
Farlowella acus

MORE PERCIFORMES

AFRICAN MOON TETRA
Bathyaethiops caudomaculatus

ALBACORE
Thunnus alalunga

BARCA SNAKEHEAD
Channa barca

BLACK DRUM
Pogonias cromis

* *Trumpetfish*

BLACKTAIL SNAPPER
Lutjanus fulvus

BLACK TETRA
Gymnocorymbus ternetzi

BLOTCHFIN DRAGONET
Callionymus filamentosus

BLUE AND YELLOW WRASSE
Anampses lennardi

BLUE ANGELFISH
Holacanthus bermudensis

BLUE HEAD COMBTOOTH BLENNY
Ecsenius lividanalis

BLUESPOT MULLET
Moolgarda seheli

BLUESTREAK CLEANER WRASSE
Labroides dimidiatus

BLUE-STRIPED DWARF GOBY
Trimma tevegae

BULLETHEAD PARROTFISH
Chlorurus sordidus

CLOWN ANEMONEFISH
Amphiprion ocellaris

COMMON DRAGONET
Callionymus lyra

CONGO TETRA
Phenacogrammus interruptus

COPPER TETRA
Hasemania melanura

CORAL GROUPER
Plectropomus leopardus

DARTFISH
Myxodagnus belone

DAY GROUPER
Epinephelus striatus

EASTERN KELPFISH
Chironemus marmoratus

FALSE CLOWN ANEMONEFISH
Entacmaea quadricolor

FIRE CLOWNFISH
Amphiprion melanopus

* *Tasselled wobbegong*

FOXFACE RABBITFISH
Siganus vulpinus

FRENCH ANGELFISH
Pomacanthus paru

FRESHWATER DRUM
Aplodinotus grunniens

GIANT GOURAMI
Osphronemus goramy

GIANT KELPFISH
Heterostichus rostratus

GRAY ANGELFISH
Pomacanthus arucatus

GULF DARTER
Etheostoma swaini

HARLEQUIN TUSK WRASSE
Choerodon fasciatus

HONEYCOMB COWFISH
Acanthostracion polygonius

HUMBUG DAMSELFISH
Dascyllus aruanus

JOHNNY DARTER
Etheostoma nigrum

JOHN'S SNAPPER
Lutjanus johnii

KENYI CICHLID
Maylandia lombardoi

LEAST DARTER
Etheostoma microperca

LEATHERJACKET
Oligoplites saurus

LEOPARD GROUPER
Mycteroperca rosacea

LINED ROCKSKIPPER
Blenniella bilitonensis

MEDITERRANEAN PARROTFISH
Sparisoma cretense

MOONTAIL BULLSEYE
Priacanthus hamrur

NAPOLEON WRASSE
Cheilinus undulates

NILE TILAPIA
Oreochromis niloticus

* *Stargazer*

ORANGE CLOWNFISH
Amphiprion percula

PEACH FAIRY BASSLET
Pseudanthias dispar

POWDER BLUE SURGEONFISH
Acanthurus leucosternon

PUNTANG GOBY
Exyrias puntang

REDBELLY TILAPIA
Tilapia zillii

RIVULATED PARROTFISH
Scarus rivulatus

SIAMESE FIGHTING FISH
Betta splendens

* *Leafy seadragon*

SMALLMOUTH BASS
Micropterus dolomieu

SNAKESKIN GOURAMI
Trichogaster pectoralis

SPEARFISH REMORA
Remora brachyptera

SPOTTED SURGEONFISH
Ctenochaetus strigothus

STRIPED BASS
Morone saxatilis

STRIPED MULLET
Mugil cephalus

STRIPED SNAKEHEAD
Channa striata

TOMATO GROUPER
Cephalopholis sonnerati

VERMICULATED SPINEFOOT
Siganus vermiculatus

WHITE BASS
Morone chrysops

WHITE GROUPER
Epinephelus aeneus

YELLOW BASS
Morone mississippiensis

YELLOW LONGNOSE BUTTERFLYFISH
Forcipiger flavissimus

YELLOWLINE GOBY
Elacatinus horsti

YELLOW PERCH
Perca flavescens

YELLOWTAIL SNAPPER
Ocyurus chrysurus

BARRACUDA FAMILY

GUACHANCHE BARRACUDA
Sphyraena guachancho

INDO-PACIFIC SAILFISH
Istiophorus platypterus

SAILFIN MOLLY
Poecillia latipinna

SWORDFISH
Xiphias gladius

SCORPIONFISH AND SCULPIN FAMILY

BLUE ROCKFISH
Sebastes mystinus

* *Razorfish*

FRINGELIP FLATHEAD
Sunagocia otaitensis

RED SEA STONEFISH
Synanceia nana

SMALL RED SCORPIONFISH
Scorpaena notate

SEAHORSES AND PIPEFISH

BELLY PIPEFISH
Hippichthys heptagonus

FRESHWATER PIPEFISH
Pseudophallus mindii

NINE-SPINED STICKLEBACK
Pungitius pungitius

SLENDER SEAHORSE
Hippocampus reidi

YELLOW SEAHORSE
Hippocampus kuda

PUFFERS AND FILEFISH

BLACK-BANDED SUNFISH
Enneacanthus chaetodon

BUFFALO TRUNKFISH
Lactophrys trigonis

FUGU FISH
Takifugu rubripes

NORTHERN PUFFER
Spheroides maculatus

OARFISH
Regalecus glesne

SPOTTED TRUNKFISH
Lactophrys bicaudalis

JAWLESS FISH

EUROPEAN RIVER LAMPREY
Lampetra fluviatilis

PACIFIC LAMPREY
Lampetra tridentate

POUCHED LAMPREY
Geotria australis

SEA LAMPREY
Petromyzon marinus

* *Crocodile fish*

* *Leaf scorpionfish*

BONY-TONGUE FISH

ARAPAIMA
Arapaima gigas

AROWANA
Osteoglossum bicirrhosum

GLASS KNIFEFISH
Eigenmannia virescens

COELACANTHS

INDONESIAN COELACANTH
Latimeria menadoensis

WEST INDIAN OCEAN COELACANTH
Latimeria chalumnae

STURGEON FAMILY

ATLANTIC STURGEON
Acipenser oxyrinchus spp. Oxyrinchus

BELUGA STURGEON
Huso huso

CHINESE PADDLEFISH
Psephurus gladius

EUROPEAN STURGEON
Acipenser sturio

LAKE STURGEON
Acipenser fulvescens

RUSSIAN STURGEON
Acipenser gueldenstaedtii

WHITE STURGEON
Acipenser transmontanus

* *Reef stonefish*

HERRING FAMILY

ATLANTIC HERRING
Clupea harengus

EUROPEAN ANCHOVY
Engraulis encrasicolus

SOUTH AMERICAN PILCHARD
Sardinops sagax

LANTERNFISH FAMILY

METALLIC LANTERNFISH
Myctophum affine

NORTHERN LAMPFISH
Stenobrachius leucopsaurus

* *Lizard fish*

COD FAMILY

ATLANTIC COD
Gadus morphua

BURBOT
Lota lota

EUROPEAN HAKE
Merluccius merluccius

HADDOCK
Melanogrammus aeglefinus

OFFSHORE SILVER HAKE
Merluccius albidus

PACIFIC COD
Gadus macrocephalus

Damselfly

Giraffe weevil

Jumping spider

Vampire crab

Trap jaw ant

Arthropods includes insects, arachnids, and crustaceans. at some point in its life; spiders can never fly; almost spiders have four pairs, millipedes can have dozens. ▶ With more than a

ARTHROPODS

Elegant grasshopper

▶ They are invertebrates—they have no backbone. ▶ Nearly every insect can fly every crustacean lives in water. ▶ Insects have three pairs of jointed legs, million species, arthropods make up Earth's biggest animal phylum.

THEY BUZZ, THEY FLY, THEY STING, they slurp, they crawl, they molt. There are many more of them than us. They live just about everywhere and come in thousands of different shapes and sizes. They are the single largest group of animals on the planet, with more than a million different species. They are . . . the arthropods.

Insects are the largest group of the arthropods. They are essential to our survival and to the health of all ecosystems. They pollinate the plants and provide food for the animals that we eat, eat the insects that can harm us, and can even help us investigate crime.

There is enormous variety within the insect class, and an even greater range of behaviors, traits, and ways of living among species within the arthropod phylum, which includes insects, arachnids, crustaceans, centipedes, and others. More than 80 percent of the world's animal species are arthropods.

LIFE CYCLE

All arthropods are born from eggs. In the case of insects, one animal might produce a single egg or millions over a lifetime. Most insect parents leave the eggs and the young insects to fend for themselves. Some wasps bring live insects into their nests for their young to feed on. Bees take great care of their young, raising them in their hives and feeding them after they come out of their eggs. Crustaceans also lay millions of eggs in their lifetimes. They do not care for their young but they do tend to their eggs.

METAMORPHOSIS

Each type of arthropod undergoes a succession of changes to its body during its life. Insects grow using one of two types of changes. In simple metamorphosis, which has three stages, an insect is hatched from an egg. It looks like a mini version of the adult and is called a nymph (or a naiad if it lives in water). As it grows, it repeatedly molts, or sheds its exoskeleton.

COMPLETE METAMORPHOSIS

Complete metamorphosis has four stages, from egg to larva to pupa to adult. An example of an insect that undergoes complete metamorphosis is the monarch butterfly.

LIVE ACTION: INSECT TALE

A green pupa is attached to a branch. It seems to wiggle, but not from the breeze. Suddenly, the skin of the pouch breaks; a leg pokes out. Then another, and another. Over the next few minutes, a beautiful monarch butterfly emerges from the pupa. Weeks earlier, it was a squishy caterpillar, eating as much milkweed plant as it could find. Now the amazing insect metamorphosis is complete. As soon as it finds a mate, the cycle starts all over again.

MOLTING AS THEY GROW

Other arthropods, including crustaceans and some insects, also start as larvae, and molt their exoskeleton as they grow and change. With each successive change, some crustaceans grow new legs, add body segments, or show off larger limbs and claws.

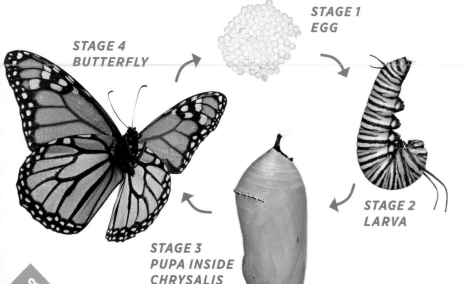

STAGE 1 EGG

STAGE 4 BUTTERFLY

STAGE 2 LARVA

STAGE 3 PUPA INSIDE CHRYSALIS

A molting green cicada emerging from its shell.

ARACHNIDS

Arachnids have several things in common with insects. They possess exoskeletons, jointed legs, and segmented bodies. There are some key differences:

▶ Two body segments rather than three

▶ Body segments are abdomen and cephalothorax

▶ Eight legs rather than six

MOUTH Insects have mouthparts that can bite, stab, or slurp, depending on the species.

EYES Most insects have compound eyes made up of thousands of tiny visual receptors.

ANTENNAE Insects use these to gather information about the world around them.

BODY An adult insect's body has three parts: head, thorax, and abdomen.

Mango tree borer

WINGS At some time in their lives, most insects have wings. Most species have four of them.

LIMBS Insects have six legs.

EXOSKELETON Most insects have hard outer shells that are both their skeleton and skin.

CRUSTACEANS

Crustaceans have hard exoskeletons, jointed limbs, and two sets of antennae. Their limbs are "biramous," which means that each limb branches off into two parts. Some crustaceans, such as crabs and lobsters, also have four "walking legs" plus large claws at the end of two additional limbs. Since most crustaceans spend their lives underwater, they are able to breathe using gills, similar to fish.

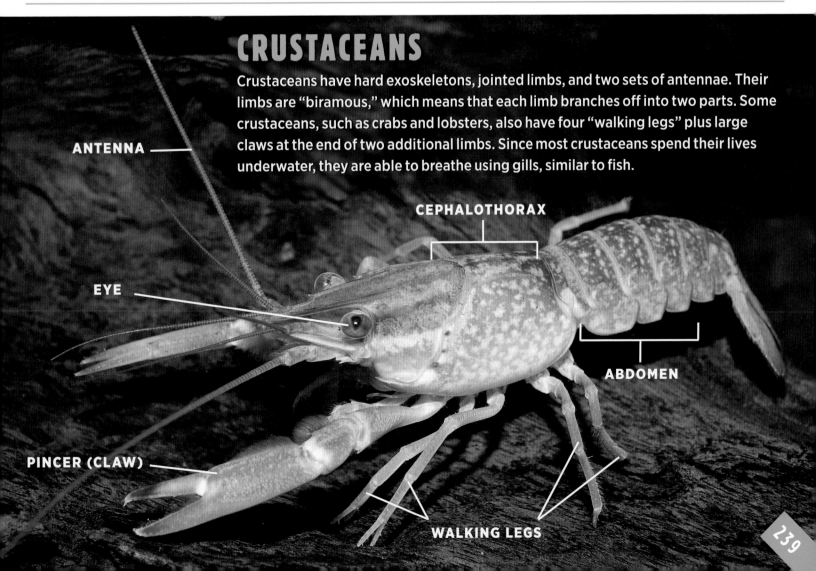

ANTENNA

CEPHALOTHORAX

EYE

ABDOMEN

PINCER (CLAW)

WALKING LEGS

SENSES

Insects have amazing ways of taking in information about the world around them. Nearly all have eyes to gather visual data. Dragonflies and damselflies have large compound eyes that can see nearly all the way around their bodies. Many insects also have simple eyes to detect light and dark. Larval crustaceans also have simple eyes and develop compound eyes as they grow. Spiders, meanwhile, generally have four pairs of eyes.

Most insects can sense sound as vibrations felt through their bodies. Insects and crustaceans use their antennae the way most animals use their noses. Insects also have some special sense organs. Bristles on the exoskeleton that transmit information to the brain are one type. Another are organs called chemoreceptors, which are used to sense chemicals left by fellow insects. Fruit flies use these to be sure they are mating with other fruit flies.

COMMUNICATION

As far as we know, insects don't have language, but they do have methods of passing information around. The most obvious way is through the remarkable range of noises they can make. Crickets chirp, cockroaches hiss, cicadas hum, and mosquitoes (and others) buzz. Living underwater, most crustaceans can't communicate well with sound or smell, so they depend on vision to connect with each other and to look for food.

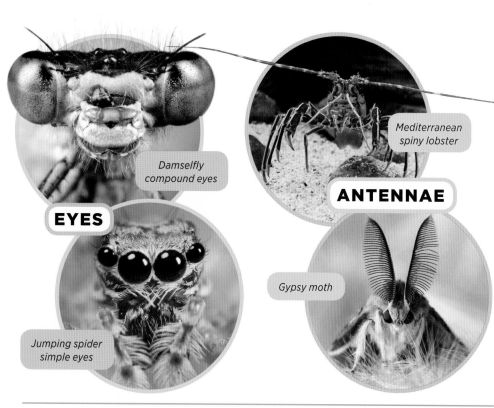

EYES

Damselfly compound eyes

Jumping spider simple eyes

ANTENNAE

Mediterranean spiny lobster

Gypsy moth

EARS

Surprisingly Human

Katydids and crickets have ears. Like the membrane in the human eardrum, it is called a tympanum, and it picks up vibrations. But on this insect, the tympanum is on its leg.

FEEDING HABITS

Insects have different foods to choose from, and different feeding tools and behaviors. Plant eaters such as milkweed bugs have strong mouthparts that can pierce plant skin. Slurpers suck nectar through a proboscis, a long mouthpart that uncoils to suck nectar from plants. And insects with strong mouthparts called mandibles use them to chomp into food.

STICK & SLURP

◀ *Butterflies drink their food through a proboscis, which acts like a straw. They feed on nectar, juices from soft fruits, and other liquids.*

▶ *The assassin bug lands on its prey and stabs a mouthpart into it, releasing a toxin that dissolves the prey's insides. That mouthpart then slurps up the goo.*

TRAP & STAB

BITE & CHOMP

▲ *Spiders are carnivores. They capture prey (usually insects), stab to inject venom, and then eat.*

EVOLUTION

Trilobite

As an animal class, insects are older than dinosaurs. The oldest fossils of insects date back more than 350 million years. Some insects of today, such as mayflies, cockroaches, and some beetles, are not that different from what has fossilized. Another way we acquire evidence of ancient insects is through preservation in amber. Amber is a mineral that was once tree sap. Ancient insects got caught in the sticky goo, which hardened over the millennia.

Many insects evolved after the growth of flowering plants, which started about 140 million years ago. The relationship between insects and flowering plants is a symbiotic one, meaning that both get something out of it. Over time, insects pollinated flowering plants, allowing them to reproduce and thrive, while the rapid development of flowering plants provided more food to sustain larger populations of insects.

Crustacean fossils have been found that are older still, dating as far back as 500 million years. The ancestors of today's crabs and shrimps probably included trilobites, one of the most common ancient fossils.

LOCOMOTION

Although the number of species of insect is enormous, the number of ways they get around is limited: Nearly all walk or fly. Some insects can move very quickly for their size on their six legs, scuttling along the ground, and some have hooks on their feet that let them climb vertical surfaces, too.

How insects get around also depends on where they are in the life cycle. Nearly all insects can fly at some point in their lives, even if it's for a short period of time. Larvae cannot fly and have to move by walking or swimming. Then there are the water bugs and aquatic beetles, which can fly but instead live mostly underwater. They can swim using paddlelike feet, though they have to breathe at the surface or from air bubbles that they bring under the water with them. Insects such as grasshoppers can leap far to reach their food or escape predators, but they can also fly.

JUMPING

Grasshopper

FLYING

Two-spotted lady bird

STRIDING

Water strider

INCHING

Green-moth caterpillar

241

THIS LARGE GROUP OF INSECTS includes some of the fastest fliers in the animal kingdom. With more than 5,600 species in Odonata, they are also a very large order. The second order in the group, Ephemeroptera, includes more than 3,000 species.

Odonata (dragonflies and damselflies) start life in the water as naiads, hatching from eggs. They live underwater until they emerge to change into adults. Spreading their wings, they become fierce predators. They are able to move each wing on its own, giving them the ability to turn quickly. Because they need to mate and lay eggs on the water, they spend most of their lives near ponds, streams, and rivers.

Ephemeroptera (mayflies) are known for their short life spans. Their naiads are well known to fishermen. Because the baby insects are sought by fish, anglers create lures designed to look like mayfly naiads.

EMPEROR DRAGONFLY
Anax imperator

SIZE: **3 inches long (7.6 cm)**
HABITAT: **Ponds, streams; Europe, Africa, central Asia, Arabian Peninsula**
FOOD: **Insects**

The emperor dragonfly is a fast flier. It captures and eats smaller insects while in flight. Female emperors lay their eggs atop plants floating on water. This helps protect the eggs from some predators. Males create small enclaves and attack other males who dare to come near. Emperors originated in North Africa but are common in most parts of Europe, too.

YELLOW MAYFLY
Potamanthus luteus

SIZE: **0.5–1 inch long (1.3–2.5 cm)**
HABITAT: **Ponds, streams; United Kingdom**
FOOD: **Plant matter**

Mayflies live as adults for only a very short time, often less than a day. They change from the nymph stage, mate, lay eggs, and die. Adults of most species do not feed. This species lives near only a few small rivers in England. Despite their proximity to water, they are weak swimmers and stay mostly on shorelines.

PACIFIC SPIKETAIL
Cordulegaster dorsalis

SIZE: **3–3.5 inches long (7.6–8.9 cm)**
HABITAT: **Mountains; western United States**
FOOD: **Insects**

Adders are also dragonflies, but with distinctive bodies. The naiads have a fuzzy appearance. They breed in water, and often live in woodlands as adults. They are especially powerful fliers, making them threatening predators of other insects.

Animal Antics Emerging mayfly swarms can be so huge that they can be picked up on radar. Low-flying planes (and highway-driving cars), should beware when traveling through the midwestern United States in the spring.

TWO-STRIPED SKIMMER
Orthetrum caffrum

SIZE: **1.5 inches long (3.8 cm)**
HABITAT: **Ponds, streams; Africa, Madagascar, Arabian Peninsula**
FOOD: **Insects**

Skimmers are one of the largest families of dragonflies. They get their name from the way they skim the surface of the ponds where they live. This species has distinctive stripes on their sides and between their wings.

COMMON BLUETAIL DAMSELFLY
Ischnura heterosticta

SIZE: 1 inch long (2.5 cm)
HABITAT: Ponds, streams; eastern and southwestern Australia
FOOD: Insects

This Australian damselfly shows off a bright blue body and tail tip. Its bright colors are typical of many species of dragonflies and damselflies. It has thin, delicate wings. A trait of damselflies, it can fold its wings back along its body.

BASKING MALACHITE DAMSELFLY
Chlorolestes apricans

SIZE: **1.5 inches long (3.8 cm)**
HABITAT: **Streams; South Africa**
FOOD: **Insects**

Cousins of the dragonfly, damselflies generally have thinner bodies and smaller wings than dragonflies. They have compound eyes and are very good fliers. Damselflies can eat and mate while flying. This species is making a comeback in its South African home after its habitat was threatened.

GREEN DARNER
Anax junius

SIZE: 2.5–3 inches long (6.4–7.6 cm)
HABITAT: Ponds, streams; North America, northern Central America, Kamchatka Peninsula, Japan, China
FOOD: Insects

Scientists have determined that darners, a species of dragonfly, can fly as much as 7 miles in one day. With a wingspan of 4-1/2 inches (11 cm), it is one of the largest dragonflies in North America. Why "darner"? Some people thought these dragonflies looked liked a darning needle, which is used to repair knitted clothing.

A LARGE NUMBER OF SIMILAR-LOOKING insects are well known for their ability to leap and for their long-limbed lankiness. Mantids are fierce predators. They have some of the fastest reflexes in the animal kingdom. As patient hunters, they wait until prey comes by before reaching out to grab it with their front legs and clamping on with powerful jaws. Stick insects eat plants, not insects, but they are certainly good at hiding. Most resemble the type of plants they live on, from flowers to branches to leaves.

Grasshoppers and crickets have long legs like the mantids and stick insects, but use theirs to get around. They can leap many times their body length, though they can also fly.

Nearly all these insects make their homes in areas with lots of plants, both for places to hide and rest and as sources for food.

GIANT PRICKLY STICK INSECT
Extatosoma tiaratum

SIZE: 6–8 inches long (15.2–20.3 cm)
HABITAT: Forest; Queensland, New South Wales, New Guinea
FOOD: Plants

This insect is a master of camouflage. Its brown coloring and the varying shapes of its body parts help it blend into trees. It lays eggs that fall to the forest floor. Ants transport them back to their colony. The eggs will still hatch, and the nymphs that emerge will smell and look like the ants. This is yet another form of mimicry in the same species.

GIANT DEAD LEAF MANTIS
Deroplatys desiccata

SIZE: 2.5–3 inches long (6.4–7.6 cm)
HABITAT: Rainforest; Malaysia
FOOD: Insects

This species gets its long name from a defensive move. When threatened, they will sometimes flop down and "play dead." They lie motionless and might not even move if touched. With an upper body that looks like a dead leaf, they also use camouflage to hide from predators.

EASTERN LUBBER GRASSHOPPER
Romalea guttatus

SIZE: 3 inches long (7.6 cm)
HABITAT: Forests, meadows; south-central United States
FOOD: Plants

While most grasshoppers get around quite well, this flightless type is slow. Its name—lubber—means "lazy." Since they can't fly, they are often run over on roadways, sometimes hundreds at a time. Lubbers can come in many colors, from black to orange. They can cause damage to crops when they arrive in large numbers.

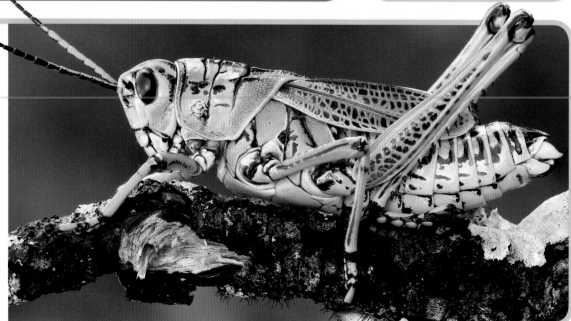

FIELD CRICKET
Gryllus pennsylvanicus

SIZE: **0.5–1 inch long (1.3–2.5 cm)**
HABITAT: **Forest or meadow floor; southern Canada to northern Mexico**
FOOD: **Plant and animal matter**

Field crickets are common insects. Like other crickets, they are best known for their song, a series of chirps created by rubbing one wing against the other. The song has its own pattern of chirps, which is used—primarily by the males—to attract mates or identify territory.

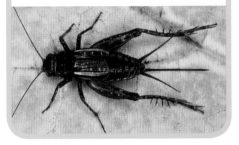

Surprisingly Human

Their upright posture and long limbs give mantids a rare humanlike look among insects. The praying mantis here looks like a person holding their hands in a moment of supplication.

BROAD-TIPPED CONEHEAD KATYDID
Neoconocephalus triops

SIZE: **1–2.5 inches long (2.5–6.4 cm)**
HABITAT: **Grasslands, near houses; southern United States, Caribbean**
FOOD: **Plant matter**

Katydids get their name from what their chirps supposedly sound like. They make sounds similar to crickets by rubbing body parts together. This species is a plant-eater. It has a triangular, cone-shaped head.

GIANT MALAYSIAN SHIELD MANTIS
Rhombodera basalis

SIZE: **4–5 inches long (10.2–12.7 cm)**
HABITAT: **Rainforest; Malaysia**
FOOD: **Insects, small reptiles**

One of the largest and most colorful of the mantids, this insect makes its home in Southeast Asia. Like others of their order, they lay their eggs in a casing called an ootheca. Its hard shell helps protect the eggs until they hatch. These insects have bright colors and a distinctive shield that aids in protection and camouflage.

PRAYING MANTIS
Mantis religiosa

SIZE: **2–3 inches long (5.1–7.6 cm)**
HABITAT: **Grasslands, forest; Europe, northern Africa, Asia, United States**
FOOD: **Insects**

From its praying-hands position, this mantis can strike out with great speed and ferocity if prey wanders nearby. It is dangerous to other insects, but poses no harm to humans. These mantises mate only once a year.

INSECTS AND PEOPLE CONNECT in many ways. Not all of those ways are enjoyable for the people, however. Cockroaches, unpopular with most people, have an important job to do in nature. They scavenge food, eating dead animals and plants that otherwise would rot. When they leave nature and come into areas where people live, they can be an enormous pest, eating anything that people eat, even burrowing into bags of food. They are one of the most ancient insects—300-million-year-old fossils similar to modern cockroaches have been found.

Another insect that causes many problems for people is the termite. These are among the only animals in the world that can eat and digest material called cellulose, which is what wood is made of. Termites can cause great damage to wooden houses and other structures. They live in nests. As social insects, individual termites have specific jobs, such as soldier or queen. Huge nests can infest a building and turn it from a home into a meal.

MARDI GRAS COCKROACH
Polyzosteria mitchelli

SIZE: **2 inches long (5.1 cm)**
HABITAT: **Forest floor; Australia**
FOOD: **Decaying plants and animals**

The mardi gras cockroach stands out for its amazing coloring. While most cockroaches are very dull in color—black or brown—this species has streaks of blue, yellow, or orange along its back. As with many cockroach species, it can spew out a nasty-smelling goo if threatened.

GERMAN COCKROACH
Blatella germanica

SIZE: **1 inch long (2.6 cm)**
HABITAT: **Human dwellings; North America, Africa, Australia, oceanic islands**
FOOD: **Human food and decaying matter**

The German cockroach is the most well-known species. They live nearly everywhere that people live, eating anything and everything they can reach. Their sticky feet allow them to climb on any surface, while a flat body helps them pass through tiny crevices in search of food.

FORMOSAN SUBTERRANEAN TERMITE
Coptotermes formosanus

SIZE: **0.5 inch long (1.3 cm)**
HABITAT: **Wood, subsoil; southern China, Taiwan, Japan, South Africa, the Americas**
FOOD: **Wood**

Living in underground nests with millions of individual termites, this species can swarm out in great numbers to mate. It is originally from the island of Taiwan, which used to be known as Formosa, and arrived in the southeast United States in the early 1900s. This destructive insect lives underground and can infest a house from its foundation.

GIANT HISSING COCKROACH
Gromphadorhina portentosa

SIZE: **2-3 inches long (5.1–7.6 cm)**
HABITAT: **Forest floor; Madagascar**
FOOD: **Decaying plants and animals**

Often seen in zoos and even classrooms as pets, this is one of the most well-known cockroaches. It looks scary, but it is harmless. It can make a loud hissing sound by forcing air through small holes in its abdomen called spiracles.

FUN FACT!
How bad is the damage from termites? The U.S. Department of Agriculture statistics show more than 600,000 homes are damaged each year. Americans spend as much as $5 billion a year to fix problems caused by these insects.

PACIFIC DAMPWOOD TERMITE
Zootermopsis angusticollis

SIZE: 0.5–1 inch long (1.3–2.5 cm)
HABITAT: Forest; Baja California, Pacific coast of United States, British Columbia
FOOD: Rotten wood

Dampwood termites aren't interested in dry wood, as most termites are. This means that they don't usually do damage to houses. Dampwood termites live in forests where they eat decaying and rotting logs and trees. They also swarm, often in late summer, moving their nests to a new location. They are the largest species of termite in North America.

HARLEQUIN COCKROACH
Neostylopyga rhombifolia

SIZE: 0.75–1 in. (20-27 mm)
HABITAT: In or near human habitation, forest; topical and subtropical areas worldwide
FOOD: Decaying animals and plant matter

An attractive cockroach? Thanks to a colorful speckled pattern on their exoskeletons, harlequins are actually kept by some people as pet insects.

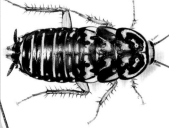

AMERICAN COCKROACH
Periplaneta americana

SIZE: 1.5–2 inches long (3.8–5.1 cm)
HABITAT: Moist areas; worldwide
FOOD: Decaying plants and animals

Like its cousin the German cockroach, this species lives where people do. However, it is more mobile and can also live outside, so it is often found in drains, steam pipes, or sewers.

GIANT COCKROACH
Blaberus giganteus

SIZE: 3–4 inches long (7.6–10.2 cm)
HABITAT: Rainforest, tropical forest; Central America, northern South America
FOOD: Decaying plants and animals

As its name suggests, this South and Central American native is one of the largest cockroaches in the world. Its large size helps it avoid some predators, while the stinky goo it lets out when grabbed scares away others. It has a flat body that allows it to burrow in slim crevasses. When a female mates, she can lay eggs for life. She lays the eggs in batches over time.

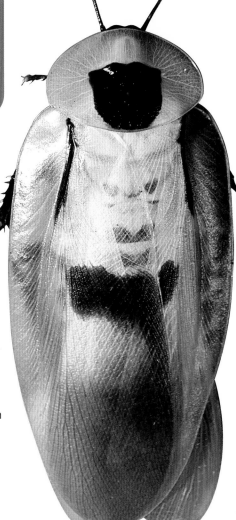

ANTS
LONG LEGS, BENT ANTENNAE, COVERING ALMOST EVERY REGION ON EARTH

THERE ARE ABOUT 7 BILLION people on Earth. There are an estimated 100 trillion ants. If they ever decided to take over, we'd be heavily outnumbered. Ants live in every habitat on Earth except water. Their enormous colonies can include millions of individual ants. They make nests underground, in huge mounds of earth, in trees, and in human structures. In the colonies, ants have different jobs. One queen ant does all the egg-laying. Worker ants bring food. Soldier ants protect against invaders.

Scientists studying ants have found some truly amazing behaviors. Ants can leave a chemical trail to help one another find food or return to the nest. Some ant species can form living bridges. Army ants can ravage a landscape, destroying plants and wildlife. Some ants can sting, causing humans a lot of pain or even death.

INCHMAN BULL ANT
Myrmecia forficata

SIZE: 0.5–1 inch long (1.3–2.5 cm)
HABITAT: Forest, woodland; southeastern Australia, Tasmania
FOOD: Insects, nectar, fruit

Visitors to southeastern Australian forests should watch where they step. Bulldog ants have a very powerful venom and can cause great pain with their stings. They may hide their nests out of sight of predators.

ARGENTINE ANT
Linepithema humile

SIZE: 0.1 inch long (0.3 cm)
HABITAT: Urban areas; northern South America, Europe, Asia, Australia, Africa
FOOD: Anything

Native to South America, these ants now live all over the globe. They are known as a "tramp" species due to their wide travel. In many places, they have become a pest, damaging crops or infesting human homes. A key to their survival is their noncompetitive nature. Unlike many other ant species, they seldom compete with one another.

BOLIVIAN ARMY ANT
Eciton hamatum

SIZE: 0.08–1 inch long (0.2–2.5 cm)
HABITAT: Tropical forest; Mexico, central Brazil, Bolivia, French Guiana
FOOD: Insects, plants

Army ants get their name from how they move: in massive groups like a marching army. This orange-colored species moves in long columns, while other species swarm over the ground. Army ants can cause great damage to a habitat, eating almost any plant, small animal, or insect in their path.

Surprisingly Human

Researchers at Arizona State University found that ants and people share similar ways of choosing a home. Ants look at several possibilities and the pick the one that fits all their needs. It's not random chance, but a careful decision.

COMMON FIRE ANT
Myrmica rubra

SIZE: 0.1–0.25 inch long (0.3–0.6 cm)
HABITAT: Meadows, riverbanks; Europe
FOOD: Insects, honeydew

Fire ants sting when threatened, and their venom can be very painful. Native to Europe, they know also live in North America, often near to human beings. Each colony is made up of several different nests.

RED HARVESTER ANT
Pogonomyrmex barbatus

SIZE: 0.5 inch long (1.3 cm)
HABITAT: Desert, scrubland; southern United States
FOOD: Seeds, dead insects

This ant can cause a lot of damage to crops and plant life. It uses its powerful jaws to grind up seeds. The resulting paste is stored in the nest to feed the colony. These ants can painfully sting or bite humans and other animals that disturb a nest.

JACK JUMPER ANT
Myrmecia pilosula

SIZE: 0.5 inch long (1.3 cm)
HABITAT: Sandy soil, woodland; Australia, Tasmania
FOOD: Insects

Jack jumpers get their name from the hops they make if disturbed. They also have a bite that can be painful to humans. Some people can get very sick from the jumper's venom, too. On the island of Tasmania, they cause more deaths than snakes and spiders.

MEXICAN LEAFCUTTER ANT
Atta Mexicana

SIZE: 1 inch long (2.5 cm)
HABITAT: Urban areas; Mexico, Arizona
FOOD: Plants

The worker ants of this species cut up leaves and carry the parts back to their nests. Other ants in the nest chew up the leaves to grow a fungus that feeds the whole colony. Leafcutter ant nests are among the largest in the ant world, filled with millions of ants doing different jobs.

NORTHERN WOOD ANT
Formica aquilonia

SIZE: 0.5 inch long (1.3 cm)
HABITAT: Forest, woodland; Scotland, Ireland, Europe
FOOD: Dead animals

Found in Europe and the largest ant in the British Isles, the Northern wood ant makes tall, cone-shaped nests covered with pine needles. They are among the ant species that "farm" aphids, eating the honeydew the aphids make while keeping the aphids alive so they keep producing this tasty liquid. They are also known as Scottish wood ants. They are red and black.

BEES AND WASPS

SEE A BEAUTIFUL FLOWER? Thank a bee. Eat some fruit for breakfast? Thank a bee. Check out a tree in bloom? Again ...thank a bee. By spreading pollen from plant to plant, bees help many growing things thrive. Experts estimate that as much as half of everything we eat is in some way helped to grow by bees.

Honey bees live in colonies around a queen, a larger bee that lays eggs to increase the colony. Some bees leave the hive to gather the pollen. Others stay behind to look after eggs or make the honey that becomes the bee's food. Human beings have kept bees for millions of years in order to harvest honey.

Wasps and hornets are similar to bees in body structure, hive life, and stinging ability. Some species do pollinate, but not nearly as much as bees do.

NORTHERN PAPER WASP
Polistes fuscatus

SIZE: 0.5–1 inch long (1.3–2.5 cm)
HABITAT: Woodland, urban areas; southern Canada, northern United States
FOOD: Nectar, insects

To create its nest, these wasps chew wood and other plants to make a kind of paste. They press this paste into sheets that make the nest. Inside the nest, small cells or chambers are used to hold their eggs. They may also put a caterpillar or small insect inside the nest to feed the hatched larvae.

EUROPEAN HONEYBEE
Apis mellifera

SIZE: 0.5 inch long (1.3 cm)
HABITAT: Meadows, gardens; Europe, Asia, Africa, the Americas
FOOD: Pollen, nectar, honey

Also called the Western honeybee, this is the main pollinator in most of Europe. A pollen basket on its rear legs helps it carry large amounts of pollen back to the colony. Once there, the bees secrete a waxy substance that forms the walls of the hive. The queen lays eggs in this wax, and the hatched larvae are tended by other bees. The European bee is also found in Asia, Africa, and the Americas.

ALFALFA LEAFCUTTER BEE
Megachile rotundata

SIZE: 0.25 inch long (0.6 cm)
HABITAT: Meadows; Europe, Asia, Australia
FOOD: Nectar, pollen

First they cut, then they build. Using their mandibles, these bees chop parts of plants into small, circular-shaped pieces. They then assemble these pieces into nests that may range up to 7 inches (18 cm) in length.

ORANGE SPIDER WASP
Priocnemis bicolor

SIZE: 1 inch long (2.5 cm)
HABITAT: Meadows; Australia
FOOD: Spiders, nectar

This wasp is bad news if you're a south Australian spider. The wasp stings and paralyzes the spider. Then it drags the spider back to its nest, buries it and lays an egg on it. After the egg hatches, the wasp larva eats the spider, which is often still alive.

EASTERN CARPENTER BEE
Xylocopa violacea

SIZE: 0.5–1.5 inches long (1.3–3.8 cm)
HABITAT: Old wood; Europe, Asia
FOOD: Pollen, nectar

This bee stands out for two reasons: Its color is often bright purple or violet, with very shiny wings; and it makes its home in trees or wood of other sorts, earning its name by boring into the wood to create space for a nest.

The U.S. government is helping farmers keep bees that pollinate their crops. In 2014, it gave $4 million to the Midwest alone to help. "The future of America's food supply depends on honeybees," said U.S. Secretary of Agriculture Tom Vilsack.

BLACK-AND-YELLOW MUD DAUBER
Sceliphron caementarium

SIZE: 1 inch long (2.5 cm)
HABITAT: Urban areas, woodland; Canada, United States, Central America, South Africa, West Indies
FOOD: Nectar, insects

To build their nests, these insects gather bits of mud from ponds and puddles. They pack it together to create hard nests, often attached to buildings or trees. In these nests, they then lay their eggs. These insects have very narrow waists, sometimes called thread waists. They rarely sting in self-defense.

BALD-FACED HORNET
Dolichovespula maculata

SIZE: 0.5–0.75 inch long (1.3–2 cm)
HABITAT: Forest, urban areas; Canada, United States
FOOD: Nectar, insects

This insect has white patches on its head that create its bald look. Though it's called a hornet, it's more closely related to a yellowjacket, which is a different type of insect. The bald-faced hornet forms a large papery nest that is often shaped like a football. These nests can be up to 3 feet long.

BUTTERFLIES AND MOTHS

BUTTERFLIES ARE SOME OF THE MOST colorful animals in the world. The bright patterns on their wings are made from individual scales that may shimmer in the light. Butterfly bodies are usually very slender, with six legs. Their antennae end in a small bulb. Butterflies go through complete metamorphosis, emerging from cocoons after changing from a larval form called a caterpillar.

Moths also change as butterflies do. Their bodies, however, are generally more round or stout. They usually have feathery, oval-shaped antennae. Though there are exceptions, most moths are more muted colors. While butterflies like to feed and fly during the day, many moths are active at night.

Both caterpillars have mouths that can bite and chew up plants. The adults have only a sipper called a proboscis that slurps up plant nectar. More than 150,000 species of butterflies and moths have been identified.

CHINESE OAK SILKMOTH
Antheraea pernyi

SIZE: **5–6 inches (12.7–15.2 cm) (wingspan)**
HABITAT: **Forest; Eastern Asia**
FOOD: **Plants, trees, shrubs (larvae)**

This moth is a member of the giant silk moth family, which have cocoons wrapped in silk. Silk from this moth is called "tussah silk," which is considered to be a "wild silk" and is darker in color compared to the white silk spun by domesticated silkmoths.

POLYPHEMUS MOTH
Antheraea polyphemus

SIZE: **6 inches (15.2 cm) (wingspan)**
HABITAT: **Forest; North America**
FOOD: **Plants (larvae)**

With one eyelike spot on each wing, this moth gets its name from a one-eyed monster in Greek mythology. It lives throughout the United States, as well as parts of Mexico and Canada. Its cocoon can be covered in leaves, so it is harder for predators to find in the branches. These moths will startle predators with a quick, violent flap of their wings.

RED CRACKER BUTTERFLY
Hamadryas amphinome

SIZE: **3–3.5 inches (7.6–8.9 cm) (wingspan)**
HABITAT: **Tropical forest; Mexico, Central America, northern South America**
FOOD: **Rotting fruit, sap**

Listen carefully and you might hear how this South American butterfly got its name (though it should perhaps be "blue cracker"). When males take off in flight, they make a crackling sound by clapping their wings together. In the evening, adults come together on individual trees, then spread apart to retire until the following morning.

There is a growing "peace silk" movement designed to protect farmed silkmoths by waiting until after they have completed metamorphosis to harvest the cocoons.

CAIRNS BIRDWING BUTTERFLY
Ornithoptera euphorion

SIZE: **5–6 inches (12.7–15.2 cm) (wingspan)**
HABITAT: **Rainforest; northeastern Australia**
FOOD: **Plants, nectar**

This colorful insect uses chemoreceptors to taste plants to make sure that they are the right kind. They often eat from a vine that is poisonous to other animals, thus defending against most predators. This is one of Australia's largest butterflies. That country has several conservation projects to help preserve its habitat.

ATLAS MOTH
Attacus atlas

SIZE: **10–12 inches (25.4–30.5 cm) (wingspan)**
HABITAT: **Tropical and subtropical forests; southeastern Asia, Malay Archipelago**
FOOD: **Plants (larvae)**

This is one of the largest species of moth in the world. However, they only live for about a week after emerging from their large cocoons. One reason: Adults do not have a mouth.

ORNATE MOTH
Utetheisa ornatrix

SIZE: **1.5 inches (3.8 cm) (wingspan)**
HABITAT: **Meadows; midwestern and eastern United States and Canada, Mexico, Central America**
FOOD: **Plants**

There are two reasons many people enjoy this moth. It's one of the most colorful species, and it flies during the day so we can observe it. Also called the bella moth, it is often seen near plants called rattlepods in parts of the United States

BLUE MORPHO BUTTERFLY
Morpho peleides

SIZE: **3–8 inches (7.6–20.3 cm) (wingspan)**
HABITAT: **Forest trails, woodland streams; Mexico, northern South America**
FOOD: **Fruit, sap**

The bright blue scales on this large Central American butterfly might seem to make it easy to spot. But it has a secret. The underside of this species' wings is a mixture of brown and white spots. The contrast between the two sides of the wings when it flies makes it harder for predators to see. This beauty is fleeting, however. Adults only live for about two to three weeks.

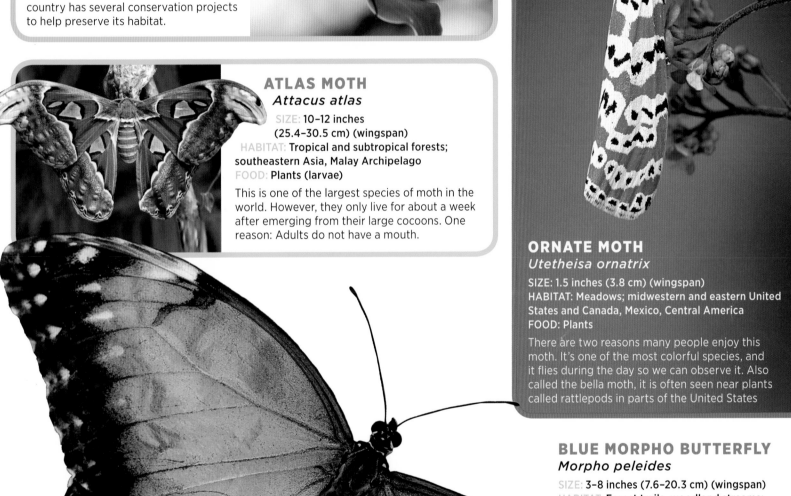

253

SPICEBUSH SWALLOWTAIL

The spicebush swallowtail caterpillar has two large spots back behind its head. When threatened, it can raise its front end up to look like a larger snake or lizard head. This caterpillar also can spin a mat of silk between leaves, making a mini shelter to rest in between meals.

While inside, the caterpillar undergoes one of nature's most amazing transformations. It emerges as a fully adult butterfly. Its lifespan, like those of many butterflies, is very short, perhaps only two weeks.

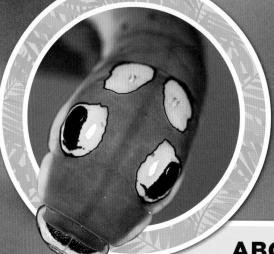

ABOUT ME!

I'm a spicebush swallowtail caterpillar. I'm a good mimic, or copycat. When I was younger, I was brown and looked like bird droppings (poop!). Now I'm green and have two large black-and-white eyelike spots. This makes me look like a snake, which keeps birds from eating me.

7 FACTS ABOUT THE SPICEBUSH SWALLOWTAIL

- ▸ Is found throughout the eastern United States
- ▸ Caterpillar was supposedly inspiration for the Pokémon character Caterpie
- ▸ Often lives on and eats spicebush plants
- ▸ Name swallowtail comes from long fringe at bottom of each wing, like that of the swallow, a kind of bird
- ▸ Caterpillar often turns yellow just before making cocoon
- ▸ Very young caterpillars sometimes resemble bird droppings as camouflage
- ▸ Male has bluish hind wing; female has greenish hind wing

MECOPTEROIDS

THIS LARGE GROUP OF INSECTS are united by the way their mouths work. Nearly all have long mouthparts that slurp up liquid food like a straw.

Flies, fleas, and mosquitoes are after big prey. They suck blood from animals many times their size by tapping directly into blood vessels or by cutting their host and lapping up the blood that pools on their skin.

Flies have four wings like most insects, but two of them are so tiny that they are useless. There are more than 150,000 types of flies, and they live in just about every habitat on Earth. Fleas are less common, but an infestation can be quite annoying. Mosquitoes are actually the deadliest creature on the planet. By transmitting germs that cause diseases such as malaria, they contribute to the deaths of a million people each year around the world.

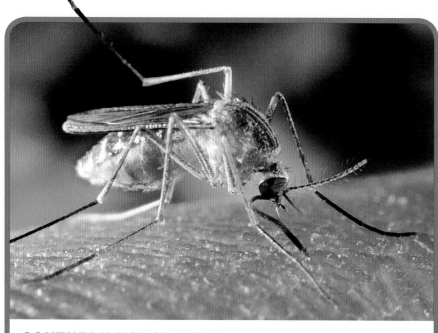

LOVEBUG
Plecia nearctica

SIZE: 0.5 inch long (1.25 cm)
HABITAT: Grassy areas; Gulf Coast of the United States, Central America
FOOD: Rotting organic material

They're not true bugs, though they earn their name, often flying in mated pairs. Swarms in Texas and the Southeast can be so massive that they make driving dangerous and can even damage automobile engines.

SOUTHERN HOUSE MOSQUITO
Culex quinquefasciatus

SIZE: 0.1 inch long (0.3 cm)
HABITAT: Tropical and subtropical regions; worldwide
FOOD: Blood, nectar

This mosquito can be found throughout the tropical and subtropical regions worldwide. It can carry the germs that cause West Nile virus and encephalitis. As with other types of mosquitos, the females are the only ones that eat blood. They need it to lay eggs, which they do on or near water.

COMMON GREEN BOTTLE FLY
Lucilia sericata

SIZE: 0.4 inch long (1 cm)
HABITAT: Temperate and tropical regions; worldwide, especially Africa and Australia
FOOD: Rotting flesh, plant fluids, feces

As adults, these flies are found around the world, dining on animal waste and decaying flesh. Females lay their eggs in these substances, as well. In fact, their taste for dead things makes them useful to humans. Crime-scene scientists "read" the age of bottle fly larvae (called maggots) to determine how long a body has been dead.

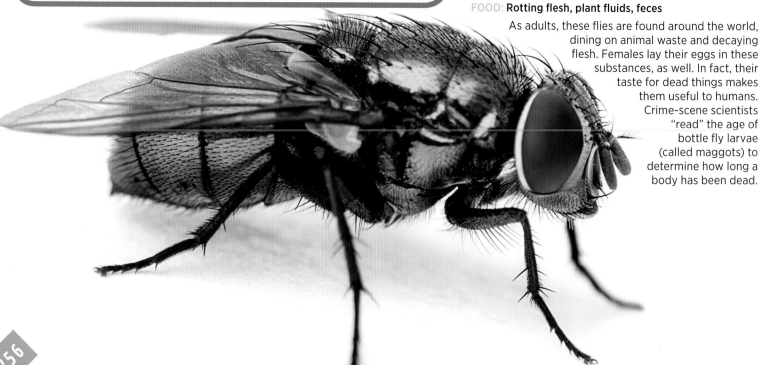

TSETSE FLY
Glossina morsitans
SIZE: **0.5 inch long (1.3 cm)**
HABITAT: **Dry areas; Africa**
FOOD: **Animal blood**

The tsetse fly is a killer, carrying the germs that cause sleeping sickness. They bite animals that have the germs and then bite humans, passing them along. Over ten thousand people in Africa die of this each year. Many efforts are underway in affected countries to control the tsetse populations and protect people.

BEE FLY
Bombylius major
SIZE: **0.5–1 inch long (1.3–2.5 cm)**
HABITAT: **Gardens, meadows, woodland; worldwide except Australasia**
FOOD: **Nectar, insect larvae**

When is a fly in disguise? When it looks like a bee. Bee flies look very much like bumblebees, with bristly yellow backs. They also feed on nectar as bees do. Bee flies will sometimes sneak their eggs into bee hives. After hatching, the larvae eat bee larvae.

BLACK-TIPPED HANGINGFLY
Hylobittacus apicalis
SIZE: **1 inch long (2.5 cm)**
HABITAT: **Forest edges, meadows; southern United States, Mexico**
FOOD: **Insects**

Unlike most of its relatives, these insects are hunters. They hang from plants and use clawlike grips on their legs to grab flying insects. Then they stab and slurp.

COMMON CAT FLEA
Ctenocephalides felis
SIZE: **0.1 inch long (0.3 cm)**
HABITAT: **Mammal skin; worldwide**
FOOD: **Mammals**

Fleas live as parasites on animals, eating skin, hair, and blood. This species is the most common on American pets (dogs as well as cats). They are hard to get rid of. Their eggs and pupae are very sticky, and adults have clawlike feet and sharp bristles that help them cling to animal hair. Americans spend more than $6 billion a year trying to get rid of them.

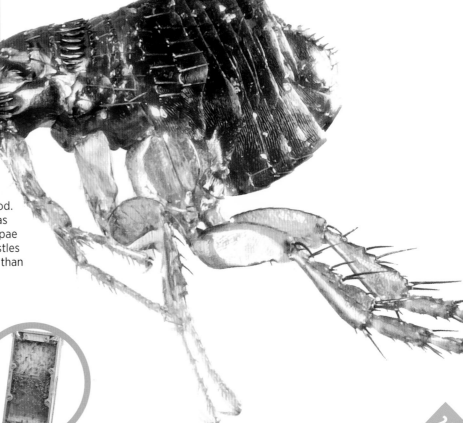

FUN FACT NASA sent fruit flies to the International Space Station. With the flies contained in special boxes, scientists observed how they reacted to zero gravity and life in space.

BEETLES

HARDENED FOREWINGS, MOUTHS FOR CHEWING, VARIED ANTENNAE

WITH MORE THAN 350,000 SPECIES, beetles have greater variety than any other order of animals in the world. Some scientists think there are hundreds of thousands of additional species waiting to be discovered.

Beetles lay eggs that hatch to become larvae. The larvae must undergo a complete metamorphosis to become adults. Beetles can be incredibly tiny or else surprisingly large, with some as wide as the palm of your hand. They live in nearly all habitats on Earth.

Like most insects, adult beetles have four wings. However, the two forewings are on top of the back and they are very hard. Called elytra, they act as a protective cover. To spot a beetle, look for the line along its back where the two wings meet. When a beetle wants to fly, the elytra open up so the hind wings have room to flap.

COWBOY BEETLE
Chondropyga dorsalis

SIZE: 0.5–1 inch long (1.3–2.5 cm)
HABITAT: Woodlands, meadows, backyards; eastern Australia
FOOD: Plants

Native to Australia, this beetle lays eggs in rotting wood. The hatched larvae can feed on the wood. As adults, they make a loud buzzing sound as they fly. Combine this with their orange-and-black coloring and they're often mistaken for wasps. In addition to wooded areas, this species is often seen in suburban gardens.

COLORADO POTATO BEETLE
Leptinotarsa decemlineata

SIZE: 0.5 inch long (1.3 cm)
HABITAT: Fields, gardens; North America, Mexico, Europe
FOOD: Plants

This beetle, native to Mexico and the American Southwest, has been found throughout the United States for more than a century. It is considered a pest, since it attacks potato crops. It is only rarely seen in Colorado, but it got that name in 1867 and it stuck. It is known for its distinctive markings, including stripes along its elytra.

Animal Antics

The deathwatch beetle lives in the walls of people's homes. It bangs it tiny head against the inside of the wood. People hearing this eerie knocking had trouble sleeping, and this reminded them of the all-night vigil—or deathwatch—at the bedside of a dying loved one. That's how this beetle got its name.

DIVING BEETLE
Dytiscus marginalis

SIZE: 1 inch long (2.5 cm)
HABITAT: Freshwater; Europe, northern Asia
FOOD: Insects and fish

This is one of several beetles adapted for living underwater. Their legs are flattened to aid in swimming. When they dive they can trap an air bubble beneath their outer wings to breathe underwater. Their larvae are known as water tigers for their fierce attack on anything they can catch. The diving beetle prefers shallow water such as ponds, streams, or the edges of lakes.

WHAT MAKES A BUG A BUG? Its mouth, according to scientists. Though many people call insects "bugs," a group of insects called true bugs are the only insects for which scientists use that word. One good way to tell is the name. If "bug" is a separate word (jewel bug), then it's usually a true bug. If "bug" is part of a single-word name (ladybug), then that animal is another kind of insect. Ladybugs are beetles, for instance.

The mouths of true bugs are like straws. They have no teeth or jaws, but only a tube that can suck up liquid from whatever they are eating. Some true bugs eat plant fluids. Some true bugs prey on insects or other animals, using their pointed mouth to stab and inject saliva that turns the prey's insides to liquid . . . and then they sip away.

GIANT WATER BUG
Lethocerus americanus

SIZE: **2–2.5 inches long (5.1–6.4 cm)**
HABITAT: **Freshwater; southern Canada, northern United States**
FOOD: **Fish, small amphibians**

People who step on giant water bugs while wading in streams feel the same sharp bite used on prey, which has given this bug its nickname, "toe biter." The giant water bug breathes underwater through tubes in the abdomen.

HAWTHORN SHIELD BUG
Acanthosoma haemorrhoidale

SIZE: **0.5 inch long (1.3 cm)**
HABITAT: **Meadows, gardens; Europe, Russia**
FOOD: **Plants**

Shield bugs get their name from the shape of their thorax and wings, which fold on their back when not flying. Like most shield bugs, the wings of this species are somewhat rectangular in shape. This species lives mostly in Great Britain, where it finds its favorite plant, the hawthorn bush.

THORN BUG
Umbonia crassicornis

SIZE: **0.5 inch long (1.3 cm)**
HABITAT: **Meadows, fields; southern United States, Central and South America**
FOOD: **Plants**

These insects love to gather in groups on branches. Their thorn like shape transforms a plain stick into a thorn-covered one. It is their best defense against predators. While they hide in plain sight, they eat the insides of the plants, and can cause great damage to some species of trees or bushes. A common food source is sap, which they suck from young trees called saplings.

MASKED HUNTER ASSASSIN BUG
Reduvius personatus

SIZE: **0.5–1 inch long (1.3–2.5 cm)**
HABITAT: **Human homes, dry fields; North America, Europe, Africa**
FOOD: **Insects**

Assassin bugs take their name from their method of attack. They pounce on other insects, stab with a sharp mouth, and suck out the insides. This species got its "masked" name from the way its nymphs hide among dust in people's homes. They camouflage themselves, emerging to hunt their prey at night.

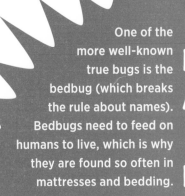

One of the more well-known true bugs is the bedbug (which breaks the rule about names). Bedbugs need to feed on humans to live, which is why they are found so often in mattresses and bedding.

SNACK ATTACK

RHINOCEROS BEETLE

Compared to humans, insects are small. But compared to other insects, most of the 300 species of rhinoceros beetle are big. Most species of rhinoceros beetle have horns that make an insect's total length from back end to point of horn add up to 6 inches (15.2 cm) or more. They don't use their horns to hunt or eat, however; rhinoceros beetles only eat plants. The big horns are used in combat with other beetles to win mates. The beetles use their horns to lift up other beetles, like Olympic wrestlers. They can even use the horns to flip enemies over onto their backs. When threatened, the beetles use the horns to dig holes in which to hide.

ABOUT ME!

I'm a rhinoceros beetle. My horn looks like a rhino's horn, and I use it for fighting and digging. I am small but very strong. I can lift objects, such as stones and sticks, that weigh 850 times as much as I do. That's like a person lifting more than 40 actual rhinos.

7 FACTS ABOUT THE RHINOCEROS BEETLE

▶ Will grunt at rivals and squeak for mates
▶ Some species spend as many as four years as larvae before finally becoming adults
▶ Females don't have horns
▶ Lives all over the world, but most species are native to Asia and Africa
▶ Is a kind of scarab beetle
▶ Each species has evolved its own style of head horn
▶ Body is nearly vertical—straight up and down—in flight

SPIDERS ARE NOT INSECTS. Like insects, though, they are arthropods, which are segmented animals with multiple legs and hard outer shells. Spiders have eight legs instead of six, and two body parts (cephalothorax in front, abdomen in back) instead of three.

Spiders are best known for the webs that most spiders weave. They eject strands of silk from a special part of their body called a spinneret. Different species weave different shapes or sizes of webs; some species don't make webs at all. For web spinners, the webs become traps to capture prey. They can also use webs to make nests to lay eggs.

Most spiders have sharp fangs and can bite their prey, injecting venom to kill or paralyze it. The venom also turns the inside of the prey to liquid that the spider can then suck out. Spiders are predators and hunters, not plant eaters.

HOBO SPIDER
Eratigena agrestis
SIZE: **0.5 inch long (1.3 cm)**
HABITAT: **Forest, grassland; Europe, northwestern United States**
FOOD: **Insects**

These funnel-web spiders mate toward the end of a two- to three-year lifespan. Small hairs on the legs help males track females to begin the mating process. After mating, females lay a clutch of eggs and then die, their mission accomplished. Hobo spiders can discern changes in air pressure through special receptors in their legs.

FUN FACT

Spiders can have as many as eight eyes, located on the top or sides of the head. They can sense light and dark and see shapes.

SYDNEY FUNNEL-WEB SPIDER
Atrax robustus
SIZE: **1–1.5 inches long (2.5–3.8 cm)**
HABITAT: **Forest, urban areas; Australia**
FOOD: **Insects, small reptiles**

Funnel-web spiders build long, cone-shaped webs. They wait inside the funnel for prey to step on a piece of webbing near the opening. Then they skitter out and pounce. This species has a bite that is very dangerous to people. They prefer to dwell in hidden spaces, such as rock crevasses or underneath houses.

FEATHER-LEGGED ORBWEAVER
Uloborus glomosus
SIZE: **0.1–0.5 inch long (0.3–1.3 cm)**
HABITAT: **Forest; North America**
FOOD: **Insects**

Short, soft bristles on the legs of this species are the reason for its name. The reason for the bristles? To comb or brush the strands of the web as it is being made, helping shape the network of lines into a circle.

BOLD JUMPING SPIDER
Phidippus audax

SIZE: 0.5 inch long (1.3 cm)
HABITAT: Urban areas, forest, grassland; Canada, United States, Mexico
FOOD: Insects

Some spiders lie in wait to eat. Jumping spiders don't need to wait, they have excellent eyesight to spot prey. Then they jump, often many times their body length, and land on the prey.

BRAZILIAN WANDERING SPIDER
Phoneutria nigriventer

SIZE: 1-1.5 inches (2.5-3.8 cm)
HABITAT: Rainforest; South America
FOOD: Small animals of all sorts

Living in the tropical rainforest of South America, this spider hardly ever encounters humans. Good thing, as its venom is considered to be one of, if not the most, deadly in the world. This spider doesn't hunt with a web, but stalks its victims in the forest.

WASP SPIDER
Argiope bruennichi

SIZE: 0.5 inch long (1.3 cm)
HABITAT: Gardens, grasslands; central and northern Europe, northern Africa
FOOD: Insects

Bright yellow stripes on its large abdomen make this spider look like a wasp. Wasp spiders are orb web spinners, usually weaving at the very beginning or end of the day.

NORTHERN BLACK WIDOW SPIDER
Latrodectus variolus

SIZE: 0.5 inch long (1.3 cm)
HABITAT: Woodpiles, forests; northeastern United States
FOOD: Insects

The red hourglass shape on the abdomen is a signal to stay away from this spider. Black widow stings can hurt or even kill humans. However, such bites are rare and only come if the spider is threatened. Only the females' bite is dangerous; they are also much larger than the males. Black widows weave strong webs, and they usually weave them close to the ground.

GOLIATH BIRD-EATING TARANTULA

Even people who are not afraid of spiders might cower in the company of this arachnid. The goliath bird-eating tarantula is one of the largest spiders in the world. It got its name because it is big enough both to bring to mind the biblical giant Goliath and to capture and eat birds. More than 1 foot (0.3 m) across (from leg to huge, hairy leg), it makes its way through the South American jungle in search of prey—and succeeds.

ABOUT ME!

I am a goliath bird-eating tarantula. When hunting prey, I pounce on things small enough to eat and inject venom with my fangs. I may bite you in self-defense if you come too close. I can stridulate, which means I make a hissing sound by rubbing the bristles on my legs and mouthparts together.

8 FACTS ABOUT THE GOLIATH BIRD-EATING TARANTULA

- ▶ Weighs about 6 ounces (170.1 g)
- ▶ Has fangs that are 1 inch (2.5 cm) long
- ▶ Makes hissing sounds by rubbing its legs and mouthparts together
- ▶ Stalks and attacks prey instead of making a web
- ▶ Releases sharp hairs that can cause great irritation if they stick to skin
- ▶ Some people catch, roast, and eat these spiders
- ▶ Female may kill male after mating
- ▶ Despite name, rarely eats birds; usual diet is lizards, snakes, amphibians, insects, and other spiders

SPIDERS ARE NOT THE ONLY ANIMALS with eight legs and fangs. The animal class Arachnida includes scorpions, ticks, and mites. A major difference between arachnids and insects is that arachnids have neither antennae nor wings.

Scorpions are among the most spiderlike in appearance, with eight long legs and a two-segmented body. However, scorpions do not spin webs, and they have a large tail with a sharp stinger on the end. They release venom from this stinger to kill or immobilize their prey.

Ticks and mites have small and flat bodies. Their body segments have evolved to look like a single unit, rather than separate sections as in other arachnids. They are also much smaller than most spiders and scorpions; in fact, many are only visible under a microscope.

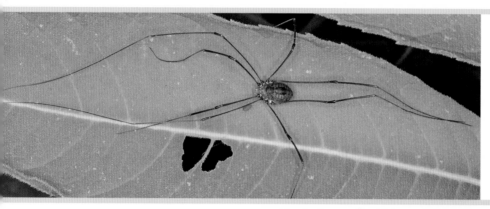

EASTERN HARVESTMAN
Leiobunum vittatum

SIZE: **0.25 inch long (0.6 cm)**
HABITAT: **Grasslands, forest; eastern United States**
FOOD: **Insects**

Often confused for spiders, these are a different kind of arachnid also called daddy longlegs. There are more than 6,500 species of harvestmen. To make things more confusing, there is a type of spider called a daddy longlegs spider. Best way to tell them apart? Spiders have two clear body parts; the harvestman has one.

AMERICAN DOG TICK
Dermacentor variabilis

SIZE: **0.1-0.25 inch long (0.25-0.6 cm)**
HABITAT: **Mammals; United States**
FOOD: **Mammals**

Ticks, like fleas, feed on host vertebrates. This species will attack a variety of mammals, including humans. Like other ticks, it has a large, shieldlike back plate called a scutum.

ATLANTIC HORSESHOE CRAB
Limulus polyphemus

SIZE: **1.5–2 feet long (0.5–0.6 m)**
HABITAT: **Coastal water; Gulf of Mexico, northern Atlantic coast of North America**
FOOD: **Worms, clams, small mollusks, algae**

A visitor from prehistoric times would recognize this animal. Living under their armored shells, horseshoe crabs are nearly unchanged from fossils dating back more than 400 million years. These are not actually crabs or crustaceans, but rather a type of arthropod. They may live to be 20 years or older.

Animal Antics

After they are born, baby Arizona bark scorpions will stay with their mother for the first few weeks. The babies climb onto their mother's back after they are born. As many as 25 or more ride on her back until they molt for the first time.

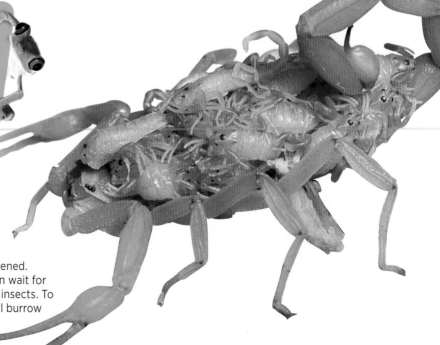

ARIZONA BARK SCORPION
Centruroides exilicauda

SIZE: **3 inches long (7.6 cm)**
HABITAT: **Desert; southwestern United States, Mexico**
FOOD: **Insects**

The venom of this scorpion is considered to be one of the most deadly in the world, and certainly in North America. Like other scorpions, it will only sting humans when threatened. Otherwise, it uses its sandy coloring as camouflage to lie in wait for passing prey. It feeds on crickets, beetles, and other small insects. To escape the desert heat during midday, these scorpions will burrow under rocks or tree bark.

THE NAMES FOR CENTIPEDES ("100 feet") and millipedes ("1,000 feet") are not very accurate. Most centipedes have far fewer than 100 legs. The most legs found on a millipede so far is about 750.

How do you tell the difference between the two types of arachnids? Look for the body segments in each type of animal. A centipede will have one leg on each side of each segment. Millipedes will have two pairs of legs for each body segment. Millipedes will curl up into a tight ball for defense, showing their hard outer shell to the predator.

When capturing their own prey, centipedes rely on sharp fangs and venom. They also have sharp claws on many of the legs. Millipedes, on the other hand, are foragers. They look for decaying plants and animals to eat.

MEDITERRANEAN BANDED CENTIPEDE
Scolopendra cingulata

SIZE: **4–6 inches long (10.2–15.2 cm)**
HABITAT: **Soft soil; southern Europe, northern Africa**
FOOD: **Insects, small vertebrates**

Found throughout southern Europe and northern Africa, this centipede is fast and will bite when threatened. The colors of this species will vary slightly depending on where it lives, such as sandy areas, rocky places, or grasslands. It burrows into moist, dark environments, often beneath piles of rotting leaves.

YELLOW SPOTTED MILLIPEDE
Harpaphe haydeniana

SIZE: **1.5–2 inches long (3.8–5.1 cm)**
HABITAT: **Forest floor; Pacific coast of North America**
FOOD: **Rotting plants**

When this insect is threatened, it curls into a ball and spews out a poison called cyanide. While this is bad for predators, in this small quantity it is not really dangerous for humans.

 FUN FACT

Ancient centipedes were even bigger than those we know today. One found in South America measured 39 inches (just over a meter). Imagine that crawling up your leg!

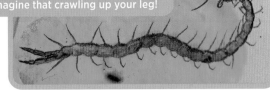

BRISTLY MILLIPEDE
Polyxenus fasciculatus

SIZE: **0.1 inch long (0.3 cm)**
HABITAT: **Forest floor; eastern United States, Caribbean Islands**
FOOD: **Rotting plants**

Unlike most millipedes, which are smooth on the outside, this species is covered with fine bristles. The bristles are neatly ordered in rows on the back and in clusters at the sides. They help in self-defense by entangling attackers. The hairs can also come off if grabbed, letting the millipede escape.

CRUSTACEANS

UNDERWATER . . . AND ARMOR-PLATED!

INSECTS ARE AMONG THE MOST numerous animals in the world . . . on land. Underwater, crustaceans take that title. Like insects, crustaceans are arthropods. They hatch from eggs, start out as larvae or nymphs, and molt their hard exoskeletons as they grow. Crustaceans have segmented bodies, too. Most species have a head, abdomen, and thorax. However, the limbs of crustaceans are "biramous," meaning split into two. Many also have a pair of limbs for each of their body segments. So while insects have six legs and spiders eight, a lobster, for example, has 10. Crustaceans have two pairs of antennae, while insects have just one.

Many of the 70,000 species of crustaceans feed on the plant life that is found underwater, while others eat their tiny fellow crustaceans. Some crustaceans live in freshwater, such as crayfish. A few spend their life on land, including woodlice and a few species of crabs. Crustaceans range in size from nearly microscopic to massive—the Japanese stone crab can be 12 feet (3.7 m) across, including the length of its legs. Alaskan king crabs can weigh more than 20 pounds (9 kg).

PELAGIC GOOSENECK BARNACLE
Lepas anatifera

SIZE: **3–6 inches long (7.6–15.2 cm)**
HABITAT: **Tropical and temperate waters worldwide**
FOOD: **Fish, marine invertebrates, plankton**

The pelagic gooseneck barnacle is composed of two distinct parts: a heart-shaped shell called a capitulum, and the peduncle, a long stalk that attaches to ships, rocks, or floating ocean debris such as driftwood.

AMANO SHRIMP
Caridina multidentata

SIZE: **2–2.5 inches long (5.1–6.4 cm)**
HABITAT: **Coastal saltwater (larval stage), freshwater streams and marshes (adults); Japan, Korea, Taiwan**
FOOD: **Decaying vegetation, algae**

Originating from the swamps of Japan, the Amano shrimp is translucent in color with reddish-brown dots and dashes along the length of its body and a tan or white stripe running down its back. It feeds on algae and is an efficient cleaner, making it a popular aquarium fish.

AMERICAN SIGNAL CRAYFISH
Pacifastacus leniusculus

SIZE: **2.5–6.5 inches long (6.4–16.5 cm)**
HABITAT: **Freshwater**
FOOD: **Decaying animals and plant matter**

Hungry and fast-moving, crayfish are a key part of many freshwater ecosystems. However, as an invasive species, they can upset the balance of a system, too. This species has invaded some European rivers and streams and caused damage.

AMERICAN LOBSTER
Homarus americanus

SIZE: **8–24 inches long (20.3–61 cm)**
HABITAT: **Atlantic coast of northeastern North America**
FOOD: **Clams, crabs, snails, small fish, algae, carrion**

The familiar claws of the lobster have been part of the American diet since at least the time of the Penobscot Nation settlements in what is now Maine. Lobsters for their part eat mostly dead and decaying marine animals that have fallen to the floor of the sea, where lobsters make their homes.

DUNGENESS CRAB
Metacarcinus magister
SIZE: 8–10 inches long (20.3–25.4 cm)
HABITAT: Coastal water, estuary; west coast of North America
FOOD: Marine animals

Females of this crab can lay 2.5 million eggs in a lifetime, which is one reason this is one of the most popular crustaceans for human food. Millions of tons of them are pulled from the Pacific Ocean each year. After hatching, the larvae of this crab sometimes attach themselves to dangling jellyfish tentacles. This provides safety while the larvae feed on passing marine plankton.

GLASS CLEANER SHRIMP
Urocaridella antonbruunii
SIZE: 1–1.5 inches long (2.5–3.8 cm)
HABITAT: Saltwater; Indo-Pacific Ocean
FOOD: Marine plants, parasites from fish

These almost see-through animals are popular with people who own saltwater aquariums. These shrimp get their name by eating the marine plants that cling to the glass of the tanks. In the wild, they will gather together in groups, and frequent sheltered spaces such as caves.

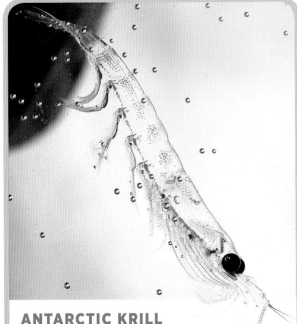

ANTARCTIC KRILL
Euphausia superba
SIZE: 1–2.5 inches long (2.5–6.4 cm)
HABITAT: Antarctic Ocean
FOOD: Phytoplankton

Individually, krill are tiny, floating through chilly water eating passing marine plants. Yet they travel in large schools, and are gathered up in great numbers by humpbacks and other whales. In addition, they are a key food source for seals, penguins, and many other members of the Antarctic ecosystem.

PINK GHOST CRAB
Ocypode ryderi
SIZE: 1–1.5 inches long (2.5–3.8 cm)
HABITAT: Sandy beaches of tropical and subtropical oceans; shorelines of southern Africa, Indian Ocean
FOOD: Insects, crustaceans, decaying flesh of animals

These square-shaped creatures are found skittering along the beaches of South Africa. *Ocypode* means "swift-footed," which suitably describes their behavior, as they can run sideways at speeds of 6 feet (2 m) per second. This makes them one of the fastest land-based crustaceans in the world.

SNACK ATTACK

A better question than "What do crustaceans eat?" is "What eats crustaceans?" Krill are the main food for many species of whales. The other species that likes to eat crustaceans is . . . us. We humans eat more than 10 million tons of crustaceans a year, including crabs, shrimp, and lobsters.

IN THE TROPICS

The tropical zone is the area on Earth that surrounds the equator. This region is home to a diverse variety of animals that thrive in the often wet, hot climate.

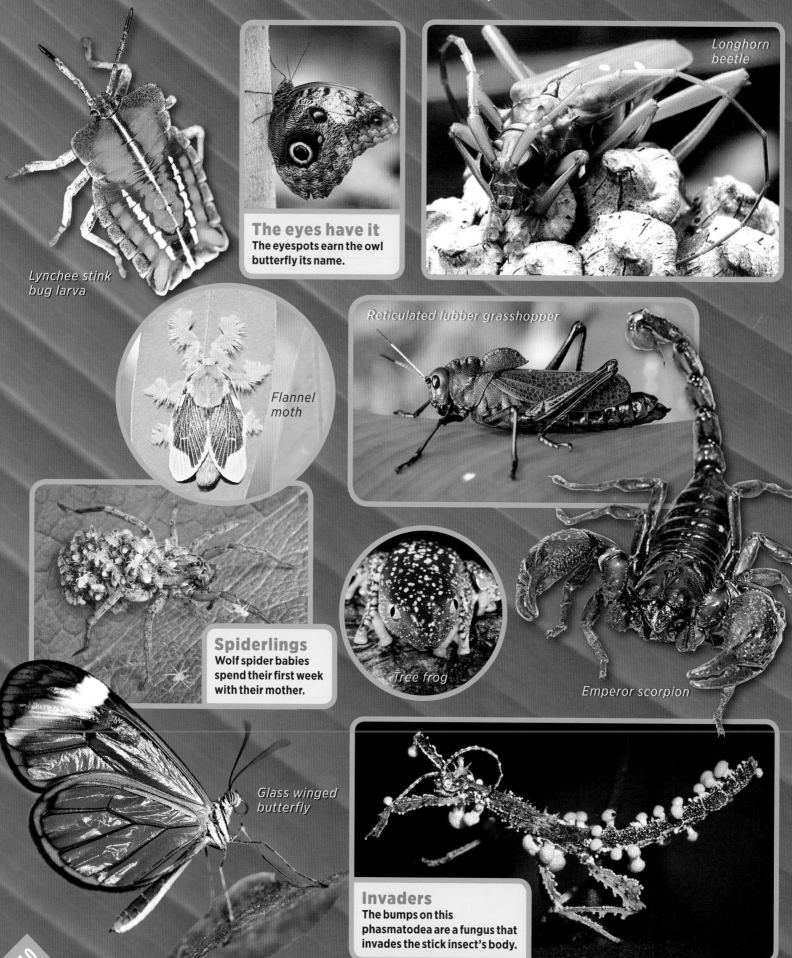

Lynchee stink bug larva

The eyes have it
The eyespots earn the owl butterfly its name.

Longhorn beetle

Flannel moth

Reticulated lubber grasshopper

Spiderlings
Wolf spider babies spend their first week with their mother.

Tree frog

Emperor scorpion

Glass winged butterfly

Invaders
The bumps on this phasmatodea are a fungus that invades the stick insect's body.

Periander
metalmark butterfly

Hornbill
bird

Tropical
swallowtail moth

Golden orb weaver

Flag-
footed
bug

One of a kind!
Basilisk lizards pump their
legs and spread their fringed
toes to run on water.

Giant metallic
ceiba borer

Transformer
This brightly striped
caterpillar will
become a tetrio
sphynx moth.

Capybara

271

MORE ARTHROPODS

There are more than 1 million known insect and arachnid species in the world. Here are some interesting ones to learn more about.

❋ Jewel bug

PRIMITIVE-WINGED INSECTS

AZURE DAMSELFLY
Coenagrion puella

BLUE DASHER
Pachydiplax longipennis

COMMON BLUE DAMSELFLY
Enallagma cyathigerum

COMMON DARTER
Sympetrum striolatum

COMMON MAYFLY
Ephemera danica

FOUR-SPOTTED CHASER DRAGONFLY
Libellula quadrimaculata

GIANT FOREST DAMSELFLY
Megaloprepus caerulatus

GIANT LACEWING
Osymlus fulvicephalus

SOUTHERN HAWKER
Aeshna cyanea

MANTIDS, STICK INSECTS, GRASSHOPPERS, AND MORE

AFRICAN CAVE CRICKET
Pholeogryllus geertsi

ANNUAL CICADA
Tibicen linnei

AUSTRALIAN PLAGUE LOCUST
Chortoicetes terminifera

DESERT LOCUST
Schistocerca gregaria

DEVIL'S FLOWER MANTIS
Idolomantis diabolicum

DIFFERENTIAL GRASSHOPPER
Melanoplus differentialis

EUROPEAN MOLE CRICKET
Gryllotalpa gryllotalpa

GIANT LEAF INSECT
Phyllium gigantea

INDIAN STICK INSECT
Carausius morosus

MIGRATORY LOCUST
Locusta migratoria

❋ Fruit fly

MILKWEED GRASSHOPPER
Phymateus morbillosus

ROESEL'S BUSH CRICKET
Metrioptera roeselii

OAK BUSH CRICKET
Meconema thalassinum

SOUTHERN TWO-STRIPED WALKING STICK
Anisomorpha buprestoides

SPECKLED BUSH CRICKET
Leptophyes punctatissima

STRIPE-WINGED GRASSHOPPER
Stenobothrus lineatus

TRUE KATYDID
Pterophylla camellifolia

❋ Leopard lacewing butterfly

COCKROACHES AND TERMITES

AUSTRAL ELLIPSIDION COCKROACH
Ellipsidion australe

CATHEDRAL MOUND TERMITE
Macrotermes bellicosus

DEATH'S HEAD COCKROACH
Blaberus craniifer

GIANT BURROWING COCKROACH
Macropanesthia rhinoceros

GREEN BANANA COCKROACH
Plachlora nivea

SOUTH ASIAN TAR BABY TERMITE
Globitermes sulphureus

❋ Picasso bug

ANTS

BULLDOG ANT
Myrmica gulosa

BULLET ANT
Paroponera clavata

EASTERN CARPENTER ANT
Camponotus pennsylvanicus

FUNGUS-GROWING ANT
Mycocepurus smithii

GHOST ANT
Tapinoma melanocephalum

HONEYPOT ANT
Myrmecocystus mimicus

LEAFCUTTER ANT
Atta sexdens

MEAT ANT
Iridomyrmex purpueus

RED WOOD ANT
Formica rufa

WEAVER ANT
Oecophylla smaragdina

BEES AND WASPS

BUFF-TAILED BUMBLEBEE
Bombus terrestris

CUCKOO BEE
Bombus vestalis

EASTERN CARPENTER BEE
Xylocopa virginica

EASTERN CICADA KILLER WASP
Sphecius specious

❋ Maggot

EUROPEAN HORNET
Vespa crabro

GIANT HORN-TAIL WASP
Urocerus gigas

GIANT ICHNEUMON WASP
Rhyssa persuasoria

ORCHARD MASON BEE
Osmia lignaria

ORCHID BEE
Eulaema bombiformus

ORGAN-PIPE MUD DAUBER
Trypoxylon politum

PARASITIC WASP
Ichneumonidae cremastinae

POTTER WASP
Eumenes fraternus

SAXON WASP
Dolichovespula saxonica

STINGLESS HONEYBEE
Meliponula ferruginea

TARANTULA HAWK WASP
Pepsis formosa

❋ Richmond birdwing butterfly

MECOPTEROIDS

BLUE BOTTLE FLY
Calliphora vomitoria

BOTFLY
Cuterebra lepivora

COMMON HORSEFLY
Tabanus bovinus

CRANE FLY
Tipula paladosa

GNAT
Culex pipiens

HOUSEFLY
Musca domestica

HORNET ROBBER FLY
Atlas crabronformis

INDO-PAKISTAN MALARIA MOSQUITO
Anopheles stephensi

SCREWWORM FLY
Cochliomyia macellaria

STALK-EYED FLY
Cyrtodiopsis whitei

❋ Halloween pennant

BUTTERFLIES AND MOTHS

AFRICAN GIANT SWALLOWTAIL
Zizina otis

AFRICAN MOON MOTH
Argema mimosae

AUSTRALIAN PAINTED LADY BUTTERFLY
Vanessa kershawi

BHUTAN GLORY BUTTERFLY
Bhutanitis lidderdalii

BOGONG MOTH
Agrotis infusa

BRAZILIAN OWL BUTTERFLY
Caligo brasiliensis

BUFF-TIP MOTH
Phalera bucephala

COCOA MORT BLEU BUTTERFLY
Caligo teucer

COMMON BUCKEYE BUTTERFLY
Junonia coenia

COMMON CASTOR BUTTERFLY
Ariadne merione

CORN EARWORM
Helicoverpa zea

COMMON HAWKER
Aeshna juncea

COMMON MORMON
Papilio polytes

DEATH'S HEAD HAWK MOTH
Acherontia atropos

GARDEN TIGER MOTH
Arctia caja

GOAT MOTH
Cossus cossus

❋ Honeybee

GREAT SPANGLED FRITILLARY
Speyria cybele

GREAT ORANGE TIP
Hebomoia glaucippe

GYPSY MOTH
Lymantria dispar

HEWITSON'S BLUE HAIRSTREAK
Thecla coronata

HIEROGLYPHIC MOTH
Diphthera festiva

HOOP PINE MOTH
Millonia isodoxa

HORNET MOTH
Sesia apiformis

INDIAN LEAF BUTTERFLY
Kallima inachus

JAPANESE EMPEROR
Sasakia charonda

KARNER BLUE BUTTERFLY
Lycaeides melissa spp. samuelis

LESSER GRASS BLUE BUTTERFLY
Carterocephalus palaemon

MAGPIE MOTH
Abraxas grossulariata

MALLOW SKIPPER
Carcharodus alceae

NUMATA LONGWING BUTTERFLY
Heliconius numata

ORANGE-BARRED SULPHUR BUTTERFLY
Phoebis philea

OWL MOTH
Brahmaea wallichiii

PALE TUSSOCK
Calliteara pudibunda

PEACOCK BUTTERFLY
Inachis io

PEPPERED MOTH
Biston betularia

POSTMAN BUTTERFLY
Heliconius melpomene

PROVENCE BURNET MOTH
Zygaena occitana

❋ Luna moth

SMALL COPPER
Lycaena phlaeas

QUEEN ALEXANDRA'S BIRDWING
Ornithoptera alexandrae

SIX-SPOT BURNET MOTH
Zygaena filipendulae

SMALL WHITE BUTTERFLY
Pieris rapae

SUNSET MOTH
Chrysiridia croesus

VERDANT SPHINX HAWK MOTH
Euchloron megaera

VICEROY BUTTERFLY
Limenitis archippus

WHITE WITCH MOTH
Thysania agrippina

WHITE-BARRED EMPEROR BUTTERFLY
Charaxes brutus

ZEBRA SWALLOWTAIL BUTTERFLY
Euprotographium marcellus

❋ Ringed paper wasp

BEETLES

ACTAEON BEETLE
Megasoma actaeon

AMERICAN BURYING BEETLE
Nicrophorus americanus

ATLAS BEETLE
Chalcosoma atlas

BOMBARDIER BEETLE
Brachinus crepitans

CARDINAL BEETLE
Pyrochroa coccinea

CHAFER BEETLE
Neptunides polychrous

* Yellow jacket

CLICK BEETLE
Semiotus angulatus

COWPEA BEETLE
Callosobruchus chinensis

DARKLING BEETLE
Onymacris candidipennis

EUROPEAN ELM BARK BEETLE
Scolytus multistriatus

FLAT-FACED LONGHORN BEETLE
Callipogon barbatus

FLOWER BEETLE
Dicronorhina derbyana

HERCULES BEETLE
Dynastes hercules

JEWEL SCARAB BEETLE
Chrysina resplendens

KING STAG BEETLE
Phalacrognathus muelleri

* Braconid wasp

MALAYAN FROG BEETLE
Sagra buqueti

MALAYSIAN BRENTID BEETLE
Eutrachelus temmincki

MEALWORM BEETLE
Tenebrio molitor

MEXICAN BEAN BEETLE
Epilachna varivestis

MOUNTAIN PINE BEETLE
Dendroctonus ponderosae

MULTICOLORED ASIAN LADY BEETLE
Harmonia axyridis

PIE-DISH BEETLE
Helea subserratus

RED FLOUR BEETLE
Tribolium castaneum

SIX-SPOTTED GIANT GROUND BEETLE
Anthia sexguttata

SNOUT BEETLE
Cyrtotrachelus dux

STAG BEETLE
Lucanus cervus

TEXAS DUNG BEETLE
Onthophagus gazella

TORTOISE BEETLE
Eugenysa regalis

VIOLIN BEETLE
Mormolyce phyllodes

WASP BEETLE
Clytus arietis

WASP MIMIC BEETLE
Clytus ruricola

* Bumblebee

TRUE BUGS

ANNUAL CICADA
Tibicen linnei

AZURE WEEVIL
Eupholus cuvieri

BEET LEAFHOPPER
Circulifer tenellus

BROWN MARMORATED STINK BUG
Halyomorpha halys

* Soldier fly larva

CABBAGE APHID
Brevicoryne brassicae

COMMON POND SKATER
Gerris lacustris

COMMON WATER STRIDER
Aquarius remigis

COTTONY CUSHION SCALE
Icerya purchasi

DOG DAY CICADA
Tibicen canicularis

FOREST SHIELD BUG
Pentatoma rufipes

GLASSY-WINGED SHARPSHOOTER
Homalodisca virtipennis

KISSING BUG
Triatoma infestans

LANTERN BUG
Fulora lanternaria

LIGHTNING BUG
Photuris pennsylvanica

* Pirate bug

MAGIC CICADA
Magicicada septendecim

MANGO TREE BORER
Batocera rufomaculata

MILKWEED ASSASSIN BUG
Zelus longipes

PERIODICAL CICADA
Magiciada septemdecim

RED APHID
Acyrthosiphon pisum

SEVEN-SPOT LADYBUG
Coccinella setempunctata

SOUTHERN GREEN STINKBUG
Nezara viridula

WATER MEASURER
Hydrometra stagnorum

SPIDERS

BROWN HUNTSMAN SPIDER
Heteropoda ventoria

BROWN RECLUSE SPIDER
Loxosceles reclusa

EUROPEAN CAVE SPIDER
Meta menardi

FISHING SPIDER
Dolomedes triton

GOLDEN WHEEL SPIDER
Carparachne aureoflava

HAWAIIAN HAPPY FACE SPIDER
Theridion grallator

INDIAN ORNAMENTAL SPIDER
Poecilotheria regais

KING BABOON SPIDER
Citharischius crawshayi

LARGE CAROLINA WOLF SPIDER
Hogna carolinensis

MEXICAN RED-KNEED TARANTULA
Brachypelma smithi

MIRROR SPIDER
Thwaitesia argentiopunctata

* Hoverfly

PINKTOE TARANTULA
Avicularia avicularia

SEA SPIDER
Colossendeis australis

SPINY-BACKED ORBWEAVER
Gasteracantha cancriformis

VAMPIRE SPIDER
Evarcha culicivora

* Earwig

OTHER ARACHNIDS

ASIAN FOREST SCORPION
Heterometrus longimanus

BARK SCORPION
Centuroides sculpturatus

DEATHSTALKER SCORPION
Leiurus quinquestriatus

DEER TICK
Ixodes scapularis

GIANT DESERT HAIRY SCORPION
Hadrurus arizonensis

GIANT INDIAN VELVET MITE
Trombidium grandissimum

HIGHLAND MIDGE
Culicoides impunctatus

HONEY BEE MITE
Acarapis woodi

IMPERIAL SCORPION
Pandinus imperator

POOR KNIGHTS WETA
Deinacrida fallai

ROCKY MOUNTAIN WOOD TICK
Dermacentor anderson

STEPHENS ISLAND WETA
Deinacrida rugosa

WATER SCORPION
Nepa cinerea

CENTIPEDES/MILLIPEDES

AFRICAN GIANT MILLIPEDE
Archispirostreptus gigas

AUSTRALIAN HOUSE CENTIPEDE
Allothereua maculata

BLACK MILLIPEDE
Tachypodoiulus niger

EUROPEAN PILL MILLIPEDE
Glomeris marginata

FLAT-BACKED MILLIPEDE
Polydesmus angustus

GARDEN CENTIPEDE
Lithobius forficatus

GIANT CENTIPEDE
Scolopendra hardwickii

GIANT DESERT CENTIPEDE
Scolopendra heros

HOUSE CENTIPEDE
Scutigera coleoptrata

NORTH AMERICAN MILLIPEDE
Narceus americanus

SHOCKING PINK DRAGON MILLIPEDE
Demoxytes purpurosea

STONE CENTIPEDE
Lithobius forficatus

CRUSTACEANS

ACORN BARNACLE
Semibalanus blanoides

AMANO SHRIMP
Caridina multidentata

AMERICAN LOBSTER
Homarus americanus

AMERICAN SIGNAL CRAYFISH
Pacifastacus leniusculus

ANTARCTIC KRILL
Euphausia superba

ATLANTIC BLUE CRAB
Callinectes sapidus

ATLANTIC GHOST CRAB
Ocypode quadrata

ATLANTIC MARSH FIDDLER CRAB
Uca pugnax

BANDED CORAL SHRIMP
Stenopus hispidus

BLUE FLORIDA CRAYFISH
Procambarus alleni

BLUE-EYED ROCK CRAB
Percnon affine

CALIFORNIA SPINY LOBSTER
Panulirus interruptus

CARIBBEAN SPINY LOBSTER
Panulirus argus

COLEMAN SHRIMP
Periclimenes colemani

DURBAN DANCING SHRIMP
Rhynchocinetes durbanensis

* Black soldier fly

EDIBLE CRAB
Cancer pagurus

GIANT FRESHWATER CRAYFISH
Astacopsis gouldi

GLASS ANEMONE SHRIMP
Periclimenes brevicarpalis

GLASS CLEANER SHRIMP
Urocaridella Antonbruunii

GOOSE-NECKED BARNACLE
Pollicipes polymerus

HAWAIIAN SWIMMING CRAB
Charybdis hawaiensis

JAPANESE SPIDER CRAB
Macrocheira kaempferi

MAGNIFICENT ANEMONE SHRIMP
Ancylomenes magnificus

NORTHERN KRILL
Meganyctiphanes norvegica

OCONEE BURROWING CRAYFISH
Cambarus truncates

ORANGE CARNIVAL CRAB
Geosesarma aristocratensis

ORANGUTAN CRAB
Achaeus japonicus

PACIFIC CLEANER SHRIMP
Lysmata amboinensis

PEACOCK MANTIS SHRIMP
Odontodactylus scyllarus

PISTOL SHRIMP
Alpheus macrocheles

POLL'S STELLATE BARNACLE
Chthamalus stellatus

RAINBOW CRAB
Cardisoma armatum

RED REEF LOBSTER
Enoplometopus occidentalis

RED SNAPPING SHRIMP
Alphaeus armatus

* Southeastern subterranean termite

RED-BANDED LOBSTER
Justitia longimanus

ROBBER CRAB
Birgus latro

SALLY LIGHTFOOT CRAB
Grapsus grapsus

SHORE CRAB
Carcinus maenas

SMOOTH GOOSENECK BARNACLE
Lepas anatifera

SPANISH SLIPPER LOBSTER
Scyllarides aequinoctialis

SPONGE DECORATOR CRAB
Hyastenus elatus

SPOTTED CLEANER SHRIMP
Periclimenes yucatanicus

SPOTTED SPINY LOBSTER
Panulirus guttatus

STRAWBERRY HERMIT CRAB
Coenobita perlatus

TADPOLE SHRIMP
Triops cancriformis

TREE LOBSTER
Dryococelus australis

WATER MEASURER
Hydrometra stagnorum

ZEBRA MANTIS SHRIMP
Lysiosquillina maculata

OTHER ARTHROPODS

COMMON EARWIG
Forficula auricularia

HORSESHOE CRAB
Limulus polyphemus

SILVERFISH (NON-WINGED HEXAPOD)
Lepisma saccharina

* Spotted ladybug

273

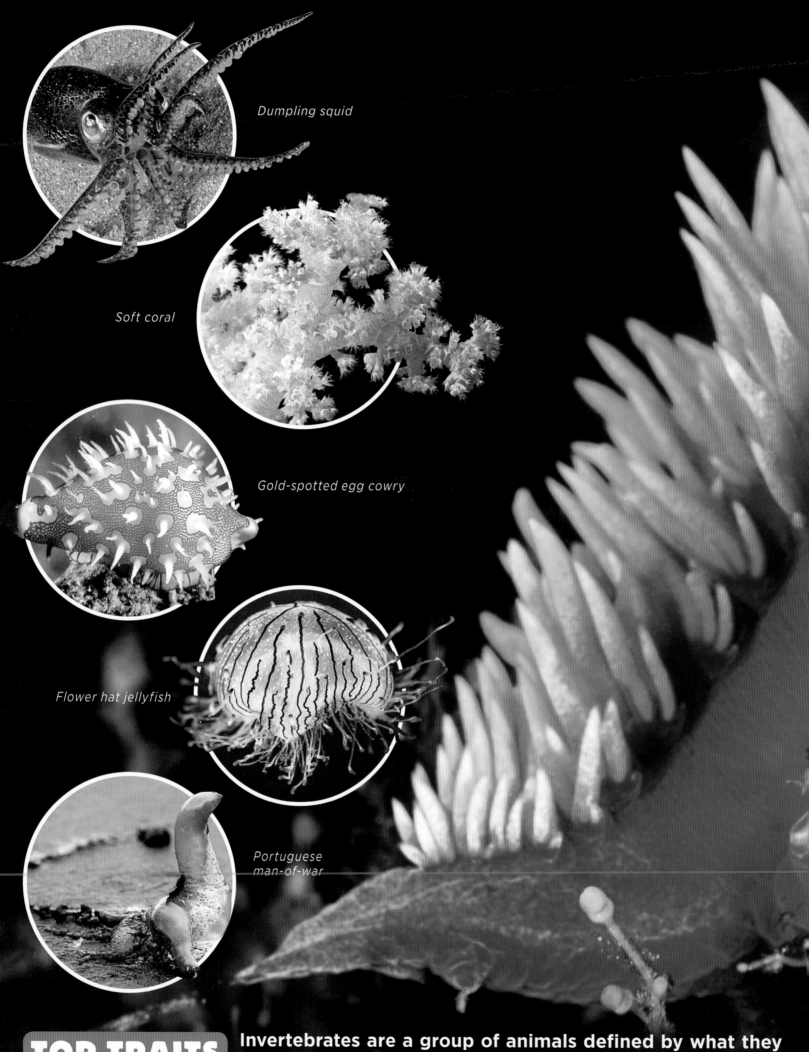

Dumpling squid

Soft coral

Gold-spotted egg cowry

Flower hat jellyfish

Portuguese
man-of-war

TOP TRAITS **Invertebrates are a group of animals defined by what they
environments. ▶ Even invertebrates that have hard shells
▶ Invertebrates breathe by passing oxygen through their skin, or in some cases by**

OTHER INVERTEBRATES

Spanish shawl nudibranch

lack—backbones. ▶ Aside from arthropods, most inhabit marine or freshwater for protection have bodies lacking a fixed shape—and sometimes even lack heads. using gills. ▶ Ninety-nine percent of all living creatures on Earth are invertebrates.

INVERTEBRATES ARE SO DIVERSE that except for being spineless—and resembling creatures from another planet—there isn't much they share in common. Not counting arthropods, there are five main groups of invertebrates. Sponges are simple animals that lack organ systems or tissues—they are a collection of cells. Most attach themselves to rock or some other hard surface and remain there for life. Cnidarians, including jellyfish, corals, and sea anemones, are animals with stinging cells, which they use to defend themselves and to catch prey. Starfish, sea urchins, and sea cucumbers are echinoderms. Echinoderms are structured in five-point symmetry. They have five sets of organs, five major arteries, and, in the case of certain starfish, five rays, or arms. Worms—flat, round, and segmented—number about 54,000 species. While many are parasitic, living off their hosts, segmented worms such as the earthworm swallow soil and digest its nutrients. Mollusks—snails, slugs, clams, octopuses, and squid, among others—are the second-largest group of invertebrates, after arthropods. A mollusk's body consists of a small head, a foot, a fleshy body, and a mantle.

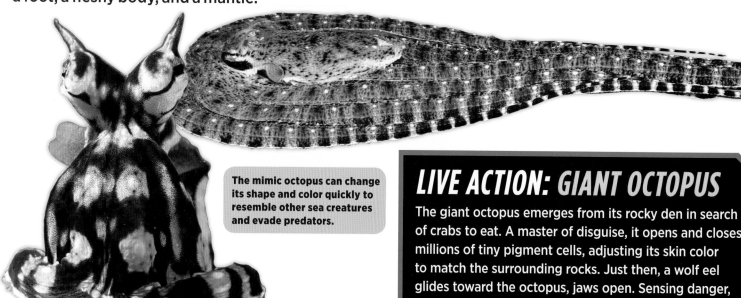

The mimic octopus can change its shape and color quickly to resemble other sea creatures and evade predators.

BEHAVIOR

If you're a spineless blob, it can be hard to protect yourself against predators. That's why invertebrates have adapted a number of ways to defend themselves. Snails and bivalves have hard shells that keep them safe. Other mollusks, such as octopuses and cuttlefish, use camouflage and/or secrete liquids at predators to divert or frighten them away. Jellyfish and other cnidarians possess stinging cells that can paralyze or kill predators that come too close. Many echinoderms, such as sea urchins, are lined with sharp spines that deter predators. Soft-bodied sea cucumbers expel some of their internal organs, sacrificing them to make a getaway. (The organs quickly grow back.) Other sea cucumbers eject sticky threads that entangle their enemies.

LIVE ACTION: *GIANT OCTOPUS*

The giant octopus emerges from its rocky den in search of crabs to eat. A master of disguise, it opens and closes millions of tiny pigment cells, adjusting its skin color to match the surrounding rocks. Just then, a wolf eel glides toward the octopus, jaws open. Sensing danger, the octopus uses its siphon to squirt a cloud of purplish ink at its predator. At the same time, the octopus rapidly propels itself backward. It does this again and again. The wolf eel, unable to see its prey in the inky dark, becomes disoriented and confused. By the time the cloud has cleared, the octopus has retreated to its den of rocks.

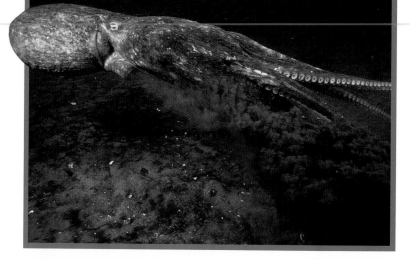

EBRATES

Giant barrel sponge

HEAD Some invertebrates, such as starfish and sponges, are headless. Octopuses and other cephalopods have small heads.

NO BACKBONE Invertebrates are animals without backbones.

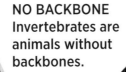

Hooded cuttlefish

BRAIN Jellyfish, starfish, and sponges lack brains. Cephalopods—the smartest class of mollusks, with subclasses including the octopus, cuttlefish, and squid—have larger and more complex brains than any other invertebrate's. They are highly mobile, active hunters.

Underside of starfish

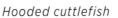

Red cushion starfish

TUBE FEET Echinoderms move using rows of tube feet located on the undersides of their bodies. Each foot extends and attaches to a surface by means of a sucker. Once the pressure is released, the echinoderm is pulled forward.

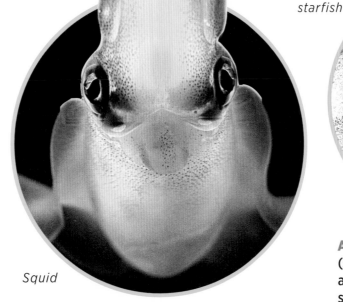

Squid

ARMS While many invertebrates (sponges, worms, and snails, among others) lack arms, others, such as octopuses and squid, have a multitude of arms. Starfish arms are called rays. Most starfish have five arms, but some species have many more.

EYES Most invertebrates have eyespots that can detect light and dark. Squid, octopuses, and cuttlefish have large eyes that are similar to the human eye.

Red sea urchin

MOUTH While sponges take in food through their cells, most other invertebrates have mouths of some sort. For some, such as jellyfish, the mouth serves as a place both to take in food and to excrete it. Cephalopods have sharp beaks that they use to break their food into small pieces.

Market squid

Spotted jellyfish

SKIN Invertebrates have soft bodies, for the most part. Snails and other mollusks are protected by shells. Starfish and sea urchins have spiny bodies. Many cephalopods can change the color of their skin to blend in with their surroundings.

FEEDING HABITS

Invertebrates will eat almost anything, and they go about getting their food in a multitude of ways. Sponges are filter feeders that take in water and filter out the small food particles within. Some echinoderms are also filter feeders. Others graze on algae or, like starfish, actively hunt their prey. Jellyfish capture plankton and small fish with stinging cells on their tentacles and then use the tentacles to bring the prey to their mouths. Cephalopods use their arms to bring prey to their mouths. Earthworms and other segmented worms are detritus feeders, dining on the decomposing organic matter found in soil, while many species of flatworm and ringworm are parasitic, feasting off the nutrients in a host's intestines. Land mollusks such as snails and slugs have tiny rows of teeth that they use to eat plants and fungi.

Roman snail

Two-spined starfish eating squid

METAMORPHOSIS

Animals that undergo metamorphosis change form as they mature. Many animals, such as humans, look like miniature versions of their parents when they are born. But the young of other animals look very different from their adult forms and go through a series of radical changes as they develop. Nearly all invertebrates, including insects, mollusks, jellyfish, and echinoderms, undergo metamorphosis. Often, the young invertebrates live in different habitats or feed on different foods than their adult counterparts do.

Purple sea urchin (adult)

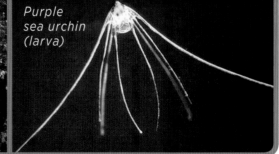
Purple sea urchin (larva)

HABITATS

While many snails, slugs, and segmented worms are land dwellers, the majority of invertebrates (excluding most arthropods) live in aquatic environments. Sponges live in fresh- and saltwater, where they attach themselves to rocks or other hard surfaces. Echinoderms are exclusively marine animals, and so are cnidarians, except for a few species that live in freshwater lakes. Octopuses, squid, clams, and many other mollusks can be found throughout the world's oceans. About 80 percent of all flatworms are parasites that make their homes on or in other living creatures, getting their nourishment from their hosts.

Surprisingly Human

When you help out a classmate with homework, it's only natural to expect a favor in return. This mutual give-and-take is also found in many animal relationships. A sponge and the bacteria that live on its body have a symbiotic relationship. Experts think the bacteria may aid the sponge in breathing and other chemical processes; in return, the sponge provides the bacteria with a safe place to live.

OCEAN

SHORELINE

CORAL REEF

SOIL

TIDE POOL

Ammonite fossil

EVOLUTION

The earliest multicellular animals were invertebrates. Scientists have found fossils of primitive soft-bodied, spongelike animals that date back to more than 600 million years ago, long before dinosaurs walked the Earth. After these early multicellular animals died out, a multitude of invertebrates came into being, many of which we'd recognize today, such as sponges, jellyfish, worms, and mollusks.

Invertebrates continue to dominate Earth today. The bulk of them are arthropods, which include insects and arachnids, but the other species in this division also pull their weight. There are about 8,000 species of sponge, 10,000 species of jellyfish and their relatives, and about 100,000 species of mollusk.

JELLYFISH

WITH BODIES THAT ARE 95 percent water, jellyfish are primitive animals that lack blood, a heart, and even a brain. What these bell-shaped sea creatures do have are stinging tentacles. Jellyfish use their tentacles to capture prey, including plankton, crustaceans, and other jellies, and defend themselves from predators.

Jellyfish are found throughout the world's oceans at every depth, from shallow bays to the deepest abysses.

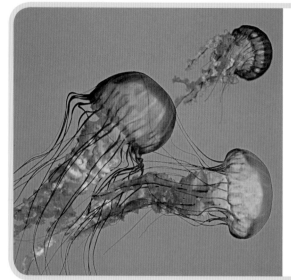

ATLANTIC SEA NETTLE
Chrysaora quinquecirrha

SIZE: 1–1.5 feet long (0.3–0.5 m)
HABITAT: Coastal temperate water, estuary; Atlantic and Indo-Pacific Oceans
FOOD: Plankton, jellyfish, small fish, crustaceans

The sting from these large jellyfish is especially painful and often leaves a rash. During the summer months, as water temperatures rise, the sea nettle population explodes on the East Coast, becoming a menace to swimmers there.

UPSIDE-DOWN JELLYFISH
Cassiopea xamachana

SIZE: 8–14 inches long (20.3–35.6 cm)
HABITAT: Coastal mangrove; western Atlantic Ocean, Caribbean Sea, Gulf of Mexico
FOOD: Plankton

As its name suggests, this jellyfish spends most of its time upside-down, sitting on the sea floor. Inside its eight upheld arms are organisms called algae. The jellyfish and algae have an unusual relationship. The algae make food, some of which the jellyfish consumes. In return, the jellyfish provides a home and food for the algae.

Jellyfish on the menu? In some countries jellyfish is considered a delicacy. Jellyfish salad is a favorite with the Chinese, and in Japan they like jellyfish sprinkled with soy sauce and vinegar.

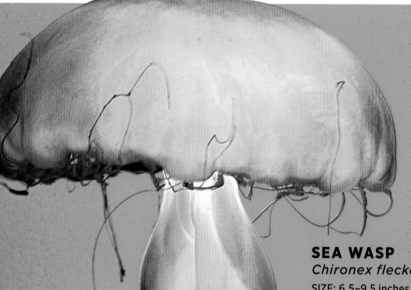

SEA WASP
Chironex fleckeri

SIZE: 6.5–9.5 inches in diameter (16.5–24.1 cm)
HABITAT: Shallow saltwater; Indian Ocean, Pacific Ocean
FOOD: Shrimp, small fish

One of the most dangerous animals in the ocean, the sea wasp has a lethal sting. Each of its long tentacles are lined with stinging cells. The venom is meant to kill the sea wasp's prey, but sometimes swimmers are stung. This jellyfish's sting is so painful that sometimes swimmers go into shock and drown before they can reach shore. It doesn't help that this square-shaped creature is transparent and therefore very hard to see.

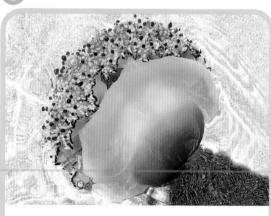

MEDITERRANEAN JELLYFISH
Cotylorhiza tuberculata

SIZE: 13–14 inches in diameter (33–35.6 cm)
HABITAT: Open water, coastal lagoon; Mediterranean, Aegean, and Adriatic Seas
FOOD: Plankton, jellyfish

Resembling a fried egg, the Mediterranean jellyfish has a weak sting. Feeding on plankton and jellyfish, it moves extremely slowly through the bay waters of the Mediterranean Sea. Young crabs sometimes live on its bell, poaching food from its tentacles.

CORALS AND ANEMONES are simple animals that are usually anchored to rocks or other hard surfaces on the ocean floor. Their mouths are surrounded with stinging tentacles, which corals and anemones use to ensnare prey and to ward off predators. While almost all species of anemones live alone, most corals live in large groups called colonies. Certain coral species with hard skeletons form reefs that can support a multitude of life.

SNAKELOCKS ANEMONE
Anemonia viridis

SIZE: 2.5–3 inches long (6.4–7.6 cm)
HABITAT: Shallow saltwater, intertidal pool; Mediterranean Sea
FOOD: Fish, mollusks, plankton

With over 200 tentacles clustered around its mouth, the snakelocks anemone sweeps the ocean floor in search of food. When prey is hard to come by, it removes itself from whatever hard surface it has attached itself to and relocates.

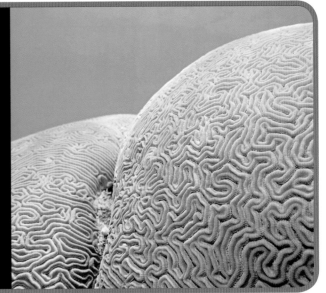

GROOVED BRAIN CORAL
Diploria labyrinthiformis

SIZE: 6–8 feet in diameter (1.8–2.4 m)
HABITAT: Outer and offshore reef; Caribbean Sea, tropical western Atlantic Ocean
FOOD: Plankton, small marine invertebrates

This coral's maze-like grooves resemble a human brain, which gives the reef-builder its name. The many polyps that make up the coral form dome-shaped colonies. Like most species that reside in shallow waters, the grooved brain coral has algae living inside its cells. The relationship is a symbiotic one, with the algae supplying the coral with nutrients while it receives protection in return.

COMMON MUSHROOM CORAL
Fungia fungites

SIZE: 11–12 inches in diameter (28–30.5 cm)
HABITAT: Reef slope, lagoon; Indo-Pacific Ocean
FOOD: Plankton, jellyfish

Unlike most other corals, the mushroom coral doesn't live in colonies. Instead, these flat or rounded animals are free-living, resting on the slopes of reefs. The young, however, do start out attached by a stalk to a rock. When they reach a certain size, they detach and are on their own.

Animal Antics
A hermit crab will invite an anemone to live on its shell by stroking its body. When the hermit crab outgrows its shell, it transfers the anemone to its new home.

HERMIT CRAB ANEMONE
Calliactis polypus

SIZE: 2.5–3 inches long (6.4–7.6 cm)
HABITAT: Hermit crab shell; Indo-Pacific Ocean, Red Sea
FOOD: Algae, animal matter

Certain sea anemones and hermit crabs form mutually beneficial relations. Carried around on the back of a hermit crab, the anemone prowls the sea floor with its partner. When the crab finds prey, the anemone shares in its host meal by stretching out its tentacles and picking up leftover bits of food the crab has shredded with its claws. For the crab, the anemone provides it with a colorful camouflage.

OCTOPUSES, SQUID, CUTTLEFISH, and nautiluses are members of a group of mollusks called cephalopods. The most intelligent of all the invertebrates, cephalopods have large brains. Octopuses have eight arms, and squid and cuttlefish have two extra tentacles that are used for grabbing prey. Most cephalopods breed by laying eggs in clusters on the ocean floor. With short life spans, the majority of cephalopods die shortly after reproducing.

COMMON OCTOPUS
Octopus vulgaris

SIZE: **1–3 feet long (0.3–0.9 m)**
HABITAT: **Tropical and temperate water; worldwide**
FOOD: **Crabs, crayfish, mollusks**

The common octopus is a master of camouflage, able to change its appearance in seconds to match the colors, patterns, and textures of its surroundings. Predators glide past unaware. If a shark or other fish does notice the octopus, it has another trick up its sleeve. Releasing a cloud of dark ink, the octopus makes its getaway.

GREATER BLUE-RINGED OCTOPUS
Hapalochlaena lunulata

SIZE: **4–8 inches long (10.2–20.3 cm)**
HABITAT: **Shallow reef, tide pool; Indo-Pacific Ocean**
FOOD: **Crabs, fish, mollusks, small marine animals**

Tiny but deadly, the greater blue-ringed octopus has extremely toxic venom that it produces in its saliva. After pouncing on its prey, the octopus uses its sharp beak to pierce a hole in its shell. Venomous saliva is then dribbled into the opening, and the prey is soon paralyzed.

FUN FACT

The name *cephalopod* is a Greek word meaning "head-foot." Its name refers to the fact that its foot (modified into arms) being situated right next to its head.

COMMON CUTTLEFISH
Sepia officinalis

SIZE: **1–1.5 feet long (0.3–0.5 m)**
HABITAT: **Shallow water; northern Atlantic Ocean, Mediterranean Sea**
FOOD: **Mollusks, small fish**

These flat-shaped mollusks have a chalky shell inside their bodies called a cuttlebone. The cuttlebone is divided into tiny gas-filled chambers that help keep the cuttlefish afloat. Cuttlefish hide from predators by changing their color to match their background.

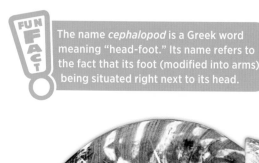

CHAMBERED NAUTILUS
Nautilus pompilius

SIZE: **6–7 inches long (15.2–17.8 cm)**
HABITAT: **Bottom of shore, coral reef; southern Indian and Pacific Oceans**
FOOD: **Crabs, fish, carrion**

Long before dinosaurs walked the earth, the nautilus jetted around the oceans. Protected from predators by its outer shell, the nautilus propels itself forward, backward, or sideways by drawing water into its mantle and shooting it out through a tube. Its shell is made up of a series of gas-filled chambers, which keep the creature afloat. Nautiluses are known as living fossils because they are virtually unchanged from their long-ago ancestors.

WITH MORE THAN 60,000 SPECIES, gastropods live in many different habitats—from oceans and lakes to rainforests and even deserts. While slugs lack a hard, protective covering, almost all other gastropods have shells. Gastropods also possess a muscular foot that in most species is used to get around. Worms are soft-bodied creatures without legs. While many worms are found in fresh or marine waters or burrow in soil, others are parasitic.

SHEEP LIVER FLUKE
Fasciola hepatica

SIZE: 1–1.5 inches long (2.5–3.8 cm)
HABITAT: Liver of sheep, cattle, human; worldwide
FOOD: Tissue of its host

This tiny flatworm is a parasite that dwells in the liver of grazing animals, primarily sheep, where they can cause much damage. Liver fluke can also infect people who eat food that is tainted with this parasite.

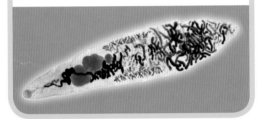

GARDEN SNAIL
Cornu aspersum

SIZE: 2.5–3 inches long (6.4–7.6 cm)
HABITAT: Garden, agricultural area; western Europe, northwestern Africa, British Isles
FOOD: Garden plants, crop vegetables, fruit trees

A garden pest, this snail's rows of tiny teeth can nibble their way through plants and fungi. Like all land snails, the garden snail prefers moist conditions. When the weather is dry, they retreat into their spiral shells and close off the opening with mucus that hardens to form a protective seal.

CHRISTMAS TREE WORM
Spirobranchus giganteus

SIZE: 1.5–2 inches long (3.8–5.1 cm)
HABITAT: Coral reef; tropical oceans worldwide
FOOD: Plankton

This marine worm is named for its resemblance to a fir tree. On top of its tube-like body the worm has two pointy-shaped spiral cones. The cones are mouthparts armed with plume-like tentacles that come in a variety of brilliant colors. With the lower part of its body anchored to its coral burrow, the worm is stationary.

Surprisingly Human

Humans have a fight-or-flight response to danger. It could be said that bivalves have a barricade or flight response. Most bivalves close their shells to protect against danger, but not the scallop: It swims away from predators by clapping its shells open and shut to move forward.

GIANT CLAM
Tridacna gigas

SIZE: 3–5 feet long (0.9–1.5 m)
HABITAT: Shallow lagoon, reef flat; tropical Indo-Pacific Ocean
FOOD: Plankton, food produced by algae

The world's largest bivalve, the giant clam can weigh more than 500 pounds (227 kg). Immobile, it anchors itself on the ocean floor and then stays put for life. While this huge giant gets some of its nourishment from filtering tiny food particles from the water through one of its siphons, it feeds primarily on the nutrients that are produced by the single-celled algae that live in the mollusk's fleshy mantle.

SEA PEN

With their feathery tops drifting in the tide while they cling to sandy seabeds, sea pens are a pretty sight for ocean explorers the world over. They are soft corals named for their fluffy polyps, which resemble quill pens. A polyp is an individual coral animal; like other corals, a sea pen is made up of multiple polyps working together to survive. One polyp is the base of the colony. It is buried in sediment to anchor the sea pen, and it emerges as the central stem. Other, smaller polyps branch out to serve a number of functions. This top feeds on plankton and other microscopic food floating in the water, using toxins to stun the plankton and secreting fluid to digest them.

ABOUT ME!

I'm a sea pen. I grow on the ocean floor, swaying gently with the motion of the water. If you look closely, you'll see lots of little polyps that end in tiny tentacles. These help me in different ways. Some take in water, and others take in food. And some are used in reproduction— making more pretty sea pens like me!

6 FACTS ABOUT THE SEA PEN

- ▶ Can deflate itself or burrow into sediment if disturbed
- ▶ Glows when touched, due to bioluminescence
- ▶ Fossils date back more than 485 million years to Cambrian period
- ▶ Can be found from shallow waters to depths of more than 1,000 feet
- ▶ Main predators are nudibranchs and starfish
- ▶ Is home to some species of porcelain crab, which camouflage well in sea pen's branches

STARFISH, SEA URCHINS, AND SEA CUCUMBERS

belong to a group of animals called echinoderms, which is a word meaning "spiny skin." But not all of the 6,000 plus species in this group have prickly spines. While starfish and sea urchins do, sea cucumbers have soft, leathery bodies. Echinoderms are ocean dwellers. They are all built similarly, with bodies that radiate outward from the center like petals on a flower.

GIANT SEA CUCUMBER
Thelenota ananas

SIZE: 1.5–2.5 feet long (0.5–0.8 m)
HABITAT: Coral reef, reef flat; Indo-Pacific Ocean
FOOD: Seaweed, plankton

Also known as the prickly redfish, this massive sea creature can weigh up to 13 pounds (6 kg). Resembling a moving rug, it crawls across the ocean floor searching for seaweed to eat. The giant sea cucumber is considered a delicacy in Asia, and the demand for it has led it to become endangered.

FIVE-KEYHOLE SAND DOLLAR
Mellita quinquiesperforata

SIZE: 3–5 inches across (7.6–12.7 cm)
HABITAT: Ocean bed; Indo-Pacific Ocean
FOOD: Plankton, detritus

The sand dollar, a type of sea urchin, burrows its body in the ocean floor, often near the shore. Tiny, fine spines cover its body. These spines trap food particles and allow the sand dollar to inch along.

PIN-CUSHION SEA STAR
Culcita novaeguineae

SIZE: 5–12 inches across (12.7–30.5 cm)
HABITAT: Coral reef, reef flat; Indo-Pacific Ocean
FOOD: Detritus, coral

With its rounded body and extremely short arms, the pin-cushion sea star is sometimes mistaken for a sea urchin rather than the starfish it is. Its unusual shape, though, helps the sea star survive by making it difficult for predators to get hold of it. Young pin-cushion sea stars are much flatter than their parents, with longer, more identifiable arms.

FUN FACT Echinoderms have hundreds of tiny tube feet arranged in rows on the underside of their arms. To move around on the ocean floor, echinoderms extend and retract each foot, which slowly pulls them forward.

COMMON STARFISH
Asterias rubens

SIZE: 4–10 inches across (10–30 cm)
HABITAT: Marine water, shallow shore; northern Atlantic Ocean
FOOD: Mussels, barnacles, carrion

The common starfish, like most starfish, uses suction tubes on the undersides of its feet to pry open the shells of its prey, often mollusks. It then pushes its stomach out through its mouth and squeezes it into the shell. After the stomach has finished digesting the mollusk's soft flesh, it withdraws back into the body. And if in the struggle the starfish loses an arm, no problem. It is able to grow another one.

SPONGES

SPONGES ARE AMONG THE SIMPLEST of all animals. They come in a variety of forms. While a few of the more than 8,000 species that exist live in freshwater, the majority can be found in marine environments, where they permanently attach themselves to rocks or the ocean floor. All sponges are porous. They feed by taking in water through tiny pores throughout their bodies, filtering it for nutrients, and then pushing the water back out.

VENUS' FLOWER BASKET
Euplectella aspergillum

SIZE: 4–12 inches tall (10.2–30.5 cm)
HABITAT: Deep sea; western Pacific Ocean
FOOD: Bacteria, plankton, ocean debris

Also known as a glass sponge, these deep-sea sponges have skeletons composed of silica, the same material that is used to make glass. Shaped like a long vase, the sponge is home to a certain species of shrimp. A male and female shrimp live and breed inside the sponge's tube, eventually growing so large inside the chamber that they can never leave.

TOUCH-ME-NOT SPONGE
Neofibularia nolitangere

SIZE: 1–4 feet tall (0.3–1.2 m)
HABITAT: Coral reef; western Atlantic Ocean, Caribbean Sea
FOOD: Plankton, bacteria, debris

This sponge's name says it all. Handling or stepping on this huge toxic sponge can cause intense burning or itching often followed by a rash. Its toxicity doesn't stop certain species of parasitic worms from living inside.

BARREL SPONGE
Xestospongia testudinaria

SIZE: 5–6 feet tall (1.5–1.8 m)
HABITAT: Coral reef; Indo-Pacific Ocean
FOOD: Plankton, bacteria

Barrel sponges are wide and tall, with a central cavity large enough for an adult to climb inside. A hard sponge with deep ridges, some species take in tremendous amounts of seawater when they feed. In one day a large barrel sponge can pump enough water to fill an Olympic-size pool. They are usually a maroon or pinkish color, with a band of white around their opening.

SNACK ATTACK

The harp sponge is a carnivorous deep-sea creature with an unusual way of trapping its food. It has many branches that are covered with sticky hooks. When tiny shrimp are swept toward the sponge by ocean currents, they become caught in the hooks and the harp sponge slowly digests them.

IN THE TIDE POOL

Teeming with life, tide pools are pockets of ocean water that form on the shore when the tide pulls out. Some are shallow puddles that support just a few plants and animals; deeper pools may offer a home to a multitude of life forms. Tide pools are found on rocky coasts around the world.

Black oystercatcher

Take that!
The California sea hare squirts sticky, purplish ink when threatened.

If I only had a brain!
Like all sponges, the marine sponge is an animal without a heart or a brain.

Cockerell's dorid

Rock sculpin

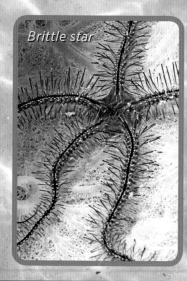
Brittle star

Small but deadly
The venom of the tiny blue-ringed octopus is potent enough to kill people.

Red sea cucumber

Red rock crab

Red starfish

288

Striped shore crab

Sea squirt

Crusher!
The frosted nudibranch has strong jaws it uses to crush snails.

Snowy egret

Blue-spotted headshield slug

What's for dinner?
The sand dollar's mouth is on its underside and it eats as it moves along the sand.

Ruby octopus

Aggregating anemone

Leather star

Check out the Animal Planet L!VE cam to see interesting invertebrates in action by scanning this code or visiting animalplanet.timeincbooks.com/invertebrates.

Invertebrates are a diverse group of animals found in every part of the world. Here are some interesting ones to learn more about.

JELLYFISH

AUSTRALIAN SPOTTED JELLYFISH
Phyllorhiza punctata

BROWN JELLYFISH
Chrysaora melanaster

CHRISTMAS TREE HYDROID
Pennaria disticha

GOLDEN JELLYFISH
Mastigias papua spp. etpisoni

LION'S MANE JELLYFISH
Cyanea capillata

* *Giant West African snail*

NOMURA'S JELLYFISH
Nemopilema nomuri

RED-SPOT COMB JELLY
Eurhamphaea vexilligera

ROOT-MOUTHED JELLYFISH
Eupilema inexpextata

SEA THIMBLE JELLYFISH
Linuche unguiculata

STINGING BUSH HYDROID
Macrorhynchia robusta

CORALS AND ANEMONES

BOWL CORAL
Favia fragum

BOULDER BRAIN CORAL
Colpophyllia natans

BRAIN SPONGE
Agelas cerebrum

BRANCHING FIRE CORAL
Millepora alcicornis

BRANCHING TUBE SPONGE
Aiolochroia crassa

BUBBLE CORAL
Plerogyra sinuosa

CAULIFLOWER CORAL
Pocillopora damicornis

* *Jumping conch*

CLONAL ANEMONE
Anthopleura elegantissima

COLORFUL SEA ROD
Diodogorgia nodulifera

COMMON RAZOR CORAL
Fungia scutaria

CONVOLUTED BARREL SPONGE
Aplysina lacunosa

CORKY SEA FINGER
Briareum asbestinum

DEEP WATER SEA FAN
Iciligorgia schrammi

ELEGANT ANEMONE
Actinoporus elegans

ELLIPTICAL STAR CORAL
Dichocoenia stokesii

ELKHORN CORAL
Acropora palmata

ERECT ROPE SPONGE
Amphimedon compressa

FEATHERY BLACK CORAL
Antipathes pennacea

* *Giant keyhole limpet*

FIRE CORAL
Millepora alcicornis

FISH-EATING ANEMONE
Urticina piscivora

FIVE-TOOTHED SEA CUCUMBER
Actinopyga agassizi

GOLFBALL CORAL
Favia fragum

GREAT STAR CORAL
Montastrea cavernosa

HALLER'S ANEMONE
Anemone halleri

KNOBBY BRAIN CORAL
Diploria clivosa

LEATHERY SEA ANEMONE
Heteractis crispa

LONG-TENTACLED SEA ANEMONE
Macrodactyla doreensis

MAT ZOANTHID
Zoanthus pulchellus

* *Common blue mussel*

MUSHROOM SOFT CORAL
Anthomastus ritteri

ORANGE BALL CORALLIMORPH
Pseudocorynactis caribbeorum

FRAGILE SAUCER CORAL
Agaricia fragilis

ORANGE CUP CORAL
Tubastraea coccinea

ORANGE SEA FAN
Antipathes gracilis

PILLAR CORAL
Dendrogyra cylindricus

PINK AND RED ENCRUSTING SPONGE
Spirastrella coccinea

PITTED SPONGE
Verongula rigida

PURPLE TUBE ANEMONE
Cerianthus membranceus

SMOOTH FLOWER CORAL
Eusmilia fastiginia

SPONGE ZOANTHID
Parazoanthus parasiticus

STAGHORN CORAL
Acropora cervicornis

STRAWBERRY VASE SPONGE
Mycale laxissima

SUN ANEMONE
Stichodactyla helianthus

SUNRAY LETTUCE CORAL
Helioseris cucullata

STARLET SEA ANEMONE
Nematostella vectensis

SWIMMING SEA ANEMONE
Stomphia coccinea

* *Tessellate cone snail*

TEN-RAY STAR CORAL
Madracis decactis

THIN LEAF LETTUCE CORAL
Agaricia tenuifolia

TUBE CORAL
Cladocora arbuscula

VENUS' FLOWER BASKET
Euplectella aspergillum

VENUS SEA FAN
Gorgonia flabellum

VISCOUS SPONGE
Plakortis angulospiculatus

WARTY SEA ANEMONE
Bunodosoma cavernata

* *Striped paper bubble snail*

CEPHALOPODS

ARGENTINE SQUID
Illex argentinus

BIG BLUE OCTOPUS
Octopus cyanea

BIG BOTTOM BOBTAIL SQUID
Austrorossia australis

BANDED PIGLET SQUID
Helicocranchia pfefferi

BROADCLUB CUTTLEFISH
Sepia latimanus

CALIFORNIA TWO-SPOT OCTOPUS
Octopus bimaculatus

CARIBBEAN REEF OCTOPUS
Octopus briareus

CARIBBEAN REEF SQUID
Sepioteuthis sepioidea

COCONUT OCTOPUS
Amphioctopus marginatus

COMMON BLANKET OCTOPUS
Tremoctopus violaceus

CURVESPINE CUTTLEFISH
Sepia recurvirostra

DEEPSEA SQUID
Bathyteuthis abyssicola

EUROPEAN SQUID
Loligo vulgaris

FLAMBOYANT CUTTLEFISH
Metasepia pfefferi

GIANT CUTTLEFISH
Sepia apama

GIANT PACIFIC OCTOPUS
Enteroctopus dofleini

GIANT SQUID
Architeuthis physeteris

GREATER HOOKED SQUID
Onykia ingens

HUMBOLDT SQUID
Dosidicus gigas

MAORI OCTOPUS
Octopus maorum

MEXICAN FOUR-EYED OCTOPUS
Octopus maya

MOON SQUID
Selenoteuthis scintillans

NEEDLE CUTTLEFISH
Sepia aculeata

NORTHERN PYGMY SQUID
Idiosepius paradoxus

OVAL SQUID
Sepioteuthis lessoniana

PINK CUTTLEFISH
Sepia orbignyana

RAM'S HORN SQUID
Spirula spirula

REAPER CUTTLEFISH
Sepia mestus

SPIDER OCTOPUS
Octopus salutii

TRIDENT CUTTLEFISH
Sepia trygonina

GASTROPODS

ANTILLEAN FILECLAM
Lima pellucida

ATLANTIC SEA SCALLOP
Placopecten magellanicus

ATLANTIC THORNY OYSTER
Spondylus americanus

AUSTRALIAN SCALLOP
Pecten australis

AUSTRALIAN TRUMPET
Syrinx auranus

BADWATER SNAIL
Assiminea infirma

BAY SCALLOP
Argopecten irradians

BLACK SLUG
Arion ater

BLUE SEA SLUG
Glaucus atlanticus

BOULDER SNAIL
Athearnia crassa

BURGUNDY SNAIL
Helicarion rubicundus

BUTTERFLY BUBBLE SHELL
Hydatina physis

CALIFORNIA MUSSEL
Mytilus californicus

CATERPILLAR SLUG
Laevicaulis haroldi

CHINA CLAM
Hippopus porcellanus

CIRCUMCISION CONE
Conus circumcisus

CLEAR SUNDIAL SNAIL
Architectonica perspectiva

COMMERCIAL TOP SHELL
Tectus niloticus

COMMON BLUE MUSSEL
Mytilus edulis

DENRODONTID NUDIBRANCH
Dendronotus frondosus

DOG WHELK
Nucella lapillus

EUROPEAN PRICKLY COCKLE
Acanthocardia echinata

* *Dog whelk*

FIRE CLAM
Ctenoides ales

FLAT OYSTER
Ostrea edulis

FLINDER'S VASE
Vasum flindersi

FLUTED GIANT CLAM
Tridacna squamosa

FLY-SPOTTED AUGER
Terebra areolata

FRESHWATER PEARL MUSSEL
Margaritifera margaritifera

FRIED-EGG NUDIBRANCH
Phyllidia varicosa

FROND OYSTER
Dendostrea frons

FUZZY CHITON
Acanthopleura granulata

GARDEN SLUG
Arion distinctus

GARDEN SNAIL
Helix aspersa

* *White-lipped snail*

GIANT AFRICAN SNAIL
Achatina funicula

GIANT FRESHWATER CLAM
Chamberlainia hainesiana

GIANT RAZOR CLAM
Ensis siliqua

GLORY OF THE SEA
Conus gloriamaris

GREAT LAKE SNAIL
Benthodorbis pawpela

GREAT POND SNAIL
Lymnaea stagnalis

GREAT SCALLOP
Pecten maximus

HEBREW CONE
Conus ebracus

✳ *Heavy bonnet snail*

HORSE'S HOOF CLAM
Hippopus hippopus

IMPERIAL HARP
Harpa costata

THE JUNONIA
Scaphella junonia

LETTUCE SEA SLUG
Elysia crispata

LISTER'S KEYHOLE
Diodora listeri

LONG FINGERNAIL CLAM
Musculium transversum

MATCHLESS CONE
Conus cedonulli

MOON SNAIL
Euspira lewisii

MOUNT MATAFAO DIFFERENT SNAIL
Diastole matafaoi

NUTTAL'S COCKLE
Clinocardium nuttallii

OCELLATE COWRIE
Cypraea ocellata

PACIFIC SIDEBAND SNAIL
Monadenia fidelis

PACIFIC THORNY OYSTER
Spondylus princeps

PAINTED ELYSIA
Thuridilla picta

PAINTED SNAKE-COILED FOREST SNAIL
Anguispira picta

PAJAMA SEA SLUG
Chromodoris quadricolor

PINK CONCH
Strombus gigas

PONTIFICAL CONE
Conus dorreensis

PRECIOUS WENTLETRAP
Epitonium scalare

PURPLE-SPOTTED SEA GODDESS
Hypselodoris marci

QUEEN CONCH
Strombus gigas

QUEEN SCALLOP
Equichlamys bifrons

RAYED PEARL OYSTER
Pinctata radiata

RED MANGROVE SHELL
Assiminea brevicula

RED SLUG
Arion rufus

SAFFRON-COLORED CLAM
Tridacna crocea

SMOOTH GIANT CLAM
Tridacna derasa

SNAKE SKIN HUNTER SLUG
Chlamydephorus dimidius

SPOTTED SEA HARE
Aplysia dactylomela

TIGER COWRY
Cypraea tigris

TIGER MAUREA
Maurea tigris

TIGHT COIN
Ammonitella yatesii

TRIUMPHANT STAR TURBAN
Guildfordia triumphans

TOWER SCREW
Turritella terebra

WAVED GOBLET
Cantharus undosus

WAVY-RAYED LAMP MUSSEL
Lampsilis fasciola

WEST INDIAN TOP SNAIL
Cittarium pica

YELLOW BANANA SLUG
Ariolimaz columbianus

ZEBRA MUSSEL
Dreissena polymorpha

WORMS

BEARDED FLATWORM
Hermodice carunculata

BEEF TAPEWORM
Taenia saginata

BLACK WORM
Lumbriculus variegatus

COMMON EARTHWORM
Lumbricus terrestris

DUGESIA FLATWORM
Dugesia sagitta

FRESHWATER LEECH
Americobdella valdiviana

FRESHWATER PLANARIAN
Schmidtea mediterranea

GIANT GIPPSLAND EARTHWORM
Megascolides australis

GREEN EARTHWORM
Allolobophora chlorotica

✳ *Tiger cowry*

GRINDAL WORM
Enchytraeus buchholzi

INDIAN FEATHER DUSTER WORM
Sabellastarte spectabilis

JAPANESE MOUNTAIN LEECH
Haemadipsa zeylanica

KENTUCKY EARTHWORM
Komarekiona eatoni

KINABALU GIANT RED LEECH
Mimobdella buettikoferi

KING RAGWORM
Nereis virens

LAKE PEDDER PLANARIAN
Romankenkius pedderensis

LEOPARD FLATWORM
Pseudobiceros pardalis

LOB WORM
Lumbricus terrestris

LOUISIANA MUD WORM
Lutodrilus multivesiculatus

MARINE FLATWORM
Pseudobiceros gloriosus

MEDICINAL LEECH
Hirudo medicinalis

NEMATODE
Caenorhabditis elegans

OREGON GIANT EARTHWORM
Driloleirus macelfreshi

PARCHMENT WORM
Chaetopterus variopedatus

PEACOCK WORM
Sabella penicillus

PORK TAPEWORM
Taenia solium

✳ *Rough cockle*

✳ *Goose-necked barnacle*

RACING STRIPE FLATWORM
Pseudoceros bifurcus

SAMOAN PALOLO WORM
Eunice viridis

SEA MOUSE
Aphrodita aculeata

SHOVEL-HEADED GARDEN WORM
Bipalium simrothi

SLUDGE WORM
Tubifex tubifex

STAR HORSESHOE WORM
Pomatostegus stellatus

TYRANT KING LEECH
Tyrannobdella rex

WANDERING BROADHEAD PLANARIAN
Bipalium adventitium

WEST INDIAN WORM
Vermicularia spirata

ECHINODERMS

ASHY SEA CUCUMBER
Holothuria cinerascens

BEAUTIFUL FEATHER STAR
Cenometra bella

BLACKSPOTTED SEA CUCUMBER
Pearsonothuria graeffei

BLUE SEA CUCUMBER
Actinopyga caerulea

BLUE SEA URCHIN
Echinothrix diadema

BLUE STARFISH
Linckia laevigata

BOTTLENECK SEA CUCUMBER
Holothuria impatiens

BROWN SEA CUCUMBER
Isostichopus fuscus

CHOCOLATE CHIP STARFISH
Protoreaster nodosus

✳ *Flamingo tongue snail*

COMET STAR
Ophidiaster guildingi

COOKIE DOUGH SEA CUCUMBER
Isostichopus badionotus

COTTON-SPINNING SEA CUCUMBER
Holothuria forskali

CROWN-OF-THORNS
Acanthaster planci

DIFFICULT SEA CUCUMBER
Holothuria dificilis

DONKEY DUNG SEA CUCUMBER
Holothuria mexicana

EUROPEAN EDIBLE SEA URCHIN
Echinus esculentus

FEATHER STAR
Antedon petasus

LEOPARD SEA CUCUMBER
Bohadschia argus

JAPANESE SPIKY SEA CUCUMBER
Apostichopus japonicus

NEW ZEALAND SEA CUCUMBER
Stichopus mollis

PEBBLE COLLECTOR URCHIN
Psuedoboletia indiana

RED HEART URCHIN
Meoma ventricosa

RED SLATE PENCIL URCHIN
Heterocentrotus mammilatus

SPONGE BRITTLE STAR
Ophiothrix suensonii

SWIMMING SEA CUCUMBER
Enypniastes eximia

THREE-ROWED SEA CUCUMBER
Isostichopus badionotus

VIOLET SEA APPLE
Pseudocolochirus violaceus

SPONGES

AZURE VASE SPONGE
Callyspongia plicifera

BLACK-BALL SPONGE
Ircinia strobilina

BREADCRUMB SPONGE
Halichondria panicea

✳ *Thorny oyster*

BROWN BOWL SPONGE
Cribrochalina vasculum

CALCAREOUS SPONGE
Sycon ciliatum

DARK VOLCANO SPONGE
Svenzea zeai

DEAD MAN'S FINGER SPONGE
Codium fragile

ELEPHANT EAR SPONGE
Ianthella basta

FAN SPONGE
Phyllospongia lamellosa

FRESHWATER SPONGE
Spongilla lacustris

GLOVE SPONGE
Spongia officinalis

GOLF BALL SPONGE
Cinachyrella australiensis

LAVENDAR ROPE SPONGE
Niphates erecta

LOGGERHEAD SPONGE
Spheciospongia vesparium

LUMPY OVERGROWING SPONGE
Monanchora unguifera

ORANGE ELEPHANT EAR SPONGE
Agelas clathrodes

ORANGE ICING SPONGE
Mycale laevis

PINK LUMPY SPONGE
Monanchora unguifera

RED BORING SPONGE
Cliona delitrix

RED ENCRUSTING SPONGE
Monanchora barbadensis

RED SPONGE
Negombata magnifica

ROW-PORE ROPE SPONGE
Aplysina cauliformis

SPONGE GOURD
Luffa aegyptiaca

STINKER SPONGE
Ircinia felix

STOVE-PIPE SPONGE
Aplysina archeri

TUBULATE SPONGE
Agelas tubulata

✳ *Fire clam*

YELLOW CALCAREOUS SPONGE
Clathrina canariensis

YELLOW TUBE SPONGE
Aplysina fistularis

GLOSSARY

adapt To change body features or behaviors, often over many generations, in response to conditions in the environment. Species that are able to adapt are more likely to survive.

alpine Mountainous.

ambush predator A predator that remains hidden while waiting for prey to pass, then makes a surprise attack and captures it.

Kodiak brown bear

▲**apex predator** A predator at the top of a food chain. An adult apex predator is not prey for any other animal.

aquatic Living in or having to do with water.

arid Very dry, because of a lack of rain.

biome A major type of ecological community. Rain forests, deserts, and coral reefs are biomes.

brackish Somewhat salty. Brackish water is saltier than freshwater but not as salty as seawater.

breed To mate and produce offspring.

camouflage A disguise, such as coloring or body shape, that helps a living thing blend in with its surroundings.

canopy The highest level of a forest, formed by the overlapping branches and leaves of the tallest trees.

▼**carnivore** An animal that eats meat.

Jumping spider

cell The smallest unit of a living thing that can function independently.

class A group of related living things that is larger than an order but smaller than a phylum. Mammals, birds, and amphibians are classes.

climate The average weather of an area over a long period of time.

cloud forest A moist, tropical mountain forest that is usually full of clouds.

Splash-backed dart frog

▲**cold-blooded** Having a body temperature that changes based on the temperature of the environment. Reptiles, amphibians, and fish are cold-blooded.

coniferous forest A forest that contains mainly conifers, trees that stay green year-round and that produce their seeds in cones. Pines, firs, and spruces are conifers.

conservation The protection of valuable things, such as wildlife or natural resources, to prevent them from being abused or destroyed.

▼**coral reef** A chain of coral just below the surface of a body of water. Coral is a substance made up of tiny sea creatures and their skeletons.

Warty frogfish

deciduous forest A forest that contains mainly deciduous trees, trees that lose their leaves at the end of a growing season. Oaks, elms, and maples are deciduous trees.

desert A dry area that receives very little rain each year and usually has few plants.

domain The largest type of group of living things. Every living thing on Earth is a member of one of three domains.

domesticate To tame and breed an animal so that it can live with or be used by humans.

ecosystem The community of all living things in a particular area, and their relationships to their environment.

Hawksbill turtle

▲**endangered** In danger of becoming extinct. If a species is endangered, there are very few members left.

estuary An area where a river joins a sea.

evolution The process of gradually changing over many generations.

▼**exoskeleton** An outer covering that supports and protects an animal's body. Insects and other arthropods have exoskeletons.

Blue crab

extinct No longer existing. If a species is extinct, it has died out completely.

family A group of related living things that is larger than a genus but smaller than an order. Cows, goats, and antelopes are members of the same family.

forage To search for food, usually plants.

genus A group of related living things that is larger than a species but smaller than a family. Different animals of the same genus are similar in many ways but cannot reproduce together. Horses and zebras are members of the same genus.

grassland A large, flat area of open land that is covered with grasses.

habitat The place or type of place where an animal usually lives and grows.

herbivore An animal that eats plants.

hibernate To spend the winter resting or sleeping, in order to conserve food and energy.

ice sheet A year-round covering of ice and snow.

incubate To keep eggs warm before they hatch.

indicator species A species whose presence or absence reflects a particular condition in its environment.

insectivore An animal that eats mainly insects.

invertebrate An animal that does not have a backbone. Insects, sponges, and worms are invertebrates.

kingdom A group of related living things that is larger than a phylum but smaller than a superkingdom. Animals and plants are kingdoms.

kleptoparasitism A way of feeding in which one animal steals food from another animal.

larva A young animal that looks different from how it will look as an adult.

marine Having to do with the ocean.

Mediterranean Near the Mediterranean Sea, which lies between Europe and Africa.

metabolism The chemical changes within cells that turn food into energy and allow living things to function and grow.

▼metamorphosis A series of changes in form and structure that certain animals go through as they develop into adults. The young of a species that undergoes metamorphosis look very different from the adults.

Monarch butterfly larva

migration The movement of a group of animals from one habitat to another at certain times of the year.

▼molt To lose an outer covering, such as feathers, shell, or skin, so that it can be replaced with a new one.

Gryfalcon

monotypic species A species that is the only member of its genus.

old-growth forest A forest that has developed over many years without experiencing a major disturbance such as fire, insect infestation, or logging.

Racoon

▲omnivore An animal that eats both plants and meat.

order A group of related living things that is larger than a family but smaller than a class. Primates and rodents are orders.

overfish To fish too much, so that a species is significantly reduced or a fishing ground is emptied.

parasitic Having to do with a relationship in which one species lives on or inside another species, usually causing harm to the host.

parthenogenetic Able to produce offspring without mating.

phylum A group of related living things that is larger than a class but smaller than a kingdom. Arthropods and mollusks are phyla.

Honeybee

▲pollinate To transfer pollen from one plant part to another, or from one plant to another, so that the plant can create seeds and reproduce.

predator An animal that hunts and eats other animals.

prehistoric From an ancient time before history was recorded in writing.

prey An animal that is hunted and eaten by another animal.

rain forest A dense, wet forest that receives a lot of rain each year.

reproduction The act of creating offspring.

savanna A flat grassland with few trees, usually in or near tropical areas.

scavenger An animal that eats dead or decaying animals or plants.

second-growth forest A forest that has regrown after experiencing a major disturbance such as fire, insect infestation, or logging.

species A group of living things of the same type, smaller than a genus. Animals of the same species can reproduce together. All humans are members of the same species.

superkingdom A group of related living things that is larger than a kingdom but smaller than a domain.

symbiotic Having to do with a relationship between two different species that is helpful to both species.

systematics The science of describing, classifying, and naming living things.

taiga A moist, cold coniferous forest that begins below the tundra.

temperate forest A forest in the regions between the tropics and the poles, where summers are warm and winters are cool but temperatures are not extreme.

territory An area that an animal or group of animals lives in, feeds in, and defends against others.

Sea wasp

▲toxic Dangerously poisonous.

tropical Having to do with the regions near the equator that are usually hot and humid.

tundra A very cold, treeless area of the Arctic with a layer of permanently frozen soil.

understory The level of a forest between the canopy and the ground.

venom Poison made by some animals, used for hunting or self-defense.

vertebrate An animal that has a backbone. Mammals, fish, and birds are examples of vertebrates.

warm-blooded Having a body temperature that stays the same, regardless of the temperature of the environment. Mammals and birds are warm-blooded.

wetland An area of land where the soil is full of water. Swamps, marshes, and bogs are wetlands.

▼zygodactyl Having two toes facing forward and two facing backward.

Hyacinth macaw

Surprisingly Human

WE HUMANS SHARE EARTH with all of its creatures—wild and domesticated, living far away in distant habitats or right in our homes. The fascination we have for animals and the joy we feel from the special human-animal connection is essential to who *we* are as animals in an interconnected world.

Some animals are highly sociable and hang out in groups, and others are loners, happier away from the crowd. Some, like lion cubs and orangutans babies, wrestle and play. And many find ways to huddle and cuddle. Whether they look happy or sad, angry or silly, we often see ourselves in their faces and behavior. That's not surprising; we're all part of the magnificent animal kingdom.

Hyacinth macaw

Red Iguana

Grizzly bear mother and cub

Long-eared owl

Polar bear

Goldfish

Jumping
spider

Nudibranch

Meerkat

Sea
gull

Red-eyed tree frog

African
elephant

INDEX

Illustrations are indicated by **boldface.** When illustrations fall within a page span, the entire span of pages is **boldface.**

Mexican giant musk turtle

Black-nosed sheep

Cape fur seals

Prairie dogs

Flying gurnard

White-headed marmoset

Water vole

Black bear

Shreve's Sarayacu treefrog

PHOTO CREDITS

Bengal tiger

ANIMALS: A VISUAL ENCYCLOPEDIA

Writers
James Buckley, Jr. (Reptiles, Arthropods)
Anita Ganeri (Introduction, The Animal Kingdom)
Beth Landis Hester (Amphibians)
Cari Jackson (Birds)
Catherine Nichols (Fish, Other Invertebrates)
Lori Stein (Mammals)

Produced by Scout Books & Media Inc
Project Director Susan Knopf
Project Manager and Editor Beth Sutinis
Assistant Editor and Photo Researcher
Brittany Gialanella
Photo and Editorial Researcher Chelsea M. Burris
Copyeditors Michael Centore, Stephanie Engel
Proofreader Brad Beatson
Editorial Interns Jaclyn Heeney, Faith Krech
Indexer Wendy Allex
Designers Dirk Kaufman, Annemarie Redmond,
Jason Snyder
Prepress by Andrij Borys Associates, LLC

SCOUT
BOOKS & MEDIA

Advisors
Special thanks to our expert reviewers, whose passion for, and willingness to share their knowledge of, the animal kingdom inspires us all.

Andy DeHart (Fish)
VP of Animal Husbandry, Patricia and Phillip Frost Museum of Science

Brendan Dunphy (Arthropods, Other Invertebrates)
Research Associate, Department of Entomology, Iowa State University

Doug Hotle (Reptiles, Amphibians)
Critical Species Biologist, Native Species Recovery Program

Douglas A. Lancaster (Birds)
Former Director of the The Cornell Laboratory of Ornithology

Diane Longenecker (Birds)
Senior Keeper-Birds, ABQ BioPark-Rio Grande Zoo

Michael Rentz, PhD (Mammals, The Animal Kingdom)
Lecturer in Mammalogy, Iowa State University

Special thanks to the Discovery and Animal Planet Creative and Licensing Teams: Tracy Conner, Elizabeta Ealy, Robert Marick, Doris Miller, Sue Perez-Jackson, and Janet Tsuei

Published by Liberty Street,
an imprint of Time Inc. Books
1271 Avenue of the Americas, 6th floor
New York, NY 10020
LIBERTY STREET is a trademark of Time Inc.

LIBERTY
STREET

ISBN 10: 1-61893-153-9
ISBN 13: 978-1-61893-153-5
Library of Congress Control Number: 2015940344

We welcome your comments and suggestions about Time Inc. Books. Please write to us at:
Time Inc. Books, Attention: Book Editors, P.O. Box 361095, Des Moines, IA 50336-1095 If you would like to order any of our hardcover Collector's Edition books, please call us at 800-327-6388, Monday through Friday, 7 a.m.-9 p.m. Central Time.